T0347169

TRANSNATIONAL BUSINESS AND CORPORATE CULTURE

PROBLEMS AND OPPORTUNITIES

edited by

STUART BRUCHEY
ALLAN NEVINS PROFESSOR EMERITUS
COLUMBIA UNIVERSITY

LOGICS OF RESISTANCE

GLOBALIZATION AND TELEPHONE UNIONISM IN MEXICO AND BRITISH COLUMBIA

STEVE DUBB

Routledge
Taylor & Francis Group
New York   London

First published by 1999 Garland Publishing, Inc.

This edition published 2013 by Routledge

Routledge
Taylor & Francis Group
711 Third Avenue
New York, NY 10017

Routledge
Taylor & Francis Group
2 Park Square, Milton Park
Abingdon, Oxon OX14 4RN

Routledge is an imprint of the Taylor & Francis Group, an informa business

Library of Congress Cataloging-in-Publication Data

Dubb, Steve.
    Logics of resistance : globalization and telephone unionism in
Mexico and British Columbia / Steve Dubb.
        p.   cm. — (Transnational business and corporate cul-
ture)
    Includes bibliographical references and index.
    ISBN 0-8153-3373-0
    1. Trade-unions—Telephone company employees—Case
studies. 2. Sindicato de Telefonistas de la República Mexicana.
3. Telecommunications Workers Union (B.C.) 4. Trade-unions—
Telephone company employees—Mexico. 5. Trade-unions—
Telephone company employees—British Columbia.
6. Privitization—Case studies. 7. Organizational change—Case
studies. I. Title. II. Series.
HD6475.T3D63 1999
331.88'11384—dc21
                                                            99-19513

In memory of my grandmother, Rita S. Gordon,
who always fought for what she believed was right.

Caminando no hay camino
el camino es andar.
—A. Machado

Contents

Tables

Foreword

To establish the character of labor's emerging response to the changes that are sweeping through global telecommunications today must be a high intellectual priority. Telecommunications systems comprise the core infrastructure, around which is proceeding a widespread process of social reorganization.

This shift goes far beyond the corporate metamorphoses that are heralded by the business press, as "networked business processes" proliferate and alterations are made to the competitive landscape on which financial and industrial organizations contend. For tele-communications restructuring has become the occasion for an attempt, as massive as it is multifaceted, to privilege further transnational capital. Initiatives that use telecommunications in order to short-change social need on behalf of private profit are globally apparent, in the changing terms of educational provision; the quality and extent of paid employment; and, of course, the character and availability of telecommunications services themselves.

For this reason, despite its admittedly often immediate aims, collective action by telecommunications workers has acquired a significance that is anything but parochial. Over the last two years or so, telecommunications workers have intermittently mobilized to resist carriers' attempts to contract out work to non-union enterprises, against state efforts to privatize national carriers, and—in some places—against IMF attacks on established living standards. From South Korea to Brazil, from France to Puerto Rico, from Canada to Sudan—even in the United States—telecommunications workers have shown their opposition to the terms of the neoliberal social settlement.

Or, at least, sometimes they have. For, as Steven Dubb shows in this important book, the collective energies of different groups of telecommunications workers, in different countries, have taken markedly distinct institutional forms historically. Not all unions behave in the same ways, either with regard to their members or in their interactions with employers and state agencies. To situate this variation historically, and to establish a baseline from which to project its strategic significance, a few additional comments may be helpful.

During the early postwar era, throughout much of the world, national telecommunications systems were set up, or re-established, as state enterprises. These government ministries of posts, telephones and telegraphs (PTTs) were created, or reconsolidated, for either of two antagonistic reasons. On one hand, the U.S.-led policy of "containment," directed first and foremost at Soviet socialism, saw telecommunications as a vital bulwark of state authority, and one that had to be shored up as quickly as possible to arrest the socialist advance. Paradoxically, given prevailing U.S. preferences, the telecommunications systems of what was to exist for four decades as West Germany, and of Japan, were reconstructed under U.S. military occupation in their old form, as PTTs. Containment harbored more purely domestic objectives within much of the Poor World but, here, again—beginning, perhaps, with Argentina in 1946—telecommunications systems often were nationalized to grant a veneer of popular legitimacy to programs of authoritarian capitalist rule.

In other countries, however, the creation of state telecommunications agencies was motivated by a more real anti-imperialist nationalism. The two or three decades following 1945 saw dozens of nations throughout Asia, Africa, the Caribbean and the Pacific emerging from the coils of colonialism as formally sovereign states committed to one or another variant of revolutionary nationalism. Throughout the already-independent countries of Latin America, concurrently, there sprang up significant resistance to "dependency" and "neocolonialism." Those that sought, against the odds, to pursue an independent path of national development tended to view direct government control of telecommunications as an essential prerequisite.

Indeed, in some cases—Cuba is the paramount one—the expropriation of a foreign- (read U.S.) owned domestic telephone system itself comprised a defining act of sovereignty, something akin to the Boston tea party. In Chile, to its people's eventual great cost, the Allende government elected in 1970 made nationalization of the ITT-owned system a key desideratum of its tragically foreshortened project of social reconstruction. Even in Mexico, exposed by the misfortune of geography to the unrelenting projection of U.S. power, during roughly a quarter century following World War Two, systems owned by Ericsson and ITT were gradually assimilated into a national, state-owned entity, Teléfonos de México. Canada, again in significant part as a result of continuing U.S. influence, never got even this far on the road to national self-determination in telecommunications.

The United States, in turn, itself remained the cardinal exception to the pattern of state-led system development. In the United States, from the Civil War era onward, telecommunications systems have been owned and administered by corporate capital. Beginning, furthermore, in the immediate aftermath of World War One, U.S. business and governmental interests began to press to introduce privately controlled telecommunications systems elsewhere around the world.

The striking thing is just how long they remained unsuccessful. First, the scourges of global depression, fascism and war intervened. Following World War Two, again, the urgent necessity became (from the perspective of the U.S. governing strata) to contain socialism, and so support was given to the reconstruction of state-run systems. During the 1970s and 1980s, however, the U.S. model finally began to metamorphose into a viable export.

Throughout scores of countries, and diverse multilateral agencies, major corporate telecommunications users succeeded in pressuring national governments to jettison established institutional arrangements in the telecommunications industry. In the first instance, they hoped merely to reduce their costs and to gain access to state-of-the-art network systems under maximally permissive conditions. The fact that the world's single largest domestic market—the United States—had already been successfully prodded to embrace telecommunications deregulation functioned as a strategic wedge: major telecommunications users in any and all industries saw a competitive need to strive to replicate around the world the liberal conditions that they benefited from within the giant U.S. market. Ultimately, however, the corporate vision of telecommunications reform was recast. By the 1980s and 1990s, telecommunications reform had become the foundation for an accelerated cycle of capitalist globalization and, relatedly, a new phase of accumulation—what Edward S. Herman calls "the deepening of the market"—in which activities previously exempt or removed from market relations were brought within the latter's sphere.

Whatever their historical basis, in consequence, state-led tele-communications systems have been rapidly all but supplanted. Literally dozens of huge telecommunications privatizations, generally shepherded by U.S. banks, lawyers, advertising agencies and management consultants, have finally established corporate ownership and control of this strategic sector as a worldwide phenomenon. Concurrently, transnationally integrated telecommunications infra-structures, beholden to investors rather than nations, have encroached dramatically on once-domestic systems—in the United States, as elsewhere.

The employees of the telecommunications industry thus confront a triad of wrenching shifts. Privatization is transforming them from state employees into employees of capital. Transnationalization is subordinating national flag carriers and nationally-organized systems of provision to a new logic of regional and global network system integration. Changes in the underlying technology of telecommunica-tions provision, as networks are digitalized to accord with the "1"s and "0"s of computers, are profoundly altering labor processes and work content throughout the industry.

What, then—to return to the question posed at the outset—is the likely character of labor's response to these fundamentally altered conditions? Steven Dubb's study is an exemplary comparative analysis of efforts by Canadian and Mexican telecommunications unions to orientate themselves and, if possible, to get in front of, these overarching changes. Canada and Mexico are of particular interest for such an inquiry, because they comprise the partners of the United States in the North American Free Trade Agreement—which in turn constitutes a vital codification of the neoliberal orthodoxy that has driven global capitalism for a generation. However, as this book shows, the two nations' union movements and, in particular, their tele-communications unions, remain unlike—the Telecommunications Workers Union, a small union based in British Columbia, is a feisty advocate of tying union goals into larger oppositional social movements, while Mexican telecommunications workers are led by a much different organization, which adheres to a familiar "bread-and-butter" orientation. Sensitive both to areas of continuing historical difference, and to converging trends and tendencies, Dubb develops a powerful comparative approach to changes occurring in and around telecommunications—from the perspective of labor's chief institution of collective action. The results are both informative and inspiring.

Dan Schiller
Professor of Communication
University of California, San Diego

Preface

Few industries have been more greatly influenced by globalization than the telephone industry. Not only has the industry been transformed from one based on national monopoly service provision to one based on international oligopolistic competition, but the industry in fact is situated at the heart of the globalization process. For without the telephone network that makes electronic communication—such as the World Wide Web and the Internet—possible, globalization would not exist.

In this book, I examine how unions, which represent tens or sometimes hundreds of thousands of workers at different telephone companies, have responded to these changes. The reason for this focus on unions was two-fold. First, unions' location at the workplace frequently makes them the first to have to confront industry changes. Patterns and settlements established between unions and corporations in the telephone industry can and do have a ripple effect on other workers and industries. For instance, the struggle of telecommunications workers at BC Tel (British Columbia Telephone) in Canada in the late 1970s and early 1980s for protections from lay-offs due to technological change led to later changes in the Canada Labour Code, resulting in the creation of federally-mandated technological change advance notice provisions. Another, albeit different, example is provided by the 1992 productivity agreement between Telmex and the Mexican Telephone Workers' Union, which was widely hailed as providing a framework for more cooperative bargaining arrangements between management and labor in Mexico.

A second reason for the focus on unions is that unions remain one of the most important collective political agents in a capitalist economy. Although much maligned both by many in business (who see unions as unnecessary fetters on management decision-making) and some on the left (who see unions as hopelessly compromised to the status quo), unions are important because they are often the only agents able to represent the collective interests of people in the workplace. Moreover, they possess a unique *capacity* to resist corporate initiatives when they find these initiatives to have a deleterious effect on their members. The reasons for this unique capacity are not hard to identify: institutional memory of prior struggles, relatively early access to information regarding industrial developments, and a stable membership base are obvious advantages that unions possess over many other political organizations. Of course, the fact that unions have the capacity to resist does not mean that they will always exercise that capacity. Indeed, the questions of whether and to what extent they do so form the heart of this study.

Key to understanding union behavior is understanding that unions optimize rather than maximize. This is, unlike businesses, which have a single maximization criterion—i.e., profit—unions have to balance multiple objectives, much as governments do. As a result, unions often make hard choices. For instance, a union that solely focuses on maximizing its members' wages may end up with a smaller membership, reducing its ability to protect the rank-and-file in the future.

The unions examined here provide a good comparative frame for the analysis of these issues. Put simply, the Mexican Telephone Workers' Union (STRM) exemplifies a form of unionism known as *business unionism* in which the union cooperates with management initiatives made in the name of globalization in exchange for "bread and butter" gains, while the Telecommunications Workers' Union (TWU) of British Columbia, Canada is a strong counter-example of a brand of unionism known as *social unionism*, which more actively resists globalization by building broad oppositional coalitions.

Comparative analysis demonstrates the effect of these strategic differences. One area where a particularly stark contrast exists is in the two unions' responses to deregulating and privatizing trends in the industry. The STRM was initially in favor of keeping the Mexican telephone company under state control, but its support for privatization was easily purchased. In exchange for a government offer to provide a low-interest loan to the union to buy 4.4% of the company at below-market prices, the union dropped its opposition to the company's sale and even cooperated by agreeing to contractual changes that eliminated management's obligation to replace retired workers and reduced the union's say in the implementation of technological change. On the positive side, STRM members profited from this arrangement with a one-time stock payment that, if cashed-out in 1993, would be worth roughly U.S. $20,000 per member, roughly twice the average STRM member's salary.

By contrast, the TWU was unwavering in its opposition to the deregulation of the Canadian telecommunications industry. When a newly elected Conservative government in 1984 sought to imitate the United States and deregulate the industry, the TWU participated in a broad coalition that succeeded in halting that effort. Among the TWU's tactics were efforts to generate public opposition, both through grass roots tactics (such as getting town councils to pass resolutions of opposition) and modern media tactics, such as buying television ads in which a person dressed up as Alexander Graham Bell denounced the deregulation plan. As a result, deregulation in Canada was stalled until 1992. Consequently, in the 1980s, while deregulation caused telephone company employment to fall by over 20% in the United States, employment remained steady in Canada.

Even after deregulation was approved, however, the TWU has continued to have notable successes. For instance, in 1993, the TWU successfully opposed a company plan to "give away" telephone inside wire (with the intention of thus making customers responsible for inside wire repair), thereby preserving TWU member work. And in 1995, the TWU successfully pushed through an "Accord" with a pro-labor British Columbia provincial government and BC Tel that commits the company to providing universal access to the internet for rural British Columbians. Ironically, the agreement was made possible by deregulation: the BC government pledged not to compete with BC Tel in telecommunications services provided that BC Tel subsidize rural internet connections. In short, the case of the TWU illustrates that, despite globalization, unions can still effectively promote social reform, especially when political circumstances are favorable.

But this work is not merely about the application of union strategy, but its creation, which is a complicated and contentious process. Here, many factors come into play, including the union's internal governance structure, factional strife, occupational divisions, and external political pressures. Strategies tend to be established in the heat of conflict. Once consolidated, they are often difficult to dislodge. Nonetheless, an external shock, such as globalization-induced industry changes *may* lead to a strategic reevaluation. In the case of the TWU, the key period of strategy formation is that of the 1977-1981 conflict over workplace technological change protection, which was marked by two strikes and a change in union leadership. The 1977-78 dispute was fought for a social unionist goal of technological change protection, but with traditional methods. While not a failure, it was costly, with the union treasury largely depleted after a five-month strike. Another such "success" and the TWU might well have given up on social unionism.

Instead, in the 1980-81 dispute, the TWU made use of three new tactics: 1) it intervened in regulatory commission hearings, thereby embarrassing management by showing how the company had failed to meet its service obligations; 2) it conducted an occupation of telephone facilities throughout the province in which the union expelled managers from the buildings but continued to provide service to the public, a militant (and illegal) tactic that nonetheless won the union considerable popular support; and 3) when forced to end the occupation by Court order, it relied on the support of fellow unions, with a citywide strike taking place in the mid-size town of Nanaimo being used to successfully pressure management to settle the strike on the union's terms. The TWU's success in the 1980-1981 dispute thus consolidated its social unionist approach.

In the case of the STRM, the key period was from 1976 to 1982. The similar timing with the TWU is not entirely coincidental, as here, too, impending computerization played a role in the conflict. Nonetheless, here disputes *within* the union were even more important than disputes between the union and Telmex management. In April 1976, operators dissatisfied with a proposed new contract organized a national wildcat work stoppage and called for a change in union leadership. As a result of this action, emergency union elections were called and an opposition slate was elected, led by a 26 year-old technician, Francisco Hernández Juárez.

Between 1978 and 1980, the STRM engaged in four short strikes. These strikes centered primarily on wage and benefit issues. In particular, the strikes aimed to increase operator wages to be more in line with the wages earned by other telephone workers. Union efforts to increase operator wages and improve operator working conditions were generally successful, but the union had less success at raising general wage levels.

Complicating matters was a split in the newly-empowered opposition slate. While Hernández Juárez sought to push for greater union autonomy vis a vis the Mexican state, but to maintain a narrow wage-and-benefits focus, a minority faction sought to push the union to embrace a broader social change agenda. In 1982, this faction, dissatisfied with union progress on negotiations regarding computerization, launched its own wildcat work stoppage. Partially successful at first, the movement nonetheless succumbed to opposition from state labor officials and other pro-government unions, which backed Hernández Juárez. Ever since, the union has maintained a strong "bread and butter" orientation. This has included a willingness to cooperate with management to boost productivity, provided workers receive associated wage and benefit increases.

Nonetheless, while both the TWU and the STRM have maintained their respective strategies since the early 1980s, these strategies are not immutable. Change has become particularly likely in the case of the STRM, where the December 1994 devaluation of the peso has disrupted not only union politics, but Mexican politics as a whole.

For the TWU, the period immediately following deregulation was marked by significant internal strife and self-doubt. This tension was evident in the field interviews I conducted among union leaders and members in the fall of 1993. Deregulation had occurred, but the effects of deregulation were still in the future and the union leadership was uncertain as to whether it could be successful in the new regulatory environment. The success of the 1995 Accord, which in hindsight may seem to be just another notch in the TWU's social unionist trajectory, was far from assured.

By contrast, in the STRM, while 1994 was the beginning of major political changes, the peso devaluation had not yet occurred and in field interviews union leaders remained quite certain that their strategy, including a strong alliance with Mexican state technocrats, was the "correct" one to follow. Three years later, however, in August 1997, the STRM split with the pro-government Labor Congress. With respect to management, the STRM still tends in a "bread and butter" direction, but this strategy is being increasingly challenged by the pressure of political events.

In short, while globalization presents unions with many challenges, not all unions choose to respond in the same manner. The process of globalization is also unpredictable—increasing pressures on unions to promote competitiveness at times, but also spawning political pressures that lead unions to adopt more militant positions. While a few years ago, unions seemed to be moving in the direction of greater cooperation, today the opposite tendency is in ascendance. If past is prologue, then further twists and turns can be expected along the way. It would appear that contrary to the positions held by some, the union movement has quite a bit of life in it still.

Acknowledgments

There are few activities that are more solitary than writing a book, yet at the same time any book is a collaborative effort, this one perhaps even more so than most. The book grew out of a class project in the winter of 1990 when I was a first-year graduate student at the University of California, San Diego (UCSD). Professor Ann Craig required that students in her class write a mock research proposal on the study of some social movement. I was vaguely interested in the labor movement, in part because my great-grandmother (who died well before I was born, but about whom I had heard many stories) had been an activist in the International Ladies' Garment Workers' Union.

Professor Craig advised me to talk to Maria Lorena Cook, who is now at Cornell, but at the time was finishing up her dissertation. Maria told me there were three unions in Mexico that were particularly important: the teachers' union (SNTE), the electricians' union (SME), and the telephone workers' union (STRM). I chose the STRM, in part because I (foolishly) thought that telephone technology was easy to understand. At the end of the quarter, I was encouraged to apply for a summer pre-dissertation grant. I applied, and to my surprise received, a Tinker Foundation grant, cosponsored by the UCSD Center for Iberian and Latin American Studies.

So with only a year of graduate studies under my belt, I brazenly set forth on my research project. Fortunately, I was aided by two people: Aslan Cohen, my senior thesis advisor at Berkeley, set me up to live in Mexico City with the Martin family, who have been very supportive of me throughout my studies; Professor Enrique de la Garza introduced me to STRM members and was of invaluable assistance in getting me started. In a short two months, I was able to collect enough information to write a paper on the opposition movement in the telephone workers' union ("Trozos de cristal"), which I presented at the Latin American Studies Association conference in Los Angeles in 1992. They've been thanked before, but it is only right to acknowledge again the assistance of Wayne Cornelius, Jeff Weldon, Ben Alpha Petrazzini, Patti Rosas, Harry Browne, and Juan Molinar Horcasitas who all commented on the paper.

By the summer of 1992, I had completed my coursework and had to come up with a research project for my dissertation. I knew I wanted to compare the Mexican telephone workers' union with another union, but which one? After picking up Elaine Bernard's book on the British Columbian telephone workers' union, though, the decision was pretty easy, as I realized the comparison of the two cases would give me a unique angle from which to address the question of globalization. Still, I knew that I would have to sell a project comparing a Canadian and a Mexican union. It is to the credit of the members of my committee that they actually let me go forward with the proposal. Ellen Comisso was particularly helpful in getting me to focus my research question in the prospectus.

I was fortunate to get grants from two research centers: The UCSD Center for Iberian & Latin American Studies and the UC-MEXUS program at UC Riverside. Their funding enabled me to spend six months in Vancouver, British Columbia, and an additional six months in Mexico City to conduct my field research. I gratefully acknowledge both organizations' support.

During my field research, I was very impressed by the welcome I received from the Telecommunications Workers' Union in Canada. I was given full access to their research library and was able to attend everything from meetings with company management to emergency executive council sessions. Sid Shniad, the TWU's Research Director, helped me track down needed documents. The telephone workers were also very supportive. The ability to go out with an installation & repair worker, or to listen in to an operator working may not yield tangible research data, but it certainly helped me gain a better feel of the people and the industry that I was researching.

While I was in British Columbia, I also hooked up with Professor Mark Thompson of the Commerce Department at UBC. Mark set me up to give a couple of informal talks about my research, which enabled me to stay in contact with an academic community while I was conducting my research.

I did not enjoy the same access at the STRM as I had at the TWU, but I am very grateful for the help that I did get. The Mexican telephone workers themselves were quite supportive and also let me tag along at different work sites. While in Mexico, I was able to attend a trinational telephone workers' conference put on by Transnational Information Exchange (TIE) which proved invaluable for getting information about the actions of other telecommunications unions in North America. Professor Enrique de la Garza provided thoughtful comments and gave me full access to his files. There are many others who helped me, but who must remain nameless here. Mil gracias.

Writing the dissertation was actually more difficult than doing the research. Fortunately, I came in contact with many people who supported me when writing was difficult, including members of the Groundwork Books collective, the UCSD student book cooperative; my fellow Political Science graduate students; and my parents.

In terms of the actual writing of this work, my dissertation committee—Wayne Cornelius, Paul Drake, Ellen Comisso, Jeffrey Haydu, and Harley Shaiken—was of great assistance, helping me sharpen the introduction as well as the sections on international political economy and Taylorism. Wayne Cornelius, my committee chair, suggested the title of this work and made sure I stayed on schedule in my writing.

In addition to my committee members, I received comments from Sid Shniad, Jeff Cowie, Scott Morgenstern, Heather Williams, Lorna Lueker, Patti Rosas, Hubert Dubb, and a group of Mexican telephone union members. Sid was particularly thorough; I had asked for comments, but Sid also copy-edited the entire nine chapters, making this book far more readable than it otherwise would have been. Jeff helped me think through some of the issues regarding the relationship of telecommunications to the wider economy. Scott helped me clarify some of the issues regarding the state-labor relationship in Mexico and pushed me to incorporate tables to this work to improve readability. Table 3-1 is a direct result of a suggestion made by Heather. Lorna, Patti, and my father provided additional feedback and editing assistance.

I also received very helpful comments from participants at four informal presentations. These were made to the Latin American democratization study group, chaired by Wayne Cornelius; to a conference of Canadian telecommunications unions; to the executive council of the TWU; and to the Center for Democratization and Economic Development group, chaired by Germaine Hoston.

In converting the dissertation into this present book, I would like to acknowledge the efforts of Professor Stuart Bruchey, who reviewed the manuscript and accepted the book for publication on behalf of Garland Press; Dan Schiller, who wrote the foreword for this book; and Damon Zucca, who has been a very thoughtful and patient editor.

Finally, and most importantly, I would liike to thank Barbara Berglund. Barbara's love, friendship and support have been invaluable to me.

Acronyms

ACTWU	Atlantic Canada Telecommunications Workers Union
AF of L	American Federation of Labor
AGT	Alberta Government Telephone
AT&T	American Telephone & Telegraph
BC Tel	British Columbia Telephone
BRC	Board of Railway Commissioners
BTE	Business Terminal Equipment
BTUC	British Trade Unions Committee
CANTV	Compañía Nacional Teléfonos de Venezuela (National Telephone Company of Venezuela)
CAW	Canadian Auto Workers
CBA	Canadian Banking Association
CBTA	Canadian Business Telecommunications Alliance
CCC	Canadian Competition Coalition
CEP	Communication, Energy & Paperworkers Union
CFCW	Canadian Federation of Communication Workers
CGT	Confederación General de Trabajadores (General Workers' Confederation)
CIO	Congress of Industrial Organizations
CLC	Canadian Labour Congress
CLRB	Canadian Labour Relations Board
Coparmex	Confederación Patronal de la República Mexicana (Employers' Confederation of the Mexican Republic)
COTC	Contracting-Out and Technological Change Committee

CROM	Confederación Regional Obrera Mexicana (Mexican Regional Worker Confederation)
CRTC	Canadian Radio-television and Telecommunications Commission
CT	Congreso del Trabajo (Labor Congress)
CTC	Canadian Transport Commission
CTM	Confederación de Trabajadores de México (Mexican Workers' Confederation)
CUPW	Canadian Union of Postal Workers
CUT	Central Unica de Trabajadores (Sole Workers' Central)
CWA	Communication Workers of America
CWC	Communication Workers of Canada
DOC	Department of Communications (Canada)
DOL	Department of Labour (Canada)
EEO	Electric Employees' Organization
FAT	Frente Auténtico de Trabajo (Authentic Labor Front)
FCC	Federal Communications Commission
Fesebes	Federación de Sindicatos de Empresas de Bienes y Servicios (Federation of Unions of Goods and Services Businesses)
Foro	Foro: El Sindicalismo frente a la Crisis y ante la Nación (The Forum: Unionism Addressing the Crisis before the Nation)
FTW	Federation of Telephone Workers
GTE	General Telephone and Electronics Corporation
IBEW	International Brotherhood of Electrical Workers
IDIA	Industrial Disputes Investigation Act
ITAC	Information Technology Association of Canada
ITT	International Telephone and Telegraph
MAS	Movimiento de Acción Sindical (Union Action Movement)
Mexicana	Compañía Telefónica Mexicana (Mexican Telephone Company)
NAFTA	North American Free Trade Agreement
NDP	New Democratic Party
OK Tel	Okinagan Telephone Company
PNR	Partido Nacional Revolucionario (National Revolutionary Party)

PRD	Partido de la Revolución Democrática (Party of the Democratic Revolution)
PRI	Partido Revolucionario Institucional (Institutional Revolutionary Party)
PRM	Partido de la Revolución Mexicana (Party of the Mexican Revolution)
PRT	Partido Revolucionario de los Trabajadores (Revolutionary Workers' Party)
PSUM	Partido Socialista Unificado de México (Unified Socialist Party of Mexico)
PTTI	Postal, Telephone & Telegraph International
SaskTel	Saskatchewan Telephone Company
SCT	Secretaría de Comunicaciones y Transporte (Ministry of Communications and Transportation)
SNTE	Sindicato Nacional de Trabajadores de la Educación (National Union of Education Workers)
SME	Sindicato Mexicano de Electricistas (Mexican Union of Electrical Workers)
STET	Società Torinese Esercizi Telefonici (Torinese Society for Telephone Enterprise)
STyPS	Secretaría de Trabajo y Previsión Social (Ministry of Labor and Social Welfare)
STRM	Sindicato de Telefonistas de la República Mexicana (Telephone Workers' Union of the Mexican Republic)
SUTERM	Sindicato Unico de Trabajadores Electricistas de la República Mexicana (Sole Union of Electrical Workers of the Mexican Republic)
Telmex	Teléfonos de México (Mexico Telephone)
TIE	Transnational Information Exchange
TOO	Telephone Operators' Organization
TSPS	Traffic Service Position System
TWU	Telecommunications Workers Union
UAW	United Auto Workers
UMW	United Mine Workers
UNT	Unión Nacional de Trabajadores (National Union of Workers)

Logics of Resistance

CHAPTER ONE

Introduction: Globalization and Labor's Search for Alternatives

The last big problem that trade unions went through is when they had to evolve from the craft unions to the industrial unions. Now we're going in the transition from the industrial union to—I don't know what that would be—the technological union? But we're leaving the industrial union stage. I don't think our pains are any different in nature than what our predecessors went through in the transition from craft to industrial unions (TWU business agent, Interview T-94-74).[1]

The principal goal is this: to organize a distinct alternative, an alternative that represents the workers' interests, that permits us to stop cold the destruction of the Collective Agreement (STRM opposition activist, Interview S-94-25).

Ultimately, this work is a study about changes and about alternatives. It focuses on changes in the sense that telecommunications is an industry in the midst of rapid transformation, in which there have been in recent years great changes in the use of computer technology, the organization of work, the structure of markets, and the role of the state. This study looks at alternatives in the sense that telecommunications trade unions, although confronted with multiple changes in their environment, have not been passive actors in the process, but rather through numerous tactics and stratagems have sought to influence the overall direction of the changes.

In arguing for the importance of the role played by unions, this work parts company with those who forecast the decline of the working class and working-class organization due to the onset of a "postindustrial age" (Gorz 1982). Indeed, discussing labor's strategic options only makes sense if labor indeed has a future.

This study seeks to address the issue of labor strategy by examining two unions' responses to globalization within the telecommunications industry. It contrasts a Canadian union, the TWU, which represents workers at British Columbia Telephone (BC Tel) with that of a Mexican union, the STRM, which represents workers at Teléfonos de México (Telmex), Mexico's primary telecommunications company. Basic statistics regarding the two unions are provided in the table below:

Table 1-1: STRM and TWU, Basic Statistics

	STRM	TWU
Formation of first predecessor union	1915	1901
Date present union was founded	1950	1944-45
		(FTW)[2]
Membership[3] at founding	6,324	2,056
Membership (1972)	15,548	8,634
Membership (1982)	27,624	11,731
Membership (1994)	40,606	11,236
Year of most recent strike	1980	1981
Union density at telephone company	64%[4]	78%[5]
Percent of union members in single company	100%	98%

The comparison between a Canadian union and a Mexican union is unusual, but the selection of these two unions facilitates the analysis of three key questions. First, the comparison highlights the issue of the impact of globalization on labor in distinct domestic contexts. According to one influential argument (Piore and Sabel 1984), globalization is currently producing a shift in the nature of production from segmented, single task, atomized work (Taylorism) to clustered, multi-task, team work (flexible specialization). Many analysts of the labor movement in academic (Heckscher 1988, Bluestone and Bluestone 1992, Hoerr 1991, Streeck 1992, Levine and Strauss 1993), union (Hernández Juárez and Xelhuantzi López 1993) and government circles (Peterson 1990) contend that these changes will compel unions to cooperate with management regarding shop-floor issues, an argument that I label "the convergence hypothesis." The findings of this study largely contradict that hypothesis. Even though the process of globalization in Canada and Mexico has been intensified through the implementation of the North American Free Trade Agreement (NAFTA) and the intervention of U.S. managers in both companies, the response of the STRM and the TWU illustrate how two unions when faced with similar work organization and technological changes can respond in sometimes starkly different ways.

Second, the comparison allows for more careful examination of the hypothesis of Mexican labor exceptionalism. This hypothesis, so often assumed in the literature (see, for instance, Bizberg 1986, Bizberg 1990, Zapata 1989, Aziz Nassif 1989, Collier 1995, Hellman 1988), has rarely been analyzed comparatively, and when it has (Collier and Collier 1991), the analysis occurs primarily in a Latin American, and not a North American, context. Put simply, this thesis argues that it is Mexico's unique system of labor control, frequently labelled in the literature "state corporatism," which is responsible for labor quiescence. There is more empirical support here than for the convergence hypothesis above. Nonetheless, the hypothesis of Mexican labor exceptionalism is flawed in two important respects. First, it underestimates the centrality of internal union struggles in determining the position a given union takes—and it is *not* always the case that the state-supported side prevails. (Nor is it the case that state officials are always unified as to which side to support). Moreover, this hypothesis ignores the ubiquity of state intervention in labor worldwide, even in countries that have a relatively permissive labor regime, such as Canada. In both Mexico and Canada, despite efforts to influence labor strategy, state officials have had limited ability to impose a particular strategic approach on labor unions. This is especially true in key industries, such as telecommunications, where the strategic importance of the industry gives union leaders greater leverage.

A third benefit of this comparison is that it allows for the analysis of two distinct union strategies with respect to globalization: one, the STRM, the example *par excellence* of union-management cooperation in Mexico; the other, the TWU, with a well-earned reputation as the "most militant [telecommunications] trade union in Canada" (Winseck 1993: 233). Although in the past decade the Canadian union has been more militant than its Mexican counterpart, historically there have been times when the Canadian TWU more closely approximated the labor quiescence seen as the Mexican norm, and there have been times when the Mexican STRM has more closely approximated the labor militancy seen as the Canadian norm. Labor unions do make strategic and tactical decisions that have consequences for their membership and, indeed, for the industries and even the economies in which they operate. While these decisions take place in specific political and economic contexts, the decisions are better explained by examining the internal logic of the individual trade union than by focusing on global economic imperatives or national political or labor-regime structures. The nature of the two unions are examined in further detail below, as are issues of labor strategy, the impact of globalization on trade unions, the relationship between trade unions and the state, and the role of internal union decision-making.

THE LOGIC OF COMPARISON

Although the Mexican STRM and the Canadian TWU operate in different national[6] labor regimes, there are important similarities that allow me as a researcher to isolate the differences and assess their importance. First of all, both unions include all non-management personnel in their bargaining unit. This often is not the case. For instance, at Bell Canada (the main telephone company in Ontario and southern Quebec), plant workers and operators are in one union while clerical workers are in a separate union. Second, both unions are single-employer unions.[7] Within North America at least, this is becoming increasingly unusual. Both the Communication, Energy & Paperworkers (CEP) union, which represents over 20,000 telephone workers in three Canadian provinces, and the Communication Workers of America (CWA) organize many workers in industries that have nothing to do with telecommunications. Dealing with a single-union, single-employer environment in both cases makes comparison much simpler. Instead of having to control for differing mixes of employers and industries, this comparison allows in-depth comparison of how two unions respond specifically to the threat posed by globalization in the telecommunications industry.[8]

Since Teléfonos de México was privatized in 1990, both unions have to deal with companies that are partially owned by foreign investors. GTE has a 50.1% share ownership in British Columbia Telephone, while both Southwestern Bell and France Telecom have minority interests (24.5% of voting capital each) in the newly privatized Teléfonos de México. While it is difficult to measure the effect of foreign ownership, the fact that American corporations have ownership stakes in the two companies helps explain why similar organizational techniques (e.g., work teams) have been attempted or are currently in effect at the two companies. Moreover, the two unions have a history of industrial militancy. In particular, they both experienced an eruption of strikes and militant activity at roughly the same time in the late seventies and early eighties. A bit more should be said about this, since it is usually asserted that Mexican labor is, in general, quiescent (Middlebrook, 1989) and even Canadian unions are often accused of excessive "industrial legalism" (Palmer 1992: 370-377).

In 1976, a wildcat strike of rank-and-file telephone workers in Mexico City led to the ousting of the old leadership and the election of a then twenty-six year-old reformist leader, Francisco Hernández Juárez. Between 1978 and 1980, the STRM engaged in four strikes rooted in both wage and non-wage issues (Unomásuno 1980, Martinez Lira 1986, Xelhuantzi López 1988). The Mexican state responded on repeated occasions by sending in the army to take over operations at the telephone company, in what is known as a *requisa*. But state officials acceded to some union demands, particularly those which increased the workplace rights of operators.

The TWU likewise had a province-wide wildcat strike in 1976, although the cause of the strike was the company's contracting-out of union work, not internal political strife. In addition, in both 1977-1978 and 1980-1981, the TWU engaged in selective strikes, targeting large business customers, which in both cases led to management-imposed lock-outs of the entire workforce. In the 1980-81 case, in an attempt to preempt an anticipated lock-out by management, the TWU occupied British Columbia Telephone facilities province-wide—thereby locking management out. Despite receiving record fines and prompting a British Columbia Supreme Court Justice to declare, "A more blatant affront to the law would be difficult to imagine," the TWU succeeded in getting the added technological-change provisions and work-jurisdiction protections that it was seeking (Bernard 1982, quote on p. 210).

But while both unions engaged in militant action in the late 1970s and early 1980s, the two unions subsequently followed divergent paths. The STRM's previously reformist leadership grew increasingly conservative, as the union sought to reach an accommodation with the Mexican government and the newly privatized company. In part, this shift was seen as an effort on the part of STRM leader Hernández

Juárez to position himself to succeed the nonogenarian Fidel Velázquez as the leader of the Mexican labor movement (Darling 1991).[9] I n exchange for signing a *convenio de concertación* with the government in April 1989, in which many pre-existing work rules were eliminated, the union and union members received 4.4% of the shares of the privatized company.[10] The STRM has endorsed such "worker participation schemes" as quality circles and work teams. Indeed, of all telecommunications unions in North America, the STRM has taken the most "accommodationist" or "cooperative" stance.

On the other hand, the TWU, which up until the late 1960s was viewed as an unusually conservative union in British Columbia (Bernard 1982: 113-131),[11] has clung more firmly to its militant stance. While no strikes have occurred since 1981, the TWU has, compared to the more moderate approaches taken by other Canadian telecommunications unions, resisted much more tenaciously the deregulation of the telephone industry in Canada, fighting a protracted eight-year battle against deregulation, including successfully suing the government in 1989 when other unions urged it to hold back (Winseck 1993: 201-260).

Still, ever since the Canadian telecommunications regulatory commission ruled in favor of deregulation in June 1992, the TWU has had to consider new methods to protect its membership. Options considered range from greater cooperation with the company to an aggressive organizing campaign to keep industry wages up in the newly competing firms and to reduce union dependence on a single company. This debate provides an excellent illustration of the distinctive paths of action available to labor, as well as an opportunity to analyze the potential consequences of these alternatives.

LABOR AND THE LOGICS OF UNION STRATEGY

> America has always been full of machines and ghosts—Taxi Ghosts, Bus Ghosts, Police Ghosts, Fire Ghosts, Meter Reader Ghosts, Tree Trimming Ghosts, Five-and-Dime Ghosts. Once upon a time the world was so thick with ghosts, I could hardly breathe (Kingston 1977: 96-97).

Academia too has its ghosts, in precisely the sense that Kingston uses the term. There are Liberal Ghosts, Pluralist Ghosts, Corporatist Ghosts, Critical Theory Ghosts, Marxist Ghosts, Social Movement

Theory Ghosts, and Poststructuralist Ghosts, to name a few.[12] And there are more than a few times when, wading through the literature, the theoretical debates becomes so stifling that one hardly has room to breathe. Indeed, as Richard Hyman wrote in his study of industrial relations, at times theory can seem "something of a dirty word" (Hyman 1975: 1). But as Hyman argues, theory is not only inescapable but necessary. Only a theoretical framework can provide a systematic "way of seeing, of understanding, and of planning" (Hyman 1975: 2), a means to generalize from specific cases and a way to interpret the cases that one is able to examine personally. Although not an attempt to provide a thorough explanation of either the nature of the state or of capitalism, this work is guided by a number of implicit theoretical understandings.

On the one hand, these theoretical understandings spring from a Marxist understanding of the centrality of capitalism in contemporary society, where capital enjoys a predominant position over labor, both directly in the workplace and indirectly through its predominance of influence over the state. On the other hand, this study does not make much use of Marxist terminology, such as the relations of production, mode of production, base, and superstructure. Whereas the problematic of this work is set by a concern about the relation between capital and labor and its influence on everyday life, the approach adopted here is to attempt to evaluate labor unions within their *own* logic, rather than analyze them externally through a Marxist logic. Thus, although I analyze the writings of Marxist theorists of the labor movement, such as Lenin and Rosa Luxembourg, I concentrate more on the works of Selig Perlman and Sidney and Beatrice Webb, which better reflect the reformist logics that have been adopted by the great majority of unions in Canada and Mexico.

In particular, Selig Perlman explains the logic of *business unionism*, a logic that seeks to maximize worker monetary gain while limiting the challenge to the rights of capital as much as possible. Sidney and Beatrice Webb explain the logic of *social unionism*, which seeks a much broader array of reforms but stops short of seeking revolutionary change. In Mexico, the dominant tendency, though named corporatism, operates according to a logic very similar to that of American business unionism; however, there are unions in Mexico that follow more of a social unionist logic. In Canada, the social and business unionist tendencies are both strong, although currently the social unionist approach is somewhat stronger. As will be seen, these two logics, while both reformist, imply very different union responses to the pressures of globalization. While the logic of business unionism implies a trend to meet the "imperatives" of global capital on its own terms—that is, to cooperate with management to increase production—the logic of social unionism involves a much more complicated mix of accommodation and resistance.

How a union will respond to globalization will depend significantly on the strategic orientation that union has adopted. Strategy is chosen based on unionists' understanding of the market and the state and how to confront the two. This understanding is largely the result of internal factors, set forth in more detail below, such as historically ingrained patterns of behavior and resolution of internal differences among different occupational strata and political tendencies. External factors, such as the economic restructuring brought about by globalization, or the specific changes unleashed by state decisions to privatize or deregulate, may or may not lead to a reassessment of union strategy. Generally, one can anticipate that the union will initially seek to respond as it has in the past and adjust only after attempts to apply tried-and-true tactics have failed.[13]

GLOBALIZATION AND THE TELECOMMUNICATIONS INDUSTRY

Although much discussion in the business press regarding globalization and the need to be "lean and mean" is thinly disguised propaganda, there can be no doubt that trade unions face new challenges in the global economy. Telecommunications is a unique case in that it is both affected by these economic changes and simultaneously an important part of them. Rules and boundaries that were once solid and clear have become blurred and uncertain. Globally, workers now find their lives connected as never before, and not just by telephone wires or satellite link-ups.[14]

At its simplest level, globalization in telecommunications can be defined as a shift from a traditional structure of national (or, in the case of Canada, provincial) monopoly provision of telephone services to a market structure based on controlled or limited international oligopolistic competition. However, this shift has been accompanied by many other changes. For instance, management structure has been altered, with middle managers losing authority while top-level managers, such as chief executive officers, gain new authority, as formerly nationally bound companies have expanded their operations internationally.

At the same time, while capital has become more and more global, labor has remained largely national, and even local in character. This puts trade unions at a significant disadvantage. There have been some preliminary efforts to build cross-national labor solidarity, but so far it remains the case that while the economy is becoming increasingly international in character, labor still focuses its activity at the national and local levels. Thus, this study does not focus on labor internationalism—which is still very limited—but rather on how trade unions organized at the national and subnational level have responded to trends resulting from globalization.[15] These trends include such factors as an increasing concentration of capital in the industry, a new market balance-of-power giving more weight to large telecommunications users (i.e., international banks and other multinational corporations), the spread of computer technology and management attempts to use new technology to reorganize the workforce, and changes in the role of the state within a rapidly evolving telecommunications market.

In this study, then, capital is clearly the first mover, the creator of the "external shocks" to which state and union officials must respond. This is true not because capital *a priori* must be the first mover, but rather because historically, in the case of the emergence of new market structures in the telecommunications sector, it was.

Although there have been many studies on globalization's effects on the organization of production,[16] there has been surprisingly little work comparing the choices made by telecommunications unions as a result of the change in economic structure. Those studies that have been done, examined in more detail in Chapter 3, have largely concluded that the changes brought about by globalization compel unions to cooperate with business to improve productivity. This study instead seeks to show how and why different telecommunications unions respond differently.

LABOR, GLOBALIZATION, AND NATIONAL LABOR REGIMES

Though globalization may reduce state officials' ability to direct economic affairs, the state's role remains substantial. First of all, the state sets up and maintains the regulatory framework for the telecommunications industry. Certainly, there are differences in the role played by the state in Canada and Mexico. Nonetheless, particularly in telecommunications, these differences have diminished considerably over the past decade. The reason for this is not difficult to understand. For the state's relationship with capital has changed from that of a coordinator that directs the overall economy to more of a mediator that adjudicates among competing business interests while maintaining a much reduced planning role.[17] When the state acted as a coordinator, then its greater degree of authority, both in terms of share of total investment and as a direct owner of major branches of the economy, meant that there would be a greater divergence in the way that authority was used. Now as a mediator among competing interests and with a reduced planning role, the state's scope of authority is reduced and so is the degree of variation in state action. This shift reflects both a relative decline in the degree of direct state influence as well as the general decline of the Keynesian state-based economic model.

As well as being a referee of capital in the regulatory arena, the state acts as an enforcer of the capitalist order (through such means as declaring strikes "non-existent" in Mexico or by issuing injunctions in Canada) in the industrial relations field. In particular, the state acts as a coordinating body of a given nation's labor regime—that is, the set of rules, norms, and institutions that govern relations among workers, capitalists, and state officials. Because labor regimes remain primarily national in character, differences in national labor regimes do influence the paths taken by unions in different countries. At the same time, it must be noted that these differences can be and are exaggerated. This matter bears emphasis since the importance of national labor regime differences is a frequent theme in the literature.

In Mexico, the labor regime is most commonly identified as state corporatist—that is, the government limits the number of unions, seeks to impose its own choice of leaders on these unions, and insists that these leaders endorse the economic and social policy preferences of the ruling political elite in return for considerable autonomy in dealing with rank-and-file union members (Collier 1992, Bizberg 1990, Trejo Delarbre 1990). In the words of David Collier, "In the face of repeated crises and challenges since the late 1960s, and notwithstanding important shifts in the relation between the party and the labor movement, the traditional corporative features of the Mexican system remained, at least until the end of 1994, a fundamental feature of national politics" (Collier 1995: 155-156). Students of the Mexican labor movement have focused on organized labor's so-called "bargain" or "alliance" with government officials (Aziz Nassif 1989). Thus, in the Mexican labor literature, there are many studies on both government controls on labor, including limits on the right to strike (Middlebrook 1995) and labor's inability, despite its links to the ruling "revolutionary family" (Brandenburg 1964), to influence policy decisions. By contrast, Canada—like the United States[18]—is said to have a labor system based on "free collective bargaining" (Palmer 1969).[19] While Mexico's labor system is characterized as top-down, government-controlled unionism, Canada's labor system is characterized by pluralism and independent unionism (Lazarus 1977, Laxer 1976, Morton 1980), though more recently scholars have placed greater emphasis on the coercive role of the Canadian state (Panitch and Swartz 1993, Palmer 1992).

There are, of course, substantial differences in the labor relations systems of the two countries—differences that are in fact important for this study. For instance, Mexico's labor regime is more centralized than Canada's. But it's worth noting that even at the height of Mexican "corporatism,"[20] roughly half of Mexican union members were not members of the Mexican Confederation of Workers or CTM. This includes some of Mexico's most important unions, including the school teachers' union, the telephone workers' union, and the oil workers' union, among others. Moreover, there are both independent unions in Mexico (Roxborough 1984, Novelo 1991, Trejo Delarbre 1990) and many dissident factions that exist even within even the most autocratic Mexican unions.[21]

Both the divisions within the official government-supported labor unions and the existence of a wide variety of dissident groups in Mexican labor pose serious questions for traditional accounts of Mexican labor and has important implications for the analysis of the cases studied here. Not only does it mean that state officials sometimes lose (as in 1976 with the rise of dissident leader Francisco Hernández Juárez in the STRM), but, more importantly, the focus on state action in the Mexican labor literature obscures some underlying similarities with unions in other countries, such as Canada. The debate in Mexico over labor strategy between so-called "corporatist" unions and "independent" unions (Roxborough 1984), for instance, parallels in many respects the debate between "business" unions and "social" unions in Canada. Canadian business unions, like Mexican corporatist unions, emphasize the importance of short-term "bread and butter" gains. Canadian social unions, like Mexican independent unions, advocate a strategy that seeks broader social reform. The outcome of these debates will affect the way labor interacts with global capital and the state in both countries.

UNION DECISION-MAKING: INTERNAL FACTORS

The internal logic of unions is built from many factors. Most important in explaining how a union will respond to globalization is its overall strategic orientation—that is, the overall, long-term strategy that is followed by a given union. This is, after all, the gist of what the political factions struggle about. Some unions, such as Canadian business unions and Mexican corporatist unions, seek to focus on wage and benefit gains and generally otherwise cooperate with management. In the past, this meant ceding to management near-unilateral authority over workplace relations; now, instead, it often means working with managers to jointly implement management-designed production techniques such as work teams. The STRM's productivity program, examined in more detail in Chapter 6, is a good example of such an approach. However, it should be noted that the STRM is not alone in such endeavors; both the CWA (Communications Workers of America) in the United States and the CEP (Communications, Energy & Paperworkers) in Canada have been advocates of team-based production. Business unionists also tend to be less vigorous in resisting state policy initiatives such as deregulation or privatization.

Other unions, such as social unions in Canada and independent unions in Mexico, pursue a broader agenda of social reform, work in conjunction with a social democratic party (where they exist, as in the case of the Canadian New Democratic Party or NDP), and seek to form community coalitions. Such unions are more likely to press management on worker control issues, even at some sacrifice to wage gains. Though not necessarily hostile to team production per se, one can expect social unions to show more resistance on these issues and demand more workplace rights in exchange for their consent than their business union counterparts. As well, social unions tend to be more aggressive in resisting state deregulatory and privatization initiatives.

These different classifications are ideal-typical. It is thus certainly possible for a union to lie between different modal types. Nevertheless, a strategic orientation is not easily established nor easily changed. It is central to the argument of this study that a union's strategic orientation influences how a union responds to a wide variety of issues, including those that are the focus of the empirical chapters: namely, technological change, the organization of work, and the way the union interacts with the state.

Changes in strategic orientation are akin to what is known as "realignment" in the political science elections literature. A major external shock, such as that provided by globalization in this study may *potentially* lead to a change in strategic orientation.[22] Indeed, as can be seen in the analysis here, though both the STRM's business unionist approach and the TWU's social unionist approaches have held so far, both have been subject to challenge due to the negative impact that globalization has had on many union members.

However, though a union's strategic orientation may be the most important factor in understanding how a union responds to the changes brought about by globalization, it is hardly the only one. Clearly, there are various factors that enter into union decision-making and it's important to identify the most important of these: namely, occupational divisions, a union's governing structure, and the role of competing political factions.

The first factor, occupational divisions, may seem trivial, particularly when compared to the immense challenge posed by globalization of the telecommunications industry. But in the same sense that one could say of U.S. politics that "all politics is local" (O'Neill 1987: 6-26), so too can one say all union politics is occupational. Of course, literally speaking, neither is all U.S. politics local nor all union politics occupational. But all U.S. politics impacts localities and likewise all union politics impacts specific occupational groups. While union leaders are typically motivated by broader concerns, they often gain rank-and-file support on the basis of what they can provide at specific work sites for specific work groups. Frequently, in the telecommunications industry, occupational and gender divisions coincide as operator positions and many clerical positions remain largely female-dominated, while most plant and technical jobs are still held by men (Cooper Tory 1989, Vallas 1993).

Some of the changes brought about by globalization, particularly those involving technological change and workplace restructuring, have widely disparate effects on different sectors of the unionized workforce.[23] On such issues, the ability of occupational groups to organize, stage shop floor walk-outs and other action, and secure central union leadership support is often key in determining how aggressively the union as a whole will respond. This is seen in particular in Chapters 5 and 6, where the issues of union response to technological change and workplace reorganization, respectively, are discussed at length.

The governing structure of the union is also important because it is through this structure that union decisions are made. A union can be democratic or authoritarian. If democratic, the union can be based on direct membership democracy[24] or, as is the case with the TWU, indirect delegate-based democracy. If authoritarian, the union can be exclusionary[25] or inclusionary, like the STRM, where the union leadership seeks the plebiscitary approval of the rank-and-file in elections held every four years. Broadly speaking, democratic unions often are slower to respond to changes, such as those brought about by globalization, but tend to be able to alter strategic approaches with less upheaval than authoritarian unions. The cases here would seem to bear this out, as major changes in STRM policy have generally occurred as a result of either government imposition or rank-and-file rebellion, while the TWU convention delegates have regularly voted members of the central union executive council out of office when they were dissatisfied with their performance, doing so most recently in January 1995.

Within the governing structure of a union, one encounters various groups struggling over the direction of union policy. In the STRM, historically various political currents have operated. In particular, there has been a struggle between those who wish to pursue a policy that aims to accommodate the changes in the global economy, by promoting cooperation with management and the government and working to boost productivity in the hope of obtaining higher wages and benefits; and those who wish to pursue a more class-based and confrontational unionism which places more emphasis in resisting what are seen as unfavorable changes in the global economy and in which a broader social agenda is pursued. In the TWU, the factions have been situated somewhat differently, as historically the faction that has had the broader social agenda has been, with some exceptions, more moderate and the faction that has had the narrower, wage-focused agenda more militant. Another distinction between the two unions is that generally the gap between the main factions in the STRM has been wider than in the TWU. In part, the narrower gap in the TWU may result from the TWU's more democratic structure. Though not always the case, it would appear that democratic unions tend to be more amenable to the striking of compromises than authoritarian unions, which may discourage polarization.

METHODOLOGY

Field research was conducted in Canada from August 1993 through January 1994 and in Mexico from February 1994 through August 1994. In Canada, over 80 field interviews were conducted. These interviews consisted of a mixture of standard questions which were posed to all respondents and specialized questions which were asked to respondents with knowledge in particular areas. As well, I asked follow-up questions as seemed appropriate. Interviews ranged in length from one hour to three hours, with most lasting about 90 minutes. In selecting interviewees, I tried to get a good cross-section of the membership (both among the locals and among different levels of the union), including people with no active union involvement, people who attend union meetings but hold no union position, shop stewards, counselors (chief shop stewards), and members of the province-wide union executive council. In addition, I interviewed a few people outside the union, including unionists from other unions, academics, and British Columbia Telephone management officials. Overall, due to the focus of my study on union strategic decision-making, the majority of people interviewed are union activists. The rank-and-file and non-TWU interviews serve as a "check" on the claims made by union activists, but the overall weight of the interviews is biased towards union activists and purposely so. The detailed interviews were extremely important in increasing my comprehension of the actual "shop floor" effects of the introduction of new technology, as well as getting an articulation of the different positions within the union regarding the proper strategy and tactics for the union to use to confront the changes brought about by globalization in telecommunications.

My field research in British Columbia also included other elements—observation of union activities, research in union archives, and perusal of the secondary literature on Canadian unionism. I was able to attend roughly a dozen different meetings of union locals, as well as several meetings of the provincial union executive council, and I attended the union's annual convention. In addition, I visited several work sites, observing the work stations of clerical and operator workers and travelling in trucks with plant workers. These experiences gave me a better feel for the occupational categories within the union and allowed me to gain a greater understanding of the operation of semi-formal political factions in the union. The primary archival and secondary research has also proved quite important. Among the key archival documents I examined are convention minutes, provincial executive council minutes, minutes of meetings for selected locals, key arbitration decisions, past collective agreements, union video tapes, union submissions to government and regulatory agencies, company strategy documents, minutes of company presentations to the union's executive board, and articles from the union periodical *The Transmitter*. Elaine Bernard had deposited her notes and the documents that she amassed in writing her 1982 book on the TWU at the University of British Columbia library, which enabled me to get a good historical overview of the union's development.

Field research in Mexico followed similar lines, but with a somewhat different strategy. During research on the STRM done in 1990 (Dubb 1992), I had already conducted about 20 field interviews and had made contacts with members of the STRM and academic researchers. This prior research focused on the internal political dynamics of the union leadership and opposition approaches to confronting globalization, in particular the privatization of the company. The 1994 field research was focused on updating earlier work and obtaining a broader pool of interview subjects. Since 1992, the secondary literature has been expanded by a half-dozen academic studies of the STRM.[26] I also got access to dozens of company and union documents. From Enrique de la Garza Toledo of the UAM-Iztapalapa, I obtained copies of studies that his students had done about the union in 1993. As well, several non-governmental union advisory groups provided recent data that compared STRM members to other telephone workers in Mexico.

In Mexico in 1994 I conducted an additional 35 interviews (for a total of 55), similar in length and scope to the Canadian interviews. My previous research consisted largely of pro-opposition unionists, mainly because most pro-leadership members refused to be interviewed. My 1994 research also included a high percentage of those critical of the union leadership, but I did have long interviews with three high-ranking union staffers and two executive committee members who were members of the pro-leadership camp. Though I was not able to attend many internal union meetings, I was able to attend inter-union conferences at which representatives of the STRM played key roles, such as the PTTI (Postal, Telegraph & Telephone International) conference held at STRM headquarters in Mexico City in March 1994 and the First National Union Productivity Conference in June 1994, in which the STRM was one of seven cosponsoring unions. In addition, I contacted members of other tendencies who I was unable to contact previously, such as the Línea Proletaria (supporters of Juárez from 1979 to 1983, until he broke with them), and members of the 1988-1992 Executive Committee. I also interviewed management officials and spoke informally to academic researchers of different political tendencies. While my access to the STRM was restricted in some ways, largely because the union is not as open or democratic in its governance as the TWU, it was nonetheless substantially greater than that which has been granted independent researchers of the STRM in the past.

ORGANIZATION OF THIS WORK

In the following chapter, the concept of globalization is defined and its impact examined. In particular, I argue that while globalization is a real and important phenomenon, its characteristics are different from what is commonly described. Especially in telecommunications, rather than globalization of competition, what has in fact occurred is that the telecommunications sector has shifted from a national monopoly structure to one based on an international oligopolistic cartelization of the market among large service providers. This chapter also analyzes how globalization has diffused similar work organization practices across national boundaries, leading to their adoption in different telecommunications companies.

Chapter 3 examines four theories of unionism—those of Lenin, Luxembourg, the Webbs, and Perlman—and sets forth an argument that each theory demonstrates a distinctive logic of unionism or strategic orientation, which may or may not characterize a given union, depending on the circumstances. Three theories regarding the specific relationship between unions and globalization are then examined: the cooperation or convergence theorists, the national labor regime theorists, and the strategic choice theorists. Each perspective is examined in detail, but I contend that each of these perspectives falls short in some measure. The decisions made by union officials are a reflection of a combination of local membership demands and a union's overall strategic orientation with respect to the market and the state.

Chapter 4 focuses in more detail on the historical development of both the STRM and the TWU, concentrating especially on changes that have taken place in the two unions since the mid-seventies. As well, this chapter looks at the extent, and the limits, of the influence exercised by different legal frameworks in Canada and Mexico on trade unions. Finally, this chapter serves to introduce the empirical data to be presented in the next three chapters.

Chapter 5 is the first of these empirical chapters and focuses on analyzing how the two unions have responded to changing technology, in particular examining the experiences of two categories of workers, technicians (central office workers) and operators. Both represent large work groups that have experienced significant automation in the past two decades. In both the TWU and the STRM, technicians were politically very important, but in the TWU technicians were aligned with the union leadership while in the STRM they led a key opposition group in the union. On the other hand, the operators in the STRM were politically aligned with the leadership, while operators were less politically central within the TWU. Through this focus, this chapter identifies both the importance of analyzing occupational and political divisions within unions in shaping specific responses to globalization, while examining a key period in the formation of the distinct union strategies adopted by union leaders in the STRM and TWU.

Chapter 6 looks at how the two unions have responded to changes in work organization. In particular, two types of work organization changes are examined. One type involves the transfer of work from one department to another. This is one area in which both the STRM and TWU ended up taking accommodationist stances, not without opposition in either case. One reason for this accommodation is the fact that company-wide work organization is an issue which is far removed from the shop floor; as a result, union influence over the process is weaker. Often the most that can be done is to ensure that workers maintain their employment in the company.

On the other hand, the difference in union behavior with regard to reorganization of work at the work site could not be greater. While the STRM has been a high-profile advocate of "participatory" work practices, the TWU has successfully staved these off. This contrast highlights an important difference between the STRM's emphasis on "pay for the family" and the TWU's embrace of social unionism.

Chapter 7 focuses on the issue of union-state relations. In particular, the relationship between the STRM and the Mexican state-PRI is examined and contrasted with the relationship between the TWU and the Canadian social democratic party, the NDP. The STRM's acquiescence in the privatization of the telephone company, in exchange for the government's agreement to step in with the granting of a super-low-interest loan to finance the union's purchase of stock in the privatized company is contrasted with the TWU's bitter, eight-year fight with the Canadian federal government over the issue of deregulation. While the STRM's tactics are in keeping with its promotion of short-term monetary gain, even at the expense of extensive concessions affecting working conditions, the TWU's tactics are consistent with a different logic, one that places a higher value on maximizing the number of jobs and building alliances with community groups.

Chapter 8 concludes the empirical case studies by evaluating the two unions' overall strategies in response to the globalization of the industry, in light of the empirical evidence and the ideas of labor union theorists discussed in Chapter 3. The various factors (institutional history, occupational sector balance of power, internal governance structure) that go into union decision making are highlighted. Finally, I provide an analysis of the challenges posed by globalization for unions, like the STRM, that follow a business unionist logic, and the very different challenges for unions, like the TWU, that follow a social unionist strategy.

The concluding chapter comments on the emerging economic structure of international oligarchic competition and its likely effects on unions and workers. This chapter reviews the key findings of this study and signals possible directions for future research.

NOTES

1. All interviews were conducted confidentially. The T stands for the British Columbian TWU (Telecommunications Workers Union) and the S stands for the Mexican STRM (Sindicato de Telefonistas de la República Mexicana or Telephone Workers' Union of the Mexican Republic). The letter U is used for interviews conducted in the United States. The second number is the year the interview was conducted. The third number refers to the number by which the specific interview was coded. As well, in Canada, I had some miscellaneous sources; these included interviews from third-party (neither management nor labor) sources, as well as notes from closed meetings I attended. These are designated "Canada-Misc Notes," followed by a number which codes the specific event or interview.

2. The FTW (Federation of Telephone Workers) was founded in 1944 with plant workers and operators only. Clerical workers were joined into the union the following year. The FTW changed its named to the TWU in 1977.

3. Membership data on STRM from Telmex 1994a and Lara Sánchez 1992a. Membership figures for TWU from TWU 1994a and Bernard 1982: 92.

4. See Lara Sánchez 1992a: 13.

5. The TWU figure is an estimate. This estimate is based on obtaining the number of total employees from BC Tel annual reports, while the number of employees is from Labour Canada reports of collective bargaining settlements (Labour Canada 1994; Statistics Canada, various years).

6. Throughout this work, I use "national" and "country" interchangeably. Thus, national here refers to the nation-state and *not* specific nationalities (i.e., Canada and Mexico, *not* French-Canadians, English-Canadians, Maya, Zapotec, etc.).

7. Technically, the TWU is not a single-employer union. However, more than 98% of TWU members are covered by its collective agreement with BC Telephone. The only collective agreement that covers an even marginally significant number of TWU members outside of BC Tel is the TWU's contract with Prism, a telecommunications equipment manufacturer located in the Vancouver metropolitan area of British Columbia.

8. As well, this study provides some insight into the response of unions to globalization in general. To be sure, telecommunications unions are stronger than most unions, since the jobs of their members are, relatively speaking, protected from capital flight. Though computer technology is eroding this protection, it remains important. This means that telecommunications unions have a greater range of options available than many other unions. Telecommunications unions have often been in the forefront of the battle for worker control over technological change (Sethi 1989).

Still, the telecommunications industry is a key industry to study because it is undergoing rapid transformation in market structure and is widely seen as a bell-weather industry for future economic development. Telecommunications unions have frequently played important roles in the labor movements of their respective countries. Moreover, examining a sector like telecommunications where unions are better able to implement their strategies makes it easier to identify key elements in union strategy formation, which could serve to facilitate future research of union strategy in other industrial sectors.

9. See also de Buen (1989) for an analysis of how Hernández Juárez's leadership style differs from the Mexican norm.

10. Technically, the union paid for the shares, with the help of a government-financed, low-interest loan. After repaying the loan in 1992, workers at Telmex retained 3.1% of Telmex stock.

11. Indeed, as late as the 1960s, the TWU (then the FTW) had to fend off charges that it was a so-called "company" (that is, company-controlled) union. See Olding 1965.

12. On the question of telephone regulation, Winseck (1993: 25-60) provides a good overview of pluralist, corporatist, and critical theory approaches. For a liberal approach, see Cowhey and Aronson 1989. For a leading example of poststructuralist theory, see Foucault 1980. For a general theoretical discussion of social movement literature, see Slater 1985 and Touraine 1988.

Regarding the social movement literature, it should be noted that labor itself is a social movement. Oddly, labor studies and social movement studies have sometimes been put in opposition to one another. It is clear that historically there have been many class-based movements, as well as many cross-class movements (such as the abolitionist movement in the United States in the 1850s). The importance of the labor movement is not that it subsumes all other social movements, but rather that unlike other social movements, it confronts capital directly instead of indirectly.

13. In her study on Italian unionism, Miriam Golden (1988: 8) states this point even more emphatically, contending that, "Officials, rather than recalculate their policies from the top at every opportunity, deliberately avoid questioning the established routines and integrity of their organization, in a perfectly (if bounded) rational allocation of intellectual and organizational resources. Only catastrophic failure or suddenly successful innovation makes it likely that the organization will reconsider the parameters of its established identity" (quoted in Robinson 1993: 23-24).

14. One analyst goes so far to state that the current ability of capital to move location around the globe means that "workers in Michigan and Morelos now have a relation like workers in Illinois and Indiana" (MacEwan 1994: 130-143). Telecommunications workers in Michigan and Morelos do *not* as yet have the same relationship as workers in Illinois and Indiana, but they are facing more and more common threats and problems due to the increasingly rapid diffusion of technology and management practices across national borders.

15. In saying this I do not wish to belittle the efforts that are being made by labor unionists. During my research, I was able to attend two multinational conferences of telephone workers, a rank-and-file grouping (consisting mostly of union local officers) organized by Transnational Information Exchange (TIE) and a peak-level grouping of the Postal, Telephone & Telegraph

International (PTTI). However, though the degree of internationalization of labor has increased, it is still far less internationalized than capital.

16. See, for instance, Piore and Sabel 1984, Zuboff 1987. In the sturdy of Mexico's relationship with globalization, much of the work focuses on the maquiladora sector; see Shaiken 1990, Carrillo 1992, Kopinak 1995, and Sklair 1989, as well as a plethora of case studies. For studies of the impact of globalization specifically in the telecommunications sector, see Arthur D. Little 1985 and Cowhey and Aronson 1989.

17. As Hamilton (1982) notes, as a coordinator the state often had to act against the immediate interests of the capitalist class, albeit thereby establishing the conditions for long-term capitalist economic development. This, of course, was particularly true during the Great Depression and, in Mexico, President Lázaro Cárdenas' embrace of stepped-up land reform and nationalization of the oil industry was emblematic of this tendency. As a mediator, the state's role is more limited. State officials still have to act against the interests of individual capitalists or even specific industrial sectors, but this is part of a process in which state officials mediate regulatory and other disputes among different industrial groups and sectors. Thus the state's relationship with capital in the global economy is more like a referee, and less like a director.

18. Incidentally, there is significant doubt as to whether "free collective bargaining" characterizes the U.S. labor system. See, for instance, Geogehan (1992) for a critique of U.S. labor law and an analysis of the central role of the National Labor Relations Board.

19. For dissenting views as to the validity of the "free collective bargaining" label in Canadian labor relations, see Winseck 1993 who describes the Canadian system as "semi-corporatist," due to the large role played by federal "conciliators" and Drache and Glasbeek (1992), whose account focuses on the ways in which the Canadian state has sought to either repress labor or channel labor disconnect into "acceptable" forms of dissent.

20. The period from the 1954 peso devaluation until the 1968 student uprising in Mexico City is generally considered to represent the apex of Mexican corporatism. See de la Garza 1988, Zapata 1981.

21. See Novelo (1991) for her analysis of a pocket of dissident activism in what was said to be the most tightly controlled of Mexico's unions, the oil workers' union under Joaquín Galicia Hernández. Better known as "La Quina," Galicia Hernández was an autocratic union leader, legendary for his corruption and brutality, who ruled the oil workers' union until he was jailed for largely political reasons in 1989. As Novelo demonstrates, Mexico City technical workers, were, for a time at least, able to maintain a considerable degree of

autonomy for the negotiation of department-level affairs, even though the oil workers' union was (and remains) one of Mexico's most undemocratic unions.

22. The argument here is thus one of punctuated equilibrium. Economic factors influence a union's adoption of a strategic orientation, but it takes a large shift in either external or internal union conditions for a change in orientation to occur, just as it takes a large shift in macroeconomic conditions for an electoral realignment to take place.

23. Telmex in particular has been the focus of many studies on the effects of technological change in the telephone industry. See, for instance, Caliz Cecilia 1984, Cruz Cervantes 1984, and Campos et al. 1989.

24. One of the most prominent examples of such a union is, ironically given its past history, the Teamsters' Union in the United States where the entire executive slate is elected by a direct rank-and-file vote.

25. A good example of this is the Mexican Workers Federation (or Confederación de Trabajadores Mexicanos, hereafter CTM). The CTM, Mexico's largest union, was led by Fidel Velázquez from 1941 to 1947 and again from 1950 until his death in 1997.

26. See Jones Tamayo 1993, Lara Sánchez 1994, Mondragón Pérez 1994, Sánchez Daza 1992, Solís Granados 1992a and Xelhuantzi López 1992.

CHAPTER TWO

Globalization in the Telecommunications Industry

In this chapter and the next, the phenomenon of globalization in the telecommunications industry and theories of unionism are examined in order to situate the empirical chapters that follow. Rather than viewing globalization as a mysterious force, the argument advanced here is that globalization, at least in how it pertains to the telecommunications industry, is a very specific phenomenon with some very specific effects. In essence, telecommunications have shifted from a market structure based on the provision of telephone service by a single, domestic provider to an increasingly oligopolistic international market in which one carrier retains a dominant position in a given national market but where other international telecommunications companies are permitted some market entry. Thus, for instance, AT&T, the dominant telecommunications carrier in the United States, has, by purchasing a 20% share in the upstart Canadian telecommunications company Unitel, become a niche-market service provider in Canada (Sutrees 1994, Marotte 1994). As a result, what were once very distinct markets patterns in Canada and Mexico have become more similar; as well, more and more frequently, the companies involved in both countries are the same.

The changes brought about by globalization are great, but are not entirely unprecedented. It's worth noting, for instance, that as of 1987, global trade as a percentage of world gross domestic product had still not recovered to the level of its pre-World War I high (Glyn and Sutcliffe 1992: 77-82). Still, some features of the current shift in economic structure have dramatic effects, especially in the financial

27

sector, where the volume of international financial transactions increased twenty-fold between the mid-1960s and the mid-1980s (Magdoff 1992: 56). This affects telecommunications because banks are major users of telecommunications services; indeed, financial institutions often lead the coalitions pushing for deregulation in the industry. At the same time, developments in the telecommunications industry itself speed the (re)internationalization of the economy by making new forms of global production possible.

Not surprisingly, these changes are affecting telecommunications labor unions in both countries. Thus, the analysis of globalization in this chapter shall be followed in the next chapter by a close look at how the union movement and different types of unions are affected by the new environment. As in past eras, different unions today have varying reactions to shifts in economic structure; however, while it is true that different union responses are possible, some union responses are likely to be more effective in meeting the needs of their members than others. Lastly, I shall discuss different ways of modelling internal union decision-making processes and why it is essential to examine internal union decision-making, and not simply macroeconomic change or national labor law, in analyzing union responses to the challenges posed by the restructuring of the global economy.

THE GLOBALIZATION OF PRODUCTION

> Since at least the Roman Empire, where an extensive road system
> proved equally suited for moving either commerce or troops,
> communications infrastructures have served to control both economy
> and polity (Beniger 1986: 20).

As pointed out in James Beniger's analysis, the role played by the communications industry has always been important in structuring the overall economy. As such, it is not surprising that the wave of technological change that has come about due to the computerization of communications since the 1970s should have a major impact on the structure of production. However, it would be a mistake to view the changes in telephone industry structure of the past twenty years as inevitable. Although it is certain that technological change has made possible certain developments that otherwise would either have been impossible or economically not viable, technological change, in and of itself, is rarely sufficient to bring structural change about.

An example from the automotive sector demonstrates how instant communications have made available new forms of corporate decision-making structures. In the era before instantaneous global communications, the automotive industry was structured along multidivisional lines, with considerable autonomy for local managers.[1] Today it is possible for all major decisions to be made in the host country. Ford Motor Company, for instance, attempted to use the new computer communications to allow for multi-country production of a single model line, the Ford Escort. Though the Ford experiment was only partially successful, communications technology has been used by central management to make decisions that before would have been delegated to divisional heads. Indeed, the centralized structure made possible by computerization has led some analysts to distinguish between this new form of corporate organization, which such analysts label as *transnational*, with the more traditional *multinational* organization that was common to nearly all enterprises with distinct national subsidiaries prior to the computer revolution.[2]

In the field of telecommunications, similar forces are at work, even though telecommunications, despite the changes of the past decade, remains less open to international competition than automobile manufacturing. The nature of this globalization of production is fairly simple and easy to understand. In essence, the globalization of production involves a shift in market organization from the national to international level. However, the impact of globalization can best be seen by examining the set of changes that have resulted from the combined effects of the introduction of computer technology and changes in the global economic structure. Although each facet of these changes will be explained in greater detail below, a brief listing of the key aspects of the new production structure would include the following: a) a new managerial structure, b) new work organization practices, c) a shift from a national monopoly industrial structure towards an international oligopoly market structure, d) a reduction in the direct role of the state, e) a new market balance-of-power, characterized by a shift from provider or "supplier" (i.e., telephone company) dominance to large corporate telecommunications user dominance (e.g., banks and large manufacturing corporations), and f) at least a short-term reduction in union power in the industry.

The above changes are, of course, interconnected. This can be seen clearly by analyzing the role of the new communications technology itself. In the 1960s, long distance communications were expensive and telephone data transfers unheard of; indeed, in some countries at that time, such as Mexico, direct dial international long distance service did not exist! Today, both long distance telephone and data communications are taken for granted. The ease of use of this communications technology has many effects on organizational hierarchies.

On the one hand, the new communications technology allows for rapid horizontal distribution of information (Zuboff 1987). This enables workers and managers at lower levels to make decisions that they couldn't make before, since now they have information that was previously unavailable to them. At the same time, however, this change makes possible an unprecedented degree of centralization of authority in the head office, as information technology increases the quantity and quality of information possessed by central executives. As a result, there is less to the "decentralization" phenomenon than the business press likes to suggest. In fact, the net effect would appear to be an increase of decisions made at the central management level.

With new computer technology, the need for managerial supervision of employees is reduced, since many supervisory functions that once were performed by management can now be performed by machines. Even more pronounced is the reduction of the need for "supervisors to supervise the supervisors," or what is more commonly known as middle management. As a result of computerization, top managers can get daily reports on first-line manager performance. Although the computers do not capture all of the information needed to evaluate managerial performance—and, of course, computer data can be intentionally entered incorrectly, leading to the commonplace problem of "garbage in, garbage out"—it is nonetheless the case that computer technology has led to a relative decline in the need for supervisory employees.[3]

Typically, the resulting centralization of managerial authority that occurs goes by the name of "levelling" or "flattening." That is, the number of levels of managers who "supervise the supervisors" is reduced (Malone and Rockart 1993: 49-50). However, by reducing the number of layers separating top management from the shop floor, this flattening actually *increases* the authority of central management.[4] This trend toward fewer management levels has been widely evident in the telecommunications industry.[5]

In telecommunications, national firms still retain their dominant positions, but there is rapid movement towards internationalization, with greater control exercised directly by leading multinational telecommunications companies' central headquarters. As the two cases in this study demonstrate, the American multinational GTE appears to be playing a more direct role in its BC Tel subsidiary since the advent of Canadian deregulation in 1992. In Mexico, the sale of 49 percent of the voting shares of Telmex in Mexico to France Telecom and Southwestern Bell of the United States has led to a restoration of direct multinational influence in Telmex affairs after a 32-year period of solely Mexican ownership. Both France Telecom and Southwestern Bell have sent hundreds of managers to Telmex to directly monitor their investment. Though direct management of the company remains in the hands of Grupo Carso, led by Mexican billionaire Carlos Slim, the role of these multinational enterprises in Telmex operations is growing (Interview S-94-33).

SHOP FLOOR IMPACT OF GLOBALIZATION

> Because information can be distributed more easily, people lower in the organization can now become well enough informed to make decisions effectively. At the same time, upper level managers can now more easily review decisions made at lower levels (Malone and Rockart 1993: 50).

Although the above statement refers to the structure of management, the above logic doesn't solely apply at the managerial level, but also at the shop floor level itself. Much has been made of information technology's potential to empower workers to make more decisions (Zuboff 1987), though others argue that computerization leads to a deskilling of work (see Shaiken 1986, Noble 1984). Over all, the field data collected here would indicate support of the skeptics over the optimists. But a better way of looking at the problem than doing a comparative statics analysis[6] of the absolute level of skill required, would be to do a contextual analysis of the changing organization of work and the skills required within that new organization of work. Stated simply, computer technology allows for workers to make greater use of skill, but without this implying an increased degree of control over the work process, unlike what the phrase "skilled work" has implied in the past.

To understand this distinction, one must be clear about the difference between *skill* and *control*. Historically, as analyzed by

Braverman (1974) and others, the two issues have been linked: that is, management has sought to gain control of skills as a means of asserting control over the workforce. Skilled workers, because of specialized experiential knowledge, were not as easily replaceable as unskilled workers. An important aspect of the "skill" possessed by many craft workers in nineteenth-century factory production was their knowledge of the intricacies of the production process. This craft knowledge, almost by definition, was not in the possession of management. Even if, as often occurred, managers were former craft workers themselves, the managers at most possessed knowledge of their particular craft and not of the entire production process on which late nineteenth-century manufacture depended. Management thus was often compelled to cut a deal (in terms of higher wages and benefits, better working conditions, etc.) with the shop-floor representatives of the workers in order to ensure smooth and efficient production. Failure to cut such a deal often meant a marked increase in the size of the scrap heap or other related industrial problems.

Taylorism, of course, was an effort to systematize shop-floor knowledge and place it under the control of management. It was also a means to make the work process more susceptible to management inspection. In addition to learning what workers were doing, Taylorism sought to place strategic elements of business operations under central management direction, break jobs into component parts, and to separate out tasks. Deskilling thus occurred for two reasons: 1) to reduce the leverage workers have over the work process by reducing their ability to make decisions, especially in strategic areas of business operations, such as the organization of production, and 2) to increase the visibility of the work process to management, thereby increasing management control through its ability to "veto" worker decisions through disciplinary action.

It's important to note that management "rationalization" of the production process through Taylorism was only partially successful. Even in automobile assembly, the Taylorist industry *par excellence*, many areas remained beyond management control, including welding, stamping, fabric trim installation, and other subassembly work (Zetka 1995). In the telephone industry, management control over the labor process was even less substantial. With the notable exception of operators, most telephone work was not Taylorized. Outside plant workers had—and, to a great extent, still have—a large amount of control over the work process and pacing. Clerical work has not been as uncontrolled as plant work, but nonetheless the degree of on-the-job autonomy of the average clerical worker has been significantly greater than that enjoyed by the average operator.

Sometimes lost in the debate over deskilling is the point that all other things being equal, it is in management's interest to *maximize* worker skill, for the simple reason that if workers know more, they can do more and increase the productivity of the business. Obviously, all other things are not equal; historically, increased skill has meant increased worker control over work pace, increased worker demands for compensation, and ultimately increased worker control over the organization of production itself. For these reasons, management historically has faced a trade-off between maximizing worker productivity (but at the cost of having to pay higher wages) and maximizing management control (but at the cost of lower productivity); often management has felt compelled to make do with less-skilled workers, even at the cost of lower productivity (Noble 1984: 265-323).

Automation, however, eases this management dilemma. Advances in communications and computing technology, in particular, have decreased on-the-job autonomy—or worker *control*—almost across the board, but the average skill level required has often increased. Take operator services. Always the most Taylorized part of the telephone business, with operators required to use set phrases and the like (Bernard 1982), automation has nonetheless further decreased worker control in two important aspects. First, prior to the advent of computerization, an operator had to physically plug in a cord to complete a call. An operator desiring a mini-break could likely get away with taking a few extra seconds to plug in. With a computerized system, operator control over pacing is further reduced, as the call is automatically piped into the operator's head-set.

A second change occurs with monitoring. Since the turn of the century, operators have been subjected to monitoring. Given the fact that operators work individually and within an easily observable work space, monitoring without sophisticated computer technology was still fairly simple. But with computer technology, monitoring can be conducted with little or no effort. With a computer, it is possible for a manager to plug into any operator's call without the operator being aware that she is being monitored (Interview S-94-23). As a result, operators experience greater stress than ever before (de la Garza and Melgoza 1985).

Automation has eliminated certain operator work tasks. For instance, operators no longer record billing information, which is handled automatically. Moreover, automated voice answer systems mean that the operator spends less time on each call, as the computer gives out the number requested to the customer after the operator has disconnected from the call. This means that an operator's contact with customers becomes more truncated and the calls fielded become more similar, increasing the monotony of the job. Before automation, a caller might have asked additional questions after a number has been given out. Most importantly, the overwhelming majority of calls are now dialed directly, requiring no operator assistance at all. But automation also introduces new functions, making it possible for an operator to perform both traditional operating functions and clerical functions. With current computing technology, operators can sell special long distance calling packages while still handling person-to-person and information calls. Presumably, this involves an *increase* in the variety of job tasks performed and hence some increase in the complexity or skill level of the job.

Similar trends are observable in other sectors of the telephone industry. Thus, the number of different types of transactions that a clerical worker may perform in a single work day has increased markedly in the last few years. With outside plant workers, the changes to date are less dramatic, though important changes appear to be in the offing. One area where automation reduces worker control is in the distribution of installation and repair jobs. Traditionally, this function was the job of a dispatcher, who, using his or her knowledge of the local roads and conditions, would distribute repair jobs among the plant workers. During my field research in British Columbia, this position was in the process of being automated, with dispatching done through the calculation of a computer algorithm based on the average time for job completion and the distance between job sites. In this system, the worker, instead of calling a dispatcher, would instead plug a hand-held computer into a phone line to receive the next order. Though this system has led to a *less* efficient allocation of installer work, it may ultimately prove to be more efficient in the sense that the resulting increase of installer time is balanced by the elimination of the dispatcher position. One skilled position is eliminated and worker control is reduced, but the actual number of functions to which a worker is assigned may actually increase.

In Mexico, a different version of this has occurred. Preparing in advance to adopt computer technology, management began reducing test staffing levels, even before the new technology had been installed. With testers thus overloaded, the accuracy of technical reports on telephone lines fell dramatically, increasing the required amount of on-the-job installer improvisation. Again, despite its apparent inefficiency, this might increase overall efficiency for management, because even though more time is required for installation, the labor time of the line testers is reduced. The need for the installation worker to exercise judgement in the performance of his or her work thus does not automatically fall and may in fact increase, but the scope of work that workers exercise collectively over the production process falls markedly. The partial solution of management's dilemma of maximizing skill and control thus becomes an added problem for the worker who finds that more is demanded while less autonomy is permitted.

Team production schemes are one method by which management seeks to meet its twin goals of maximizing the input of worker knowledge while minimizing management's loss of control over the work process. Team production has been particularly common in the automobile industry (see Parker and Slaughter 1988). But various forms of team production have been tried out in the telecommunications industry as well. As is examined in Chapter 6, both Telmex and BC Tel have experimented with team production. With the union's cooperation, at Telmex, management has implemented "analysis groups" that seek to bilaterally direct resources toward districts that are in greatest need of line repairs. At BC Tel, management, with very limited union cooperation, sought to restructure the business customer service division to set up a two-track process in which large company special orders would be handled by special service teams. Though neither of these efforts has had the same degree of success enjoyed by the automotive industry, mainly because there are a greater number of functions in the telecommunications industry that still cannot be automated, team production is an attempt by management to use automating technology to meet its twin goals of getting workers to perform a greater number of tasks while maximizing the amount of management control.

Unlike the auto industry, where a clear pattern of work based on multi-skilling and so-called "flexible" work organization has emerged, the development of new work practices in the telecommunications industry remains more uncertain and uneven. One key difference, of course, is that telecommunications is largely a "service" industry. Unlike automobile manufacture, there is no single "product" produced; rather, a host of telecommunications services are provided. While the more routine services are easily automated, the more complex services are not so easily susceptible to multi-skilled, flexible work organization; the variety of services produced often frustrates efforts to "rationalize" work organization in such areas. For instance, as seen in Chapter 6 of this study, attempts to automate more complex sections of the telecommunications business, such as business account servicing, have foundered due to company dependence on worker discretion to put together customized orders. Still, the effort to introduce greater multi-tasking is evident not only in the emerging global economy in general, but in the telecommunications industry in particular, and, thus is most certainly an important change spurred by globalization in the industry.

GLOBALIZATION AND MARKET STRUCTURE

While the impact of globalization *inside* the firm has been dramatic in its alteration of internal firm organization, its impact *outside* the firm has been even more far-reaching. In 1944, just prior to the end of World War II, a set of institutions, including the World Bank, the International Monetary Fund, and a system of fixed exchange rates was established at Bretton Woods in an effort to regulate the international economy. Emerging from the social struggles of the Great Depression, this system also included certain norms or guiding principles, including an informal "social compact" between labor unions and large corporations at the nation-state level in leading industrial economies, an international system of currencies pegged to the U.S. dollar, and, importantly, Keynesian regulation of domestic economies.[7] A basic understanding underlying Keynesian-type regulation was that capitalists, if acting on their own initiative, would engage in short-term, profit-maximizing behavior that would lead to economic crisis, including, possibly, a repeat of the Great Depression.[8] In this model, the paternalistic capitalist state would sometimes have to constrain capitalists' pursuit of short-term profits "for their own good."

Neither capitalists nor labor unions were ever fully satisfied with this "social compact" or "class compromise." In particular, a declining rate of profit in the late 1960s and 1970s led to increased efforts by corporations to reduce costs.[9] In the effort of leading firms to reduce their costs, communications technology played an important role. Billions of dollars could be transferred across borders overnight electronically, international investments became easier to manage, and thus capital gained greater leverage over national governments.[10] The ability of the state to manage the affairs of national capitalists in a paternalistic fashion declined, although even today the nation-state's ability to manage the national economy is far greater than it was in the Depression years when the governments of different countries had yet to establish the bureaucracy necessary to manage a national economy. If for no other reason, the state's capacity to influence the economy today remains greater because the percentage of each national economy under state control is far greater than it was in the 1930s.

Still, the decline in state control from its height in the late 1960s and 1970s is dramatic. These changes were facilitated by technological developments. Within the field of telecommunications transmission, the development of microwave technology enabled MCI in the United States to set up its initial long distance telecommunications operations in the late 1960s (Horwitz 1988; see also Cooke 1992: 688, Batten and Schoonmaker 1987: 314-316). Equally important, the explosion in computer technology and the change in organization in manufacturing and financial services industries had a ripple effect on the telecommunications industry, leading to a marked increase in demand for telecommunications services. Though perhaps not immediately obvious, these changes have had a major impact not just on telecommunications technology, but on the organization of the telecommunications industry itself. Both the development of cheaper long-distance transmission technology and increased demand for telecommunications services have led to increased political pressures to deregulate throughout the industrialized world, as large users of telecommunications organize for better access to cheaper and more specialized digital telephone services.

Telephone service providers might be expected to defend their monopoly position against such user groups, but often telephone companies have eyed enviously the possibility of leveraging their telephone service monopoly into a dominant competitive position in a broader market in which the boundaries between separate services such as cable, telephony, computing, and electronics become blurred. Such a possibility has often led telephone companies to mute their criticisms of deregulation and to focus their efforts instead on positioning themselves to profit from the "convergence" of these distinct, but related, industrial sectors.[11]

Different explanations have been given for the widespread movement from a monopoly to an oligopoly structure in the industry. One explanation, offered by Eli Noam, suggests that the key factor is the level of telephone penetration (Noam 1992). According to Noam, when the percentage of households with telephone service is low, business in general benefits by subsidizing telephone line expansion, since more customers can contact them by telephone and they can contact customers more easily. On the other hand, Noam argues, when the rate of telephone penetration becomes very high (over 90 percent), then the cost to business of the subsidy is greater than what they gain in access to new telephone subscribers. As a result, at this stage, Noam contends, business will begin to balk at the prices they pay for telephone service and demand changes. This explanation works well for countries like the United States and Japan, which deregulated early and in which over 90 percent of the population had telephone service prior to deregulation. It does not fit so well the cases of other countries such as Great Britain, where the percentage of the population with telephone service was considerably lower, but which also deregulated earlier.

While there is some truth to Noam's theory, I would argue that business, if given a choice, will opt not for universal service, but rather *universal service to the middle class*: that is, universal service to those people who would be likely to buy business' products and services and, perhaps secondarily, who are likely to be recruited to fill company jobs.[12] After reaching near-universal coverage of the middle class, business will press for full deregulation. Mexico provides a prime example of this strategy. At the time of privatization, the number of telephone lines in Mexico was 6.4 per 100 individuals (Székely and del Palacio 1995: 80). By contrast, in the United States, the telephone penetration rate is over 93% and there are more than 50 lines per 100 individuals (Halarn 1993: 9, Székely and del Palacio 1995: 42). According to the Mexican Communications and Transport ministry, as recently as 1988, only 18% of Mexican households had telephone service (SCT 1990: 3). As part of the privatization, Telmex's monopoly in basic telephone service was extended for six years. Even by the end of the extended-monopoly period, however, the number of lines per 100 inhabitants was projected to be at best 11.2 per 100 (Székely and del Palacio 1995: 118) and more than half of all Mexican households still lack direct telephone service. Nonetheless, this should be sufficient to serve as a customer base for those who had pressed for the changes, and business thus may well find deregulation preferable to the maintenance of the cross-subsidization necessary to ensure universal telephone service.

But even to the extent that business interests shift from favoring a monopoly structure designed to provide "infrastructure" and subsidize the overall expansion of the network to an oligopoly structure that caters more directly to their short-term economic interests, this change in attitudes alone would not have been sufficient to effect the necessary political changes to make the emergence of an oligopoly structure possible. To see this, one need look no further than the postal service. Like telecommunications, "universal service" in this sector was achieved long ago. Price competition, if instituted, would force postal companies to shut down service in small rural communities and concentrate on mass orders from larger businesses located in urban centers. Prices would go down and the quality of service would go up for corporate customers, while prices would climb and the quality of service would decline for rural residential customers. But large corporations haven't organized to push for the privatization of the post office.

There are, however, several differences that explain why a business interest in privatization and oligopolistic competition has been realized in telecommunications, in countries as diverse as Great Britain, the United States, Canada, Japan, and Mexico, while there has been no similar wave of privatizations in postal services.[13] First, the scale of the telecommunications sector is greater: simply put, users of postal services have less to gain by pressing for privatization. Second, the telecommunications industry is expanding and in the process of merging with "competitive sectors" of the economy such as computers; indeed, a key reason why AT&T supported divestiture was in order to gain entry into the computer market,[14] while expansion in the postal service market is minimal and chances for market convergence between the postal sector and other sectors nonexistent. As a result, in telecommunications, unlike the postal service, monopoly carrier managers have strong incentives to acquiesce in relinquishing their monopoly control, as they can be compensated for lost market leverage by being given the opportunity to leverage their capital into related sectors, instead of providing expensive telecommunications infrastructure on a universal, affordable basis. Third, in telecommunications a small group of large corporate customers[15]—in particular banks, as well as a few, very large service and manufacturing multinational corporations—form a significant portion of the telecommunications consumer base. As Székely and del Palacio indicate, "The general rule is that fewer than 5% of a national telephone company's clients generate over half the demand for long distance service . . . These big clients have the financial influence and political skill to organize themselves and can attack traditional telephone price and service provision structures" (1995: 20).[16] Much has been made of the financial impact of telecommunications on these companies' bottom line, though as Dwayne Winseck (1993:221) has shown, this impact can be exaggerated.[17] But the advantage for major corporate customers in securing an oligopolistic market structure is not solely, or even primarily, financial; rather, the main benefit is an increase in the level of service and attention to their specialized needs that they can secure due to the added customer leverage that a semi-competitive market brings. The empirical evidence shows that telephone companies are willing to go to great lengths to satisfy large corporate customers' demands in order to avoid losing a major account to a competitor. While such a logic would operate in postal services as well, the benefits for large corporate customers would be considerably less and likely not worth the market disruption that a major restructuring would entail. A final difference with the postal service is that in telecommunications, it is more feasible, though still probably not terribly cost efficient, for a major corporate customer to set up its own "in house" global telecommunications network, as has been done by Banamex in Mexico and General Motors in the United States; no similar threat exists in the postal service.[18] Though the extent of bypass is often exaggerated (Boulter et al. 1990:195-251), the threat of major corporations' defection from the "public" telecommunications network has been a lever used to encourage reluctant governments to acquiesce to opening the sector to greater competition.[19] In short, in the postal service, competition would require a major restructuring, while providing large corporate customers with only limited service and cost gains. In telecommunications, on the other hand, the gains for corporate customers are clear and, due to the higher market share that corporate consumers have in this sector, corporations have greater leverage with which to bring about the desired change.

Despite the multiple factors that strengthen the economic and political clout of those pushing for an oligopolistic market structure, the move toward competition has neither been uniform nor universal. In particular, where a strong public sector exists, such as in continental Europe, pressures for competition and deregulation have been significantly restrained. While some "advanced" sectors, such as cellular telephones were opened to competition in nearly all countries, until recently basic long-distance service remained under monopoly control in most European Union countries. Even critics have designated the 1990s as the "golden age of PTOs [public telecommunications operators]," though they see this golden age as a kind of "last hurrah" for the monopoly telecommunications companies (Noam and Kramer 1994).

Indeed, the likelihood of greater competition is fairly high in the near future, though it is likely that an overwhelming percentage of the market will remain under the control of the former national monopoly telephone service providers, just as AT&T continues to control over 60% of the U.S. long distance telecommunications market in 1995, eleven years after "full-scale" competition is said to have begun. Under the conditions of the 1987 Green Paper, long distance competition within the European Union is slated to commence in 1998, while each national company maintains a "local" monopoly within national boundaries (Fuchs 1993: 19, BTUC 1991: 3-7, Noam 1992: 306, Renaud 1992: 84-85, Winseck 1993: 114, PTTI 1992: 6). Such a structure would somewhat parallel the U.S. market structure, where, until the passage of the 1996 Telecommunications Act, local "Baby Bell" monopoly companies functioned within an overall system of national competition, with the important difference that in Europe the national companies would, through alliances with other national companies, also act as competitors in the European realm, rather than being banned from entering long distance competition as had been the case in the United States.

Regardless of possible future developments, the current global telecommunications market is still a mixture of national near-monopolies and monopolies and international oligopolistic markets. This is uncharted corporate territory, with mergers and so-called "strategic" alliances made and unmade on a regular, recurring basis. In an era less friendly to capital, such phenomena might be labelled trusts or cartels. Shifting from a market anchored in strong state regulation or, more commonly, direct state ownership toward an emerging oligopolistic competition framework, there is plenty of maneuvering for advantage. Central to the jockeying for position is the fear that the current period of international expansion may be followed by a shakeout period if the emerging international oligopoly market pattern takes hold.[20]

At present, what prevails is a form of regulated oligopolistic competition, with national state regulatory bodies apportioning market shares to "competing" firms.[21] Such cartelization is a violation of the principles of idealized competition, but does serve an important purpose of ensuring a more stable provision of important telecommunications infrastructure than would be provided by a purely competitive regime. After all, if an airline fails, other airlines can quickly pick up the slack and add new routes. This is not so easy in telecommunications. First of all, the size of a major telecommunications carrier itself is enormous. An additional problem results from the dual role played by a large telecommunications company such as BC Tel in British Columbia or Telmex in Mexico, serving as both the dominant carriers of telephone calls and the primary companies responsible for the building and maintenance of the telephone network infrastructure in their respective regions—this latter function being akin to that played by the public air control system in the airline industry. A failure of a dominant telephone carrier could thus threaten the integrity of the telephone network itself.[22]

Of course, like any cartel-like arrangement, the present market structure is potentially unstable as firms are always tempted to engage in cutthroat price competition to increase market share. Within this regulated oligopolistic structure, other practices common to the new global telecommunications industry have emerged—creation of strategic alliances; concentration of competitive efforts on large business customers; an increase in the concentration of capital in the industry,[23] and a reconstituted role of state regulation. All of these phenomena can be seen in the cases of both BC Tel in British Columbia, Canada, and Telmex in Mexico.

TRADITIONAL TELECOMMUNICATIONS ORGANIZATION IN CANADA AND MEXICO

Historically, Mexican and Canadian telecommunications can hardly be said to have followed similar paths. First, of course, there are tremendous differences in their national economies. While Mexican telecommunications operates in the arena of a developing economy, Canadian telecommunications serves the seventh largest national economy in the world. While Canada is among those countries that most rapidly developed basic telephone service, Mexico has been slow to expand telephone service, even when compared to some of its Latin American counterparts. In terms of ownership, Canada and Mexico followed very distinct—though equally eclectic—routes. Until a 1989 Canadian Supreme Court decision (Globeman 1992: 53, Winseck 1993: 236-237) placed all private telephone service under federal regulatory authority, Canadian telecommunications consisted of a mix of three distinct ownership and regulatory forms: federally regulated, private telephone companies (Bell Canada, BC Tel); provincially regulated, private telephone companies, which operated in the Maritimes provinces; and publicly-owned, provincial and municipal companies (in Alberta, Manitoba, and Saskatchewan). Mexican telecommunications was unusual in a different respect, in that it maintained separate, competing private telephone companies until 1950.[24] Afterward, a single privately owned company persisted until 1972, when the government bought up enough shares to become a 51% owner of the national telephone company, Telmex.

Additional differences between the two countries are evident in the degree of technological modernization and in the role played by the state. BC Tel in Canada has consistently been at the forefront in the use of technology. Rate of return regulation, which guaranteed a fixed percentage of profit on investment, combined with regulated prices, encouraged high expenditure on new technology, even if this wasn't the most cost-efficient method of providing service, since the only way for BC Tel to increase the absolute amount of its profits was to increase the asset base on which those profits were earned.

Mexico has been much slower to implement new telecommunications technology. In essence, Mexico followed a mixed strategy, choosing to invest in high-profile technology projects in specific areas, while maintaining a low level of investment elsewhere. Thus, while Mexico began to install digital switching technology in 1979, roughly at the same time as in Canada and the United States, and was the first Latin American nation to have its own satellite system, the Mexican telephone system continued to utilize electromechanical switches, a few of which dated back to the 1920s (Barrera 1992). In some areas, delapidated copper cabling remained in place, causing frequent crossing of lines and other service problems. In short, outside of certain high-profile modernization projects, investment in the rest of the telephone network was allowed to lag, especially after the onset of an economic crisis in 1982. A key example of the resulting technological gap is in the area of operating equipment. While operating was computerized in British Columbia in 1979 and 1980, the switch-over to computer technology at Telmex did not take place until the early 1990s (see STRM 1992a).

The role played by the state in the two countries affected the extent and pace of technological modernization. There was, of course, a difference in ownership structure in the two countries. In Mexico, from 1972 to 1990, Telmex was a 51% state-owned company.[25] In Canada, on the other hand, telephone ownership has consistently remained in private hands, except for the provincially owned systems in the Prairie Provinces (Alberta, Saskatchewan, and Manitoba). Generally, one could expect public ownership to lead to a greater state role in the industry, but in many ways the state-regulated private monopolies performed like quasi-state enterprises. So the differences between Canada's publicly-owned and privately-owned telephone companies are much less than what might otherwise be expected.

As agents of the majority owner, Mexican state officials had a greater ability to intervene in telephone company operations, all other things being equal. Indeed, Mexican state officials *did* intervene in telephone company operations and in STRM internal union politics, as is explained in later chapters. But overall the Mexican state's impact was less than what might be expected, because the Mexican government was unwilling to dedicate the resources needed to fund rapid telecommunications development. Thus, unlike some publicly owned telecommunications companies, such as France Telecom, there were no grand national telecommunications development plans.[26] To the extent that Mexican telephone company followed any kind of strategy at all during the 18 years of majority state ownership, it was that of a government "cash cow," in which money that otherwise could have been utilized to finance investment was siphoned off by the government to pay general state expenses (Cowhey and Aronson 1989: 8). Ironically, the first serious national development plan was contained in the Concession Title of 1990 that was part of the conditions of Telmex's privatization. The development plan set forth in the Concession Title had been largely written by Telmex officials by 1987, three years before privatization occurred (Solís Granados 1992).[27]

By contrast, the state in Canada, though generally not in direct control, had a more coherent and consistent telecommunications development policy. Although most of Canada's telephone companies were private, the Canadian state acted through the regulatory process to enforce high service-quality requirements through a system of fines, and it promoted universal service. As mentioned above, the rate-of-return regulation encouraged a high level of investment in construction and technological modernization. As well, the example of the publicly owned companies in the Prairie provinces, which worked aggressively to extend universal service to rural communities, helped to spur the privately run Bell Canada and BC Tel to meet the high standard set by these publicly owned companies (Winseck 1993: 223).

CANADA AND MEXICO IN THE EMERGING GLOBAL TELECOMMUNICATIONS MARKET

There are major differences between Canada's and Mexico's levels of telephone line penetration, pace of introduction of new technology, regulatory systems, and telephone sector ownership structure. But these differences have declined since the mid-1980s. On such distinct matters as the role of the state, the role of private capital, the use of computer technology, and corporate strategy, there has been a significant degree of convergence in practices as the industry becomes organized along North American, if not global, lines. In both countries, strategic alliances have been formed, telecommunications businesses have increased the attention they pay to large business customers, the role played by private capital has increased, and the role of state regulation has become more similar.

The role of the state in both countries will be examined in more detail in Chapter 7, but here it is important to look at how specific changes in state policy have led to a shift in the type of market in both countries, from separate national monopoly structures toward a North American regional, and even global, oligopolistic telecommunications market. One step taken in this direction has been an increase, in both countries, in the role played by private capital in the industry. In Mexico, the sale of Telmex to private interests in December 1990 and the establishment, for the first time, of a set of regulatory requirements, through the terms of the Concession Title, have made the structure of the Mexican telecommunications industry more similar to that of Canada and the United States. Within the Concession Title, Telmex must meet specified expansion and service quality standards or pay fines, much as has been the case for U.S. and Canadian telephone companies since World War I. Although Telmex maintained its monopoly until 1997, other parts of the Mexican telecommunications sector, such as cellular telephone service and paging, were opened to competition in 1990 (SCT 1990).

But the privatization trend extends further. While Canadian telecommunications has always been largely private, privatizations of some of the government-owned systems that did exist took place in the 1980s. The most important of these was the privatization of AGT (Alberta Government Telephone) in Alberta (Winseck 1993). More importantly, the nature of Canadian telecommunications regulation underwent a significant change, as state policy shifted more and more in the direction of promoting competition, culminating in the 1992 regulatory decision to allow competition in Canada's long distance telephone network. But even during the 1980s, there was a gradual turning away from socially oriented regulation toward an approach to regulation that enabled telecommunications enterprises to emphasize the specialized needs of large corporate customers while de-emphasizing the needs of small residential users. As analyzed by Winseck (1993: 227-228), during the 1980s, a series of regulatory changes allowed telephone companies to "rebalance" their rates so that they could charge corporate customers less and residential subscribers more. To further encourage rate reductions, competition in specialized services was permitted.[28]

In Mexico, a similar emphasis on satisfying corporate customers was made explicit through the establishment of requirements that Telmex create the institutional capacity to meet the specialized data-transmission requirements of larger businesses, though this is balanced by expansion targets placed on the privatized company so that it may "catch up" with the developed world.[29] Prior to privatization, tariffs[30] on local calls were raised sharply, especially in 1990, resulting in local telephone bills of roughly U.S. $18 a month (including local measured-service fees), while international rates were lowered; as well, taxes on the telephone company were lowered (Petrazzini 1995: 116-117, Francés 1993: 366, Telmex 1993a: 2-3, 23-25). These policy changes enabled the privatized Telmex to finance well over half its U.S. $2 billion a year investment program though internally-generated revenue to meet the line quality and service extension targets of the Concession Title (Telmex 1993a: 28-31, Cerezo P. 1994, Jeremy et al. 1991: 51, SCT 1990).

Nonetheless, Telmex had difficulties in meeting its residential service quality requirements.[31] Although Telmex's residential service has improved somewhat, it remains highly unpopular. The complaint of one customer in a letter to a Mexico City newspaper was typical. "Telmex," she wrote, "now in private hands, continues to be equally inept and very unreliable, only now it is among the most expensive [telephone service providers] in the world" (Cisneros Luján 1994).

In both Canada and Mexico, in addition to the shift to private capital, the role of foreign capital has also increased. In Canada, foreign ownership in any one telecommunications company is limited by federal legislation to 20 percent. BC Tel is an exception to this rule because the American multinational GTE purchased 50.1% of the company before this legislation limiting foreign ownership was enacted. More recently, though, American multinationals have increased their involvement in the Canadian telecommunications market. AT&T purchased a 20% share of Unitel, a company that is seeking to go head-to-head against Canada's traditional telecommunications companies in long distance service. For its part, MCI has formed a strategic alliance with Bell Canada, BC Tel, and Canada's other traditional telephone companies (Enchin 1993).

In Mexico, foreign ownership is limited to 49 percent of the voting shares of any one telecommunications company.[32] At Telmex, 24.5 percent of voting shares are controlled by the American company Southwestern Bell and another 24.5 percent of these shares are controlled by France Telecom (Corona et al. 1992, Tandon 1994). As well, other American firms such as Bell South have invested in Mexican cellular companies (Symonds 1990). MCI formed a strategic alliance with Banamex to compete with Telmex in long distance telephone service (Aguilar and Hernández 1994, Rebollo Pinal 1994) and AT&T has greatly expanded its manufacturing operations in Mexico and has become, along with Telmex's traditional suppliers, Alcatel and Ericsson, a leading supplier of digital equipment to Telmex (Petrazzini 1995: 180).

Although the influence of foreign capital is indirect, it is important in that it facilitates the diffusion of common management practices and the common use of technology across national boundaries. For instance, in Telmex there is a distribution of authority among the different partners who jointly hold the controlling bloc of shares. Thus, Southwestern Bell is in charge of operations—central office, outside plant, marketing; France Telecom is in charge of planning, communications service, and long distance; systems organization is shared between Southwestern Bell and France Telecom; and the Mexican-controlled Grupo Carso is in charge of personnel, government relations, and all other aspects of the business (Interview S-94-33, Solís Granados 1992a). According to this division of authority, Southwestern Bell and France Telecom do not have direct responsibility for industrial relations. Nevertheless, they influence the organization of work by advising management in their designated areas of expertise, even though the two companies do occasionally come into conflict with each other, as well as with Grupo Carso management (Interview S-94-33).

At BC Tel, GTE's majority ownership of the company has had a profound impact on industrial relations. Although GTE is limited by the Canadian government to having two seats on BC Tel's Board of Directors,[33] it is widely believed by union representatives that the hard line taken by management against the union in the 1970s was part of a general GTE-wide corporate strategy (Interview T-93-68). In the 1990s, an additional influence has been felt in the formation of strategic alliances. The most important of these is Stentor, led by Bell Canada and including all of the traditional telephone companies across Canada. The Stentor alliance has sought to coordinate marketing functions (BC Tel 1992a) and may soon expand its influence to cover other areas, such as by establishing a national testing center.

The effects of these strategic alliances are multiple. Generally, strategic alliances are used by corporations as a means to share risk and reduce uncertainty through "collaborative competition" or "precompetitive collaboration" (Cooke 1992: 694). Strategic alliances also allow for joint provisioning of services. Thus, the traditional Canadian telephone companies in Stentor collaborate to provide common long distance service marketing. As well, strategic alliances can be a means of sharing costs in expensive joint ventures (Moss Kanter 1991), allowing corporations to more easily afford expensive research and development projects, enter new market segments, and set product standards (Cooke 1992: 697).[34] According to one analyst, "The *national* technological paths of development will to a large extent disappear" (Fuchs 1993: 23, emphasis in original), as joint ventures and other forms of strategic alliances become more common. As can be seen in the table below, the controlling companies at both BC Tel (GTE)[35] and Telmex (Grupo Carso, Southwestern Bell, and France Telecom) have been active in expanding their operations, both through strategic alliances (such as the creation of the Telmex controlling group itself), as well as through traditional mergers and acquisitions.

Table 2-1: Strategic Alliances and Mergers of Telmex and BC Tel Controlling Companies[36]

1990	Consortium led by France Telecom and STET (Italian telecommunications firm) purchases 60% of shares in newly privatized Telecom Argentina.
1990	Consortium led by Mexican Grupo Carso, France Telecom and Southwestern Bell purchases controlling share of Telmex.
1991	Telecel, 23% owned by Pacific Telesis (acquired by Southwestern Bell in 1996), receives license to run Portugal's new mobile telephone network.
1991	Consortium led by GTE, AT&T and Telefónica Española (Spain's partially state-owned telephone company) purchases controlling share of Venezuelan national phone company, CANTV.
1992	Formation of Stentor Resource Centre ("Stentor") alliance of traditional Canadian telephone companies, led by Bell Canada and GTE-owned BC Tel.
1994	France Telecom and Deutsche Telekom form strategic alliance and jointly purchase a 20% share of U.S. Sprint.
1996	Southwestern Bell purchases Pacific Telesis, one of its sister "Baby Bell" companies.
1996	International Wireless, 20% owned by Grupo Carso, purchases Prodigy, the fourth largest U.S. internet service provider.
1997	Bell Atlantic purchases NYNEX, one of its sister Baby Bell companies.
1998	Southwestern Bell purchases Southern New England Telecommunications Corp., Connecticut's main local phone company.
1998	Southwestern Bell announces agreement to purchase Ameritech, another of its sister Baby Bell companies.
1998	Bell Atlantic announces agreement to purchase GTE.

Clearly, strategic alliances and mergers can lead to a homogenization of practices, as more decisions are made by international corporations and fewer by local companies or state-run enterprises. In the case of BC Tel, however, although a majority of its shares have been held by the U.S. multinational GTE for decades, it has, with a few exceptions, been run in a fairly autonomous fashion.[37]

But that is changing for two reasons. First, with the 1992 decision to allow competition in long distance telephone service in Canada, GTE wants to make sure its subsidiary avoids the reorganization delays that the parent company experienced when deregulation took place in the United States in the 1980s. Second, the formation of the Stentor alliance results in greater homogenization of corporate practices across Canada, as well as greater coordination with the U.S. MCI firm, thanks to the alliance between MCI and the Stentor group that has also been formed. The Stentor alliance has also had an effect on the equipment market; in particular, Northern Telecom, a majority of whose stock is owned by Bell Canada, has been a major beneficiary. Northern has been able to boost its sales to BC Tel as a result of the need for greater equipment compatibility among Stentor partners (Interview T-93-2).

The Canada-U.S. Free Trade Agreement and NAFTA also portend the likelihood of increased international diffusion effects, as international investments by GTE, AT&T, MCI, Sprint, Northern Telecom and the Baby Bells have expanded in a variety of areas including telephone equipment manufacturing, specialized telecommunications service provision (paging, cellular, etc.), and regular telephone service. On the other hand, smaller companies are feeling the pinch (Janisch and Romanuk 1994) and are starting to be squeezed out in the process. Thus, with fewer companies located in more countries and operating in more market segments, what were once three separate national markets—and, in Canada, further sub-divided into provincial markets—are more and more being molded into a single North American telecommunications market.

Technology has also played a role in the internationalization of the industry. Because telecommunications is a service industry, there are aspects that are immobile and must remain (relatively) local. But even here computer technology makes it possible for much more work to be controlled remotely. Thus, while central-office line testing used to require workers on site, now testing throughout a country can be centralized in a single location. In the United States, it is done nationally; indeed, technologically there is no reason why all Canadian line-testing could not be done remotely from the United States, a fear of many Canadian workers. Operating and clerical offices, which used to field local calls, can and do field calls remotely. Thus, in British Columbia, there is a province-wide Automatic Call Distribution system in place, so a customer calling in a service order from Victoria might have his or her call answered by a clerical service representative working more than 500 miles away in Kelowna (Interviews T-93-2, T-93-34). Although digitalization hasn't proceeded quite as far in Mexico, there are now four main testing centers for Telmex in Mexico, though by 1994 construction of a single central testing center had at least reached the planning stages (Interview S-93-32). While the testing of telephone lines has yet to be shifted abroad in the same manner as automobile production has been, the traditional isolation of the telecommunications industry from global pressures is declining.

UNION RESPONSE TO GLOBALIZATION

Obviously, the above changes—a greater emphasis on satisfying the needs of large corporate customers, the shift from a monopoly domestic market structure to an oligopolistic international market structure, the formation of corporate "strategic alliances," an increase in the role of private capital, and an increasing concentration of capital in the industry—have all impacted telecommunications unions in North America. One obvious result is that the increased mobility of capital, the increased cooperation (alliances) between telecommunications companies, and the increased concentration of capital all, ceteris paribus, diminish labor leverage and union power. Indeed, in a study of 18 industrialized countries, the percentage of the workforce organized by unions was calculated to have fallen from a high of 37 percent in 1975 to 28 percent in 1988 (Rojot and Torgeist 1992: 11). However, as shall be seen in the chapters that follow, there are different strategies and tactics that labor unions can and do use to confront these changes.

Interestingly, while corporate practices are becoming more similar across national boundaries, so far labor practices of different unions remain quite distinctive. One key reason for this is while all corporations have a similar goal-oriented behavior (i.e, profit maximization),[38] unions pursue a variety of both political and economic objectives. As shall be explained in the following chapter, these distinct objectives help to shape distinct union responses. Because of this, even when confronted with very similar problems, one can continue to anticipate that different unions will respond very differently to the problems posed by the globalization of the industry.

NOTES

1. Note, however, that "local" does not necessarily mean native. A common business strategy has been to send high-ranking officials from the

parent company to the subsidiary country precisely to maintain an acceptable level of central control.

2. STRM union advisor María Xelhuantzi López, for instance, made this distinction at an international PTTI conference held in Mexico City in March 1994.

3. This problem is particularly important at Telmex. Under the production bonus scheme implemented in 1993 (see Chapter 6 for greater detail), workers receive bonuses only if production targets are met while managers receive promotions based on their ability to meet production quotas. Not surprisingly, collusion between front-line managers and workers to change the figures in order to "meet" production targets is quite common.

4. Note too that this change is reflected in compensation patterns, as the ratio of CEO pay to shop floor worker pay has skyrocketed between the 1970s and 1990s. While there are many social reasons why one might want to advocate a reversal of this trend (and I would consider myself one of these advocates), from a capitalist shareholder standpoint, the change does make some sense. Because computer technology permits greater centralization of decision-making authority, the CEO actually *does* make more decisions that affect firm performance than was previously the case.

5. One illustration of this is that the CWA (Communications Workers of America) was not given prior notice when AT&T announced plans to "downsize" by 40,000 workers in December 1995 (Conversation with CWA rep, 1996). The reason for the lack of notice was that no unionized employees were involved! Rather, the lay-offs and early retirements were designed to thin the ranks of middle management.

6. Comparative statics is an economic modelling technique involving analysis of a variable in two discrete time periods. This allows one to compare events at one time period with another, but often fails to capture the dynamic nature of the changes taking place between the two measurement points.

7. The international postwar "class compromise" has been analyzed by many academics (Nissen 1990). See Gordon, Edwards and Reich (1982) for a Marxist analysis of the class compromise in United States. For an analysis of the class compromise in Scandinavia, see Esping-Andersen (1985), especially pp. 82-88. For an international comparison of five advanced industrial countries, see Gourevitch 1986. Various efforts are made to apply similar analyses to developing countries. See Haggard (1990) for a statist approach to the study of Third World economic policy response to changes in the international economy. While the above authors disagree on many things, all approach the topic of macroeconomic policy from a standpoint that involves a focus on the formation of social coalitions and the role of state policy-makers.

There is also a consensus that the 1970s marked a period in which the "historic compromise" that had prevailed in industrial economies during the postwar period came undone (Gourevitch 1986: 81, 181-217).

8. See Hamilton (1982) for a study of the extent and limits of such state "autonomy," as applied to the study of the presidency of Lázaro Cárdenas in Mexico (1934–1940).

9. In the United States, for instance, the average rate of return in the manufacturing sector fell from 12% in 1965 to a low of 3% in 1974, before rebounding subsequently (Brenner 1995: 113). See also Gordon, Edwards and Reich 1982.

10. As Székely and del Palacio (1995: 20) note, "In the 1970s, given the advance of world finances toward massive currency trade, in the context of a new world characterized by floating exchange rates, the most important banks needed information quickly . . . It is no accident that the first revolutionary changes in the regulation of telecommunications occurred in the 'troika' of the most important financial centers of the world: the United States, Great Britain, and Japan."

11. Note that in some countries, such as France, cable and telephone service are under the control of the same monopoly company. It is not surprising that privatization in France was much slower in coming, since unlike the U.S. or Canada, there was no cable market for France Telecom to gain in exchange for acquiescing to greater competition in telephone service.

12. A direct implication of Noam's analysis is that a monopoly structure in telecommunications is preferable when the goal is to construct a telephone network, since monopoly profits are a convenient way to finance expansion, but that a competitive structure is to be preferred when the telephone network is fully constructed and service universally available. However, as is evidenced by the case of Mexico, business will frequently press for deregulation well before the telephone network is complete.

13. An important distinction in the United States—and most of Canada—is that the traditional telephone market structure was a state-regulated private monopoly, rather than a state-provided service. Nonetheless, during the long monopoly period (1910s to early 1980s) in the United States, AT&T functioned in many ways similarly to its publicly-owned counterparts, with an "engineering" focus and a high rate of investment (Keefe and Baroff 1994).

14. Ironically, the attempt of AT&T to enter the computer sector was a dismal failure, leading AT&T to spin-off its computer sector, Global Information Systems, in 1996. Needless to say, this was not the result AT&T anticipated at the time of divestiture!

15. Four key groups behind the push for deregulation in Canada were the CBTA (Canadian Business Telecommunications Alliance), representing 340 businesses and nonprofit agencies; the ITAC (Information Technology Association of Canada), representing 300 high technology business; the CCC (Communications Competition Coalition, representing 40 of the largest corporations in Canada; and the CBA (Canadian Banking Association), representing the six largest banks in Canada (Winseck 1993: 207).

16. In the United States, for instance, it is estimated that 3% of telecommunications users provide 50% of telephone revenue (Noam 1992: 45). For BC Tel, 3% of its customers provide 49% of total revenue (GTE 1992).

17. According to Winseck (1993: 221), while it is true that Canada's six largest banks spend C$470-million a year on telecommunications, this figure still represents only 0.81% of their C$52.1-billion of annual operating expenses. In terms of profits, Canada's six largest banks earned C$3.7-billion in 1990, a sum equal to 52% of the total profits reported by the Toronto Stock Exchange 300 index.

18. As Vincent Mosco notes, General Motors operates the world's largest private telecommunications network, consisting of 8,000,000 kilometers of cable; 300 mainframes; 2,000 minicomputers; 300,000 computer terminals; and 250,000 telephones. According to Mosco, the GM network handles 12 million long-distance telephone calls a year (Mosco 1990: 9).

19. Additionally, given the fact that roughly 90% of the Canadian population lives within 100 miles of the U.S. border, deregulation in the United States enabled large corporate telephone customers to bypass the Canadian telephone network (Boulter 1985). According to a 1985 Canadian Department of Communications document, "Lower toll rates in the U.S. will encourage big customers to bypass the Canadian system. This is significant, since big customers represent about one-third of Bell's [Bell Canada's] long distance revenues" (DOC 1985: 2). See also Robert Crandell's and William Davidson's submissions to CRTC notice 92-78 regarding cable/telephone convergence (Crandall 1993: 2, Davidson 1993: 85) for further discussion of the bypass threat that can arise from differences in phone rates. On the bypass issue in the Mexican context, see Guadarrama H. 1994.

20. This is precisely what happened in the airline industry in both Canada and the United States. Prior to deregulation, access to routes was regulated and limited. When the limits to entry were relaxed, an initial period of competitive frenzy was followed by a series of airline bankruptcies and mergers of failing companies with stronger ones, leading to a markedly higher level of market concentration.

So far, deregulation in telecommunications has taken the form of "regulated oligopolistic competition," a far cry from true deregulation. For instance, in Great Britain, 90% of the long-distance telephone service market remained under British Telecom's control nearly a decade after privatization and deregulation began in 1984 (Farmer et al 1994: 1, Williams 1993). In the United States, AT&T retains a lesser, but still dominant, position, collecting 62% of total long-distance revenues and serving 75% of all households (Keefe and Boroff 1994: 34; see also Cywith 1990, Unitel 1992). However, if the regulated oligopolistic regime breaks down into true deregulation, as now seems possible, one can anticipate similar market dynamics to operate.

21. Though somewhat unusual in the United States, this is not the only case of such a market structure. A similar form of regulated oligopolistic competition existed in the U.S. auto industry from 1945 until the mid-1970s, when a rise in Japanese auto imports led to its demise (Zetka 1995).

22. Because there has been no divestiture (separation of local and national calling) in either Mexico or Canada, Telmex and BC Tel serve not only as their country's (or, in the case of BC Tel, region's) equivalent of AT&T, but also of the Baby Bells at the same time. Thus, like the Baby Bells, in British Columbia, the overwhelming majority of calls, including a majority of calls from competing telephone companies, are routed through BC Tel facilities. Ironically, Unitel, which is the second largest provider of long distance service, is also one of BC Tel's largest customers! Since Unitel has a very limited independent network, a majority of the service it provides involves purchasing discounted dedicated BC Tel and Bell Canada lines and reselling those lines at a 15% cut rate to the public (CRTC 1992).

23. In Canada, there have been trends toward privatization and concentration among the remaining private owners. In 1981, 68% of telecommunications industry revenues were generated in the private sector and 63% of all revenues were generated by Bell Canada and BC Tel. In 1993, 81% of telecommunications revenues were generated in the private sector and 73% of all revenues were generated by Bell Canada and BC Tel (Winseck 1993: 275-276). A similar trend is evident in Mexico, as the Telmex privatization, in which Southwestern Bell owns 24.5% of the dominant consortium's stock, provides an example of the increasing internationalization of capital in an industry previously dominated by national (often publicly-owned) monopolies. The 1984 divestiture of AT&T in the United States marks an exception to this trend; however, mergers and acquisitions since the passage of the 1996 Telecommunications Act, such as Southwestern Bell's purchase of Pacific Telesis in March 1996, indicate that industry concentration is now rising in the United States as well (Noll 1996).

24. Thanks to Vanda Rideout, a researcher at Carleton University in Ontario, for pointing out the unique nature of this arrangement to me.

25. Technically, after the 1982 bank nationalizations, the Mexican government share rose much higher, since many banks were major private stockholders in Telmex. The government quickly sold off most of these new share holdings, although the government's percentage remained a somewhat-higher 56% until the sale of 20% of Telmex stock in December 1990.

26. The Nora and Minc 1979 report, which became the foundation of France's 1980s national telecommunications strategy is the classic example of this type of national development planning. Spain, Singapore and Hong Kong have also followed a national development model of telecommunications policy (Cowhey and Aronson 1989: 9-14).

27. These plans are laid out in such documents as Telmex 1987a and Telmex 1987b.

28. Nevertheless, Canadian long distance rates remained higher than in the United States, while local service rates remained much lower. In 1992, Bell Canada long distance telephone rates were 40% higher than in the United States; at the same time, local rates were roughly 45% lower (Bagnall 1992).

29. This is one area where Mexico's lower level of economic development is an important explanatory factor. The Mexican business elite and Mexican government have promoted high-tech telecommunications services for the business sector in the hope that these services will enable Mexico to serve as a telecommunications gateway between the United States and Latin America. See Baur 1995, Segovia 1993, Cepeda Salinas 1993, and Zornilla 1993.

30. A tariff is the technical term for the rate set by a telecommunications regulatory body.

31. For instance, on June 9, 1993, Telmex was fined N$60,000,000 (approximately U.S.$20,000,000 at the time) for failure to meet the service quality targets set forth in the company's Concession Title (Lovera 1993, SCT 1993). As well, between January and June of 1994, Telmex ran up a fine total in excess of N$4,500,000 (U.S. $1,500,000) for billing errors investigated by Mexico's consumer protection agency, Profeco (Aguilar 1994).

32. However, by May 1992, 55.7 percent of total Telmex stock (voting and nonvoting) was in foreign hands (Petrazzini 1995: 121).

33. GTE agreed to this arrangement in exchange for an exemption to Canadian law limiting foreign ownership of telecommunications firms operating in the country.

34. Strategic alliances are also politically important in that their existence serves as a pressure mechanism for further lifting of government regulations in the telecommunications industry. As Crandall and Flamm (1989: 10) note,

"Multinational alliances undercut explicitly nationalist policies with increasing frequency."

35. At the time of writing, Bell Atlantic's announced plans to purchase GTE were still subject to regulatory approval. Evidently, if approval is obtained as expected, BC Tel's new parent company would be Bell Atlantic.

36. Chart based on information culled from Petrazzini 1995, Aguilar and Guadarrama H. 1994, PTTI 1992, Francés 1993, Noll 1996, Apodaca 1996, Serrill 1996, Holson 1998, and Schiesel and Holson 1998. Though not covered here, mergers and strategic alliances are also common in the telecommunications equipment market. See, for example, Rosablanda Rojas 1994, Sánchez Daza 1992, Lara Sánchez 1992b, Rueda 1986.

37. As this book was going to press, BC Tel itself was participating in a merger with Telus, Alberta's main phone company. GTE's percentage in the new combined company is slated to be 26.7% (Evans 1999).

38. Of course, there are different theories of corporate goals, including Herbert Simon's analysis of satisficing behavior, according to which corporations seek a satisfactory rate of return, rather than aggressively maximize profits. See Tirole (1988: 48-49) for a concise discussion of this issue. However, at a minimum all corporations pursue primarily financial objectives. The case for unions is more complicated, as shall be explained in Chapter 3.

CHAPTER THREE

Unions and the Globalization Challenge

The challenge posed by globalization is clear. With a domestic monopoly market situation, telecommunications unions were shielded from the economic turmoil that unions in more competitive sectors have had to confront. In Canada, telephone companies could afford to pay above-average wages and benefits since profit rates were capped by government regulators. In Mexico, no such cap existed, but whether the majority of shares were owned by private capitalists (1950-1972) or the state (1972-1990), workers were able to press the PRI and the state labor bureaucracy to put pressure on management to make contract concessions. In both Canada and Mexico, telephone workers are among the workers with the strongest union contracts.

Because globalization allows for greater capital mobility, intensifies competition (and thus makes companies more cost sensitive), and increases the concentration of capital (thereby making it easier for a single company to withstand a strike or other industrial action), it tends to reduce union leverage. Moreover, the automation of much of the switching technology makes it possible for the telephone network to operate with limited maintenance for weeks or even months, as has been evident in several U.S. and Canadian strikes in the 1980s.

Some analysts contend that unions need to adjust to changing times by cooperating more closely with management. Accordingly, they argue, different unions will have to converge on this common strategy because union survival depends on it. A second group of analysts argue that, conversely, national differences will persist because of the distinct labor laws that exist in each country; thus, this view predicts widely disparate union responses to globalization. A third group argues that the actual solution in each country will vary according to the strategic choices made by unions in different countries. As shall be seen further on, I am largely in accord with this third group. However, it does little good to talk about union strategic choices without clearly outlining the strategic options available.

WHAT DO UNIONS DO?

In their analysis of U.S. unionism, Freeman and Medoff (1984) asked the above question regarding the *economic* effects of unions. Here, however, I want to ask the same question about unions' *political* effects. This has been a topic of long-standing debate, going back as far as some of the early writings of Marx and Engels. For some, unions are purely economic pressure groups, while for others unions are agents of revolutionary change. There are unions that have followed each of these characterizations, as well as varying gradations in between. Indeed, when examining unions' strategic choices, one of the most important questions to ask is how a given union chooses to orient itself toward the state and toward the capitalist economy. In both Mexico and Canada there have, historically, been both revolutionary unions and "business" unions of the purely economic pressure group variety. To understand the range of options available to unions it is necessary to examine the strengths and limitations of each type.

There have been many important analysts of the labor movement. Here, however, I shall concentrate on the arguments put forth by Sidney and Beatrice Webb, Vladamir Lenin, Rosa Luxembourg, and Selig Perlman. These authors are important here not because of their direct influence on the labor movement, though each in his or her own way has had some degree of influence, but rather because each exposes a different *logic* of unionism. Within the confines of each logical framework, it is possible to explain a given union's response to a change in the structure of the capitalist economy, as is currently happening in the telecommunications industry. However, unions operating within different logical frameworks will react quite differently. That is, not surprisingly, a given union's orientation vis a vis the state and the capitalist economy will greatly affect the way it responds to changes in either the state or the economy.

Table 3-1: Types of Union Strategic Orientations

	Reformist	Revolutionary
Society focus	Social unionism (Webbs)	Leninist unionism (Lenin)
Workplace focus	Business unionism (Perlman)	Mass strike (Luxembourg)

While the four union logics outlined in the above chart are "ideal type" constructions, never perfectly realized in practice, they nonetheless are enormously helpful in explaining the variety of union strategies that have operated in the context of a globalizing economy. Each type is explained in further detail below.

REVOLUTIONARY REBELS: UNIONS AS ANTI-CAPITALIST BASTIONS

I discuss the logics of revolutionary unionism first, principally because it is frequently forgotten that unions are *potentially* revolutionary organizations.[1] Moreover, in Latin America at least, it was not all that long ago that union action brought down governments.[2] Karl Marx and Frederick Engels were among those who anticipated that unions would play an important role in fostering socialist revolution. While most unions have followed the reformist paths that I will describe below, a significant minority of unions have followed more revolutionary trajectories. Two of the most important theorists of revolutionary unionism are Vladamir Lenin and Rosa Luxembourg. Though agreeing on the need for unions to be revolutionary, there are important differences between Lenin's and Luxembourg's theories. While Lenin saw unions being led by a socialist party and focused primarily on working to seize state power, Luxembourg saw the impetus for revolutionary activity coming from workers acting much more autonomously, with the party playing a coordinating role after the workers had taken the lead. This split remains among radical union activists today, with some seeking to work within a party structure and others rejecting links with parties. Both tendencies have been present in Canada and Mexico, with the more syndicalist (non-party) radicalism more important in Mexico and the party-linked radicalism more important in Canada.

Both Lenin and Luxembourg took their cue from questions posed in the analysis of Marx and Engels. For Marx and Engels, unions, as the base organization of workers, were the training ground of political activity by the working class. For them, the key factor was not the economic struggles that union engage in themselves, important though they may be, but that unions help prepare workers for class struggle and socialist revolutionary activity. As Marx and Engels write in *The Communist Manifesto*, "The real fruit of their [unions'] battle lies, not in the immediate result, but in the ever-expanding union of workers" (Marx and Engels 1978: 481). Historically, though, unions in the 1850s and 1860s tended to be craft-based and not revolutionary. As Richard Hyman notes, though neither Marx nor Engels ever systematically revisited the question of unionism, they did comment in different letters in their later correspondence that under certain circumstances unions could be led in a reformist direction. Different possible causes were suggested, including the existence of a "labor aristocracy" of workers, passivity among the rank and file which leads to a corruption or embourgeoisement of the workers, or workers being "bought off" through capitalists sharing the gains of imperialist colonialism (Hyman 1987: 41-43).

The strength of reformist tendencies within trade unions was at least one of the factors that made Lenin skeptical of the ability for unions, on their own, to engage in revolutionary activity. Like Marx and Engels, Lenin saw unions as providing a potentially important training ground of revolutionary activity. As Lenin argued, "A strike teaches workers to understand what the strength of the employers and what the strength of the workers consists in; it teaches them not to think of their own employer alone and not of their own immediate workmates alone but of all the employers, the whole class of capitalists and the whole class of workers" (Lenin 1978: 63). But, according to Lenin, the key weakness of the union is that it represents not the working class, but a given group of workers in relation with a given employer or group of employers. Only a socialist party can represent the working class "in relation to all classes of modern society and to the state as an organised political force" (Lenin 1978: 95).[3]

According to Lenin, without the guidance provided by a class-based party, workers will fall into a narrow trade union consciousness, instead of a class consciousness (Hammond 1978). As Lenin put it, "Class political consciousness can be brought to the workers *only from without*, that is, only from outside the economic struggle, from outside the sphere of relations between workers and employers." (Lenin 1978: 110, italics in original). The dilemma, of course, is that most workers only come to socialism via the path of unionism, but in unionism lies the possibility of cooptation. Indeed, in Lenin's view, a certain level of trade union development was consistent with the development of capitalism. Lenin's contemporary Antonio Gramsci[4] makes clear how this is often the case. As Gramsci writes regarding the establishment of works councils in early Mussolini Italy (1923), "Capitalists, for industrial reasons, cannot want all forms of organization to be destroyed. In the factory, discipline and the smooth flow of production is only possible if there exists at least a minimum degree of constitutionality, a minimum degree of consent on the part of the workers" (Gramsci 1990: 167).

Though its influence has waned dramatically, the influence of the Leninist model of party-linked union organization should not be underestimated. Outside of the Soviet bloc, Community Party-linked unions have played a major role in Spain, France, and Italy and in much of Central and South America, and, though less significant, they have been present in both Canada and Mexico as well.[5] Obviously, much of the performance of day-to-day unionism, such as grievance resolution or even local walk-outs, is not revolutionary, no matter what the strategic orientation of union leaders. Also, there are plenty of historical examples when Leninist unions were "instructed" to act in concert with the bourgeois state.[6] But despite its weaknesses, this model of revolutionary party-linked unionism has been important and, on occasion, quite effective. Outside the Russian Revolution, union action per se has never been a major factor in the revolutionary seizure of power. Most communist parties that succeeded in taking state power did so on the basis of a peasant-linked movements (China, Vietnam, Cuba), through occupation by troops of the Soviet Union, or through resistance to external aggression (the former Yugoslavia). Nevertheless, the revolutionary party-linked strategy has had significant successes in promoting the interests of workers through militant confrontations with state authorities on issues of political and economic importance.

Another, very different, model of revolutionary trade unionism is suggested by Rosa Luxembourg. Here, the primacy of the struggle is in the union movement itself, with the party following, rather than the other way around. Luxembourg developed her views on trade unionism most fully in an essay entitled *The Mass Strike, the Political Party and Trade Unions*. Luxembourg's tract on the role of the mass strike was laid out as a critique of anarchism, from which syndicalism developed. Although Luxembourg criticizes anarchists and syndicalists for their ahistoricism and their overreliance on "imagination" and "goodwill and courage" (Luxembourg 1970: 159), she defends the need for union-led revolutionary action, as opposed to the Leninist model of party-led action.[7]

Luxembourg wrote her tract in response to the short-lived but dramatic 1905 Russian Revolution. In a very short period, Russian workers had changed from being the least organized portion of the working class in Europe to the most organized, whose activity was characterized by frequent general strikes. Luxembourg's description of one of these general strikes in the Black Sea city of Odessa illustrates the speed at which worker outbursts would occur:

> . . . a meeting took place of all the strikers, seven or eight thousand men; they formed a procession that went from factory to factory, growing like an avalanche, and presently a crowd of forty to fifty thousand betook themselves to the docks in order to bring all work there to a standstill. A general strike soon reigned throughout the whole city (Luxembourg 1970: 167).

For Luxembourg, the 1905 Russian revolution pointed to a need to alter the traditional (read German) relationship between a social democratic party and the union movement. First, Luxembourg argues mass strikes by necessity must be "organized for the most part spontaneously" (Luxembourg 1970: 183). One-day general strikes planned by a party are not useless, but lacking the spontaneity of the mass strike, they also lack its intensity and are less threatening to capital. Second, mass strikes arise not from general political principles and thus cannot be instigated by a political party, but rather arise from specific local economic grievances, only later building into a political struggle; in the mass strike, economic and political issues conflate and are joined together (Luxembourg 1970: 184-185). Third, the mass strike is important not because it provokes police violence, but rather because it results in a "thoroughgoing internal reversal of social relations" (Luxembourg 1970: 186). Thus, the mass strike is a key element in consciousness-building and in creating a revolution itself. Finally, then, the party cannot operate through the issuance of commands to its cadres, but rather must show the "most adroit adaptability to the given situation, and the closest possible contact with the mood of the masses" (Luxembourg 1970: 188).

Note the difference with the Leninist model. For Lenin, unionists focus solely on their own particular struggles, while for Luxembourg strikes have sometimes revolutionary "spill-over" effects. For Lenin, the party plays a vanguard role; for Luxembourg, the party plays a coordinating and facilitating role, but the leading role falls to the workers who initiate, largely on their own, revolutionary action. For Lenin, class consciousness can only come from the party; for Luxembourg, revolutionary class consciousness comes from participation in strikes and the revolutionary struggle itself.

A key reason for these differences is their different views of the structure of power within the union itself. Lenin focuses on the union leadership and, not surprisingly, finds them tending towards bureaucratization, as revolutionary advocacy is tempered by the need to ensure day-to-day organizational stability. Like Lenin, Luxembourg criticizes union leaders for their conservatism, accepting the development of a union officialdom only as "a historically necessary evil" (Luxembourg 1970: 214). But unlike Lenin, Luxembourg believes the rank-and-file workers are capable of leading the struggle, despite possible resistance from trade union officials. Union officials that stand in the way would, according to Luxembourg, simply be overrun. Hence Luxembourg contends, "A revolutionary period in Germany would so alter the character of the trade-union struggle and develop its potentialities to such an extent that the present guerrilla warfare of the trade unions would be child's play in comparison" (Luxembourg 1970: 195).

By necessity, the "mass strike" in union history is fairly uncommon. But neither is the mass strike merely an ancient historical artifact.[8] The snowballing effect described by Luxembourg in the Odessa general strike does indeed occur—and in the manner Luxembourg describes—in other cases. Though not a true general strike since it involved workers in only one industry, the rank-and-file uprising that began among the operators in April 1976 in the Mexican telephone workers' union in this study (see Chapter 4 for a more detailed description) involved a similar dynamic. As described in an issue of the union's periodical, a wildcat strike that began with operators stopping work at one exchange in Mexico City spread quickly throughout the country:

The pressures that centered around them were not important; with valor and decisiveness they announced to the whole country that the moment to act had came and from one to the next, they initiated a chain reaction that no one could stop, from Mexico City to Guadalajara and Monterrey, from Guadalajara to La Paz, from Monterrey to Chihuahua, from La Paz to Morelia and like that all the switchboards in the country were listening to the voice that without hesitancy pushed forward the struggle (STRM 1981).

In addition to her analysis of spontaneous outbursts, Luxembourg's analysis also illustrates an important form of unionism: that is, non-party revolutionary unionism. Syndicalist unions, of course, have been important in a variety of countries, including Spain, Argentina, and even in Mexico during the period of the Mexican Revolution. But beyond purely syndicalist unions, there are a number of radical unions which act much more along the lines advocated by Luxembourg than by Lenin—that is, operating largely independently of the party with which they are nominally affiliated and placing a strong emphasis on rank-and-file militancy, mass mobilizations, and wild-cat actions. Such unions tend to focus in particular on control over shop-floor issues, since it is here, rather than at the state level, where the union is strongest. In the absence of a strong revolutionary party, union militancy at the plant level often becomes a default strategy of union activists with strong anti-capitalist views. Many of the unions in Mexico's small "independent" union sector have sought to follow this strategy of non-party radicalism.

Neither the British Columbian telephone workers' union nor the Mexican telephone workers' union have followed the revolutionary strategies of either direct confrontation led by a party directed at the level of the state or of direct confrontation on local labor control issues. But both unions have, at times, flirted with such radical or revolutionary demands,[9] and in the case of the Mexican telephone workers' union, some opposition groups have insisted that the union should pursue revolutionary tactics and goals.

However, as a whole, both unions have followed reformist strategies. One reason for the prevalence of reformist strategies is that they attract less ire from capitalists and the state; they avoid this ire at the cost of ceding ground on many issues to state and corporate officials. As shall be seen, though, not all reformist strategies are the same. Two especially important reformist strategies are the social unionist strategy and the business unionist strategy, both of which are examined below.

THE LOGICS OF REFORM UNIONISM

> A labor movement must, from its very nature, be an organized campaign against the rights of private property, even when it stops short of embracing a radical program seeking the elimination, gradual or abrupt, "constitutional" or violent, of the private entrepreneur (Perlman 1928: 155-156).

The revolutionary unionist impulse may often lurk beneath the surface, but unions tend more often towards reformism than revolutionary unionism. This orientation is based on both fear of retribution and repression for taking too confrontational a stance[10] as well as honest belief that the interests of workers can best be achieved through reforms within a capitalist economy. As none other than Selig Perlman himself, an advocate of business unionism, acknowledged, however, regardless of how reformist labor chooses to be, it cannot avoid at least some degree of confrontation with those who would advocate unlimited, or nearly absolute, capitalist private property rights. Thus, the reformist union doesn't avoid battles with capital; it merely seeks to limit the scope of issues on which such battles will occur.

Reformist unionism includes two very distinct approaches. One, frequently labelled social unionism, ties labor unions to a social democratic party and seeks to effect reforms by engaging in community politics and, ultimately, the setting of state policy. In certain respects, the tie to the party is similar to the tie between Leninist parties and a revolutionary social democratic party. That is, the focus of social unionism is not so much on the local concerns of the factory or work site, but rather of the labor movement and its relation to the state as a whole. Through the formation of community-wide alliances and in coordination with a social democratic party, social unionism seeks to alter relations of power in the state and economy to the benefit of labor, without challenging the existence of private property relations on which the capitalist system itself depends.

The alternative approach is labelled business unionism. In this strategy, the role of the political party is much less important. Just as social unionism shares a certain affinity in its link to a party with party-led revolutionary unionism, so business unionism shares certain aspects with non-party revolutionary unionism, avoiding most entanglements with state-level politics. Though business unions do interact with the state to a certain degree, the extent of this interaction is much more limited; instead of working with an independent labor party to effect reforms, business unions act more as a pressure group within established business-dominated political parties. Rather than work on large-scale community campaigns and seek to alter relations of power, the focus of the business union is more concentrated on the local work site and dealing with basic issues like wages and working conditions. This "bread and butter" focus of business unionism led one of its proponents, University of Wisconsin researcher John Commons, to describe this form of union activity as "pure and simple unionism" (Perlman 1928: viii, Larson and Nissen 1987: 131-133). By looking at both social unionism and business unionism below, the dilemmas faced by any union embracing a reformist strategy become evident.

Describing the rise of "new unionism"[11] in Great Britain at the turn of the century, Beatrice and Sidney Webb, members of the Fabian group which would a few years later help form the social democratic Labour Party, explained the logic of social unionist strategy. According to the Webbs, a union's main objective has to be to alter the global relations between capital and labor in the economy; in particular, unions can and must interfere with the "freedom of contract" extolled by classic liberalism, since *"wherever the economic conditions of the parties concerned are unequal, legal freedom of contract merely enables the superior in strategic strength to dictate the terms"* (Webb and Webb 1965: 217, italics in original). For the Webbs, there are three main union goals: achievement of a standard wage rate, fixed limits to the working day, and regulation of workplace health and safety (Webb and Webb 1965: 279-324). Of course, many other issues come into play in obtaining benefits in these areas. For instance, technological change, if implemented unilaterally by management, become a means for the employer to undermine the standard wage rate. As well, unions must organize the unorganized since failure to do so will result in the union being undermined by nonunion competition; indeed, one key element of social unionism, in contrast with business unionism, is its emphasis on the need for unions to continually organize the unorganized to spread the benefits of unionism, rather than simply seeking to preserve the benefits of current union members.

According to the Webbs, unions had three main instruments that they could use to pursue their goals. One of these was the provision of mutual insurance, which in Britain had been an important means used by unions to build up their membership. The Webbs felt, however, that this instrument was destined to fade away, except for unemployment insurance (Webb and Webb 1965: 828).[12] The other key means available to unionists are collective bargaining and legislative enactment. While the Webbs believed that collective bargaining was a necessary method to use, particularly to deal with trade or industry-specific issues, they saw legislative enactment as being "superior where applicable," since state legislation ensures universality and avoids industrial strife (Webb and Webb 1965: 802-803).

The reasons for the Webbs' preference for action at the level of the state becomes clearer when one delves a bit more deeply into their social unionist philosophy. According to the Webbs, unions engage in essentially two forms of rule-making that restrict capital. One form relies on restricting numbers while the other form involves setting common standards. The Webbs label this latter approach the "common rule" (Webb and Webb 1965: 560).

According to the Webbs, union restrictions that attempt to benefit members by restricting numbers are a mixed bag. This method does allow insiders to make a better bargain with employers and maintains higher skill and efficiency than that which would prevail in the absence of unionism. But at the same time, restricting the entry of new workers means that the most capable workers may end up being excluded from the workforce; as well, it reduces efforts at maintaining production efficiency and transfers employment to non-unionized sectors. Overall, the Webbs contend, such union rules are better than having no union at all, but restricting numbers is not an ideal way to protect workers. Moreover, the Webbs assert, the number of trades where entry could feasibly be restricted had fallen rapidly due to the increased mobility of capital (Webb and Webb 1965: 704-715).[13]

The common rule method of regulation, on the other hand, provides all of the benefits with relatively few costs. By setting a common wage and thereby taking wages out of the competition, capitalists can no longer compete on the basis of paying workers less, so instead there is significant pressure on employers to compete on the basis of who works more (Webb and Webb 1965: 716-717). As a result, employers are compelled to respond by implementing technological change that increases productivity and hence total economic output (Webb and Webb 1965: 730, 749). In late twentieth century parlance, this is known as a "high-wage, high value-added" economic strategy.[14]

Implementing the common rule, however, requires state action in such areas as setting the minimum wage, state support of health and education, maximum working hours standards, mandated vacation time, restrictions on child labor, and other measures (Webb and Webb 1965: 839). According to the Webbs, the pursuit of the common rule and such national social programs will ensure that unions succeed at providing everyone with a living wage, which, they assert, should be unions' primary goal (Webb and Webb 1965: 599).

As they readily admit, there are alternatives available to the union other than pursuit of a living wage. A union can instead choose to defend traditional privileges, a path that the Webbs label as the "vested interests" doctrine, or by the "law of supply and demand." The Webbs acknowledge that unionism arose out of a defense of vested interests of artisans (Webb and Webb 1965: 562-570). In essence, such unions seek to defend established expectations, or a moral economy, [15] that has come under attack. This method works well in certain occasions, but is primarily defensive in character. Setting wages by the "law of supply and demand" entailed, in essence, a form of what in the late twentieth century would be called gainsharing; that is, workers would be paid according to a "sliding scale," earning higher wages when profits were high and lower wages when profits were low. Under this doctrine, higher wages were considered justified for workers who worked in highly-productive industries. While this form of payment did take hold in some English craft unions in the period from 1840 to 1880, it fell into disfavor among unionists who experienced lower wages when profits fell. According to the Webbs, though the collectivist idea of a "living wage" had been gaining in popularity in Britain since 1880, some concessions to the more traditional conceptions of union defense of vested interests and the level of productivity of a given industry would have to be made. Still, the gist of the Webbs' advocacy of social unionism is clear: a strong focus on parliamentary state action to ensure the creation of economy-wide minimum standards, a focus on the collectivist ideal of the living wage, a de-emphasis on the use of restrictions on entry to work as a means to pursue union goals and an increased emphasis instead on organizing the unorganized, and a view of labor unions as being part of a *movement*—and not simply a collection of individual craft organizations.

The social unionist conception has been very influential and is the dominant model of union organization in most Western European countries, Australia, and Canada. The Telecommunications Workers'

Union of British Columbia studied here, in particular, provides a clear example of the social unionist approach. Social unionism has also been influential in the United States and Mexico, especially in the 1930s and 1940s.[16] And, as shall be seen in Chapter 8, in Mexico, too, there are still some unions that continue to be influenced by social unionism. Of course, some unions have had more success with social unionist strategies than others. Because of its dependence on state action, social unionism tends to work best where there is a strong social democratic or labor political party and a centralized labor movement that can act quickly and decisively in the political sphere. In Canada, where labor is decentralized and the labor-backed New Democratic Party is fairly weak, unions have nevertheless faired, comparatively speaking, reasonably well in terms of maintaining contract benefits and membership levels in the face of globalization.[17]

A very different type of union reformism is business unionism. Writing near the end of a period of economic growth characterized by declining union membership (1928), Selig Perlman laid out some of the fundamental principles of business unionism. For Perlman, unionism is an "essentially pragmatic" (Perlman 1928: 5) response to the conditions faced by the worker at the factory or work site. In the United States, Perlman asserts, the only labor consciousness that is common to the highly heterogeneous U.S. working class is "job consciousness," which involves a limited objective of wage and job control (Perlman 1928: 169). These involve a very limited challenge to the rights of private property. As a result, the reforms which are sought by business unionism are both more local and more limited than the reforms sought by social unionists.

As opposed to social unionism, business unionism has limited objectives at the level of the state. Rather than participating in a social democratic labor party, business unionists choose to carry out politics in the form of a pressure group, "trading off labor votes as payment to pledges made by regular party politicians to carry out, if elected to office" (Perlman 1928: 173). Thus, rather than acting as a social movement, business unionism seeks out individual deals with individual politicians. This type of deal making necessarily narrows the scope of a union's political agenda; instead of engaging in the political work necessary to build a majority coalition, business unionism cedes this task to the politicians, seeking to ensure that basic concerns are addressed.[18]

For the business unionist, the primary concern is to ensure the "right to job opportunities of self-conscious groups, say a craft . . . and of the individuals within such groups" (Perlman 1928: 298). For Perlman, the drive to unionize comes not from a worker's consciousness of his or her class, but rather out of the worker's sense of a lack of job opportunities and hence the need for protection, which Perlman deems "a consciousness of job scarcity" (Perlman 1928: 8). Consequently, business unionism places primary emphasis on promoting higher wages and better working conditions for the members of a particular union, but shows very little concern for altering overall social conditions.

But in the United States, business unionism a la Gompers was having its problems at the time Perlman was writing, as Perlman himself was well aware (Perlman 1928: 231-233). Indeed, in the United States, the late 1920s were a time not unlike the 1980s and early 1990s, marked by increasing class inequality and declining union power (Geoghegan 1992). Perlman himself grudgingly admits to business unionism's faults, conceding that the "revolutionary solidarity" exhibited by social unionists in the United States in his day, such as Sidney Hillman of the garment workers "has cemented together a body of otherwise individualistic workers" (Perlman 1928: 228) and that such unions display a "real 'will to organize' and to increase . . . membership to the maximum."[19] By contrast, the majority of business unionist leaders had chosen to "settle down to a smug survey of the well oiled machinery of their little organizations, which suggests at least a suspicion that these leaders might not entirely welcome too many new members, whose alignment in the politics of the union would at best be uncertain" (Perlman 1928: 232).

Despite these comments, Perlman does not pause long to analyze these tendencies of business unionism. But it should be noted that, although few unions are entirely absent bureaucratic tendencies, the very conservatism of business unionism tends to heighten the degree of bureaucratization. As Perlman notes, the philosophy of the business unionist A.F. of L. was profoundly "pessimistic" (Perlman 1928: 252), focusing as it did with the problem of how to deal with a scarcity of opportunity. With such an outlook, it is not surprising that business union officials would seek to cut deals "behind closed doors" and avoid challenging the political status quo; that they would be reluctant to support any activity, such as wild cat strikes, that went beyond the union leadership's direct control (Perlman 1928: 163-164); and that they would be wary about dedicating significant resources for the organization of new members. By contrast, social unionism, not to mention the various brands of revolutionary unionism, has a much more optimistic attitude regarding the possibilities of labor action. Not surprisingly, then, social unions are typically willing to open themselves to more membership control and participation and devote greater resources to organizing new members. This, then, is where a core weakness of business unionism lies: though it avoids certain types of ideological conflict and its repercussions among the rank-and-file and avoids direct confrontation with capital, at the same time its pessimism and narrow breadth tends to cut it off from the pursuit of objectives that would be beneficial to workers, as well as restricting the overall success and growth of the labor movement as a whole. In purely economic terms, one could say that business unionism results in a lowering of short-term risk, but at the cost of lower long-term return. As shall be seen in this study, the Mexican telephone workers' union exhibits many of these tendencies of business unionism.

WHAT *CAN* UNIONS DO?

> England may have its Trade Unions, its growing regulation of private industry and its income-tax and death duties, but Germany has its revolutionary Social Democracy, France its political instability, the United States its tariff and currency troubles, India its famines, Cuba its chronic rebellion, and South America its revolutions (Webb and Webb 1965: 631).

The question of whether trade unions can maintain their members' high wages in the face of global competition is not a new one. The Webbs' answer, published originally in 1897, suggested that many factors influence when and where a capitalist firm will invest and that the level of wages and benefits is only one of these. This view is echoed by more contemporary analysts (Freeman and Medoff 1984, Streeck 1992). While there are striking parallels with the past,[20] there are also some significant differences between the globalization of the late twentieth century and the explosive growth of international commerce in the late nineteenth century. Factors listed in the previous chapter, such as the creation of a world telecommunications infrastructure that can transmit data across the globe instantaneously, certainly imply that present-day globalization entails a level of international economic integration of a much greater magnitude.

There are three principal theories regarding the possibilities for labor action in the new globalized environment. The first holds that there will be a convergence in types of unionism due to the competitive imperative of globalization. Generally speaking, the convergence is supposed to be toward greater labor-management cooperation, which is seen as necessary for labor to survive in an environment characterized by intensified global competition. A second view holds that national differences will continue to play an important role in determining the strategies of labor in each country. Of particular importance in the context of this study, many Mexican labor specialists assert that the Mexican labor regime is exceptional. According to this outlook, one would expect labor strategy to be similarly exceptional. Finally, a third view holds that strategic choices of unions, corporate managers, and state officials are key. I shall examine each of these schools of thought below and conclude with an analysis of how a union's strategic orientation, as outlined above, both impacts its response to globalization and influences globalization itself.

THE CONVERGENCE HYPOTHESIS

> There is a substantial consensus . . . that increased involvement of
> employees is important for economic progress. The disagreement
> comes in trying to work out a form for that involvement (Heckscher
> 1988: 251).

The convergence hypothesis is a prediction of long standing. Coming out of the academic literature of the late 1950s proclaiming an "end of ideology" (Bell 1960) it was predicted that the logic of industrialization would lead to a convergence between Soviet Union-style central planning and U.S.-style private enterprise. In place of two competing systems, adherents, such as Clark Kerr, believed a single common system would emerge, characterized by what Kerr termed a "web of rules" of "tripartite constitutionalism" in which labor, business, and state officials would jointly decide industrial relations and macroeconomic policy issues (Kerr 1983: 19, see also Kerr et al. 1960). This view was echoed by other analysts, such as Philippe Schmitter (1974) who argued that the twentieth century was the "century of corporatism." Obviously, events in the past twenty years have moved in quite a different direction. Not only has Leninism collapsed in the Soviet Union and Eastern Europe, but there has been a general trend away from corporatism, with some notable exceptions, as in Germany (Wever 1995).

But the convergence hypothesis of old has been replaced with a revised convergence hypothesis, one that sees unions and corporate managers as moving uniformly, albeit perhaps unevenly, in a cooperative direction. The new convergence hypothesis is usually made implicitly, as indicated by the Heckscher quote at the beginning of this section, rather than being explicitly spelled out. But it is nevertheless omnipresent in today's industrial relations literature.

Simply put, the argument is that labor and management *must* cooperate, since the days when "adversarial" labor-management relations could reign have ended. Though approaching the question from a variety of perspectives—including government officials, union leaders, former labor officials, business writers, and academics—Heckscher (1988), Bluestone and Bluestone (1992), Hoerr (1991), Levine and Strauss (1993), Peterson (1990), Streeck (1992), Hernández Juárez and Xelhuantzi López (1993) all deliver a similar message: in a globalized economy, labor and management must cooperate in order to effectively compete; conflict over distribution may be inevitable, but this must be subordinated to the greater good of global competition. Whether the solution is called "associational unionism" (Heckscher), the "enterprise compact" (Bluestone and Bluestone), "new unionism" (Hernández Juárez and Xelhuantzi López), or simply involves a more general advocacy of union-company cooperation (Peterson, Levine and Strauss, Hoerr), all agree that unions must "adapt" to the new capitalist environment, which must, by and large, be accepted as given. Though few go so far as to argue that the labor movements of every country will converge to the extent that they will be exactly alike, the gist of the argument is that the ultimate criterion of success for unions is their ability to promote competitiveness rather than, for instance, their ability to promote the interests of union members. But of course, central to the argument is that unions, by assuring the competitiveness of industry, are also best able to promote the interests of the rank and file. Though short-term conflicts of interest obviously exist, this is subsumed under a logic of liberal harmony in which the long-term interest of both labor and industry are satisfied by the cooperative pursuit of competitiveness.

This theory of a tendency toward cooperative convergence begins with the premise, accurate enough, that globalization has had a disruptive effect on industrial relations systems, particularly those that have historically been characterized as "adversarial." Focused on the United States, but with corresponding arguments made in Canada (Peterson 1990) and Mexico as well (Fesebes 1992, Lovera 1993, Hernández Juárez and Xelhuantzi López 1993), the argument is that a key reason for insufficient U.S. (or Canadian or Mexican) competitiveness lies in the inability of labor and management to form "cooperative" partnerships to boost productivity (Bluestone and Bluestone 1992: 5-8). In particular, the asserted lack of cooperation in North America[21] is contrasted with the cooperative practices said to be in place in many countries of Western Europe and Japan. Although different authors tender different "solutions," the overall message is remarkably consistent: North American unions (and companies) need to remake themselves within the framework of the Japanese/European system[22] in order to be able to compete effectively in the global economy.

Common to the vision of adherents of the convergence approach is the notion that unions periodically need to adjust to shifts in the global capitalist system. The current period is seen, correctly, as a period of restructuring of the capitalist economy, and thus it is anticipated that changes in labor relations will also need to occur. For instance, Heckscher states, "My thesis, then, is that we are approaching a new juncture, analogous to that of the 1920s and 1930s. I predict, not the end of unionism, but its reemergence in a changed form" (Heckscher 1988: 8).

In and of itself, the argument that a reorganization of labor relations must occur is reasonable. In fact, some sort of reorganization is to be expected, as such reorganizations have occurred before. As Heckscher argues, the Great Depression of the 1930s and the war that followed marked one such period of adjustment. Out of that period, in fact, there *did* emerge a new institutional framework between labor, capital, and the state. In Mexico, Canada, and the United States, that period was indeed characterized by great changes in industrial relations.

In Mexico, for example, a new labor federation, the Confederation of Mexican Workers (Confederación de Trabajadores de México, hereafter CTM) was formed in 1936 by the breakaway of a faction of the main labor confederation of the time, the Mexican Regional Worker Confederation (Confederación Regional Obrera Mexicana, hereafter CROM). The breakaway organization was led by Vicente Lombardo Toledano, in alliance with President Lázaro Cárdenas. Two years later,

Cárdenas, with CTM support, nationalized the petroleum industry. This proved to be a key event in consolidating labor support for the regime (Collier and Collier 1991). In exchange for labor peace, the government undertook to ensure the provision of key benefits to labor union members and to ensure state control of strategic industries through selective nationalizations (Aziz Nassif 1989: 52-53, 79-81).

However, the current system of Mexican labor relations wasn't fully institutionalized until later. In 1947, the more militant Lombardo Toledano was ousted from the CTM and replaced by the more acquiescent Fidel Velázquez. There followed a brief period in which roughly half the membership of the CTM, led by Lombardo Toledano, seceded from the CTM and formed a rival federation (Central Unica de Trabajadores or Sole Workers' Central, hereafter CUT), but the CUT was brutally repressed through the use of troops by President Miguel Alemán (president of Mexico from 1946 to 1952). By the end of Alemán's term, the current overall framework of Mexican labor relations had been consolidated (Aziz Nassif 1989: 97-102, de la Garza 1988: 53-64).

Likewise, in Canada and the United States, the 1930s was marked by the formation of a new labor confederation, the Congress of Industrial Organizations (CIO).[23] Led by John Lewis, President of the United Mine Workers (UMW), the CIO launched mass union organizing drives in basic manufacturing industries. The success of these efforts led to spectacular increases in union membership, especially in the United States, where union membership rose from roughly 10% of all workers in the early 1930s to 35% by 1945. Key government actions during this period were the passage of the Wagner Act in the United States in 1935 and the Industrial Relations and Dispute Investigation Act in Canada in 1948, which created a semicorporatist system of labor regulation recognizing unions' increased economic and political clout. In addition, in both countries, World War II served to increase the government's role in regulating industrial relations. An important difference between the United States and Canada, however, was the 1947 passage in the United States of the Taft-Hartley Act, which took back some of U.S. labor's gains, and, most importantly, consolidated the position of nonunion employers in the South. This move would contribute significantly to a later decline in U.S. union membership, as companies located new production facilities in the largely nonunion South while closing facilities in the unionized industrial states (Cowie 1996). Furthermore, in both the United States and Canada, as in Mexico, the late 1940s were marked by an attempt to purge communists, though the purge was most severe in the United States (Palmer 1992: 290-298). Again, as in Mexico, by the early 1950s, a more or less stable pattern of industrial relations system had been established.

The notion, then, that economic change may lead to changes in labor relations is not in question. Although very different in terms of their levels of economic development, form of government, level of foreign economic investment, level of state intervention, and so forth, Canada, Mexico, and the United States all experienced great changes in labor relations in the period between 1935 and 1955. While the changes experienced in Mexico are different than those in the United States and Canada, there are some broad similarities. In Mexico, as in the United States and Canada, the 1930s were marked by rising union membership and labor activism. The nationalization of the petroleum fields in 1938 solidified labor support for the PRI in Mexico in much the same way as the Wagner Act in the United States consolidated labor's allegiance to the Democratic Party. In the late 1940s, there was a retrenchment in union power in Mexico and a purge of leftists, a pattern also evident in Canada and especially the United States. Given the contemporary shift in the economic environment from Keynesian-style national economic policies of government intervention and demand management to global international oligopolistic competition, change in labor relations in North America is once again to be expected. However, although the notion of a convergence or cooperation imperative approach is superficially plausible, it suffers from a number of flaws.

One problem is that no tendency in labor relations ever achieves complete dominance. In both Mexico and Canada, there have always existed some unions that acted quite different from the tendencies that are nationally most common. Even in the heyday of Mexican corporatism, there were always two major competing tendencies (Xelhauntzi López 1992), one representing the CTM and the other representing many of the national industrial unions; since the 1970s, there has also been a small, but not insignificant tendency of more militant, "independent" unions.[24] In Canada, there have always been the competing tendencies of social unionism and business unionism, as well as a fair number of Communist Party-led unions or unions that followed syndicalist-like mass mobilization tactics.

A more serious problem with the convergence model lies in its lack of analysis of power dynamics. The extent of this problem becomes obvious as soon as one thinks about *how* labor relations models come into being. Few unions (and few corporations, for that matter) consciously pursue a *model* of development or labor relations. Unions and corporations (as well as worker confederations and national employer associations) pursue their *interests*, as they perceive them. Only through the interaction of state, labor, and business actions is it even possible that some sort of an equilibrium or "model" is reached. Even then, the equilibrium or model reached is only an ideal type, glossing over significant particularities and differences. And of course, such models are always subject to further, indeed continuous, challenge if one or more of the actors is not satisfied. Thus, in their enthusiasm to propose new industrial relations laws and policy, to achieve (relative) labor relations harmony, and to promote industrial competitiveness, scholars advocating various versions of the convergence models neglect the fundamental fact that it is the struggle between labor and capital that defines that the contours of a given "model."

This oversight has serious consequences. It leads analysts to focus solely on the ideal of cooperation, rather than examine the overall dynamics of a labor relations system. This is what leads advocates of convergence to make the common error of seeing German and Japanese systems of labor relations as being similar, when in fact in many respects they are polar opposites. While the German and Japanese labor relations systems are similar in that both are characterized by a higher level of shop floor union-management cooperation than the U.S. labor relations system, the bases for this cooperation are very different. In Germany, social unionism triumphed. In Japan, militant social unionism was *defeated* by a concerted employer offensive in the 1950s. Thus, in Germany there exist legislated union representation rights (codetermination), while in Japan unions have no role in strategic corporate decision making. German unions often pursue coordinated national strategies to force corporations to make concessions on such items as a shorter work week. In Japan, the nearly exclusive emphasis of coordinated union activity is on wage levels (the spring offensive). Thus, in the terms used above to describe types of unionism, Japanese unionism follows more of a "business unionist" approach, while German unionism follows a "social unionist" approach.[25] In short, it is not solely the fact that cooperation exists that matters. The balance of power among the different actors strongly influences what the parties cooperate about. Clearly, labor is a much more powerful actor in Germany than in Japan and this power enables German trade unions to ensure a greater responsiveness by the state to labor concerns in the shaping of the German economy. This has led to the alteration of some of the features of the country's macroeconomic structure, to the benefit of German workers.

Despite these flaws, convergence theorists do raise some important points. They accurately assert that economic changes may lead to changes in labor relations. They rightfully insist that labor unions need to examine these economic changes and adjust their tactics accordingly. And indeed they are right to argue that these changes are often international in character. But in their tendency to overgeneralize and, more importantly, in their tendency to shy away from analysis of labor-capital conflict and to abstract away from a serious analysis of the separate, and often conflicting, interests of the parties, there is an almost magical aura to the models that are proposed to bring labor relations harmony to the twenty-first century. For better or worse, there is no reason to suspect that the formation of a new model(s) of industrial relations will be less conflictual in the twenty-first century than it has been in our own.

THE "MEXICAN EXCEPTIONALISM" HYPOTHESIS: THE ROLE OF NATIONAL LABOR REGIMES

Not all analysts are persuaded by the argument that there will be a global convergence in labor relations regimes. To the contrary, some contend that unique features dependent on such factors as national labor law, national political structure, national level of economic development, and the distribution of jobs among different national industrial sectors will ensure continued divergence in terms of labor relations regimes. In many respects, this hypothesis is the opposite of the convergence thesis examined above. As the title of this section suggests, it has been popular among academics who study Mexico to view that country's system of labor relations as unique or exceptional. As explained above, there are many historical parallels in the history of labor relations in Mexico and Canada. But this is not to deny the existence of some substantial differences.

Analysts of Mexican labor exceptionalism, generally speaking, focus on two unique factors: the revolutionary legacy of the labor movement and the unique relationship between labor unions and Mexican party-state dominated by the PRI (Partido Revolucionario Institucional or Institutionalized Revolutionary Party) that was created out of political compromises reached in the 1930s and 1940s. As a result of these factors, it is asserted, Mexican unions enjoy unique benefits and suffer from unique restrictions not experienced by unions in other countries. In the Mexican Revolution, labor played a limited, but important role. At one crucial point in 1915, 7,000 to 10,000 followers of the moderate (or "collaborationist") labor leader Luis Morones enlisted on the side of "the Constitutionalist" forces and formed the "Red Batallions" that helped the forces of Venustiano Carranza and Alvaro Obregón defeat the peasant rebels, led by Emiliano Zapata and Pancho Villa (Hart 1989: 309). In the 1917 Constitution drafted by the Revolutionary victors, labor gained, on paper, constitutional protections in Article 123 which arguably formed "the most progressive piece of labor legislation in any country of the world of 1917" (Hellman 1988: 20). However, by the time of the Constitution's drafting, labor's fortunes had already passed their high-water mark; few labor representatives attended the Constitutional convention. As one historian put it, "Article 123 descended from on high, like a Mosaic tablet conferred by a stern deity on a chastened, disgruntled people: at best, it offered future salvation, conditional upon present good behaviour" (Knight 1990: 435). As Ramón Ruiz points out, though Article 123 contained many favorable provisions, including the right to join unions, the right to strike, the right to equal pay for equal work, the right to an eight-hour working day, limits on child labor, a guaranteed minimum wage, and mandated health and accident insurance, among other provisions, the same Article also ensured that "The state, the new leviathan, had the authority to supervise and control relations between the two parties [capital and labor] and to decide what was in the public interest" (Ruiz 1980: 356).

The role conferred upon the state has proven to be key. In particular, it has led Mexican labor leaders to place a great deal of emphasis on their relations with state labor officials and relatively less emphasis on relations with employers. The powers granted to Mexican state officials by Article 123 of the 1917 Constitution and later implementing legislation, such as the 1931 Federal Labor Law (*Ley Federal de Trabajo*), including the power to grant or deny union registration and the power to declare a strike legal or illegal (Bizberg 1986: 133) have resulted in a system of labor relations in which state bureaucrats play an often determining role in the resolution of labor disputes. Actions of individual businesses and unions are correspondingly less important than in Canada.

It is not particularly unusual for the state to play a major, even central, role in labor relations (Schmitter 1974). What is said to be unique about Mexico is not the central role of the state per se, but the *nature* of this role. As mentioned above, the 1930s and 1940s saw in Mexico, as in Canada, a major reconfiguration of the national labor relations system. But the Mexican labor relations system differed from the system that developed in Canada. First, Mexico as a country was significantly poorer; this meant (and, to a significant degree, continues to mean) that to have an industrial job in Mexico was to enjoy a relatively privileged position. Mexican unions thus are marked by more of a "craft consciousness" or "labor aristocracy" outlook than their Canadian counterparts. This labor aristocracy position certainly explains why Mexican corporatism, with its affinities to business unionism in terms of labor strategy, has been a viable option. At the same time, though, a craft consciousness quite often forms the basis of strong labor solidarity and even radicalism (E. Thompson 1966, Haydu 1988, Nash 1979). This, too, has sometimes been true in Mexico.

Not only the labor regulation system, but the entire Mexican political framework, had yet to be consolidated when the Great Depression of 1929-1939 hit. Indeed, it was only in 1929 that General Plutarco Elías Calles brought Mexican elite factions together to form a "national revolutionary party," (the Partido Nacional Revolucionario or PNR), a predecessor to the PRI-state formation that dominates Mexican politics to this day. The PNR was sharply divided between a faction led by Calles and another led by Lázaro Cárdenas.[26] As a result of this split—as well as the considerable discretionary powers granted to the Mexican state under Article 123—labor leaders were able to extract major concessions. However, as the PRI party-state apparatus solidified, these same constitutional powers were used to rein in the influence of labor, as Kevin Middlebrook's recent study indicates (Middlebrook 1995).

The political compromise that resulted from this struggle between labor and the state led to an unusual relationship, misleadingly named the labor-state "alliance" (Aziz Nassif 1989). On the one hand, measures were introduced to reinforce the conservative face of the Mexican industrial worker's relatively-privileged position. This included the provision of social security—initially set up in 1942 and greatly extended during the presidencies of Adolfo López Mateos (1958-1964) and Luis Echeverría Alvárez (1971-1976)—which includes generous pension, health care, and (later on) day care benefits;

the creation of a right to profit sharing in 1963; and the establishment of union-only stores and recreation facilities.

On the other hand, measures were also taken to restrain the more radical face of the Mexican industrial workforce. Often, the same presidents who initiated many of labor's benefits were among the most heavy-handed users of repression. Thus, López Mateos gave workers profit sharing, but his government was also responsible for arresting the leaders of the rail workers' union in 1959. His government also ousted the reformist leadership of the telephone workers' union in 1962 in a less violent, but nonetheless state-imposed, coup d'etat, after the government-supported slate lost in union elections. Likewise, the Echeverría government, though recognizing some "independent" unions, crushed the Democratic Tendency movement led by the longtime electricians' union leader, Rafael Galván. As a result of this two-pronged policy of repression of dissident currents and the use of a high level of non-cash benefits to encourage a conservative orientation among Mexican workers, Mexico has not seen the formation of major labor-backed parties of either a social democratic or communist persuasion—a marked contrast to the path taken by labor in most other Latin American countries.[27] The overall system was consolidated by guaranteeing labor union leaders a certain number of seats in Congress, thus formally incorporating labor as a junior partner in the PRI. In 1979, labor representation reached its highest level ever with 86 out of 300 congressional seats (i.e., 29%); labor representation in the Mexican Congress has, however, fallen significantly since then (Zapata 1989).[28]

The Mexican labor relations system is characterized, misleadingly, as corporatist (Aguilar García 1990, Suárez Azueta 1989, Corona Armiento 1992: 60). Of course, if all one means by corporatism is that state officials are able to frequently impose their will on labor leaders, then Mexico can be said to be corporatist. But while formal tripartite bargaining in Mexico is common, the Mexican system is more *dirigiste* [state-directed] than corporatist. While the state is centralized, business and labor are only partially centralized. In the labor sector in particular, there are a number of independent, quasi-independent, and semi-official federations that co-exist with the PRI-sanctioned labor sector peak organization, the CTM. The way in which Mexican state officials exercise their control over labor thus has less to do with the issuing of top-down commands via the CTM, than by using tactics of *divide and rule* to play one labor union (and one labor union leadership group) off against the others.[29] This distinction is important since it is labor's division—not state control over a single, unified, hierarchically-ordered, labor federation—which enables state officials to impose terms on labor leaders.[30]

The Mexican labor system does have some unique features. The combination of a powerful state apparatus and a divided labor movement has allowed state officials to restrain labor's reaction against policy initiatives that are unfavorable to unions, such as the imposition of rapidly declining real minimum wage levels in the mid-1980s (Bolívar and Sánchez 1987). Labor's early incorporation into the Mexican PRI-state has helped to prevent the emergence of labor-backed, oppositional social democratic or communist movements (Collier and Collier 1991, Collier 1992). And while his influence had waned by the early 1990s, it is nonetheless true that Fidel Velázquez— leader of Mexico's single largest union federation, the CTM, from 1941 to 1947 and again from 1947 to 1997—had cast an imposing shadow on the labor movement (Darling 1991). The notion that Mexican labor is unique and unchangeable is popular not just among academics, but among union activists as well. As one such activist explained, "The Mexican state is very wise . . . In Mexico, everyone has his quota [sphere of influence]. It is very unlikely that in Mexico they are going to permit independent unionism" (Interview S-94-6).

Nonetheless, there is reason to believe that there is less to the thesis of Mexican exceptionalism than meets the eye. Despite its unique characteristics, Mexican unions exhibit many traits that are quite similar to those found in their U.S. and Canadian counterparts. Like many U.S. unions, most Mexican unions have formed an implicit alliance with a business-dominated political party. Like the majority of U.S. unions and a minority of Canadian unions as well, most Mexican unions have followed a business unionist strategy in the post-World War II era, pursuing, in the words of one telephone workers' staff member, "pay for the family" (Interview S-94-14) and accepting the overall capitalist economic framework. Nor is Mexican unionism as monolithic as it is sometimes portrayed. The electricians' union of the central Mexico company Luz y Fuerzas (Light and Power), the Sindicato Mexicano de Electricistas (SME), has frequently had a leadership that has pursued a moderate social unionist policy based on a logic of gradual reformism, acting on the margins of the PRI's "left wing" (M. Thompson 1966: 229). As well, the 1970s saw the emergence of a small, but not insignificant, independent union sector

(Roxborough 1984), which has acted as militantly as the most militant Canadian unions.

Of course, the Mexican labor regime *does* structure the labor environment in which union leaders operate. But despite the predominance of many so-called corporatist (i.e, strongly state-aligned) unions, there are also independent (i.e., not state-aligned) unions, as well as a few "semi-independent" national industrial unions that seek to straddle the line between the two camps—the SME and the telephone workers' union among them. Of these independent and semi-independent unions, some choose to follow a "bread and butter" business unionist strategy while others are more oriented towards a social unionist strategy. Mexican labor officials frequently seek to use state power to push unions in a more conservative direction, thereby aiming to limit the sphere of union action, but these actions are only partially successful. Moreover, it must be noted that the Canadian state has also acted on occasion to arrest union leaders for leading "illegal strikes," as in the case of the 1978 arrest of postal worker leader Jean Claude Parrot (Laidlaw and Curtis 1986). During the 1940s and 1950s, the Canadian state frequently intervened against Communist-led unions (Palmer 1992: 290-298, 355-356). More recently, in the 1980s, state interventions in labor conflicts in Canada have increased markedly, through the frequent resort to "back-to-work" legislation in response to public sector strikes (Panitch and Swartz 1993). In short, the use of state repression to restrain labor is not a uniquely Mexican phenomenon.

Of course, the importance of national labor differences could be defended by instead focusing on unique features of the Canada's labor regime. Such an argument is full of holes as well, but it is not entirely without foundation. After closely paralleling U.S. unionism for nearly 100 years, Canadian labor diverged from the U.S. pattern in the 1960s, as French-Canadian union membership exploded as part of Quebec's "Quiet Revolution" (Lipsig-Mummé 1990) and public sector unionism grew rapidly throughout Canada (Thompson 1981). As a result of these changes, and of breakaways from U.S.-led international unions, the percentage of Canadian union members in Canadian unions rose from only 30% of the unionized workforce as late as 1966 to 61% twenty years later (Heron 1989: 147-173).[31] While U.S. unionization rates fell steadily, Canadian unionization rates increased, peaking at 40% in 1983 and holding at roughly 36% in 1995. As Alan Gladstone notes, Canada is unique among the major industrial nations in that there has been little movement toward either more enterprise-specific bargaining or greater labor-management cooperation. Instead, Gladstone asserts, Canada is an example "of systemic stability and lack of change in industrial relations" (Gladstone 1992: 8). As will be seen below, the Canadian divergence from the U.S. pattern and subsequent attempts to explain Canadian labor's relatively stronger position led to the creation of a whole new approach to the study of labor relations: the strategic choice approach. But, despite its unique growth spurt, the reality is that Canadian unionism has been subjected to similar calls to get with the labor-management cooperation program (Hecker and Hallock 1991, Peterson 1990). As well, there have been numerous attempts to introduce quality circles, work teams, and other "flexible" work practices, as the case of the telephone workers' union in British Columbia under study here illustrates well. In some cases, such as with the larger CEP (Communication, Energy and Paperworkers) union at Bell Canada, the union has been an active participant and advocate of greater shop floor cooperation with management (CWC 1992, TIE 1994). Thus, the notion of Canadian exceptionalism carries even less weight than that of Mexican exceptionalism.

This is not to deny that those who call attention to national distinctions, particularly the unique revolutionary heritage of the Mexican union movement and its subordination to the state, are calling attention to some important distinctive features. These differences can help explain overall historical trends affecting national labor movements. In particular, looking at national labor regimes is important since while capital is global, labor is still national, as the international coordination of labor is far less developed than that of capital. But analyzing national labor regimes, though useful in explaining overall trends in a given country, is less effective as a means of explaining the strategic orientation of individual unions, particularly in key sectors such as telecommunications where greater economic clout gives the union a greater ability to shape its own path. Of course, given a specific labor regime, one can expect it to influence, at least somewhat, the way in which a union with a given strategic orientation responds tactically. But as will be seen in Chapters 4 through 8, the problems faced by telecommunications unions in Mexico and Canada are remarkably similar. While national labor regimes do provide one reason why one should not expect to see convergence in labor relations result from globalization, there is a much more basic factor at work: not all unions are pursuing the same ends.

THE STRATEGIC CHOICE HYPOTHESIS

The strategic choice perspective developed out of two very simple observations: 1) the U.S. union movement, which once represented over 30% of all workers, had fallen to barely half that level, and 2) after nearly 100 years in which U.S. and Canadian unionization rates were nearly identical, between 1960 and 1984 a sharp divergence emerged. This second observation was particularly difficult to explain using conventional analysis. From a common level of roughly 30% in 1960, by 1984 U.S. unionization had fallen to 19% while Canadian unionization had risen to 40% (Perusek and Worcester 1995: 14, Thwaites 1989: 104-105, Hecker and Hallock 1991: 2-4).[32] There were differences in the national labor regime. Most importantly, passage of Taft-Hartley in 1947 in the United States consolidated the position of nonunion employers in the U.S. South by financially weakening unions that did exist (by allowing states to pass "right to work" laws forbidding mandatory dues check-off), requiring elections to be held after card counts, and by banning powerful union organizing tactics, such as the sit-down strike (Geoghegan 1990: 51-53). As well, certification of labor unions in Canada is easier, with some provinces permitting labor unions to be certified if 55% of eligible workers sign cards and a pay a small fee indicating their desire to be represented (Rogaw 1989).[33]

Other arguments have focused more on specific features of Canadian history or culture. For instance, it has been argued that an older tradition of state intervention in the Canadian labor market, dating back to the 1907 Industrial Disputes and Investigation Act, allowed the Wagner Act-like legislation passed in Canada to be more effective (Kettler et al. 1990: 177-179). Canada is also said to have a somewhat more "social democratic political culture, at least by North American standards" (Watkins 1991: 31). On the other hand, one author contends that Canadian labor's strength vis a vis U.S. labor stems not from Canadian state support, but rather the greater state resistance Canadian workers had to confront to secure rights similar to those obtained in 1935 by U.S. workers (Robinson 1993: 23-29).

In their 1986 book on the decline of U.S. unionism, *The Transformation of American Industrial Relations*, Thomas Kochan, Harry Katz and Robert McKersie (hereafter Kochan et al.) suggest that the differences in labor regime structure identified above are too small to explain such a wide divergence in outcomes. Rather, they assert,

"We wish to develop a more *strategic* perspective on U.S. industrial relations and thereby demonstrate that future patterns are not unalterably predetermined by economic, technological, or some other forces in the American environment" (Kochan et al. 1986: 4-5, italics in original).

In this approach, one looks at decisions made by "American managers, union leaders [and] public policy decision makers" (Kochan et al. 1986: 5) at the workplace, in collective bargaining, and outside the realm of collective bargaining. This last category is the level of strategic decision making. For employers, strategic decisions include such matters as investment, marketing, and overall human relations strategy; for unions, this would include a union's political strategy and organizing strategy; for government, this would include the setting of macroeconomic policies (Kochan et al. 1986: 17). Changes at the strategic level can alter the balance of power at the negotiating table and thus alter established collective bargaining patterns. Contrary to the systems theory approach of such writers as John Dunlop and Clark Kerr, which analyzed developments within the national labor regime, Kochan et al. claim that their framework is able to explain a change in the framework itself (Kochan et al. 1986: 7).

At the core of their argument is the contention that unions in the United States were outmaneuvered by a change in management strategy (Kochan et al. 1986: 13), in which management successfully opened up nonunion facilities, then shut down older, unionized plants (Kochan et al. 1986: 72-108). Meanwhile, labor was stuck in a business unionist mode that placed little emphasis on organizing and a higher emphasis on satisfying current membership demands. This approach may have proved satisfactory for many members up through the 1970s.[34] But it left them vulnerable to hostile managers when severe economic recession hit in the 1980s (Kochan et al.: 23-41, 113).[35] According to their prognosis, there were four feasible scenarios for U.S. unions— continued decline, labor law reform followed by more gradual decline,[36] diffusion of labor-management innovations, or new organizing, which the authors saw as the "least likely" scenario (Kochan et al. 1986: 251-253). Not mentioned, but implicit in the analysis—and further developed by Kochan in later writings—is that Canadian labor engaged in much more aggressive organizing; thus, according to this view, Canadian industrial relations need not follow the U.S. path (Hecker and Hallock 1991: 4-5; see also Kochan and Verma 1992).

There are some important strengths in the strategic choice approach, not the least of which is that it attempts to take into account the actions of the actual actors involved, rather than basing all explanation on the structural imperatives of national labor regimes or globalization. However, the approach does have a few key weaknesses. Chief among these are its failure to account adequately for the interrelationship of structure and agency; a tendency to lend itself, perhaps unconsciously, toward taking a managerial embrace of an competitive ethic; and an inadequate distinction between strategy and tactics, which is particularly important if one is to understand the difference in the nature of strategic decision-making within corporations and labor.

These shortcomings stand out in a more recent book adopting a strategic choice approach, in which Thomas Kochan teams with Paul Osterman to propose the establishment of what they call the *mutual gains enterprise.* According to Kochan and Osterman, U.S. industry in the 1980s improved its competitiveness, but did so in a bad (i.e., not self-sustaining) way—by reducing wages and devaluing its currency. Thus, between 1982 and 1990, real (inflation-adjusted) wages in the United States fell by 2.7%, while rising 3% in Canada, 18.4% in Japan and 26.9% in Germany (Kochan and Osterman 1994: 22-24). To alter this, Kochan and Osterman propose a series of measures that can be undertaken by management to promote workplace cooperation (Kochan and Osterman 1994: 46-53). As well, Kochan and Osterman recommend that changes be made to national labor laws to promote labor-management cooperation and rectify the current "low trust" industrial relations atmosphere (Kochan and Osterman 1994: 13, 203-209).

So-called "traditional" or "adversarial" unionism is, in their view, simply not an option. The structure of the new globalized economy has already, apparently, been set. Labor's task is simply to adapt itself to the new structural imperatives. As Kochan and Osterman put it, "The void in worker representation in American society is not likely to be filled in a way that contributes to the competitiveness of the economy by a resurgence of traditional-style unions" (Kochan and Osterman 1994: 166-167). Only via the joint action of managers, labor leaders, and government representatives can a "high-productivity/high-wage economy" be created (Kochan and Osterman 1994: 213). Either labor becomes a "positive and visible champion" of the mutual gains approach or "management and public policy makers will continue to view labor as a largely negative or, at best, irrelevant force at the workplace and in economic and social affairs" (Kochan and Osterman 220). Briefly stated, labor's strategic options are narrowed down to two: *cooperate—or else.*

Ironically, Kochan and Osterman don't explore the implications of such a choice. For if labor's strategic options are truly limited to cooperate or else, it's easy to understand why true labor-management cooperation becomes nearly impossible. Indeed, one might expect management to respond by seeking to press its strategic advantage, given the wide range of choices available to management, and take a hard line with union leaders to obtain the best possible deal.[37] Faced with this strategic disadvantage, one can expect many labor leaders to recoil from cooperation, since the "else" appears like the lesser of the two evils, as it at least allows the union leadership to maintain its sense of honor (Golden 1990). In fact, such a response by U.S. unions in the eighties and nineties has not been uncommon.[38]

The strategic choice approach thus addresses the key question of how labor is to respond to the development of a global economy. There's no doubt that labor's position in the United States, the focus of much of the strategic choice literature, is particularly weak. But the strategic choice literature rarely examines the range of options available to union leaders.[39] As a result, despite its stated intentions (Kochan et al. 1986:7), strategic choice theory does much better at explaining, in ad hoc fashion, the logic of past strategic decisions than it does at explaining how labor makes choices when the final result is not predetermined.

Underlying this shortcoming are two related problems. One is that the strategic choice approach tends to have a managerial focus. Though not anti-union per se—indeed, most strategic choice writers at least favor having unions in the workplace—the central problematic of the strategic choice approach is the managerial question of how best to organize work so as to increase the quantity and quality of goods and services produced. This should not be surprising, given that the notion of strategic choice traces its origins back to corporate strategy research (Kochan et al. 1986: 11). A strategic focus thus often tends toward emphasizing corporate priorities over those of labor.

Furthermore, strategic choice theory fails to recognize that "strategy" for labor means something very different than "strategy" for capital, since the nature of strategic choices for labor is different from that for management (Offe and Wiesenthal 1985). Management's ultimate strategic goal is clear: the maximization of profit. Corporate strategy amounts to the choosing of long-term tactics designed to maximize corporate profitability. This is not to deny the complexity of corporate decision making (Streeck 1992: 76-104), but compared to labor, which has no single strategic criterion, capital is at an advantage. While it is true that U.S. business unionism has attempted to counter the business notion of profitability with the union notion of "more," this strategy has had notable pitfalls. For as Kochan et al. (1986) note, this strategy left U.S. labor unprepared and largely undefended when the management assault of the 1980s arrived.

Thus, although strategic choice theory has opened up new lines of research—some of which are pursued, in fact, in this study—it nonetheless suffers from important flaws: it is subject to a managerial bias; it tends to take the economic structure as given, rather than explain the interaction among structure, workers, and unions; and it fails to recognize the distinctive nature of strategic decision making in unions from strategic decision making in the corporate environment. By correcting these errors and taking into account the lessons of the globalization and national labor regime approaches explored above, it is possible to set up the problematic of this paper: that is, the relationship between globalization and union strategic choice.

UNIONISM AND GLOBALIZATION: TOWARDS A THEORY OF *LABOR* STRATEGY

In Chapter 2, the distinct effects of globalization were detailed, particularly as it has manifested itself in the telecommunications industry. Though the concept of globalization is subject to much mystification and mythologizing (the end of history, postindustrialism, the information age, etc.), there are nonetheless very real and profound changes occurring in the global economy that require a union response.

In this chapter, four key theories of the labor movement were reviewed: those of Lenin (party-led revolutionary unionism), Luxembourg (independent revolutionary unionism) the Webbs (party-led social democratic reformism or social unionism), and Perlman (business unionism). Each of these theories embody distinctive *logics* of unionism as it has existed, though clearly many unions embrace a combination of elements from different approaches. In the past, these distinctive union logics have led unions to respond quite differently to similar economic phenomena.

I then examined three theories of unionism that focus not on the nature of unionism per se, but rather on how unions interact with their environment, concentrating on the current economic changes brought about by globalization. According to the proponents of the convergence or cooperation school, globalization is likely to lead to a convergence in labor regimes that enhance managerial flexibility and shop floor cooperation between unions and management. On the other hand, the approach taken by the national labor regime writers suggests that one should expect national differences in industrial relations to persist, despite the internationalizing tendencies of global economic oligopolistic competition. Finally, adherents of the strategic choice approach argue that results can vary according to the strategic choices made by union leaders, corporate managers, and government officials. Nonetheless, the managerial perspective underlying much of this literature leads to similar conclusions as the cooperation school, the only issue being whether the labor movement will wise up and cooperate or choose to commit suicide. As a result, this approach can easily degenerate into a discussion of how best to adjust to the imperatives of the global economy.

The distinctive logics of the four ideal types of unionism described above will lead different unions to respond differently to globalization. For instance, a business union in Mexico is likely to act in a more similar manner to a business union in Canada than to a social union in Mexico. This is not to suggest that national labor regimes are unimportant; they certainly influence the choice of tactics and they are, at least, one of the factors that help to determine a given union's overall strategic orientation. However, few, if any, countries have labor regimes that are so uniform that only a single type of unionism can be found within their boundaries. In both Canada and Mexico, there is considerable variation in unions' strategic orientations.

The reasons for this variation necessarily have to do with local factors, such as the particular union's institutional history, the balance of power among occupational groups, and the structure of internal union governance. In the chapters that follow, it will be seen that internal union politics, though typically focusing on more immediate concerns can—and, at times does—extend into a struggle over whether to shift from one strategic orientation or another, over whether to be a business union, a reformist social democratic union, or a more revolutionary socialist union. More frequently, though, a single viewpoint or strategic orientation does predominate. This is why unions are not quite as unstable of organizations as the analysis of Offe and Wiesenthal would suggest (Offe and Wiesenthal 1985). Nonetheless, a union's strategic orientation is not immutable. Debate regarding overall strategy may arise due to external factors, like a shift in economic structure, technological change, or the formation of a new state regime,[40] or internal factors, such as the emergence of a newly-mobilized occupational sector, as occurred among operators in the Mexican telephone workers' union in 1970s. In either case, the union's strategic orientation may well be subjected to internal questioning, debate and possibly major alteration, with all the instability that is inherent in that process.

The changes in economic structure brought about by globalization, deregulation, and privatization are certainly of sufficient significance to *potentially* lead telecommunications unions that long ago settled this question of strategic orientation to open that debate anew. Indeed, this debate has been engaged in both the Mexican and British Columbian telephone worker unions examined here. Though the actual clashes usually occur over tactical issues (e.g., whether or not to agree to cooperate with management to introduce a team work organization structure), the debates reveal very different conceptions of what a union is about and what a union's ultimate ends are.

While it may be difficult to predict how the debate will be resolved in any particular union—although, as shall be seen, there are some pretty clear tendencies emerging in both unions in this study—it is safe to predict that the debate will not be resolved the same way in every union. As a result, different unions will likely pursue different ends and will mount different responses to the question of globalization.

In concrete terms, one can expect a business union to move in the direction of cooperation with management, as suggested by cooperation school theorists and as advocated by some strategic choice theorists. In other words, the *mutual gains enterprise*, the *enterprise compact*, *associational unionism*, and the Mexican *new unionism* are different versions of *one* possible route for unions to follow, involving, essentially, an adaptation of the logic of business unionism to globalization. As such, it shares both many of the strengths, but also many of the weaknesses, of traditional business unionism.

To understand this, it is necessary to cut away one of the myths held by many analysts of business unionism: namely, that business unionism is a peculiarly *adversarial* form of unionism.[41] In fact, business unionism is a highly cooperative form of unionism, although it is, to be sure, fiercely adversarial in its fight over wages and benefits, and, to a lesser degree, over the governance of shop floor working conditions. Even though, as Perlman acknowledges, *all* forms of unionism, by definition, involve some challenge to the absolute rights of capital (Perlman 1928: 155-156), business unionism involves explicitly *limiting* the field of contestation to a narrow field of concerns, involving, in Perlman's words, an exchange of "class consciousness for a job consciousness" (Perlman 1928: 232). Thus, the prototypical business union, unlike the social union, limited its political involvement and focused its demands at the workplace to largely "bread and butter" (i.e., wage and benefits) concerns.

These tendencies are evident in a recent analysis of the U.S. auto industry. In his study of the UAW, James Zetka shows that during the 1950s, a period when a system of supposedly "adversarial" business unionism had been consolidated, the central UAW leadership *opposed* militant shop floor action, particularly in plants which were considered to be vulnerable to being closed down. As Zetka points out, "The UAW International was especially hostile to militant shop-floor demands from workers in the firms hardest hit by the intensifying competition. The International accepted management's utilitarian rationalization for their speedups" (Zetka 1995: 162).[42] As well, the bureaucratic grievance mechanisms that are sometimes said today to be a legacy of adversarial unionism were in fact set up to prevent "local conflicts from disrupting production schedules by legitimating peaceful step-by-step mechanisms for resolving disputes" (Zetka 1995: 37).

The logic of business unionism is thus a simple one: *the union would work to push up the wage and benefit levels of the membership, while allowing management near-unilateral control over the work process.* As Heckscher argues, the business unionist A. F. of L.'s "eventual triumph involved in large measure the recognition of the need to cooperate with management" (Heckscher 1988: 26). Through wildcat actions, shop floor workers, particularly those who worked in trades that involved "solidarity-generating work processes" (Zetka 1995: 58)—that is, work processes that require giving workers a degree of on-the-job group autonomy—were able to substantially restrict management's "unilateral" control. But these were, nonetheless, limited incursions on the rule of union cooperation with management on working conditions issues, including explicit trade-offs involving increased wages and pension benefits in exchange for union cooperation in the introduction of new technology (Moody 1988: 67).

In new work systems involving team production and other collaborative practices that have stemmed from the globalization of the telecommunications industry, more is asked of the workforce. Rather than simply obeying the supervisor, workers are supposed to work aggressively to problem-solve for the company. Some of this, of course, has always occurred. But the goal of new work reorganization schemes is to institutionalize and make better use of this worker adaptability.[43] According to Kochan and Osterman, "A high-conflict/low-trust relationship" is inimical to high productivity in such a schema (Kochan and Osterman 1994: 51). Under such circumstances, the new deal—for a union with a strategic orientation that seeks to "manage the conflict" between labor and capital (Moody 1988: 68)—is to move from giving management quasi-unilateral control over working conditions in exchange for higher wages to *agreeing to work bilaterally with management to increase productivity in exchange for higher wages*. As shall be seen in Chapter 6, this is precisely what has occurred with the telephone workers in Mexico.

This form of unionism goes by different names. In Japan, it is known as enterprise unionism. The Mexican variant, advocated by the telephone workers' union, among others, is known as new unionism or neo-corporatism. Note that neo-corporatist unions differ from corporatist unions in the same manner that "mutual gains" unionism differs from traditional business unionism. This is not to imply that business unionism and Mexican "corporatist" (state-aligned) unions are the same. As Enrique de la Garza points out, the "corporatist" union is "a type of union that has subordinated its functioning in collective bargaining to state political functions" (de la Garza 1993: 21), while business unions are relatively independent from the state. However, the *logics* of these two types of unions in terms of economic and workplace activity are rather similar. Both corporatist and business unions accept the constraints of the capitalist system and concentrate their energies on extracting wage and benefit gains, while relinquishing most control over working conditions to management. Oddly, despite their largely accommodationist efforts, both corporatist and business unions also get routinely chided for being too "adversarial" and are urged to adopt more "modern" union structures.

There is one further similarity in the logics of Mexican "corporatist" and U.S. "business" unions that merits emphasis: the activities of both reinforce the existence of a significant "wage gap" between unionized and nonunion sectors. In the United States, the wage gap between union and nonunion workers reached close to 30% in the late 1970s (Freeman and Medoff 1984: 53); in Mexico, accurate figures are hard to come by, but there is no doubt that union workers make far more than their counterparts in the informal sector, low as union wages may be. This wage gap tends to result in a gradual decline in the rate of unionization over time, both because such unions devote fewer resources to organizing new members and because business moves to nonunion worksites—to the border states or by contracting out to the "informal sector" in the case of Mexican capitalists; to the U.S. South and abroad in the case of U.S. capitalists. Over time, the reduction in union coverage affects overall union strength, which goes a long way towards explaining the relative lack of union resistance to wage decline in the United States and declining wages in Mexico, in comparison with the much more active resistance witnessed in countries with strong solidaristic labor movements, as in France,[44] Belgium, and, to a lesser degree, Canada.[45] In other words, business unionism and Mexican corporatist unions, in the wake of their own success, sow the seeds of their gradual dissolution.

UNION STRATEGIC ALTERNATIVES AND GLOBALIZATION

> The problem is that workers can neither fully submit to the logic of the market, nor can they escape from the market. Caught in this trap, workers and workers' organizations are involved constantly in the immensely complicated process of finding out what their interests are and how they can be pursued in a way that does not turn out to be self-contradictory and self-defeating (Offe and Wiesenthal 1985: 213-214).

Fortunately for the trade union movement, there actually are alternatives other than "cooperation or else" in the new global economy. But unfortunately, as Offe and Wiesenthal make clear, this doesn't mean they are easy to act upon or that success is automatic. In this section, I shall focus on two of these alternatives: non-party revolutionary or radical unionism and social unionism. I am excluding an analysis of party-led revolutionary unionism because, although important in the past (de la Garza 1993: 15-18), there appear to be few parties of appreciable size in the world currently advocating revolutionary activity.[46]

The non-party revolutionary approach in which union leaders seek to act as revolutionary agents rarely is present in its pure form, though historically strong syndicalist unions have existed in many countries, including Spain, Argentina, France, and Italy, as well as Mexico during the Revolutionary War period in which the Casa del Obrero Mundial (House of the World Worker) played an important role, despite its eventual defeat (Hart 1989: 276-326). More common is a variation on the syndicalist theme in which militant activists eschew reformist party politics and instead exhibit a more effusive general radical or revolutionary socialist political outlook, focusing primarily on aggressively pursuing shop-floor control issues. For instance, in Italy in 1968 workers established factory councils to gain more direct control over the production process. Typical demands included "direct control over working conditions, defense of health . . . and influence in the organization of work" (de la Garza 1993: 26). Such unions tend to support radical or revolutionary causes,[47] but often reject political parties for being hopelessly reformist. These unions can have great appeal, since they tackle important immediate workplace issues in a manner that is easily visible to the entire membership. But there is a tendency for such unions to be myopic. As de la Garza explains, one of the problems faced by the councils in Italy was that they "had to confront extrafactory institutions that took them away from their terrain and their purposes" (de la Garza 1993: 26). Capitalist restructuring and a capitalist offensive in 1982 led to their demise (de la Garza 1993: 27).

The allure of this form of unionism should not be underestimated. Indeed, workplace militancy in response to working conditions is common to most unions, even when union leaders would rather see such practices go away. Even in the most conservative corporatist or business union, there is some degree of shop floor militancy. *Indeed, when business leaders or academics complain about the "traditional adversarial" system of unionism, it is most like this type of shop floor militancy—which is most frequently opposed by business unionist leaders—to which they object.* Unlike business unionism, radical shop floor activism truly is strongly adversarial. Ironically, then, what is being objected to is not business unionism per se, but business unionism's inability to tend to its "business," i.e., maintain shop floor discipline.[48]

Sometimes, shop floor militancy does in fact become a union-wide priority as part of a wider social unionist vision (i.e., a revolutionary, or at least radical, vision that goes beyond the factory gates). This appears to be the case with the postal workers' union in Canada—whose bitter fights with Canada Post management over speed-ups led to repeated strike actions, resulting in over 1,500,000 worker-days on strike between 1975 and 1981. It is certainly the case with some independent unions in Mexico. Often, this combination of a limited degree of party or movement-linked activity, with a strong local workplace focus, is the result of either the lack of a strong social democratic party (as in the United States or Mexico) or a perception that the existing social democratic or "Eurocommunist" party is not articulating an adequate social vision (as in Canada or Italy). Among the Mexican telephone workers, as shall be seen, there are tendencies representative of both the pure syndicalist vision and the syndicalist-social unionist hybrid I describe here. Due to the weakness of Mexico's quasi-social democratic party, the PRD (Partido de la Revolución Democrática or Party of the Democratic Revolution), many opposition activists are reluctant to be connected with any party or specific social movement and advocate instead simple disengagement from the state and a focus on militant job control.

How would a strategy of nonparty radicalism or a syndicalist-social unionist hybrid (revolutionary unionism with limited party or movement links) interact with globalization? One hint is provided by the actions of opposition activists in the telephone workers' union in Mexico. *In essence, these activists have sought to wrest control of the telephone servicing process from management by using the forms of participation, designed primarily to speed up work, to instead assert worker control over the labor process.* As shall be seen in Chapter 6, while their efforts have been largely unsuccessful, the speed-up by management has not been terribly successful either. Nonetheless, in specific work areas where workers have always maintained considerable on-the-job autonomy, such as telephone line construction, it is conceivable that considerable gains could be made through this strategy. Though a new wave of syndicalism or workers' councils is not terribly likely, a new emphasis on shop floor issues may well occur. Ironically, the new team work and other so-called cooperative work practices might bring an upswing in militancy, rather than its opposite. As Joseph and Suzy Fucini argue in their book analyzing a Mazda factory in Michigan, "The history of JIT/team plants that are unionized indicates that workers at these facilities want an independent union to counter management's power" (Fucini and Fucini 1990: 226-227). This is not surprising. After all, the less the protection provided by the

Collective Bargaining Agreement, the more working conditions depend on the ability of shop floor workers to enforce a "moral economy" on their own.

SOCIAL UNIONISM AND GLOBALIZATION

Another alternative to the "cooperation or else" logic so common to today's industrial relations literature is the social unionist approach. As covered earlier in this chapter, a social union focuses on obtaining wide-ranging social reforms, but does so within the logic of the capitalist system. Kim Moody describes its basic premise: "While no degree of working-class organization can change the fundamental social structure of capitalism or erase the laws of political economy, mass, combative organization can affect social policy" (Moody 1988: 335). At the level of the state, a social union seeks to work with a social democratic party to establish a broad array of legislative minimums and social reforms, as described by the Webbs. At the level of the firm, social unionism embraces a broader array of issues than does business unionism. Especially important here is worker control over technological change. In terms of tactics, social unionism values the building of community coalitions. That is, in social unionism, "Unions form only one part of the labor movement, which typically includes political parties, cooperatives, cultural, social and athletic organizations" (Moody 1988: 341).

The historical achievements of social democracy and social unionism are significant (Esping-Andersen 1985). As Wever explains in the case of Germany, the action of trade unions and social democratic party action has helped to create a "social market" economy, which includes social expenditures on a per capita basis that are two to three times as high as those in the United States. As well, Germany enjoys the shortest work week of any major industrial country (Wever 1995: 32-49). Another important contribution of social unionism, in Sweden and Germany, has been the advent of codetermination (Swenson 1989).

It is important to examine codetermination briefly, since it is not uncommon for "pale imitations" (Moody 1988: 191) of codetermination to be suggested as the cooperative remedy to all that ails labor relations in the Americas. Social unionism is, in fact, not adverse to the cooperation promoted by cooperation school theorists. The basis of the cooperation, however, is quite different from the form of cooperation that is most frequently prescribed by the cooperation school.

As Lowell Turner analysis makes clear, there is a profound difference between the German and the Japanese models of industrial organization. Not all cooperation is alike. As Turner notes:

> . . . it also makes a big difference whether labor's integration into managerial decision making is backed up by law or corporatist bargaining arrangements, which include a cohesive labor movement. When this is true (as in West Germany), labor participates in firms' decision making from a base that is independent of management; unions are in a position to assess the needs of the work force and market requirements independently and to bring a new perspective to the discussion and perhaps even an independent, worker-oriented vision . . . By contrast, where no such statutory or bargaining arrangements exist and the labor movement is fragmented (as in Japan) . . . labor is integrated into managerial decision making in a decidedly subordinate way. (Turner 1991: 12-13)

Turner chooses the German telecommunications workers' union as one of the secondary cases in his study. Turner finds that the union bargains successfully on a wide range of issues including "full employment security, a measured introduction of new technology, new opportunities and training for the displaced, better working conditions, environment, and ergonomics with new technology, improved job design, widespread opportunities for training." As well, the German telecommunications workers' union is "actively engaged in decision making regarding the process and shape of change from the bottom to the top levels of the organization" (Turner 1991: 188). Though the German telecommunications workers' union must take the market into account, the pursuit of competitiveness falls nowhere on its list of priorities. Rather, it strives to ensure that the capitalists and state officials in Germany's social market economy continue to include social criteria—and not just market competitiveness—among *their* priorities.

The number of strikes in Germany and other countries with strong social democratic union movements tends to be low due to the more stable balance of power. But this does not mean that strikes do not happen or that the labor relations system is not adversarial. Kathleen Thelen's review of the 1984 dispute between the IG Metall metalworkers' union, the largest union in Germany, and the Gesamtmetall employers' federation makes this clear. (See also Swenson 1989: 216-222).[49] Against considerable employer and government opposition, the union sought a reduction in the work week for its members from 40 to 35 hours as a way of fighting unemployment and forestalling possible lay-offs.

At the time, German labor leaders worried about waning union influence, as they were faced with both an economic recession and the recent election of a conservative government. As one German union leader explained, "We openly admit that . . . we are . . . defending our strength to defend workers' interests . . . [this] strength cannot be sealed up in a bottle and saved for better times." After a six week confrontation in which 60,000 were on strike, 150,000 were locked out, and 310,000 more were laid idle due to parts and supply shortages, a settlement was reached. The terms of the settlement included a reduction in the work week from 40 to 38.5 hours. By continuing to push on this issue through two more rounds of bargaining in 1987 and 1990—this time without strikes or lock-outs—IG Metall reached an agreement which achieved its initial goal of a 35-hour week (Thelen 1991: 161-175, quote on 162).[50]

Despite its impressive achievements, there is no doubt that social unionism requires a difficult balancing act on the part of both union leaders and the rank and file, even in the best of times. As Offe and Wiesenthal point out, unions operate on the basis of two very different logics of power: one logic is material or resource based; the other logic is motivational or solidarity based. In terms of material resources, unions are always at a disadvantage; in terms of motivational resources, unions are at an advantage, but it is much more difficult to motivate people to act with collective solidarity than to spend money! (Offe and Wiesenthal 1985: 187). Indeed, in the process of determining union priorities, it is sometimes the case that the membership will be divided on an issue pursued by a progressive union leadership. For instance, in the British Columbian telephone workers' union, both the issues of comparable worth (pay equity) and same sex spousal benefits have sharply divided the union. In 1990, a contract offer was turned down by a narrow majority (51%) of the membership, in part because of opposition among male telephone workers to the comparable worth part of the agreement. In 1994, there was nearly a repetition of the 1990 contract rejection as a provision granting spousal benefits to same sex partners generated considerable rank and file opposition. In the event, the contract was approved by a 51% majority (TWU 1990a, 1994b).[51]

There are often reasons for union leaders to strike compromises that may not be popular with the rank and file. After all, one of the strongest chits that a union has in its negotiation arsenal is its ability to provide labor peace in exchange for management concessions at the bargaining table: in other words, its promise *not to strike* in exchange for concessions. Once the immediate objectives have been achieved in a new agreement, absent a strong sense of class consciousness, the tendency to demobilize is always present. Mobilization is messy; it involves conflicts over divergent interests, can cause organizational instability, and requires passing up the short-term gains that can be had in exchange for demobilizing. Gaining bureaucratic benefits such as greater resources in exchange for demobilizing and deradicalizing is thus, in Offe and Wiesenthal's view, not simply the result of union leaders "selling out," but frequently a result of the difficulties inherent in maintaining an organization that must challenge some of the values of capitalism within a capitalistic economy. At the same time, however, seemingly good reasons for compromise can weaken the solidaristic support for the union, on which its power ultimately depends (Offe and Wiesenthal 1985: 215-219).

Though Offe and Wiesenthal's analysis can be applied to business unionism (Zetka 1995: 39-40), the primary target of their criticism was none other than German social unionism whose achievements were outlined above. Canadian social unionism is subjected to similar criticism. Thus, Brian Palmer criticizes former CAW (Canadian Auto Worker) President—and current Canadian Labour Congress leader— Bob White as simply playing the role of "good cop" (Palmer 1992: 370-377). Palmer argues that "The job of union bureaucracies is . . . making sure that workplaces of the land do not rampage out of control" (Palmer 1992: 377). In an important sense, Palmer's criticism is apt. Social unionism, after all, *is* reformist and reformism implies a need to institutionalize and, at least to some extent, bureaucratize. Social unionism, as well as business unionism, is forced to strike compromises. The key difference with social unionism is that there is a community-outreach and mobilization arm that counters the bureaucratizing tendencies; put bluntly, business unionism (or Mexican corporatist unionism) allows bureaucracy to proceed unchecked, while social unionism provides important restraint upon the organizational bureaucracy.

In the context of globalization, social unionism, like business unionism, must make some adjustments. It is clear that, despite the fact that there are many social democratic government in the world,[52] in many respects social democracy is on the defensive. It is not difficult to understand why: while social democracy places heavy reliance on using the state to regulate capitalism, there is no state mechanism capable of regulating international capitalism. With globalization, then, the ability to impose reforms through state activity is reduced. While reduced, this ability has not been eliminated. As will be shown in Chapter 7, in 1995 the British Columbian telephone workers' union was successful in negotiating with the state and company management an accord to assure universal access to the "information highway," thus promoting the traditional goal of universal service provision in the era of electronic services and ensuring the preservation of jobs for the union rank and file. As well, social unionism doesn't solely depend on state action for its strength, but rather also on community and worker mobilization. While it is true that globalization poses a challenge for social unionism, it would be an exaggeration to say that globalization makes a social unionist response impossible.[53] Because social unionism refuses simply to adapt to market imperatives, the interaction of social unionism with globalization is highly unlikely to generate the results proposed by the cooperation theorists. Instead, *what one can expect is for social unionism to shift its tactical emphasis from state-level action to more community-level and workplace-level action in pursuit of its egalitarian social goals.* In other words, social unionism will continue to seek to avoid being confined to the realm of collective bargaining. In a sense then, just as some syndicalist approaches adopt elements of social unionism, social unionism can be expected to adopt a few of the elements of syndicalism. One can also expect social unionism to pursue goals that involve reaching out to the entire community—such as the fight for a shorter work week—and to place less emphasis on the wage "gains" from a "mutual gains" framework. However, because social unionism doesn't challenge the overall capitalist framework, but rather seeks to insert social values within that framework, one must expect that there will nonetheless be some accommodation to the forces of globalization on the part of social unionists. As will be seen, finding the appropriate balance between accommodation and confrontation is very much an issue with which workers in the British Columbian telephone workers' union must grapple.

CONCLUSION

Both this chapter and the previous one have sought to set up the foundation for analyzing the main question of this study: the response of unions to globalization. While the last chapter concentrated on the globalization end of the equation, this chapter has examined the unionism end. In particular, I have sought to show there are different forms of unionism that exist internationally and behave differently. While not denying the existence of distinct tendencies within individual nations and the impact of globalization, such a focus necessarily insists on the importance of understanding the existence and persistence of the question of labor identity or strategic orientation in framing the decisions that individual labor unions make. In the empirical part of this study—by analyzing the Mexican and British Columbian telecommunications unions' institutional histories and their responses to technological change, workplace reorganization, and state action—I shall seek to demonstrate how different strategic orientations lead to the adoption of different tactics, as well as analyze how the different notions of unionism are implemented, the obstacles the two unions face, and the response of internal opposition movements to union leadership strategy and tactics.

NOTES

1. A reminder that unions were once seen as revolutionary organizations is provided by Charles Lindblom's 1949 analysis of U.S. unionism (Lindblom 1949). Lindblom contends that unions are *necessarily* revolutionary, even when they consciously follow an entirely reformist path, since unions act according to a monopoly logic that is contrary to the competition mechanism of the capitalist economy.

   This study takes a different tack. Unions can be revolutionary, but most often are not. Though reformist unions' actions theoretically can have revolutionary effects, the history of the postwar period clearly indicates that such instances are exceptional.

2. The Central Obrera Boliviana (COB) in Bolivia in 1982 illustrates one such example of a union that made use of frequent general strikes in order to further its pursuit of revolutionary goals (de la Garza 1994a, Conaghan and Malloy 1994: 122-124).

3. Note that, regardless of one's view of how unions should approach the state and economy, Lenin's distinction here is a valid one. One cannot sensibly treat every struggle of a single union or unions in a single industry as the

struggle of "the working class." Of course, a strike in a key industry may have important effects, for good or for ill, on the entire working class (e.g., the PATCO strike in the United States in 1981, the Cananea miners' strike in Mexico in 1989, the 1978 postal workers strike in Canada). But a specific workers' struggle is only a struggle of "the working class" to the extent that there actually is solidarity action by a multitude of working class organizations or that the result has a demonstrable "ripple" effect on other working class organizations.

4. Gramsci and Lenin differ on many points, but they agree on the need for unions to be linked to a political party in order to effect a revolutionary shift in the social relations of production. Gramsci's emphasis on the potentially revolutionary role of works councils (see Schecter 1991) has been used as inspiration for a very different type of unionism, based more on syndicalist ideals, as shall be set forth in the discussion of Luxembourg and revolutionary non-party trade unionism below.

5. In Canada, Communist-led unions were either suppressed, as was the case with the Seamen's union in eastern Canada or eventually folded into the social democratic New Democratic Party by the early 1960s. (see Palmer 1992: 290-297). In Mexico, Communist-led unions were less important, but some individual Communists did play a large role. Not the least of these was Vicente Lombardo Toledano, the first leader of Mexico's largest union central, the Confederación de Trabajadores de México (CTM).

6. This was most clearly the case during the Popular Front Period of the Spanish Civil War and then during World War II from 1941 to 1945, though many other cases have been demonstrated. See Kelley (1990) for a fine historical study of the strengths and weaknesses of Communist Party organization in organizing the civil rights movement in Alabama during the 1930s.

7. Luxembourg is important in examining syndicalism for another reason as well. Absent the rhetorical flourish of Bakunin and some other anarchists, Luxembourg presents a stronger case for those who argue that an aggressively mobilizational trade union strategy can be effective, and not merely a romantic revolutionary ideal.

8. Indeed, the December 1995 French public sector strike is an example of a recent mass strike. Originally, the French rail workers walked out over a threatened changes in pension benefits and their retirement age, but the strike was soon joined by many other groups, leading the government to withdraw its proposals to quell the dissent (Seager and Phelan 1996, Seager 1996).

9. In British Columbia, for instance, the telephone workers' union staged an occupation of telephone switching facilities and called on the government to

nationalize the company. This action is covered in more detail in Chapters 5 and 7.

10. This fear of repression, of course, is well justified. Repression against union radicals was common throughout Canada, the United States (many more unionists were affected by the McCarthy-period purges than Hollywood writers), and Mexico in the immediate post-WW II period. As well, the United States experienced a period of severe labor repression after World War I with the Palmer raids and the accompanying "Red Scare."

11. The new unionism in Great Britain is distinguished from its predecessor in that British unions between the passage of the 1832 Reform Act and the 1885 Reform Act largely followed a craft or business unionist policy, not unlike that followed to this day by many unions in the United States in particular, and also, to a lesser extent, by many unions elsewhere, including in Mexico and Canada. The onset of economic stagnation in the 1880s, due to the rise of Germany and other competitors, led unions in Britain to turn toward social unionism, which has remained the dominant form of unionism in Britain ever since (Perlman 1928: 124-153). See also Frederick Engels' introduction to the 1892 English edition of *The Condition of the Working Class in England* (Engels 1958: 360-371).

12. Unemployment insurance has indeed since been taken over by the state in nearly every country. Interestingly, however, unemployment insurance is still distributed by unions in Belgium and in some Scandinavian countries. Not surprisingly, these countries place high among those which have the world's strongest union movements. See, for instance, Ebbinghaus and Visser 1996.

13. The Webbs are wrong on this point. While traditional guilds of the type common earlier in the nineteenth century were indeed breaking down, there are many ways in which unions continue to use restrictions on entry to maintain their members' standard of living. Indeed, restricting entry is often a key component of business unionist strategy, as opposed to the social unionist emphasis on extending common rules to all industry.

14. Note that in this aspect, the argument advanced by the Webbs has been more recently reiterated by Freeman and Medoff 1984.

15. For further description of the links between the birth of English unions and efforts to defend the moral economy of the artisan class, see E. Thompson 1966.

16. With the election of the New Voice ticket led by John Sweeney, Richard Trumpka, and Linda Chavez-Thompson in the U.S. AFL-CIO in October 1995, there is some reason to believe that social unionism may be regaining influence in the United States.

17. Nonetheless, Canadian workers have been hurt by the Canada-U.S. free trade agreement of 1988. From January 1989, when the agreement was implemented, to June 1992, manufacturing employment fell from 2,048,990 to 1,632,251, a 20.3% decline in just three-and-a-half years (Grinspun 1993: 108).

18. The reason this leads to a narrowing of scope should be clear: a social movement seeks to become the majority by creating a broad agenda that represents the desires of many groups; an interest group, on the other hand, seeks to ensure that it is "cut in" on the deal, even if it must give up many of its demands. In the constructing of a coalition of social movements, trade-offs must be made too, but the nature of the trade-off is different. While the interest group seeks to cut a deal between it and a ruler seeking to maintain social control (in an authoritarian political system) or a politician seeking to gain the votes of the "median voter" (Downs 1957), in coalition building, *social movements try to alter the agenda itself*, and hence the scope of the political sphere. In democratic regimes, this involves an explicit attempt to change the location at which the "median voter" chooses to sit. Obviously, the interest group can affect the agenda, but does so in a passive manner (i.e., the unintended consequence of the interactions of many interest groups and politicians), rather than in an active and direct manner (i.e., the conscious shaping of a new political agenda). On the logic of social movements, see Midwest Academy 1984.

19. As is evidenced by the above quote regarding the garment workers, historically, in the United States and Canada, social unionism has been responsible for organizing new branches of the economy. Thus, business unions were originally concentrated in skilled trades, while social unions were concentrated among unskilled workers in mass production industries. In part, this is a product of social unions' greater willingness to devote resources to organize; in part, this is a product of the greater ability of skilled trades workers to obtain benefits through collective bargaining without state aid. There is still some legacy of this history. However, social unionist and business unionist tendencies have frequently coexisted in the same union, as demonstrated, for instance in Seymour Lipset's classic study of the typographers' union (Lipset et al. 1956). Moreover, once organized, low-wage workers are often more interested in business-unionism's "bread and butter" focus than higher wage workers. In both unions in this study, the better paid workers are the ones who have shown greater support for the social unionist approach.

20. In both the late nineteenth and late twentieth century, the position of a previously dominant capitalist nation (Britain in the nineteenth century, the United States in the twentieth) is challenged by the emergence of new economic powers (Germany and the United States in the late nineteenth

century, the European Union and Japan in the late twentieth century), in the context of a steady rise in the level of overall international trade.

21. For the purpose of this section, Mexico is included in "North America." Of course, Mexico is geographically located in North America, but culturally in many respects is more similar to the rest of Latin America than to either the United States or Canada. Nonetheless, as discussed below in the section of this chapter on the thesis of Mexican labor exceptionalism, the Mexican system of labor relations shares many elements with the U.S./Canadian system and indeed periods of militancy and retrenchment in the three countries often occur at similar time periods.

22. Of course, this is a problem since the European/Japanese system doesn't really exist, given that the Japanese system of labor relations is quite distinct from those in, say, Germany or Scandinavia. Nonetheless, the tendency is to see differences between Europe and Japan as relatively minor. Thus, for instance, Wever argues that there is a "shared logic underlying the organization of the German and Japanese political economies" and that "compared to the United States, both Germany and Japan feature more cooperative labor relations than adversarial ones; both share a traditional focus on product quality and the work process rather than output; and both give training pride of place" (Wever 1995: 11).

23. Developments in Canadian unionism *very* closely parallel those in U.S. unionism until the 1960s. This should not be surprising, given that roughly 70% of all unionists in Canada prior to the 1960s expansion of Canadian national unions were members of American-led "international" unions. The Canadian equivalent of the A.F. of L. was the TLC (Trades and Labour Council). The Canadian equivalent of the CIO was the CCL (Canadian Confederation of Labour). When the A.F. of L. and CIO merged in the 1955 to form the AFL-CIO, the TLC and CCL merged to formed the CLC (Canadian Labour Congress). The reasons for Canadian divergence from the American pattern in the 1960s are explained below.

24. Indeed, according to Mexican labor historians, much as in the United States, during a brief period in the late 1930s and early 1940s, the more social unionist tendency was dominant (Aziz Nassif 1989, Bizberg 1990). One author goes further, arguing that it was only after Lombardo Toledano was forced out of the CTM in 1947 that "the broad social reform issues gave way to the immediate concerns for economic gains" (Kofas 1992: 59).

25. Unionism in Japan is frequently referred to as "enterprise unionism" (Watanabe and Price 1994: 234), which is indeed distinct from U.S. business unionism in that the latter is usually taken to include a greater degree of implicit industry-wide (pattern) bargaining in key manufacturing industries (e.g.

automobile production), as well as a greater degree of struggle over rules defining different tasks at the shop floor level. However, both American business unionism and Japanese enterprise unionism share a general acceptance of the capitalist economic framework and eschew active collaboration with social democratic parties.

26. Cárdenas' eventual victory was symbolically acknowledged in 1938, when the party changed its name to the PRM (Partido de la Revolución Mexicana). In 1946, the party acquired its current name as the PRI (Partido Revolucionario Institucional). This name change again reflected a change of internal power relations within the party—in this case the reduction of Cárdenas' influence (Ruiz 1992: 406, 423).

27. The PRD, formed by Cuahtémoc Cárdenas in 1988, could be considered a social democratic party. But it notably lacks major labor backing.

28. The role of the legislature in Mexican politics, however, is limited, as most policy-making occurs outside of the Mexican Congress, either through executive department negotiations or internal party (PRI) negotiations. As a result, labor's representation in the legislature has been of minimal policy-making significance. Since 1988, the role of the legislature in Mexican politics has increased; however, executive dominance remains the rule.

29. To some degree, albeit often with limited success, labor union leaders in Mexico attempt to do the reverse: that is, they seek to exploit divisions within the PRI and among different state ministries and state officials. See Cook (1990) for one such example. According to Cook, dissident union activists within the national teachers' union (Sindicato Nacional de Trabajadores Educativos or SNTE) were most successful when Education Ministry officials and SNTE officials were divided and least successful when the two groups closed ranks.

30. To see what can happen when the labor sector in fact is organizationally unified, see Waisman (1987) on the Argentine labor movement. The reason why Mexico hasn't suffered a similar "paradox of corporatism" (in which corporatist labor relations turn on the state and labor takes advantage of its unified structure to engage in general strikes and the like) is because Mexican state officials have succeeded in keeping labor fragmented, turning their support *away* from official state-sponsored official labor unions when these threaten to become too strong.

31. For a discussion of the rise of English-Canadian nationalism and the separation of Canadian sections from U.S.-headquartered international unions, see Jenson and Mahon 1993.

32. Since the early 1980s, both countries have seen union rates decline, but the decline in the U.S. has been more rapid. By 1993, the U.S. unionization rate

had fallen to 16%, representing another 15% decline. In Canada, the current unionization rate is roughly 37%. Since the election of Bill Clinton as President in the United States, the decline in U.S. unionization has been halted and for the first time since 1979 the absolute number of American workers in unions is rising; however, the percentage of total workers unionized has not risen. See Church 1994.

33. In British Columbia, union certification takes place according to the card count method described above. However, because telecommunications falls under federal jurisdiction, the TWU is governed by the less accommodating Canada Labour Code, which, like U.S. labor law, requires elections to be held after cards are turned in.

34. As noted in a study of British unionism, unions succeeded in the United States in raising the wage gap between earnings of their members and nonunion workers from 10-15% in the 1950s and 1960s to 20-30% by the late 1970s, while the wage gap in Great Britain between union and nonunion workers is 7-11% (Beaumont 1992).

35. Freeman and Medoff view direct management opposition to labor organizing as being more significant than the decline in labor organizing per se. They do confirm Kochan et al.'s argument in part, however. The authors cite a 1982 study by Paula Voos showing that real union organizing expenditures fell by 30% between 1953 and 1974. Accordingly, Freeman and Medoff contend that "perhaps as much as a third of the decline in union [organizing] success through NLRB elections is linked to reduced organizing activity" (Freeman and Medoff 1984: 229). Moreover, the two explanations (management hostility and union failure to organize) are complimentary; unions' lack of organizing allowed the gap in compensation between union and non-union workers to rise. As Kochan et al (1986: 70) note, this increased differential helps to explain increased U.S. employer resistance to unionism.

36. Some writers have a more optimistic view of the potential for labor law reform to lead to a change in the fortunes of U.S. labor. For instance, Freeman and Medoff contend that "Under a different legal environment, U.S. employers would behave differently and unions might fare better in organizing the workforce" (Freeman and Medoff 1984: 243). Thomas Geoghegan states the case for labor law reform even more strongly. In Geoghegan's view, "if the labor laws changed . . . Americans would join unions like crazy, simply out of self-interest, raw, Reaganite self-interest" (Geoghegan 1992: 267).

37. Kochan and Osterman, argue, however, that such an approach is not in management's best interests, since over time this will lead to declining national competitiveness (Kochan and Osterman 1994: 19-43).

38. The Eastern Airlines strike against Frank Lorenzo in the late 1980s is one obvious example of this sort of union behavior.

39. Lipsig-Mummé (1990) provides a rare example of a strategic choice approach being used to evaluate how unions choose from among different strategic approaches. In a 1990 working paper, Lipsig-Mummé analyzes the Quebec labor movement and identifies four strategic options (pursuit of corporatism, building of new community alliances, defensive accommodation, and depoliticization/fragmentation) and explains why what she considers to be the least desirable option (depoliticization) has taken hold. Golden (1990) addresses a narrower question, using a microfoundational (rational choice) approach to argue that unions are most likely to resist concessions if management threatens to lay-off personnel in a way that fails to protect union shop steward organization.

40. As analyzed by O'Donnell, Schmitter and Whitehead (1986), a change of regime refers to a change in the *form* of government—e.g., military dictatorship to democracy—and not simply a change in government (such as from Tory to Labour).

41. It is true that U.S. business unions demonstrated, prior to the 1980s, a moderately high level of strike activity, though generally not as high as Canadian social unions. In the 1960s, strikes in the United States were actually slightly more common (.591 days lost per year per worker v. .547); however, in the 1970s, Canadian strike rates were three times higher (.912 v. .274) than in the United States (See Ponale and Falkenberg 1989: 264).

   As discussed earlier in this Chapter, shop floor cooperation seems to require the establishment of a balance of power between the parties, not a particular type of unionism. Thus, in Japan, stable plant-level cooperation was established by the imposition of enterprise-specific bargaining, while in Germany such cooperation was the product of a strong social democratic (social unionist) trade movement's ability to gain legislated protections.

42. As can be seen, the idea of "concession bargaining" is not new.

43. This is the explicit goal, at any rate. There may be other, less friendly (hidden) goals, such as speeding up the work of those who continue to work along the lines of the old system as a prelude to downsizing (i.e., see how many people you can waste away on work team experiments while keeping operations going at full capacity, then lay off the "surplus" workers) or breaking up informal work groups as a way of reducing worker on-the-job autonomy. These themes are covered in more detail in Chapter 6.

44. France has one of the lowest unionization rates among advanced industrial countries, but the low number is misleading. Workers who are not union members frequently participate in union-led strike actions, unlike in

North America. The December 1995 public sector general strike is a recent example of a long tradition of French labor militancy.

45. In December 1995 there was a one day general strike in London, Ontario, to protest social service and program cuts. Previous acts of national resistance in Canada include a one-day walk-out in June 1983 (Palmer 1992). As will be seen in Chapter 5, in 1981 there was a general strike in Nanaimo, British Columbia, in support of the British Columbian telephone workers' strike. By contrast, there have been *no* general strikes in the United States since the passage of Taft-Hartley in 1947. In Mexico, there were two *paros cívicos* (civic walk-outs) in 1983 and 1984, which were *not* supported by state-aligned corporatist unions. Otherwise, Mexico, too, has been entirely without general strike movements, in marked contrast with much of Latin America.

46. Although this might change, at present, even parties to the left of Social Democrats (e.g., Cause Radical [Radical Cause] in Venezuela, Frente Amplio [Broad Front] in Uruguay, Refundacion Comunista [Refounded Communism] in Italy, etc.) seem to be issuing a call for social democracy to return to its more radical roots, not a takeover of the means of production. See Castañeda 1993.

47. Not surprisingly, such activity can be risky. An example of this is the Ruta Cien (Route 100) bus drivers' union in Mexico City. When government officials discovered that the union was donating money to the Zapatista guerrillas, they declared the business to be bankrupt, effectively firing all of the bus drivers.

48. Indeed, Zetka argues that it is often it is the union's failure to address working conditions that leads to wildcat action. When the UAW leadership started to address workplace grievances in collective bargaining negotiations during the 1960s, wildcat action declined (Zetka 1995: 226).

49. According to Swenson, IG Metall's attempt to reduce unemployment through a reduction in working hours also involved an explicit rejection of using export-led growth as an alternative means of generating employment (Swenson 1989: 229). In other words, IG Metall rejected the pursuit of "competitiveness" as a tactic for achieving greater employment.

50. Note that in the 1990s the Canadian Auto Workers (CAW) has followed in the footsteps of its social unionist IG Metall counterpart. In its 1993 master agreement with the Big Three, the CAW obtained added paid days off and other provisions estimated to create over 4,000 new jobs. See CAW 1993, Cross 1993 and Walcom 1993. The British Columbian telephone workers' union studied here has made negotiating a reduction in work time a priority in negotiations for a 1996-1997 contract (TWU 1995a).

51. Of course, there are plenty of other reasons why union members vote against contracts, such as insufficient wage increases, inadequate contract

provisions, a climate of generally poor labor relations at the shop floor, and so forth. However, there is little doubt that at least a sizeable minority of those voting against the contracts in 1990 and 1994 did so for the reasons indicated, illustrating the difficulty noted by Offe and Wiesenthal that for a union to articulate a collective vision for individual members with sometimes widely diverging views is not an easy task.

52. As of December 1998, social democratic governments exist in the provinces of Saskatchewan, British Columbia, and Quebec in Canada and in most European Union countries, including France, Germany, Italy, and Great Britain.

53. For an alternative view, see Mészáros 1995. According to this Hungarian Marxist theorist, "The historical moment of reformist social democracy was terminated with the end of capital's global expansionary phase, as the system's structural crisis erupted in the early 1970s" (Mészáros 1995: 665).

CHAPTER FOUR

History and Choice in Telecommunications Unionism

In the previous two chapters, I sought to provide a framework for examining what globalization means for telecommunications unions and why some unions respond to globalization quite differently than others. In this chapter, key features of the two empirical cases are outlined to provide a road map for the more detailed empirical chapters that follow. This requires first describing the general structure and key historical data of the two unions. Though more recent history (1970s-present) will be examined in greater detail in later chapters, here I simply set out the key features that distinguish the two unions. Next, the legal framework within which each union operates is examined. This is necessary to correct for common misperceptions about the nature of Canadian pluralism and Mexican corporatism. In reality, neither is Mexico fully corporatist nor is Canada fully pluralist. Rather, both have a combination of features and in distinguishing Canada and Mexico and, in particular, in evaluating the impact of the state in each country on unions, it's important to examine not only the differences, but also the *similarities* in the two systems. Arguing that the Mexican telephone union's behavior is determined by corporatism, for instance, is not a sufficient explanation of the strategic path it has followed. Lastly, this chapter provides an overview of the empirical chapters that follow.

THE DEVELOPMENT OF TELEPHONE UNIONISM IN BRITISH COLUMBIA

In both Mexico and in British Columbia, telephone industry unionization efforts go back to the early twentieth century. In British Columbia, unionization began in 1901 when outside plant workers from Vancouver chartered Local 213, affiliated with the International Brotherhood of Electrical Workers (IBEW). A second local, Local 230, was founded the following year in the nearby city of New Westminster. In 1902, Vancouver operators founded a "women's auxiliary" which acted as a sub-local of Local 213. In September of that year, linemen went out on their first strike. Management quickly responded by recognizing the union. However, after recognizing the union on paper, management refused to follow through on its commitment to negotiate with the union, resulting two months later in a joint strike by operators and linemen. Union leverage was high because direct dialing did not yet exist, meaning that every call required an operator's intervention. Furthermore, telephone lines required constant maintenance and larger businesses relied heavily on telephone service for their communications. The strikers enjoyed considerable public support, especially after management spurned a union offer to return to work without a contract and to continue negotiations mediated by local business representatives. After two-and-a-half weeks, a settlement to the strike was reached which included a closed shop provision for the union and a one-year collective agreement with the company (Bernard 1982: 17-27).

The closed shop provisions are noteworthy, since similar contract provisions still exist, especially among construction or dock workers' unions. As well, the Mexican telephone workers' union maintains a similar arrangement in its current collective bargaining agreement with Telmex. Bernard explains that the way this system worked is that "the company would contact the union when it wanted to hire new employees and the union would send the workers. If the union did not have the required workers, then the company could hire them directly, provided the new employees joined the union" (Bernard 1982: 30).

Unfortunately for the IBEW, the union was unable to extend its closed shop beyond Vancouver and New Westminster. The IBEW had organized some workers in Victoria, the provincial capital, but a four-month strike of Victoria line workers ended with a return-to-work agreement and no closed shop. In addition, it was difficult for the operators, who faced the problems of sexism within the IBEW and high turn-over, to maintain their union organization. In January 1906, the IBEW Vancouver local reached an agreement with BC Tel management to maintain the closed shop provisions for linemen, while allowing an open shop for operators. Shortly thereafter, management stepped up its harassment of operators, threatening to fire those who refused to drop out of the union. As a result, the union struck in late February. This time, though, the company was prepared and imported strike-breakers to restore service. By November, union linemen returned to work without an agreement and the union local had been broken (Bernard 1982: 31-36).

By 1910, the IBEW local had been largely rebuilt by organizing among BC Tel contractors first, then reorganizing BC Tel proper. This entailed organizing first among electrical workers (wiremen), though without achieving a closed shop provision. In 1913, the first province-wide telephone strike in British Columbia took place. Involving over 300 workers and lasting ten days, the strike was largely successful. Worker gains included the establishment of rules that reduced the ratio of apprentices to journeymen (thus increasing the company's need to hire permanent staff), a wage increase, and double payment (double time) for overtime work.

Operators remained outside the union, however. Company policy towards the operators involved both strict workplace discipline and paternalistic benefits, such as an illness benefit program, instituted in 1914. But the labor shortage created by World War One facilitated a renewal of union activity among operators by 1916. Management responded by increasing sick benefits, raising wages slightly, and creating a recreation camp for operators. Such efforts were unsuccessful, however, and by 1918 the operators once again had affiliated with the IBEW. In 1918, without a strike, the IBEW regained the closed shop for linemen, but operators were left out, mainly because it was felt that the operators were not yet fully organized (Bernard 1982: 44-49, 62-71).

Things quickly came unravelled in 1919. In that year, a general strike which aimed to form "one big union" began in Winnipeg and quickly spread throughout Western Canada. Electrical workers and operators supported the strike, but line workers only grudgingly went along. When the general strike failed to create a united industrial union in western Canada, the linemen decided to split from the electrical workers and form their own local, local 310. In the midst of this dissension, the operators' local slowly fizzled out. A factor in the split within the IBEW was that, as the telephone company grew, workers became permanent employees of the telephone company rather than splitting their time among different utility companies under contract with the IBEW, as had been true in earlier years. By the mid-twenties, BC Tel had over 60,000 subscribers and more than 2,000 workers; in 1902, there had been only 2,000 telephones province-wide. The combination of newfound job security working for a company in an expanding business and internal squabbling within the IBEW eventually led the line workers' union itself to fizzle out without a strike in 1929 (Bernard 1982: 57-71).

As part of its successful effort to oust the union, BC Tel management had created a company-controlled and financed organization known as the Electric Employees' Organization (EEO), which represented both inside plant (wire) and outside plant (line) workers.[1] This organization remained in place throughout the Great Depression. Indeed, the company union structure continued to exist at BC Tel until World War II, when increased labor militancy nationwide in the wartime, labor-shortage economy led to rapid change throughout the labor movement. The Canadian government responded to the increased militancy by implementing wartime labor measures, patterned after the Wagner Act in the United States, that "discouraged" (Bernard 1982: 89) company unions. As a result of the shift in state policy, the EEO gained financial independence and began to evolve from being a "company union" to a union that operated entirely independent of BC Tel management.[2]

The wartime labor shortage and new labor legislation also made union organizing among operators easier. In 1943, operators organized their own union—the Telephone Operators' Organization (TOO)—which enjoyed overwhelming member support, with 950 of 1100 operators (86%) in Vancouver signing on and 97% of all operators in Victoria joining as well. In 1944, the TOO and EOO merged to become the Federation of Telephone Workers (FTW). The following year clerical workers, at the time only 176 in number, joined the union (Bernard 1982: 78-92).

From 1945 until 1977, the telephone workers' union structure remained largely the same, with each of the three divisions—plant, clerical, and traffic (operator services)—maintaining a high degree of autonomy in the day-to-day affairs of the union. In 1977, a new more unified structure was created. Along with the change in structure came a change in name. As a result, the FTW became the Telecommunications Workers' Union, the TWU (Bernard 1982: 176). At this point, one could say that the contemporary era of the TWU had begun.

Some parts of the TWU's history have more or less faded away, but in reviewing the record, a few things stand out. One key feature is the dramatic divisions among different occupations. Sometimes, this is along sectoral lines; sometimes, strictly along gender lines. What is clear, though, is that the divisional structure of the union, going back to the separate locals of the IBEW period, makes gender and occupational conflict within the union more visible, if not also more pronounced. Calls to split the union back into its original component divisions are not unusual, although the likelihood of success of such efforts is low.[3] This conflict has at times become a major source of strain on the union, though the union leadership has consistently managed to reach compromises that keep everyone together in a single organization.

A second key feature is isolation. Since their split from the IBEW in the 1920s, BC Tel workers have remained organizationally separated from other Canadian telephone workers. While the U.S.-based Communications Workers of America (CWA) sought to organize BC Tel workers into the CWA in the late fifties and early sixties, the drive failed to generate sufficient worker support (Bernard 1982: 119-124).[4] Although the TWU has consistently pursued a social unionist strategy of coalition building since the 1970s, there has always been a significant minority current within the union that has advocated a go-it-alone approach and which has resisted ties to the NDP, other telecommunications unions, and community movements.

This isolation points to a third feature, which is probably the most important legacy of the TWU's historical trajectory—that is, the legacy of emerging from a company union. Though not a unique feature of the TWU (both the CWA and the United Steel Workers in the United States trace their origins to company unions), the influence of the TWU's company union past is greater since the TWU remains tied overwhelmingly to a single company, BC Tel. Unlike the CWA, which, partly compelled by the division of AT&T into eight companies in 1984 and partly through outside organizing, has branched out beyond AT&T and even beyond the telecommunications industry, in 1995 more than 98% of the workers represented by the TWU still worked for BC Tel.

The legacy of company unionism is not all negative. In particular, the TWU's history of company unionism helps to explain its tenacity on job control issues, such as contracting-out. Unlike other unions, which might just seek to organize the subcontractor firms, the TWU fought to prevent subcontracting in the first place. The union has also been fairly successful in building union loyalty by piggy-backing on company identification—i.e., this is our company and we should run it right—leading to fierce challenges on some management rights issues.

Still, the TWU's legacy of company unionism carries with it some major disadvantages. These disadvantages were perhaps not so important during the regulated monopoly era, but have become more important recently, as deregulation increases the union's vulnerability to forces external to the company. In particular, the TWU's near-exclusive focus with a single company has made it slow to adjust to changes in the structure of the industry. In part, the TWU's slow reaction is a result of placing all of its concerns on what is happening at a single company, a nearly inevitable result of its current membership distribution. In addition, there is a strong tendency to see the TWU and the BC Tel as, in the words of one union member, "joined at the hip" (Interview T-93-21c). Or, as a financial services clerk none too charitably put it, "The union could be considered a parasite of the company" (Interview T-93-36). Highly dependent on a company which is now considerably less constrained by government regulation than in the past, the TWU clearly occupies a difficult position.

THE DEVELOPMENT OF TELEPHONE UNIONISM IN MEXICO

In Mexico, as in British Columbia, the history of telephone unionism goes back to nearly the beginning of the twentieth century. In Mexico's case though, the key factor behind the formation of telephone worker unions was the Mexican Revolution. And the Mexican story is complicated by the unusual feature that, as late as 1950, Mexico had two competing telephone companies—one owned by the Swedish multinational Ericsson and the other, named Compañía Telefónica Mexicana (Mexicana), owned by the U.S. multinational ITT.[5] These two companies were roughly equal in size, so larger companies were forced to maintain both Ericsson lines, which were all listed by all-digit phone numbers, and Mexicana lines, which were listed in telephone directories with a mixed letter and digit combination, as was the case with the Bell companies in the United States at the time (Telmex 1991a: 84). The influence of these two companies still is present. Both companies maintained preferential supplier relationship with Telmex in the provisioning of switching equipment during the period of private ownership (1950-1958), the period of minority government ownership (1958-1972), and the period of majority government ownership (1972-1990).[6] Only in the 1990s, after Telmex had been privatized, did these preferential purchasing arrangements begin to break down, with the Canadian multinational Northern Telecom winning a contract to provide computerized operator equipment and the U.S. multinational AT&T becoming a "third" supplier of switching equipment.

During the first half of the century, just as there were two telephone companies, there were also two telephone workers' unions. The first company to be unionized was Mexicana, which was organized by the central Mexico electricians' union, the SME (Sindicato Mexicana de Electricistas) in 1915, in the midst of Mexico's revolution and civil war, although the telephone workers split from the SME shortly afterward. Telephone workers initiated a strike in 1915 that lasted from January 20 to February 8. On February 8, General Alvaro Obregón intervened by declaring that the Mexicana telephone company would be run by the workers until the war was over. Luis Morones, later to become the leading labor leader in Mexico during the 1920s, was made temporary manager of the company. A separate Ericsson union formed the same year, but its demands for an 8-hour day, sick pay, replacement of a manager, and higher wages were satisfied without the drama of the Mexicana strike (Jones Tamayo 1993: 85, Martínez 1988: 4-5).

Formal collective agreements came later, after the Mexican revolutionary war ended. The first such agreement in the telephone industry was reached at Mexicana. The agreement included such features as the 8-hour day, sick pay, life insurance, severance pay, a rudimentary grievance procedure, a workers' compensation policy, and double pay for working overtime or on Sunday. The contract also contained provisions to address specific workplace grievances such as a provision that a male manager in the operator services division was to be replaced by a "woman of greater seniority" (Martínez 1988: 12-13). The Ericsson union achieved a similar collective agreement in 1928, after holding a 3-day strike (Martínez 1988: 19).

Cooperation between the unions at Mexicana and Ericsson was minimal. The Mexicana union affiliated with the moderate CROM

(Confederación Revolucionaria de Obreros Mexicanos), led by Luis Morones, which largely cooperated with Mexican government officials. Indeed, at one point, Morones was the government's Secretary of Labor. This resulted in the union being run in an increasingly authoritarian manner. As one student of the STRM comments, "The designation of the union representatives was done normally from the top and specifically with leaders tied to the methods of the CROMista structure" (Jones Tamayo 1993: 86).

Later on, in the 1930s, a major fissure within the ruling PRI developed between President Lázaro Cárdenas and labor leader Vicente Lombardo Toledano on the one hand, and former President Plutarco Elías Calles and labor leader Luis Morones on the other. Cárdenas and Lombardo Toledano won, and in 1934 the Mexicana union jumped to the winning side, making substantial contractual gains in a 1935 strike in which the work week was reduced from 48 to 44 hours. After an internal union struggle, a "pro-business" slate gained temporary control of the union executive committee in 1943. But the pro-business executive committee slate was ousted just months later by a rank-and-file revolt. In 1944, when the new union leadership led a strike to pursue wage and benefit gains; the government responded with a *requisa*, a military occupation of the telephone facilities, in order to maintain service, as permitted under the authority of the 1942 Communications Law which allowed such action if "national security" were threatened. In 1945, wildcat strikes occurred at Mexicana which reflected the "incorporation of a union organization of department delegates." (These are roughly equivalent to counsellors in the British Columbian TWU). The department delegates focused on increasing worker control within the work process and marked a significant organizational gain for the Mexicana union (Martínez 1988).

The Ericsson union proceeded along a different path, affiliating with the anarcho-syndicalist CGT (Confederación General de Trabajadores or General Workers' Confederation) and earning a reputation as being the more militant of the two unions (Jones Tamayo 1993: 86, Martinez de Ita 1982: 93). The Ericsson union went on strike in 1928, 1929, 1932, 1939, 1945, and 1949. At times, the Ericsson union faced considerable hostility, as in 1939, when the government declared an Ericsson strike "non-existent." By striking, the Ericsson union succeeded in extending their union throughout the company nationwide and achieved significant improvements in seniority protection and other areas, but wage gains were less impressive, with salaries less than half those received by electrical workers. Nonetheless, structurally, the Ericsson union maintained "a dynamic union, more participative and democratic" than the top-down unionism of the Mexicana union (Martinez 1988: 19-71, quote on 31; see also Mercado Maldonado 1993: 160).

In 1950, the Mexicana and Ericsson networks, with government approval and assistance, were joined, with Telmex emerging as the new monopoly entity.[7] The fusion of the companies forced the merger of the two unions and from this merger emerged the STRM. The early years of the STRM were dominated by conflict between Ericsson workers and Mexicana workers. Indeed both unions had undertaken strikes in 1949 and 1950, largely to position their activists as the ones best able to run what was to be the new, combined union. The Mexicana union was smaller and its collective agreement was weaker. However, with government help, the more pro-government Mexicana union leader, Fernando Raúl Murrieta, became secretary general of the union and the more centralized structure of the Mexicana union was adopted as the STRM's own. In this era, management made major gains in contract language, acquiring the right to contract out work more or less indiscriminately and the right to increase the percentage of management employees as a percentage of the overall Telmex workforce.

In 1959, a rank-and-file wildcat strike toppled the leadership of the Mexicana faction, and the Ericsson dissidents were elevated to union leadership positions. The union sought under its new secretary general, Agustín Avecia, to revise union bylaws to allow for greater decentralization of authority and to limit contractually the number of management employees and the amount of work contracted out (Martínez 1988: 143-148).[8] In 1961, the STRM went on strike briefly; the government responded by using the *requisa* and the army maintained most service, but the agreement reached did result in renewed hiring of telephone workers to cover vacant posts in the company (Martínez 1988: 159-160). In union elections later that year, an Avecia ally, Alberto Velasco Velardi, won with 2943 votes against 1678 for the government-supported candidate, Manuel Guzmán Perales, with other candidates receiving a total of 1210 votes (Xelhuantzi 1988: 18).[9] In 1962, the STRM went on strike again. This time, the government responded by declaring the strike "non-existent" and sought to remove the union's leadership. On July 2, two months after the April strike had been called, Guzmán Perales was installed by government officials as the union's new secretary general (Martínez

1988: 174). In order to buy the complacency of the membership, union members were offered a wage package worth $64-million pesos over two years (at the time, US$5,120,000, equivalent to more than US$500 per worker).[10]

This government-imposed union leadership remained in control from 1962 to 1976. Despite one challenge stemming from the negotiation of a department-level work agreement in 1967, the union leadership was successful in sustaining centralized control. In 1970, a new leader, Salustio Salgado, followed in the footsteps of Guzmán Perales. This period was a time of moderate gains in real wages (not just for the STRM, but for the Mexican labor movement as a whole), but there was little progress on job control issues. As well, "the participation of the rank and file through its delegates in bargaining the Collective Agreement was nil" (Martínez 1988: 183), leading to widespread dissatisfaction. This discontent, coupled with the union leadership's neglect of workplace issues and increasing focus on pursuing national political posts for themselves, led to a nationwide wildcat strike in 1976 and the installation of a new union leadership, under Francisco Hernández Juárez, who has remained the secretary general of the union ever since.

Again, as with the TWU, it is important to examine the key aspects of the union's history that continue to influence the STRM's behavior today. One important trait of the STRM is the tension between its centralized policy structure and its decentralized administrative structure, built in the 1940s with the growth of an extensive network of local union shop stewards and counsellors[11] at the shop floor. Indeed, until a 1989 agreement between the union, management, and the government drastically altered the situation, it was department union activists who were responsible as commissioned union representatives for negotiating department-level *convenios* [accords] that specified working conditions in their departments. By the 1980s, the STRM had 63 departments and work was subdivided at Telmex among 63 different divisions with 63 separate convenios.

Much of the past two decades of STRM history has been marked, on the one hand, by efforts of Hernández Juárez and his group to centralize control and, on the other hand, by continuing resistance to centralization from union shop stewards and counsellors. Ironically, many of the successes of the STRM under Hernández Juárez can be traced to the fact that efforts to centralize have had only limited success. Despite the fact that the authority of department union activists to negotiate local agreements has been removed and even though major strategic decisions in the STRM are made by very few people, sometimes as few as five (Interview S-94-1), the huge extension of Mexican territory and the enormity of the company as a whole still require that many day-to-day decisions be carried out by union shop stewards and counsellors.

By contrast, the TWU, due to its smaller size, can enjoy the benefits of centralization while, at the same time, union officials are able to remain closer to the rank-and-file membership. Also assisting the TWU in this regard is that the union has never been divided into many separate sections as was the STRM. While the STRM was divided into 63 separate departments, many of which have fought fiercely to maintain their distance from the central union office, the TWU was never divided into more than three divisions. And negotiation of the contract provisions for these three divisions has been centralized since the late 1970s. Thus, although the TWU experiences considerable conflict among occupational groups, conflict over the degree of centralization is less frequent and less severe.

A second trait stemming from the STRM's historical development comes from its two union ancestors. Not only did the two unions' distinctive political tendencies shape political conflict in the STRM in the 1950s, but opposition movements strongly reflect certain aspects of the Ericsson union in their political philosophy, in particular the 1959-1962 period when the Ericsson union faction briefly held the secretary general post. Though identifiable Ericsson and Mexicana factions have not existed for decades, the nature of political conflict between Hernández Juárez and his supporters and opposition movements within the STRM largely reflects differing interpretations of the 1959-62 period. Thus, supporters of opposition movements, such as the Línea Democrática, have sought to restore the 1959-62 period's emphasis on no reelection and strict union democracy. That is, the 1959-62 period gives opponents of Hernández Juárez a specific experience to emulate. On the other hand, Hernández Juárez and his allies focus on the denouement of the 1959-62 period of union democracy under the Ericsson faction leadership and argue that compromise with state authorities is the only way to avoid a similar fate.

This brings up a third tendency that continues into the modern period, which is state intervention in internal union affairs. Though the STRM is not now, nor has it ever been, fully state-run (though the STRM came close to this extreme during the 1962-1976 period), state officials have intervened in internal union affairs frequently, especially during the 1976-1982 period. Since 1982, state intervention has been less visible, but is nonetheless present. A quid pro quo for union "autonomy" has been support for PRI (Partido Revolucionario Institucional, the official Mexican state party) policies and PRI candidates.

By contrast, the Canadian state interacts with the TWU via the judiciary, the labor "conciliation" system, the legislature, and through the state regulatory body, the CRTC. But state officials do not concern themselves with internal union politics per se. State control over the Canadian union is exercised through regulation of union tactics and treatment of union-management disputes, not through a direct attempt to influence the overall course of the union leadership. The TWU's relationship with the NDP (New Democratic Party), as seen in Chapter 7, does in some ways parallel the STRM's relationship with the PRI, but the TWU's relations with the NDP are not marked by direct coercion in the same way as the STRM's relationship with the PRI is.

A fourth tendency evident in the STRM's history is the tension between focusing on wage increases versus job control issues. Typically, the union leadership has focused on wages, while the opposition has focused on job control. Thus, if the opposition in the STRM were to gain control over the central union executive, one would expect the STRM to function more like the TWU or like the Mexican union, the SME, where a social unionist slate was elected into office in 1993. But this is more complicated, since there are many militants in the union who wish to pursue wage gains to an even greater extent than does the current STRM leadership.

A final facet of the STRM's history that is important in explaining its present behavior is that it, like the TWU, is a single company union. This has many of the same advantages and disadvantages for the STRM, as it has for the TWU, with one key difference. This difference is that Telmex has also developed into a double-breasted company, with union and non-union subsidiaries. Though a normal development in the United States, this is highly unusual in Mexico. The effect of the large non-union portion of the company has been to weaken the union's leverage to make gains on contracting-out language. Having lost strong contracting-out language two years after Telmex's creation in 1952, the STRM has never really fully recovered. As a result, the union, as a single-employer union, often has to settle for monetary benefits. Now that deregulation has commenced, the union is in an even more vulnerable position, competing for work not only within Telmex, but also with companies outside Telmex. If its failure to gain a toehold in the cellular market is any indication, the STRM has a difficult road ahead.

TELECOMMUNICATIONS UNIONS AND THE LEGAL FRAMEWORK

We can talk 'culture' until we all go mad. But isn't it possible that the law itself may help create the culture? (Geoghegan 1992: 267).

In some ways, unions in Mexico and Canada face quite similar legal structures. Unlike in Europe, where multiple unions exist at a single workplace, in both countries a single union gains an exclusive certification and negotiates an agreement with a single business.[12] Neither country has works councils. In both countries, government mediators are brought in when negotiation comes to an impasse. But this is not to underestimate the substantial differences. Stated simply, in Mexico the state has greater authority and individual unions and businesses have less authority. This, as U.S. labor lawyer Thomas Geoghegan would predict, affects the "culture" of labor relations in each country.

In analyzing comparatively the labor codes confronted by unions that are under federal jurisdiction in Mexico and Canada,[13] one can distinguish three distinct sets of issues: relations between union organizations and their members, relations between unions and individual businesses, and relations between unions and the state. In all three areas, substantial differences are evident.

In Mexico, unions in core sectors have significantly more authority vis a vis individual members than in Canada. This centralized authority brings with it both an increased ability of union leaders to enforce membership discipline and an increased potential for abuse of those powers. On the positive side, union membership does confer a greater number of benefits in Mexico than in Canada. These benefits have significant positive effects on workers' lives. At the same time, union leaders are able to exercise discretion and withhold these benefits from individual union members who have fallen in disfavor, making rank-and-file union members much more susceptible to discipline. One place where this dual effect is most visible is with the closed shop.

Although not required by Mexican labor law, in the core unionized sectors, including the telephone company, the closed shop prevails. This means that not only must all members pay dues to the union (this is true in the Canadian TWU as well as the Mexican STRM), but that the union also serves as a hiring hall.[14] If management wishes to hire new workers, it must recruit them through the union, which maintains a list of people awaiting jobs. These people, should they pass the required exams, must be hired by management.

This closed shop system has a profound impact on the entire scope of labor relations. On the union side, the closed shop system provides members one of their most important benefits, namely the power to recommend a family member for a job. This benefit is awarded on the basis of seniority, with those who are most senior able to recommend a candidate to fill the first vacancy and so on down the list until all of the vacancies are filled. Given that telephone work is relatively well paid in Mexico, these jobs are in high demand and there is a long waiting list.[15]

The union is also responsible for training the workers who are on this list to pass the required exams. Thus, unlike the TWU, the STRM must train workers to be operators, to type, to climb telephone polls and so forth, and a significant portion of union resources are dedicated to this end. If the union agrees there are no trained workers available for a given vacancy, then management has the right to hire directly (at which time the worker must enroll with the union). When this happens, the waiting list of family members for jobs remains just as long, so it is to the union's advantage to make sure there is a reservoir of trained applicants available for jobs.

However, this closed shop mechanism is also an important method by which union leaders can "discipline" members and punish dissidents. For not only must management go through the union to hire employees, but management is also legally bound to fire workers who have been expelled by the union from its membership. Since union membership is a condition of employment, a worker who is expelled by the union is, simultaneously, expelled from the company.

In practice, things don't always work as the law would prescribe. Management, for instance, might like an employee who has been expelled by the union (perhaps, for instance, because the worker was conspiring with management against the union leadership). In such a case, management may refuse to recognize the expulsion and hence the worker's employment is preserved. The situation is different, however, if the union expels a worker who management also dislikes. In such a case, the firing does take place.

According to Mexican labor law, an expulsion can only occur if there is a two-thirds vote of a union judicial assembly. Such proceedings are rarely abided by, meaning that a worker who chooses to fight the expulsion almost always is reinstated by Mexican labor courts, but usually three or four years later (Interview S-90-12). Penalties assessed to unions that fail to abide by the required proceedings are light and thus it is not uncommon for union leaders to expel a member for political reasons. Although workers who fight the expulsion are usually reinstated, the energy spent fighting for reinstatement is energy that is not spent working to change practices within the union. As a result, illegal expulsions are an effective means of controlling internal dissent.

A more common, and less severe, step for the union leadership to take is to simply suspend the rights of dissident union members. Such workers do not lose their jobs, but do lose their access to union benefits, such as the right to recommend a family member for a job. Given the importance of this benefit to union members, this can often serve as an effective means for silencing union members who may be sympathetic to points of view that differ from those held by union leaders.

Further strengthening the power of this disciplinary tool of suspension is the fact that benefits are administered by the union. This is unlike the Canadian system where, with some exceptions, the union intercedes only when there is a problem in obtaining a benefit guaranteed by the collective agreement. Thus, a TWU member would go directly to his or her first line supervisor to request a day of unpaid leave; a union shop steward would only intercede if, for some reason, the worker felt the request had been unjustly denied. An STRM member, on the other hand, would go to a shop steward to request a day of unpaid leave. It would then be the responsibility of the shop steward to *tramitar* or process the request and notify the first-line supervisor. If a dissident's union rights have been suspended, the request would not be processed.

On a small matter like a day of unpaid leave, a dissident on good terms with a first-line supervisor could approach that supervisor directly for permission. But there are other, more substantial benefits that are also administered by the union. These include such benefits as low-interest loans to purchase cars or houses from a union-run savings fund, to which contributions are made by both the worker and the employer. As one STRM shop steward explained, the time required for processing of requests varies according to how closely connected one is to the union leadership. "For the favored ones, these are resolved in a week, two weeks. The others are resolved in four-and-a-half months, up to a year-and-a-half" (Interview S-90-13a).

As a result of these arrangements, the Mexican STRM is active in the workplace on a daily basis, in a way that the Canadian TWU is not, affecting members' daily lives through such things as processing minor leave requests, providing loans for family durable goods purchases, and scheduling work. As a result of past conflicts in the late 1970s, the STRM gained the right to hold meetings on site at the workplace; these meetings are officially mandatory, ensuring relatively high attendance, though absences are rarely penalized.

In the TWU, the union does play an important scheduling role for plant and traffic workers, but otherwise the average member has little daily interaction with the union. Most TWU members come into contact with the union only if they choose to attend a local meeting off-site (on average, such meetings are attended by fewer than 10% of members) or if they file a grievance against the company. In political science terms (McCubbins and Weingast 1989), the STRM follows a "police patrol" model, intervening in every interaction between manager and worker (or at least seeking to do so), while the TWU follows a "fire alarm" model, intervening when a member makes a complaint. While the TWU's interventions are largely successful—and, as shall be seen in the following chapters, often more effective than those of the STRM—the STRM is clearly more visible and omnipresent in the workplace. A TWU member might not know who his or her shop steward is and might not have a need to know. A STRM member will most certainly know who his or her shop steward is.

Not only does the STRM play a greater role vis a vis its individual members; the union also benefits from provisions in Mexican labor law that give it leverage over business that would be unimaginable to the TWU. Some of these benefits are implicit in the items described above. For instance, since the union has a significant influence over who is hired, management is largely unable to use recruitment practices to choose specific types of workers and reject others. As well, since the union intercedes on a regular basis on everyday workplace matters, the union can maintain a greater shop-floor presence. On paper, though, the most impressive power of the STRM stems from a provision of

Mexican labor law that, in the event that there is a strike, the business must cease all operations. So not only is it the case that management is not allowed to hire scab workers, but management itself is legally compelled to stay away from work for the duration of a legally sanctioned strike.

The phrase "legally sanctioned" is crucial here, however. A legally recognized strike has not occurred in Mexican telecommunications in the past 50 years. But nearly a dozen "non-existent" strikes have taken place during that time period. For while Mexican labor law makes the union quite powerful with respect to both individual members and even management, the same labor law leaves the union quite weak vis a vis the state.

To understand how important the power of the Mexican state is vis a vis unions, a comparison with the more limited role of the state in Canada is quite instructive. In Canada, state officials have the power to issue a court injunction to limit unions' protest activities or employers' labor practices. State officials have the power to mediate resolutions to workplace disputes and can put political pressure on the parties to accept proposed settlements. As well, state officials have the power to change the regulatory framework or labor laws and thereby alter the environment in which both unions and management operate. In other words, Canadian state officials can prod the parties, they can forbid specific actions, and they can alter labor law or industry structure.

The role of the Canadian state is important, but its powers are limited. While altering the structure of the industry or changing labor laws can dramatically affect the parties, the impact of such actions is too slow to have a decisive effect in any single dispute. Injunctions and mediation can impact individual disputes, but both parties are often able to work around state restrictions. In response to these limitations, Canadian legislatures in the past two decades have increasingly resorted to legislative "back-to-work" orders against individual strikes,[16] particularly in the public sector and, at times when inflation was high, wage and price control measures. Although these measures should be sufficient to shatter any notion of Canadian state neutrality in collective bargaining, even in the case of legislated back-to-work orders, the state's ability to impose terms has frequently been frustrated by dogged union resistance.

Compare the above with the situation of the Mexican state. Two important powers of the Mexican state are its ability to accept or deny a certification and its ability to accept or deny a strike petition (STRM

1991, Middlebrook 1995). The first power gives Mexican state officials the ability to reward unions that politically favor the party-state PRI (by expanding their membership base and hence their financial resources), while restricting the ability of unions that oppose the PRI. Mexican state officials, if they so choose, can decide to not recognize an election victory of a particular union leadership, as occurred in 1962 in the STRM. Unless those so opposed are able to mount substantial public pressure on state officials to reverse their ruling, the position of those targeted can quickly become untenable. Just as union leaders are able to exercise pressure on dissidents by denying them union benefits, so too are state officials, by denying unions the legal authority to act as a union, able to exert significant pressure on union leaders who go "astray."

The power of the state to declare strikes "non-existent" is even more important. No need to resort to politically controversial "back-to-work" measures here. Generally speaking, roughly 98% of all strike petitions are denied (Middlebrook 1995). As this figure suggests, the Mexican state, especially during the terms of Presidents Miguel de la Madrid and Carlos Salinas de Gortari, has had a very strong anti-labor record. Since a declaration of strike legality is rarely granted, Mexican labor must often rely on currying party favor to extract benefits for union members.

The only benefit of this system for labor is that Mexican labor law makes a legal strike almost impossible for a union to lose. As a result, the government can support a politically-friendly union by jaw-boning company managers into making concessions. This path of relying on friendly state officials to extract company concessions has been frequently used by the STRM. Because Telmex had majority state ownership from 1972 to 1990, the STRM had to get state labor officials to overrule state mangers of the company, instead of pressuring managers of a private company, but the process largely paralleled the private-sector bargaining process. Indeed, the collective bargaining process has remained largely the same since Telmex was privatized.

In the end, while the mediation process exists and is used frequently in both Canada and Mexico, the dynamics of the interaction are quite different in the two countries. Unlike Canada, where it is not uncommon for either the union or management to reject a state mediator's recommendation, a formal rejection of a state mediator's "recommendation" in Mexico is simply not done. The reason for this difference is not hard to understand. If a Canadian mediator's settlement is rejected, the mediator may lobby the employers' groups or union federations, as well as lobby political leaders. But a mediator cannot impose a settlement. In Mexico, the state's ability to declare a strike legal or "non-existent" imbues it with the power to nearly unilaterally declare the winner in the dispute. A party disagreeing with the state mediator's conclusion is not only likely to be declared the loser, but to be penalized for lacking proper decorum. Not surprisingly, then, open opposition to the government mediator's position is rare. Because of these powers, the Mexican state is much more able to bring a resolution to disputes in a manner that meets state officials' liking than is the case with their Canadian counterparts.

This, however, does overstate the state's authority in Mexico somewhat. While *legally*[17] the state's authority to declare a strike existent or non-existent and to recognize or not recognize union leaders would make the state's authority nearly absolute, there is necessarily a level of illegality, or at best extralegality, in union-management relations. This is true in both Canada and Mexico, but in Mexico such "extralegality" plays a larger role.[18] The absolute quality of the Mexican state's power makes its actual use rather clumsy and heightens the need for such "extralegal" mechanisms. In other words, the existence of such state powers does not allow for deft, light-handed intervention. The state, for instance, cannot allow workers to go off the job, while allowing management to continue working: either both cease to work or neither can cease to work. But what if state labor officials want to pressure Telmex management—perhaps to punish a manager who is suspected of corruption or one whose ruthlessness is counterproductive, causing low worker morale and low productivity—but without shutting the entire telephone system down? The solution, of course, is to permit, or even encourage, wildcat action, union slowdown tactics, or general workplace indiscipline.

Labor leaders face a similar dilemma. They know they can encourage wildcat actions, slowdown tactics, and so forth—and get away with it. The state, after all, cannot punish every indiscretion if it hopes to have intermediaries in the labor movement. But these practices must be carried out within limits. Thus, union leaders in Mexico walk a tightrope between maintaining labor discipline and maintaining the threat of a labor force, that, were it not for the labor leader's close "rapport" with the rank-and-file, would be taking to the streets.

Both discipline and indiscipline are necessary. Too much repression can lead to a rank-and-file revolt against the union leadership. Too permissive of a stance, on the other hand, can lead to state retaliation, including the attempt by state officials to replace the union's leadership. In this situation, the labor leader seeks to persuade state officials that the threat of indiscipline is real, but controllable, provided that management concedes to the union's reasonable demands. Thus, an important part of the labor leader's leverage comes from the existence of the threat of indiscipline. Indeed, without the threat of indiscipline such as a rank-and-file revolt, the labor leader's role as moderator of membership demands is undermined, lessening the union leader's ability to extract concessions from management and deliver for the rank and file.

In Canada, some of this "extralegality" also exists, though it is less marked. Legally speaking, wildcat strikes are not permitted. Indeed, no strikes are permitted during the life of a collective bargaining agreement. In reality, there is no union where unauthorized strikes do not occur. The difference is that in Canada the state's response is more measured. Typically, state officials respond to wildcat actions by issuing a "cease and desist" order. Only if this order is not obeyed is punitive action taken, generally in the form of fines, though in a few exceptional cases, union leaders have been jailed.[19] The Canadian system also makes heavy use of compulsory, binding arbitration, in which both management and the union name a representative and these two name a third representative. Because the parties each have one representative on the arbitration panel, both parties retain some control over the process. As a result, this more straight-forward legal mechanism is used rather frequently, though arbitration is sufficiently expensive that both parties seek to informally resolve most matters before they get to an arbitration board. In Mexico, it is the employers' association (Coparmex) and the labor federation—labor sector of the PRI, mostly the Confederación de Trabajadores Mexicanos (CTM)— who appoint the members of standing arbitration boards, meaning that neither the company management nor the union involved necessarily have influence over the process. As a result, the parties are much less comfortable with the arbitration process and it is largely avoided by both union and management. Thus, disputes tend to be resolved by informal negotiation or through direct confrontation, in the form of wildcat strikes or work slow-downs.

EVALUATING THE LIMITS AND IMPACT OF LEGAL STRUCTURE AND HISTORY

As illustrated above, there are substantial differences in the legal environments the two unions face. Despite these differences, the legal framework governing labor relations in both countries permits different responses by these two unions to the phenomenon of globalization. More important in determining an individual union's response to globalization is its historical institutional legacy. To see this requires reviewing some of the key aspects of the legal structure set out above and then showing how institutional history, the political balance of power among occupational sectors within the union, and union decision-making structures interact with outside forces such as the state and the international economy to shape labor behavior in the increasingly internationalized telecommunications industry.

In modelling labor behavior in Mexico and Canada, one frequently finds the terms "corporatist" or "pluralist" used, but these terms provide a very incomplete picture of the nature of labor relations in the two countries. Pluralism is usually characterized as the existence of a multiplicity of unions, a high degree of decentralization in labor relations, and minimal involvement of the state. Canada imperfectly fits this definition: though the system is highly decentralized, unions are given unique jurisdictional areas of certification (unlike either Great Britain or continental Europe) and the state's role is fairly significant. Corporatism is usually characterized by having a structure consisting of single, centralized labor and employers' federations, a concomitantly high degree of centralization in labor relations, and maximal involvement of the state. Again, Mexico imperfectly fits this definition. Though there is a high degree of state intervention, labor relations are only partially centralized, with many decisions made at the individual company level. Rather than having one federation, there are multiple federations. Though the CTM may be the dominant player, it is at the same time subjected to continued competition. Indeed, over the past 50 years, the smaller union federations have been strong enough to form a strong counterweight to CTM influence and to thereby prevent full CTM dominance. Thus, one could view the comparison between the two countries as follows:

Table 4-1: State-Labor Relations in Mexico and Canada[20]

	Mexico	Canada
Degree of centralization	Moderately high	Low
Degree of state intervention	High	Moderate
Degree of labor concentration	Moderately high	Moderately low

Mexico is thus more corporatist, relatively speaking, than Canada, but the difference is less dramatic than is often presupposed. Clearly, this difference does affect the nature of choices available to Mexican unions like the STRM. Simply put, the range of strategic choice available to Mexican labor unions is more limited than in Canada, because unions face greater state intervention in their affairs. Nonetheless, the degree of choice available to Mexican unions is greater than it would be under a pure corporatist regime. By the same logic, the existence of a significant, albeit lesser, degree of state intervention in Canada means that the range of strategic choices available to Canadian unions is more limited than it would be under a purely pluralist regime. By examining the two systems, one can see that the choices confronted by unions within these systems are characterized by important similarities, though also exhibiting some important differences. This can be seen by comparing the typical options presented to Mexican unions—"corporatism" vs. "independent" unionism—with the typical options presented to Canadian unions— "social unionism" vs. "business unionism." While there are other options available, it is important to understand the two most common forms of unionism in each country to understand the framework in which union activists operate.

In Mexico, the two most common types of unions are the "corporatist" unions and the "independent" unions, with the former being far more frequent than the latter.[21] The corporatist unions, of which the CTM is the example *par excellence*, focus on political negotiations with government officials to obtain benefits for the membership.[22] Here it is important to recall the way the state uses discretion in granting strike petitions. State officials nearly always reject strike petitions, but they are willing to use their power to grant strike petitions as a way to extract benefits for those union leaders who are politically aligned with the PRI party-state. Corporatist union leaders know they are dependent on the beneficence of state officials, but there are enough gains to be made that pursuing such a strategy remains at least a marginally viable option.

The independent union leaders take a different approach. Independent unions are independent both of the government and of opposition movements. Outright opposition to the regime is not tolerated.[23] In return for maintaining an "apolitical" stance, independent unions are allowed to seek benefits for their members, within a collective bargaining context. The independent union movement was strongest in the 1970s (Ortiz Pérez and Morales Pineda 1991), when most automobile sector unions functioned in an independent manner (Roxborough 1984). In the 1980s, labor conditions worsened due to Mexico's prolonged economic crisis, the number of strike petitions granted fell, and the automotive industry moved to northern Mexico, where it was organized by corporatist unions. As a result, the position of independent unions weakened considerably. Nonetheless, some independent unions remain, especially among university professors and administrative workers. These unions are also very visible and thus are able to maintain an importance beyond that indicated by their numbers.

In Canada, the two most common union orientations are social unionism and business unionism. Social unionism focuses on the formation of an alliance with a social democratic party (in Canada, the New Democratic Party or NDP), in forming alliances with community groups, and in general seeking to promote social change within a reformist framework. Social unions tend to place a greater emphasis on workplace control issues and on the promotion of union rights, such as union control over benefits plans. Business unionism is, on the other hand, more narrowly oriented toward satisfying "interest group" needs. Rather than participating in broad political coalitions, business unions focus on collective bargaining, particularly wage and benefit issues. Business unions are not apolitical, as they work within the political system to promote their particular interests. But business unions take a narrower view of what the political arena is and are more willing to strike compromises and, in many cases, work directly with business-dominated political parties.

MODELLING STRATEGIC CHOICES IN THE TWU AND THE STRM

Neither of the above pairs—corporatism versus independent unionism in Mexico, or social unionism versus business unionism in Canada— fully encompass all of the options faced by the TWU and STRM, but both unions are, not surprisingly, influenced by the most common types of unionism that exist in their own countries. As described in the previous chapter, other types of unions, such as craft unions, Leninist unions, or anarcho-syndicalist unions do exist or have existed in both Mexico and Canada. In looking at the actual decisions made by the TWU and the STRM when confronting the globalization of their industry, it is necessary to evaluate a multitude of factors, not just external ones (such as management or state actions, state labor laws, and national labor political tendencies), but internal ones as well, the most important of which are a) the occupational balance of political power within the union, b) the institutional history of the union, and c) the decision-making rules by which the union operates. By looking at the internal political dynamics of the two unions, one can uncover some important factors that generate the formation of new types of union strategic action as well as more firmly understand the extents and limits of external control over internal union behavior.

While the initial impulse for a change in union strategy generally comes from forces outside the union, a union's response often depends far more on how that impulse is mediated within the union decision-making structure than on the nature of the external change itself. In particular, both the internal distribution of power among occupational sectors and the legacy of past union decisions regarding their strategic outlook often play a determining role in the shaping of a given union's response. The internal decision-making rules are important since these impact on how easily a transfer in authority can occur between different factions within the unions which represent different occupational sectors or different ideologies, how easily new factions or alliances can be formed, whether the union is run in a majoritarian or consensual fashion, and the nature of debate that occurs on issues when they arise.

As can be seen from Table 4-2 below, the exact lines of occupational differences are not the same in the two unions:

Table 4-2: Occupational Organization at BC Tel and Telmex

STRM/Telmex category	TWU/BC Tel category
Outside plant	Plant
Technician (switching/transmission)	Plant
Sales/Marketing	Clerical
Administrative	Clerical
Traffic/Operators: 01, 02, 04, 09	Operator Services/Traffic
Traffic/Operators: 05	Clerical (customer service reps)

As well as having somewhat different dividing lines between occupations, the two unions also have different percentages of personnel in the different categories. In particular, there is a higher percentage of operators at Telmex than BC Tel because operator services was not fully computerized until 1994. There are also fewer clerical workers at Telmex than BC Tel, because many plant functions that have been computerized and transferred to clerical workers in British Columbia remain plant functions in Mexico. While the existence of different job categories makes direct comparison difficult, the below table makes clear some of the differences in occupational distribution in the two telephone companies.

Table 4-3: Occupational Sector Divisions at BC Tel and TWU[24]

	STRM ('94)		TWU (1972)	TWU (1982)	TWU (1991)
Plant	37.34%	Plant	43.62%	49.69%	45.10%
Operators	25.20%	Operators	26.59%	15.98%	13.47%
Technicians	15.36%[25]	Clerical	29.79%	34.33%	41.43%
Admin.	11.56%				
Marketing	9.70%				
Other	0.84%[26]				

Despite the differences in dividing lines, there are some parallels in the occupational make-up of factions in the two unions. That is, one faction is stronger among outside plant workers, low-level clerical workers, and operators, while the other faction is stronger among administrative, more high-grade clerical workers, and inside plant workers. That such a split exists is not altogether surprising. This is because the operator, low-level clerical positions and outside plant jobs, especially construction crew work and cable splicers, are "blue collar" professions and generally have lower educational pre-requisites. On the other hand, office and inside plant jobs, especially "technician" or "engineer" positions, tend to have higher educational prerequisites and are seen as more akin to "white collar" positions.[27]

While factional differences do not follow directly from occupational lines, they are influenced by them. One can indeed find members from all occupational sectors in different political factions of both unions (Interview T-94-72, Interview S-90-1), but, not surprisingly, some factions are stronger among some occupational sectors than others (Interviews S-94-6, S-94-28, S-94-29, T-93-30). This is true not only because of the cultural differences that result from workers' different educational backgrounds and the different nature of the work (mental versus physical) but also because these workers' economic interests are often different, or at least are perceived to be different. As well, local union traditions play an important role.[28]

On the whole, operators and outside plant workers earn less than technicians and thus tend to place a greater importance on wage and benefit issues. Technicians, inside plant, and higher-wage clerical workers tend to place more emphasis on job control issues. Typically, outside plant workers and operators tend to be willing to take more aggressive or "militant" action than their more highly paid and highly educated counterparts, who tend to emphasize worker control issues and job creation issues over wage issues, but are less likely to take militant action. However, technicians in the STRM and TWU did become militant when their positions became threatened with deskilling due to the digitalization of telephone switch maintenance work.[29]

There is, however, no unique relationship between immediate, short-term economic interest and an overarching philosophy, vision, or ideology that seeks to provide a long-term framework in which to situate short-term action. Rather, there are different possible frameworks that can be used to try to make sense of workers' immediate experience. For this reason, it is pointless to argue whether workers are essentially class conscious and thus betrayed when union leaders pursue craft aims or, as the contrary argument would have it, essentially craft conscious and thus duped when union leaders pursue socialist aims.

The vision a union adopts tends to be based, to a large degree, on how events unfold during a key period of conflict in the union's history. Such a period is often marked by a high degree of internal union conflict, a high degree of conflict between the union and management, and sometimes between the union and the state as well. This process is in some respects similar to the evolution of state labor regimes as a whole (Collier and Collier 1991) or of a political realignment in electoral politics (Geoghegan 1992), in which a key period of class conflict shapes the framework of industrial relations for decades. Once the key period or "critical juncture" (Collier and Collier 1991) has passed, the same vision, philosophy, or ideology continues to frame actions, by both union leaders and opponents of the union leadership, for a long time to come (see also Golden 1988). Thus, the specific issues that lead to this period of conflict are important and may lead to different coalitions being formed than those described above. For instance, in the STRM, technicians have traditionally been among the most militant workers, largely because they were the first to face digital technology, which substantially altered the nature of work they performed and led to much workplace conflict.

When another major shock comes along (such as deregulation, technological change, or a major change in state labor law) and the union finds itself having to confront change, initially both union leaders and opposition activists will seek to operate within the framework with which they are familiar. However, when old methods fail, it is possible that a new shift will occur. In the 1970s, the key issue in Canadian telecommunications was technological change, the onset of which signalled the end of a long period of growth in the BC Tel workforce, threatening job security. This conflict occurred during a period marked by a national upswing in labor militancy, as the 1970s were a period of high strike activity throughout Canada. Only after two strike/lock-out disputes (1977-1978, 1980-1981), both several months long, and a change in union leadership, was a new equilibrium established between BC Tel management and the TWU.

In Mexico, a change in the political labor environment—namely, the reemergence of a strong, independent labor movement—was an important impetus for change (Trejo Delarbre 1990, Unomásuno 1980). Technological change also played an important role in prompting the changes within the STRM, though the main thrust of technological change would occur a decade later. Again, only after six years (1976-1982) of frequent strikes and wildcat actions, as well as substantial intra-union strife, was a new equilibrium established between Telmex management and the STRM. This arrangement was restructured greatly, but not overturned, in 1989, when Mexican state officials and

Telmex managers struck a deal with the union in which the union made substantial workplace concessions in exchange for economic benefits, primarily the receipt of stock in the soon-to-be-privatized company.

To date, both the TWU and the STRM continue to function within the framework of the political tendencies that emerged during their high-conflict periods of the late seventies and early eighties. At the same time, the changes being brought about by globalization are providing growing challenges to the traditional modes of action in both unions. For the TWU, key to its social unionist strategy has been the use of leverage in the regulatory arena to force the company to meet social obligations. As well, BC Tel's monopoly position permitted the union to maintain a dominant position in the industry simply by doggedly fighting to maintain the union's jurisdiction over telephone work performed by the company. BC Tel's monopoly status made things easier for the union in another way too. Since BC Tel rate of return (i.e., profit) was regulated by the CTRC, management could pass on wage increases to consumers; to a certain extent, this made it easier for the TWU to focus on non-wage issues, since it knew that the relatively high industry wage levels were not at risk. But now, with long-distance service opened to competition, the TWU's dominant position within the industry in British Columbia has also begun to decline slightly. Furthermore, the role of the regulatory board, the CRTC, itself has been weakened, and in the new regulatory environment, the CRTC is encouraging BC Tel and other former monopoly providers to cut labor costs.

For the STRM, a key element of its approach has been cooperation with the state. This has included endorsing many PRI economic policy initiatives, even when workers are called upon to make disproportionate sacrifices. In the late 1980s, with privatization, the strategy was augmented to include cooperating with management on non-wage issues (especially increasing productivity) in exchange for better earnings and benefits for the membership. Although the threat faced by the STRM is less obvious, it is no less severe. Because of Telmex's protected monopoly position, real wage declines of STRM members have been substantially less than for members of many other Mexican unions and far less than for Mexican workers that don't belong to a union. Prior to the December 1994 peso devaluation, STRM workers earned on average three times more than the average Mexican wage of N$26 (then US $8) a day (Calva 1994).

Now that Mexican telecommunications is being opened to competition, the STRM is in great danger of fading into irrelevance, as it will be very easy for competing companies to undercut STRM wage and benefit levels while still paying substantially above Mexican wage norms. In a sense, this wage gap problem is similar, albeit on a much larger scale, to that faced by U.S. unions in the 1980s (Moody 1988), even though the union/non-union wage gap there was only 20-30% (Freeman and Medoff 1984). Thus, both the STRM and the TWU, albeit for different reasons, face vulnerabilities as single-employer unions and will need to undergo significant change to successfully confront the pressures forced upon them by increasing globalization.

Internal decision-making rules, as mentioned above, are important since these impact how change and adjustment to the stresses of globalization is likely to occur. Some central characteristics of the two unions' internal structures are listed below:

Table 4-4: TWU and STRM—Internal Structure[30]

	TWU	STRM
No. of sections/locals	43 locals	131 sections
Structure of locals/sections	Regional, but often also occupational	Regional, but Mexico City subdivided by work site
Members in largest city	66% (Vancouver)	37% (Mexico City)
Frequency of elections	Every 2 or 3 years[31]	Every 4 years
Form of elections	Parliamentary	Direct membership
Reelection permitted?	Yes, all offices	Secretary General only

From the above table, one can glance many key features of the two unions, not the least of which is the dominance of the Vancouver/Lower Mainland locals in the TWU and the Mexico City section (known as the *sección matriz*)[32] in the STRM. While both unions are formally structured on geographical lines, in reality occupational lines are more important. In the TWU, there are a few "combined" locals, but mostly plant, clerical, and traffic workers maintain separate locals. In the STRM, the main Mexico City section is subdivided into occupationally-based groups that vie for influence in union conventions and assemblies. Another important feature to note from the above table is that only the secretary general can be reelected in the STRM.[33] This is one factor that helps ensure secretary general dominance within the STRM central executive (Dubb 1992).

These mechanisms help explain how regular conflicts are handled, but major shifts in strategy need not occur by such formal mechanisms. Indeed, the STRM's history indicates that there are two ways that a major shift in strategy occurs: by rank-and-file work stoppage and by government imposition. Clearly, then, no mechanism of institutionalized change has been created. Elections in the STRM occur, but the electoral process is slanted to virtually guarantee the victory of the incumbents (Interview S-93-29). This is done by giving the slate backed by the incumbent secretary general, (including a certain number of opposition activists who are allowed entry to discourage the formation of a united opposition front), nearly a year-long period on union payroll to "train" them, prior to the holding of elections. Hernández Juárez has run the union's elections in this manner in 1983, 1988, 1992, and 1996, thus maintaining his control over the union.[34]

This method is distinct from the TWU, where changes generally occur through elections at union conventions. The TWU also has norms that encourage greater debate and discussion of minority viewpoints. Incumbents are regularly voted out of office, most recently at the TWU's 1995 Convention, when two incumbent members of union's 15-member executive council lost their posts (TWU 1995b).

However, the difference in internal decision-making is more than just the absence or presence of electoral democracy. Notably different is the form that participation within each union takes. While the TWU operates very democratically, it is mainly a democracy of activists. Election of representatives to union conventions is made at union local meetings at which the average attendance rate has fallen steadily since the early 1980s and is now below 10%; member contact, even with shop stewards, is limited. Since 1992, rank-and-file activism has begun to climb again, but is still relatively low.

In the STRM, on the other hand, member contact with shop stewards is high by necessity (due to the rules regarding receipt of benefits), union meetings occur on company time, and all members are eligible to vote directly in elections. In 1992, for instance, turn-out for electing the union executive council was roughly 70%. This tendency to periodically mobilize the membership, albeit in a controlled-PRIista fashion, does raise union member consciousness and may enable the union to respond to shop floor member concerns better than the TWU leadership which, although in better touch with union activists, is not necessarily better tuned in to member concerns. At the same time, however, the controlled atmosphere of the STRM has lead to member cynicism regarding overall union strategy (Interview S-94-25).

The TWU's democratic traditions would seem to place it in a better position to have an open discussion about strategy, but it will need to substantially increase membership participation if this is to occur. With a limited level of participation, inertia and a reluctance to try new tactics tend to predominate. Until and unless a major strike or lock-out occurs or the union undergoes structural change, it is likely the TWU will continue to muddle through, seeking to maintain a social unionist strategy as a single-employer union, with minor moves to organize other companies and to work with the NDP to push for some maintenance of social commitments in telecommunication policies.

The STRM's anti-democratic tradition, on the other hand, is a definite handicap. However, the STRM's high level of membership participation means that, should the STRM confront a logjam, a rank-and-file uprising like that of 1976 is not impossible. In the meantime, though, one should expect the STRM to continue to follow its current path of cooperation with the company to improve productivity in exchange for continued—relative to average Mexican levels—high wages and benefits. In the chapters that follow, I shall seek to document how the two unions have responded to key aspects of globalization—namely, technological change, changes in the organization of work, and changes in state policy—and evaluate their efforts to respond, analyzing the effects of these changes on specific occupational sectors and on overall union tactics and strategy.

PLAN OF EMPIRICAL CHAPTERS

The empirical work is divided into four main chapters. The first three examine specific issue areas while the last empirical chapter provides a more general analysis of the cases. By looking at the empirical evidence, the importance of internal union decision-making becomes clear. As well, the empirical chapters provide a detailed account of the dynamics of internal union political decision-making as it applies to workplace issues. Though globalization does compel a union response, the range of union response on most issues is substantial. While the state labor regime can play an important role in some circumstances, more often the differences encountered in responses of the two unions can be better explained by examining internal union political factors.

In Chapter 5, technological change is examined, focusing on two groups of workers in particular—operators and inside plant workers (also known as "technicians"). Here, both internal ideological and occupational divisions are important. In the TWU, the leadership's base of support is based largely on inside plant crafts, such as technical workers, while the STRM leadership relies more heavily on the operators. As a result, the TWU has gone to extraordinary lengths to protect technicians. By contrast, the efforts made on behalf of operators, though not insubstantial, were less intense. With the STRM, the reverse is the case. Indeed, because technicians were aligned with opposition activists, the STRM union leadership took a hostile attitude to technicians, which contrasts greatly to the efforts made by union leaders a decade later to work to accommodate operators' demands regarding the modernization of operator services.

Chapter 6 addresses the issue of work reorganization, splitting the topic into an analysis of issues regarding the shifting of work *among* different parts of the company with the issue of reorganizing *within* specific parts of the company. Regarding the former, unions have a limited ability to act, beyond preserving their members' employment in the company. Both unions have had to centralize operations simply to cope with the pace of these changes. Here, then, is an area where globalization does seem to demand a significant level of union accommodation, regardless of state labor regime or factors internal to the union. Interestingly though, because the shifting of work involves the breaking down of traditional work boundaries, such shifts can be expected to have substantial impacts on internal union politics. For instance, the need to transfer plant workers into clerical and operator positions in the TWU in the early 1980s permanently altered the relations among plant workers, clerical workers, and operators in that union. Still, such changes are the unintended consequence of union attempts to cope with the shifting boundaries of work functions and not an intentional union strategy to promote its members' welfare.

On the issue of altering work within a specific part of the company, however, the TWU and the STRM provide a stark contrast, as the STRM has sought to participate to the hilt in cooperation programs, while the TWU has gone farther in resisting such programs than any other North American communications union. So far at least, the TWU, by sticking to "traditional, confrontational unionism" has preserved more members' jobs. Contrary to the conventional wisdom, such a strategy has not been inconsistent with the company's ability to maintain profitable operations.

Relations among unions, political parties, and the state are the focus of Chapter 7. As covered both here and in Chapter 3, much has been written about the exceptional nature of Mexican state-labor relations. This exceptionalism has always been greatly overstated, but even the differences that did exist have decreased during the past two decades. In part, this is true because over the past two decades the state and political parties in Canada have taken a more interventionist role (Panitch and Swartz 1993). On the other hand, in Mexico, direct intervention by the state in collective bargaining has declined, while the state's role as a regulator of the industry, always key in Canada, has become more important. As a result, the differences between the way the Canadian state and the Mexican state relate to telecommunications unions, have declined, although they have hardly been eliminated. Despite this partial convergence, the TWU and the STRM approach the state quite differently, with the STRM taking a highly cooperative path with the so-called *técnico* group in the Mexican government (not to be confused with STRM technicians), supporting the privatization of the company, while the TWU has openly resisted state regulatory policy initiatives on repeated occasions.

Finally, Chapter 8 assesses how the two unions respond to the sum of these changes in technology, work organization, and state regulation that stem from the phenomenon of globalization. To date, both unions have sought to incrementally adjust their tactics and strategy within their overall philosophical visions—social unionism for the TWU, a focus on bread-and-butter unionism within the framework of the old labor-PRI "alliance" for the STRM. This incremental response is not surprising and it illustrates that rather than all unions responding to the phenomenon of globalization in the same way, one can expect different unions to react differently according to which occupational sectors are most strongly represented in the union executive, the overall philosophy and history of the union, and the union's internal decision-making structure. Moreover, as a brief analysis of the social unionist SME (Sindicato Mexicano de Electricistas) in Mexico and the more bread-and-butter unionism of the CEP (Communications, Energy & Paperworkers) union in Canada demonstrate, these differences in union strategy tend to be tied to internal factors, rather than being a direct response to prevailing trends in the national labor regime.

Despite the unions' differences, however, in reviewing their responses to the issues they are currently facing, one is struck by how much globalization has affected these two unions. The issues globalization raises may be solved by further incremental adjustment, but it seems likely that more substantial changes will be required. Because the unions' strategic orientations are different, they define the problems that globalization poses differently as well. By looking at the ways the TWU and the STRM are seeking to confront globalization, this chapter attempts to provide an explanation of how the options available to unions pursuing a social unionist strategy are different than those available to unions pursuing a more "bread-and-butter" form of unionism. While the bread-and-butter union may opt for a cooperation program tying productivity gains to wage gains, a social union will need to work to build more comprehensive counter-market strategies, through such tactics as community coalition-building, joint bargaining with other unions (including possible mergers), and/or aggressive organizing. Thus, while globalization does not demand that all unions respond the same way, it does demand that they respond. This chapter, then, seeks to outline in detail what some of these different possible responses might entail.

NOTES

1. In doing so, the actions of BC Tel management were similar to those initiated by AT&T management after it had successfully blocked IBEW organizing efforts in the United States. See Vallas 1993: 58-65.

2. These wartime labor measures were later consolidated by the passage by the Canadian Parliament in 1948 of the Industrial Relations and Dispute Investigation Act (Carter and McIntosh 1990: 33).

3. Indeed, more moderate proposals to give occupational sectors more autonomy are almost routine. For instance, in December 1994, a joint plant and clerical local (but plant-dominated) in Vancouver proposed, among other measures, "Allowing the contract to be ratified only if a majority in each division (Plant, Clerical and Operator Service) vote in favor of it" (Parizeau and de Pencier 1994).

4. Until 1972, when the Communications Workers of Canada was formed, the CWA, in addition to its U.S. members, represented Canadian telephone workers at SaskTel.

5. Competition in telephony was widespread in some areas, particularly in larger U.S. cities at the turn of the century. See, for instance, Shiver 1995 and

Baur 1995. However, by the end of World War I, the regulated monopoly or state-owned telephone company had become the norm in almost every country, Mexico being a rare exception.

6. The French multinational Alcatel bought out ITT's Mexican operations in the early 1980s and thus took over its half of the Mexican telecommunications switching equipment market.

7. Initially, 51.24% of the shares in Telmex were held by ITT (which had owned Mexicana), 48.75 by Ericsson and 0.05 percent by 3 Mexican shareholders (Székely and del Palacio 1995: 46); however, the Mexican government initiated a process of "Mexicanization," so that, by 1958, all shares were Mexican held (with a minority held by the government, until 1972 when the Mexican government obtained a majority of the shares). Both IT&T and Ericsson remained the primary suppliers of telecommunications equipment for Telmex for decades. When the French company Alcatel bought IT&T in the early 1980s, it became, alongside Ericsson, the other primary supplier of digitalized exchanges for Telmex. Since Telmex was privatized in 1990, it has begun to diversify its supplier base, purchasing operator stations from the Canadian firm Northern Telecom and purchasing some digital switches from AT&T. See, for instance, Petrazzini 1995.

8. The STRM also signed a solidarity pact with the SME in 1960, a pact that would be restored in 1978, but that in practice has been of limited effectiveness, as neither union has ever followed through on the pledge contained in the pact to carry out a sympathy strike on behalf of the other; less dramatic sympathy actions, such as demonstrations, have taken place occasionally (Martínez 1988: 150-152).

9. Avecia didn't run for re-election, since one of the new union bylaws inserted by the Ericsson group prohibited reelection. Avecia's action contrasts with that of Hernández Juárez in 1978 who, when faced with a similar obstacle in the union bylaws, pushed through an exception to the bylaws to enable him to run for reelection.

10. (Membership figures are from Martínez de Ita et al. 1982: 28; monetary amount is from Martínez 1988: 174).

11. Shop stewards and counsellors are terms used for local union representatives in the Canadian TWU. (In many U.S. and Canadian unions, the term "chief shop steward" is used instead of counsellor). In the STRM, a local union representative is called a *delegado departmental* (department delegate). The functions of department delegates vary, with some performing functions more similar to TWU shop stewards and others, generally with more union experience, acting in more of a counsellor role. Throughout this work, I use the

terms shop stewards and/or counsellors to refer to local union representatives, whether they are from the TWU or the STRM.

12. This isn't always the case. In Mexico, there are a few sectors that are governed by sectoral bargaining arrangements, known as contract-law (*contrato-ley*). In Canada, there are some moves toward sectoral bargaining, but so far these have been modest.

13. In Canada, unlike Mexico, most unions fall under provincial, not federal, jurisdiction. However, telecommunications is an exception to this rule in Canada, and most telecommunications workers, except those working for provincially-owned telephone companies, fall under federal jurisdiction. Thus, the governing labor code for the workers at BC Tel represented by the TWU is the Canada Labour Code, not the more labor-friendly British Columbia Labour Code.

14 The hiring hall is not unheard of in Canadian labor (and indeed was present in the telephone industry itself prior to the 1920s), but currently exists in a few sectors, primarily among construction and dock workers.

15. Part of the 1989 negotiations involving the *convenio de concertación* signed by the union, the government, and Telmex management was an implicit "no hire, no fire" agreement (Interview S-94-27). As a result, hirings made since then have been exceptional and the waiting list has become much longer than it previously was.

16. From 1965 to 1992, there have been a total of 105 back-to-work measures passed by federal and state parliaments in Canada, an average of 3.75 bills a year (Panitch and Swartz 1993: 81).

17. Perhaps I should say *quasi-legally* here. If one took the Mexican Labor Code at its word, of course, then certifications should be granted more or less automatically, provided the requisite number of workers have agreed they want to unionize, and strikes should be recognized if the workers' cause is "just." Not only does such vagueness leave plenty of room for state officials to find a given strike "unjust," but in fact consideration of justice is hardly an important factor in the decision of whether or not a strike petition is granted. Rather, political considerations are far more important.

18. Though not discussed here, illegality on the management side is at least as common, throughout North America. In the United States, for instance, according to the U.S. Department of Labor, over 11,000 workers were illegally fired in 1990 for participating in union organizing efforts (Díaz 1994).

19. The Canadian Union of Postal Workers (CUPW), in particular, has been forced to confront such hard-line Canadian government actions on repeated occasions in the 1970s and 1980s. In 1978, CUPW leader Jean Claude Parrot was jailed for three months for refusing to order postal workers back to work.

This created a wave of sympathy, so subsequent government actions against the union have aimed penalties at individual shop stewards and union counsellors. See Drache and Glasbeek 1992: 184-188.

20. Degree of centralization refers to where most labor negotiations take place. A labor system in which most negotiations take place at the level of the entire economy is highly centralized; a labor system in which most negotiations take place at the level of an individual business is highly decentralized.

State intervention refers to the degree to which the state plays a determining role in negotiation outcomes. A system in which the state acts to directly determine outcomes is highly interventionist, a system in which the state intervenes in only exceptional circumstances has a low degree of intervention.

Labor concentration refers to the degree to which union members are concentrated in a single union or are dispersed in many unions. A system in which all union members belonged to a single union would be completely concentrated; a system in which all unionized workers belonged to plant or company-specific unions would be very highly decentralized. In Canada, labor concentration is currently rising, but it is still low compared to other large industrial economies.

21. Though I shall not cover such unions in detail, there are also employer-controlled unions known as *sindicatos blancos* (literally, white unions, though "rat unions" would be a more apt translation), especially in the Monterrey region. Such unions often "represent" workers without the workers even being aware that a union exists (de la Garza 1992).

22. It is, of course, frequently the case that union leaders in Mexico pursue benefits for themselves (seats in Congress, perks, etc.) with more vigor than they pursue benefits for the membership. Such corruption has made most Mexican union members very cynical about the union movement. However, a corruption-free corporatist union is at least theoretically possible. The key factor behind a corporatist union is not its corruption, but rather the manner in which it negotiates with state officials. See de la Garza 1993.

23. When the Ruta-100 Mexico City union was discovered to be supporting groups favorable to the Zapatista rebel cause in Chiapas in 1995, for instance, the Mexican government declared the entire bus company bankrupt as a way to deprive all union members of their jobs.

24. STRM figures are calculated from STRM 1994a, which lists the number of workers for each job specialty and Telmex and STRM 1993a which groups the job specialties into the five categories listed above. TWU figures are from TWU 1984a and TWU 1991a.

25. Under the Telmex-STRM productivity program, many types of transmission workers are clumped together with technicians. Defining technicians more narrowly as switch maintenance workers (centrales mantenimiento) would result in the technician figure dropping to roughly 8%, as reported in Jeremy et al. 1991.

26. There are 350 positions known as *vacantes*. These are essentially "floater" positions, to fill in for workers who are on vacation or on leave.

27. Similar occupational divisions also appear to show up as a cleavage in union politics in the CWA (Communication Workers of America). See Keefe and Boroff 1994: 42.

28. For instance, in the TWU, union locals on Vancouver Island (where Victoria, the provincial capital, is located, but not Vancouver) tend to be more militant (Interview T-94-82). This is especially the case in Nanaimo, a city on Vancouver Island with a long history of labor militancy (Bernard 1982). In the STRM, many large urban centers outside Mexico City have generally been supportive of opposition movements, especially Monterrey, Guaymas, Puebla, Hermosillo, Guadalajara, Jalapa and Veracruz (Interview S-94-8).

29. Interestingly, an outbreak of militancy among Australian technicians also occured in the late 1970s, a trend also evident among Australian telecommunications workers at the same time (Dreery 1989: 284, Matthews 1987: 142, Davis and Lansbury 1989: 112, Reinecke and Schultz 1983, Reinecke 1985, Davis 1993). More recently, similar issues have also been the cause of workplace disputes in Japan (Wada 1993). To some extent, the attempts of technicians to interject their unions into the arena of technological change parallel developments among craft workers who were facing deskilling at the hands of improved machinery and Taylorization at the turn of the century. For an analysis of U.S. and British engineers and machinists during this period, see Haydu 1988.

30. For data, on the geographic distribution of union membership in Mexico, see STRM 1994a. For data on number of sections, see STRM 1990. For TWU data on these matters, see TWU 1994c. Vancouver percentage includes entire Vancouver metro area (Lower Mainland), including Abbottsford, North Vancouver, Burnaby, and New Westminster.

31. President, Vice President, and Secretary-Treasurer "table officer" positions have 3-year terms. All 12 other executive council positions (Business Agents) have 2-year terms.

32. The word *matriz* literally means "womb," but is commonly used as a term for headquarters or head office.

33. Formally, no officer can be re-elected. However, there has always been an exception made. When the time comes to elect a slate for the next 4-year

term, there is always "a union sister that says, 'We propose that Brother Francisco Hernández Juárez return [for another term]'. The process—very manipulated if you like—serves Hernández Juárez perfectly" (Interview S-94-9).

34. Hernández Juárez explained this procedure in a 1987 newspaper interview. "Next year we have to hold elections in the union and here it is customary that a year-and-a-half early a slate of the workers themselves on a national level is organized. They are named so that they can participate and as it is the slate the workers support, it is the one that has the greatest likelihood of winning; then they are trained for 6 months to a year so they may now [before the elections] participate in leadership positions, such as negotiations or union and political activities, so that as soon as they win the elections they will have sufficient experience and preparation to ensure they don't enter green" (Hernández Juárez quoted in Guzmán G. 1987a).

CHAPTER FIVE

Union Politics and Technological Change

Technological change encompasses a broad range of issues concerning the techniques of production. As defined herein, technology refers to both the physical machinery of production (e.g., the computer equipment responsible for the routing of telephone calls) and the organization of production (e.g, work teams, Taylorist production, etc.). While the correspondence between the two is not always direct, a change in machinery often does result in a corresponding adjustment in workplace organization.

Generally, a union responds to changes in the machinery of production in a reactive manner. That is, management moves first, introducing the technological change, or at best presents to the union its plans for technological change. This is even true in countries where codetermination gives unions (or works councils) greater rights with respect to technological innovation (Turner 1991). Even when, because of legal or contractual restrictions, there is prior notice of the change, the ability of the union to impede the introduction of new technology is often quite limited. As one TWU counsellor put it, "The company steers the ship, drives the bus—the best we can hope for is to tilt the wheel a bit" (Interview T-93-10).

In examining the issues of the role of occupational divisions and a union's overall strategic orientation in union decision-making in the telecommunications industry, two specific technological changes merit special attention. One is the period of initial implementation of digital switching technology, which occurred in both Mexico and British Columbia in the late seventies. The other is the computerization of operator stations, which occurred in British Columbia in the first half of the eighties and in Mexico in the first half of the nineties. While there are other important cases of technological change, these two changes affect a large number of telephone workers and the technologies involved have now been fully implemented in both countries. This contrasts with other technologies in which the Mexican telephone company remains behind its Canadian counterpart.

How the two unions have approached the challenges posed by the substitution of one set of machines for another is, as indicated in the previous chapter, influenced strongly by the institutional histories of the two unions. At the same time, however, the political problems that arise due to technological change can occasionally result in shifts in union strategy. This in particular turned out to be the case with the issue of the digitalization of switching equipment. Digitalization was the first of a wave of technological changes to hit the telecommunications industry. Because the impact of the digitalization of the switching equipment was so great on both the industry and telephone workers, the two unions' overall strategies came into question. Though both unions had fairly conservative histories, the 1970s were marked by heightened labor-management conflict, and internal union conflict as well. Out of this dispute, there emerged in the TWU a strong social unionist philosophy which has continued to guide decision-making to this day. In the STRM, on the other hand, opposition currents—strongest amongst the technicians themselves—advocated an approach along the lines of Mexican "independent unionism;" these groups, however, were defeated and a more accommodating business unionist orientation triumphed.

The computerization of operating equipment occurred subsequently and demonstrates both the extents and limits of the impact of institutional history. While the STRM leadership here also sought accommodation with management, it was put under tremendous pressure in this case, since operators formed part of the union leadership's support base and it was operators whose jobs were at stake. Due to operator persistence and application of political pressure within the union, the operators were largely successful in obtaining the right to transfer into other departments, and no direct lay-offs of operators were carried out. Though the technological change resulted in a reduction in the number of operators from a peak of 13,000 in 1988 to 7,000 by the end of 1994, the loss of jobs was handled by a combination of attrition

(1,000), early retirement (500) and transfers (4,500). (See STRM 1993a, 1994b).

In the case of the TWU, consistent with the social unionist orientation that had emerged through the technician struggle, the union fought to maintain a larger number of operator work stations through community campaigns and arbitration cases designed to discourage the closure of offices in smaller cities. The union's efforts were, however, only partially successful. The company did, after 1986, halt the centralization of work stations (Interview T-94-80), but before this happened, many operators were "constructively laid off"—that is, given the option to transfer hundreds of miles away (which would often mean living apart from their families) or lose their jobs. Because of contractual gains made during the 1970s, B.C. operators overall did as well as their Mexican counterparts, but the 1980s were marked by more limited union achievements.

In looking at the cases of both the TWU and the STRM below, it is clear that alternative paths of accommodation and confrontation were available to union activists and union leaders. The decision to accommodate or confront management was not prescribed by economic or political conditions in either of the two countries, even though global economic pressures have came to play a larger role, especially in Mexico after the privatization in 1990. Moreover, while national labor laws and economic pressures do influence the manner in which unions cooperate or resist, whether the unions in fact do cooperate or resist appears to depend more on such factors as the union's overall strategic orientation and the occupational balance of power within the union.

THE DIGITALIZATION DILEMMA

Technologically, the concept of digitalization is rather simple. First, there is the change in equipment from electro-mechanical to computerized switching. With the electro-mechanical or step-by-step switching system, the call was extended step-by-step to the desired line under direct control of pulses which emanated from the customer's dial or from a central office pulse emitter (Bolton and Chaykowski 1990: 4). Electro-mechanical switching required frequent maintenance, since there were physical jumper cables that handled all of the telephone traffic. These cables would frequently wear out and much of the technicians' work involved locating faults and then replacing the faulty cable.

Digital technology, by contrast, requires very little maintenance, since it has both electronic control (allowing for "touch tone" dialing, instead of the emitting of dial pulses) and an electronic network, meaning that there were circuits connecting the different nodes of the switch, rather than jumper cables (Bolton and Chaykowski, 1990: 5; see also Rueda 1986).[1] Digital technology divides technician work into two types of jobs: highly-skilled workers who work on computers terminals and unskilled card-changers. With card changing, the technician, rather than fixing the fault, simply removes the faulty electronic "card" when a light is lit indicating that the card is faulty, and plugs in a new card. As Elaine Bernard writes, the digital switches "did not need the same routine of maintenance as the old electro-mechanical step-by-step equipment. Much of the central office craft job of troubleshooting, switch repairs and maintenance became a matter of 'card pulling'. The diagnoses of troubles now amounted to identifying and replacing individual cards containing the malfunctioning integrated circuits" (Bernard 1982: 155). Given that technicians are situated at the heart of the central nervous system of the telephone network, it was to be expected that a change of this magnitude would not come without conflict. In fact, conflict marked the digitalization of the switching network in both Mexico and British Columbia.

A second change relating to digitalization was in the transmission of the telephone signal from the residence or business site to this central switching system. In the sixties, this transmission was by means of copper cabling. By the late sixties in Canada and in the seventies in Mexico, this cabling began to be upgraded by a new transmission technique known as pulse-code modulation (PCM). This is a system where 24 channels or conservations can be placed on one pair of wires (FTW 1972: 9). In the eighties, further technological change resulted in the introduction of fibre optic cabling which increases transmission capacity, while simultaneously reducing outside plant maintenance costs.

From an efficiency standpoint, the reasons for digitalization of the telephone equipment were clear. As stated in an internal Telmex memo circulated in 1979 (see Solís Granados 1992a: 110-112), among the benefits of digitalization, it was expected that there would be a 30% decrease in the amount of investment required for switch installation, lower operating costs, as well as the possibility of offering additional services (such as call-waiting), better sound quality, greater capacity per switch, and reduced time for switch construction. Neither the

Mexican union nor the British Columbian union opposed the change-over of technology per se; however, in both cases, technicians feared for their jobs and wanted protections.

The difference in the technologies was substantial. Analog, semi-electronic exchanges serve up to 10,000 lines and require eight full-time employees to service. By comparison, digital equipment requires only two people to operate one exchange serving as many as 100,000 lines. In both Mexico and British Columbia, workers feared the worst. According to a TWU presentation in 1983, the digitalization technology was expected to result in a reduction of central office maintenance jobs from 900 to 200 and, when combined with the introduction of computer technology throughout the company, threatened to lead to a reduction of the entire unionized telephone workforce from 12,000 to 5,600 by 1993 (TWU 1983a). Though no estimates as specific as these were made in Mexico, similar fears prevailed, especially among the technicians whose work would be directly affected.

Not surprisingly, corporate management often plays on these fears. As one worker notes, in Mexico "The company treats it [new technology] as if it were a black box [secret]" (Interview S-94-5). Often, the actual impact on jobs of the technological change is less dramatic than is initially expected—both because of the creation of new jobs and because the new equipment is never as "trouble-free" as advertised. In the case of the TWU, instead of having 5,600 members in 1993, as it had feared, it had over 11,000. The number of central office maintenance workers also fell less rapidly than feared. As of 1991, there were still 584 workers classified as central office maintenance workers, and numbers have only fallen slightly since (TWU 1991a). Of course, the 40% decline in central office maintenance workers that did occur is far from insignificant. Moreover, the union (and the company as well, though management generally has greater access to information) must make policy decisions prospectively and does not have the benefit of hindsight when setting out its strategies. Thus, in both cases, the fear that prevailed had a major impact on union activists and their responses.

In neither case did union activists believe that halting the use of new technology was either desirable or possible. As TWU activist Linda Hebert put it at a regulatory hearing in 1980, "It is not the Union's purpose to stop technological change, but rather to ensure that our trades people are not put in the unemployment ranks because their particular job skills have been by-passed by technology" (Bernard

1982: 158). In essence, unions have three options available to achieve this goal:

1. *Expand union jurisdiction*: Seek the amalgamation of more management jobs into the bargaining unit, thereby expanding the jurisdiction of the union. A good measure of union success in this area is a low ratio of management to union employees.

2. *Reduce outsourcing*: Seek to limit the "out-sourcing" of work and to keep the amount of work done "in-house" as high as possible. Assuming comparable profitability and service levels, a high number of workers per 10,000 lines is a good measure of union success here.

3. *Retraining and lay-off protection*: Bargain for transfer rights to expanding sections of the company. Here, to measure union success, one needs to examine the strength of contractual provisions that oblige the company to retrain workers for other positions within the company and assess the strength of lay-off protection mechanisms.

If the union does not succeed in any of the above measures, the union can seek to cushion the impact of the change by agreeing to a reduction of the workforce in exchange for the augmentation of pension payments (early retirement incentives) or severance pay benefits, or use its temporary leverage during the uncertain period of the technological change to push for higher wages for the union membership as a whole. Both unions have pursued a combination of the above methods. But the TWU has placed greater emphasis on non-wage issues, while the STRM's emphasis has been more focused on wage increases.

At the center of this tactical debate, union activists have had to confront the digitalization dilemma. That is, the extent and complexity of the changes often results in a short-term increase in the amount of work and hence a temporary increase in worker leverage. But once the change-over is complete, worker leverage over the company is greatly reduced. The way both unions responded to this dilemma is set forth below.

DIGITALIZATION AND LABOR STRIFE IN BRITISH COLUMBIA

"Lately you may have noticed some tension between the phone company and its unionized employees. Relations between BC Tel and the TWU aren't quite as bad as those between Iran and Iraq; their tempers aren't quite as hot as Mount St. Helens."

Tom Barnet, *Vancouver Sun*, November 3, 1980

Relations between the telephone company and the telephone workers' union in British Columbia had slowly deteriorated in the sixties and early seventies, but the level of strife increased markedly in the mid-seventies, as the company's desire to unilaterally implement technological changes clashed with a union seeking to protect its members from the negative impact that such a unilateral imposition could cause. Central to the dispute was that the digitalization of the technology made it easier for management to shift work from some categories of workers to others. In one area, work contracting, the collective bargaining agreement provided a mechanism for the union to resist; here, the company pressed to have the restrictions on "out-sourcing" removed. On the other hand, the contract had very weak language defining jurisdictional lines, permitting the company to shift job functions from unionized workers to management employees; here, the union pressed for new language. In addition, the union fought for specific mechanisms that would give it a greater say over the implementation of technological change. In short, a range of disputes between BC Tel and the TWU centered over job control issues.

But there was more to these disputes than job control. At the heart of the conflict was the union's attempt to force the company to recognize that the era of paternalism had ended. In this respect, developments within the STRM were very similar during the same period. Subsequent to the confrontations of the late seventies and the early eighties, management's use of new technology not only did not stop, but actually accelerated. Yet militancy at the TWU subsided—as it did at the STRM as well. So any explanation of labor's response to technological change needs to take into account not only the initially militant response, but also the subsequent period of calm that followed. In part, the two unions followed national trends. The TWU's period of militancy coincided largely with that of the Canadian labor movement as a whole (the late sixties to early eighties). The STRM's period of militancy (1976-1982) came in at the tail end of the period of militancy of Mexican labor (1971-1976). Key in both cases was a change in the political balance of power in the two unions, which coincided with the beginning of a new wave of telecommunications technology.[2]

In the TWU, the rise of more militant leadership was a gradual process, with Bert Johns, who led what was the first strike at BC Tel in half a century (Bernard 1982: 132-151), being elected plant general secretary in 1963. In 1971, Bert Johns retired and Bill Clark was elected to replace him. At the time, it was already evident that developments of satellite and transistor technology were going to have a major effect on the industry. Under Clark and then Bob Donnelly, plant general secretary from 1973 to 1974 and union president from 1974 to 1980,[3] the union grew more militant. The ability of management to keep the telephone system running during the six-week long 1969 strike had alerted the TWU to the importance of automation, leading the union to press early on for protections for the membership regarding the pending wave of technological change. Union priorities were pensions, protection against out-sourcing, and protection from lay-offs due to technological change. As one former union official put it, "In 1971, we realized that we were going to have to negotiate pensions because early retirement was going to come and cost money. We were going to have to negotiate a new and modern contracting-out clause. We were going to have to negotiate a different type of lay-off clause for technological change" (Interview T-93-12). In June 1971 an automation committee was formed and in January 1972, the BC Tel plant workers accepted the automation committee's recommendations that the issues of contracting, employment security, and pension benefits be made union priorities (FTW 1972: 9). In the 1971 contract, the union had already gained the right to veto the company's contracting-out of work "regularly performed" by TWU union members and the stipulation that the work that was contracted-out had to be done by a union firm. In 1973, the TWU struck OK Telephone, a 100%-owned subsidiary of BC Tel that employed roughly 500 workers. Because the workers at OK Tel comprised about 5% of the total union membership, the union was able to pay high strike benefits and maintain those benefits more or less indefinitely (Bernard 1982: 147-151). After a five strike, the company agreed to set up a jointly-trusteed union pension fund at OK Tel. Once that benefit was won at OK Tel, it was added to the main contract with BC Tel as well. Shortly after the strike, OK Tel operations were consolidated with those of BC Tel. Also won in the 1975 contract at BC Tel was the union's right to receive 12-months notice regarding lay-offs that were due to technological change (Bernard 1982: 166, Schreiner 1977).

Because BC Tel was a regulated monopoly, which earned a very stable annual rate of return, it could afford to be generous. When pressed, BC Tel would generally, albeit very grudgingly, make concessions. But as the pace of technological change picked up, BC Tel came under pressure from other employers in the industry to roll back the contracting-out clause. This pressure came, in particular, from Bell Canada, whose operators and plant workers were unionized by the Communications Workers of Canada (CWC) in 1975 (CFCW 1975). Bell Canada feared that a similar clause might force it to substantially alter its operations and to cut back on its use of subcontracted work. Moreover, even in the mid-seventies, telephone companies were beginning to prepare for competition, at least in telephone sets and other "terminal equipment." In 1974, BC Tel began the long process of removing hard jacks and replacing them with plug-in jacks that would permit customers to install their own phones (Bernard 1982: 160). In a competitive environment, clearly, BC Tel could be at a disadvantage if it was compelled to pay higher wage rates due to strict contractual requirements to do work in-house, at union rates. At the same time, the TWU felt it needed to have protections, given the likelihood of accelerating technological change (Peitchinis 1983).

Throughout the sixties and early seventies, negotiations between BC Tel and the TWU frequently reached an impasse, but usually a government-appointed mediator would propose a settlement, which would be accepted by both sides (e.g., Ladner 1973, 1975). In 1977, however, when BC Tel and the TWU reached an impasse again, BC Tel refused to accept the "conciliation report" (Hall 1977) from the government labor ministry, and so the battle was on.[4]

In the TWU at the time, there were two key evenly-matched factions, which advocated somewhat different responses to the company's intransigence. Both were in full agreement with the need to resist the company's attempt to take away contracting-out provisions. But they had their tactical differences. Politics in the TWU has always been highly based on personalities, since almost all decisions of importance—except for strike votes, contract votes, dues increase votes, and constitution votes—are made via the parliamentary forum of union conventions. This means that 51 votes out of 100 are sufficient to be elected president of the union. Bob Donnelly worked in BC Tel as a private branch exchange (PBX) maintenance worker and then for a few years as a technician before taking full-time union office; the work involved maintaining and repairing local switchboards that private companies with multiple lines operated (Bernard 1982: 175).[5] Bill Clark was a lineman prior to taking a full-time union position (Bernard 1982: 145). But it was Donnelly whose main base of support came from what might be considered the more "blue collar" professions— that is, union delegates who were maintenance workers, cable splicers, construction workers, and some operators (whose positions are by far the most factory-like of all telephone work). Clark's base of support, on the other hand, came from those in more "white collar" professions, such as sales (part of the clerical division), installation & repair, and technicians.

In addition to their different occupational bases of support, there were ideological differences. These were reflected in the priorities they placed on bargaining issues: Donnelly was more of a militant, "business unionist," more than willing to lead a strike, but focusing primarily on preserving the contract's contracting-out language and aiming for high wages and benefits, particularly for plant workers. Clark was more of a negotiator than Donnelly, but also more of an innovator. A self-defined "socialist trade unionist" (Clark 1984), Clark followed more closely a "social unionist" philosophy. In terms of technological change issues, one key goal was to create new contract language that would protect work jurisdiction. In particular, union activists feared that union members in high wage positions, such as technicians and salespeople, were at risk of having their jobs converting into management positions. Other social unionist goals pursued by Clark included the pursuit of employment security and the creation of a jointly-trusteed pension fund.

When faced with the company's rejection of the government's conciliation offer in June 1977, the TWU held a strike vote and obtained 73% support. On September 20, the union began a work-to-rule campaign. The next day, all Vancouver-area construction workers drove their trucks downtown, circling the downtown BC Tel building for half an hour and creating a major traffic snarl at rush hour. Further union tactics involved rotating work stoppages and mass picketing of key company worksites. Management responded by initiating selective lock-outs. By mid-October, more than 20% of all workers had been locked out. On November 24, the union called all the remaining workers out, initiating a full-scale strike. Management responded by declaring that these workers were not welcome back, thereby locking them out. The company then proceeded to operate with management employees.[6] The union responded with the further use of mass picketing and "flying picket" squads, in which picket lines would be dispatched to shut down another company's operations whenever a BC Tel supervisor entered that company's premises to do telephone repair work. Ferry depots were often shut down this way, as the ferry workers would honor the TWU's pickets. BC Tel management and the management of the picketed companies would respond by seeking court injunctions against the picketing (Bernard 1982: 173-192, Schreiner 1977, Canada notes: Misc 1).

After further government mediation, a tentative agreement was reached in early February (Hutcheon 1978). The union maintained most of its contracting-out protection, but instead of having a quick resolution procedure in which a single arbitrator was required to render a decision on complaints within 72 hours, a joint contracting-out committee with a neutral umpire was established. In exchange, the union got a guarantee that employees with more than two years' seniority could not be laid off due to technological change. The scope of the contracting-out committee was extended to include the authority to discuss, but not to resolve, issues arising from technological change. As a result, the committee was named the Contracting Out and Technological Change Committee. The bitter strike/lock-out ended on a sour note a few days later, when management rescinded its demand that each striker sign an individual interim agreement promising good behavior before coming back to work. Management dropped its insistence on this point only after the union threatened to return to work *en masse* without an agreement. On February 13, 1978, the dispute finally came to a conclusion, 81 days after the full-scale strike/lock-out had begun. But few thought the new collective bargaining agreement was anything more than a truce. Sure enough, the next round of bargaining saw both sides escalate their tactics to try to gain the upper hand in the conflict over technological change (Bernard 1982: 182-191).

Though the union's actions had the support of most members, this is not to say that the winter strike and lock-out, and mass picketing in the face of a cold British Columbia winter was highly popular. As one rank-and-filer recalled, "It was bad, really bad. Freezing cold. It was really exceptionally cold in 1977-78. It was horrible . . . But I think most people knew that we had to do something. We couldn't just lie down and play dead" (Interview T-93-4). Morale was low as a result of the costliness of the strike, as well as the knowledge that more strife was on its way. As President Donnelly said when addressing the TWU's June 1978 Convention, "It has now been five months since we successfully concluded the most bitter battle in the history of our union. Never in the past were we faced with the vicious attack on the major provisions of our Collective Agreement as we just experienced and I do not consider it unwarranted pessimism to conclude that we will have to fight similar battles in the future" (TWU 1978). By the time of the June 1979 Convention, the union was already preparing for what it was convinced would be another dispute of similar magnitude. Though bargaining had yet to reach an impasse, further preparations for the upcoming dispute were made at the January 1980 Convention, including the appointment of leaders of local tactical zone committees (TWU 1979, 1980a).

At the June 1980 convention, Bill Clark challenged Bob Donnelly for the presidency of the union, prevailing by a narrow margin (TWU 1980b).[7] One of the key issues at the time was work jurisdiction, "especially over whether analysts (technicians) would be management or bargaining unit positions" (Interview T-93-12).[8] In August 1980, Ed Peck, a government conciliator, presented his recommendation for a settlement; the company accepted 69 recommendations, but rejected 4 key items concerning accumulated time off, wages, work jurisdiction, and scheduling rights for out-of-town work assignments by union shop committees in the plant division. The union voted to accept the Peck report in its entirety by a 91% margin in September (Peck 1980, TWU 1980c). Mindful of the difficulty of striking in an industry as highly automated as telephony, especially given the fact that more than 20% of all company employees occupied management positions, the union turned to slowdown tactics (which it called "super service") and to selectively striking areas of the company that served large business customers. The selective strike of 530 workers began on September 22. As luck (and a bit of poor planning on BC Tel management's part) would have it, a hearing on the company's application for a rate increase began September 30. The union intervened in the hearings, arguing that any rate increase should be contingent on improvements in service quality. Tactically, the union sought to drag out the hearings as long as possible, as the union felt locking out workers likely would hurt the chances that the CRTC, Canada's federal telecommunications regulatory body, would grant BC Tel's request for a rate hike. So the union used the period of the hearings to attack the company through the selective strike, while being temporarily shielded from management counter-attack (Interview T-93-1, Bernard 1982: 196-199). As well, the hearing provided a forum for the union to publicly air its side of the story (Hiebert et al. 1980), generating support among consumer groups (Roman 1980) and in the press (Persky 1980, Stacey 1981).

The selective strike "produced a significant backlog in construction and switchboard installation and repair" (Bernard 1982: 199). But it was not terribly popular with the membership. As one union executive council member of the time remarked, "There was a lot of rank-and-file dissention. They viewed this [the selective strike] as a division . . . they thought we should all be out together" (Interview T-93-12). The 530 who were out on strike were to be paid 70% of wages, funded by a collection of $13 per member per week of the rest of the membership. But 40% refused to pay (TWU 1981a). One illustration of the level of members' frustration with the lack of a settlement occurred on October 19, 1980, when two linemen barricaded themselves into rooms containing electronic telephone switching equipment and threatened to sabotage the equipment by throwing water on it, unless a settlement was reached. Eventually, with the help of a local radio broadcaster, an amnesty agreement was reached for the two linemen in exchange for an agreement that they stay out of the building for the duration of the dispute (Bernard 1982: 200).

On December 4, the CRTC hearing concluded. BC Tel management began to fight back, suspending over 1,000 workers for wearing buttons calling for the nationalization of the phone company. In January 1981, BC Tel initiated a policy of selective lock-outs, sending home over 1,000 more employees by the end of the month. On January 29, BC Tel was granted the full amount of the rate increase it had requested, though the CRTC did issue a warning that it would take action if service levels did not improve by the end of the year (TWU 1981b).

The union responded by occupying the telephone facilities in Nanaimo, on the east coast of Vancouver Island, on February 3. The occupation was extended to the entire province two days later (TWU 1981c). Telephone workers continued to provide operator and clerical services to the public, while supervisors were relegated to the ground floor of the buildings, with most choosing to go home. This action was highly popular with the membership (Interview T-93-12) and received considerable public support. In part, this was because of the impact of the TWU's airing of the company's dirty laundry at the CRTC regulatory hearings the previous fall; in part, this was because management had rejected a government settlement offer which the union had accepted; and in part because of positive press coverage of similar occupations being carried out by the Polish trade union Solidarity at the same time (Bernard 1982: 214). But when BC Tel management filed a complaint in Court, claiming that the occupation was a violation of a previous Court injunction prohibiting sit-ins on company property, the Court was not impressed by the union's counter-arguments. Indeed, the judge of the case wrote in his order to vacate company premises that "a more blatant affront to the authority of this Court, the law, and the basic principles of an ordered society would be difficult to imagine" (Bernard 1982: 215-216). Faced with the likelihood of jail sentences for union executive officers for further defiance of the Court order, the union vacated the premises on February 10, making sure that police officers and journalists toured the buildings first to verify that there had been no damage to company property.[9]

The conflict took further bizarre twists and turns before a final resolution was reached. When a new federal mediator tried to mediate a settlement, the company demanded a further rate increase in exchange for acceding to the union's demands. This caused management to lose whatever remaining public support it had. On March 2, a tentative agreement was reached, with compromises worked out on scheduling, jurisdiction, and wages, and with the union receiving the increase it had sought in accumulated time off days. But management wanted the union to agree to the dismissal of 24 of the striking workers, alleged by management to have engaged in misconduct during the strike, as a condition of signing an agreement. Instead, the TWU appealed to the BC Federation of Labor, which organized a one-day general strike in the city of Nanaimo on March 6 and threatened similar regional one-day general strikes elsewhere in British Columbia every two weeks until there was a successful resolution to the dispute. Finally, on March 14, a back to work agreement was reached, stipulating that the fate of the 24 employees would be decided by an arbitrator. The arbitrator decided in favor of the union three weeks later (Bernard 1982: 218-222, Hope 1981).

Shortly afterward, the parent company GTE decided that a change of approach was in order. As one union activist explained, "Within three or fourth months, four or five [prominent] managers plus the head of [industrial relations] were retired" (Interview T-93-12). As a result, more disputes were resolved by the formal contractual mechanism of the Contracting-Out and Technological Change (COTC) committee. Though conflict between management and the union would continue, the level of acrimony declined markedly.[10]

TELMEX: FROM BUSINESS PATERNALISM TO UNION-BUSINESS "COOPERATION"

> One has to understand that to transform a structure is not only administrative, it is social. It is cultural. It does not occur overnight. A business is a structure of social relations, relations of power. It is also a culture. Is this a unique case? No, the labor culture varies case by case. What is certain is that in the case of Telmex, there are certain characteristics that explain the complexity of the change.
>
> STRM advisor (Interview S-94-14)

> You always negotiate with the union. There is no change that one does without talking to the union. This is much more of a shared power environment than in the U.S. The union has a much stronger voice here than what the U.S. experiences.
>
> Southwestern Bell manager, Telmex (Interview S-94-33)

As the above statement from the STRM advisor makes clear, the process of change in the Mexican telephone workers' union has been unusually complicated. This has to do with the intensity of internal union political disputes, on the one hand, and the technological complexity of the telephone industry on the other. The intensity of the internal political battles has led both the leftist union opposition and the union leadership to cut deals with Telmex management in efforts to weaken their political opponents. The technological complexity of the industry has also had an enormous effect on STRM politics.

In particular, the technological complexity of telecommunications has had two key effects on the STRM that distinguish it from many other Mexican unions. First, in order for the union leadership to be effective in negotiations with management, it has had to develop at least a moderate level of technological competency; this need for technological competence provides a limited, but real, shield from Labor Ministry interference. Second, the need to monitor technological change at the shop floor has led to an increased role for shop stewards.

The efforts by the telephone workers' union leadership over the past two decades to contain and control shop stewards' actions are quite elaborate. But despite union leadership efforts to centralize decision-making power, the shop stewards retain considerable authority on workplace issues. And it is this factor, more than any other, that explains the continuing strength of the union that the Southwestern Bell manager found so unlike the situation in Southwestern Bell's U.S. operations.

In April 1976, a rank-and-file rebellion ousted the old *charro*[11] leadership of Salustio Salgado, which had been unconditionally supportive of the Mexican state. In its place there arose a new leadership comprised of both moderate PRI dissidents, led by the new secretary general of the union, Francisco Hernández Juárez, more radical activists from the PSUM (Partido Socialista Unido de México) and PRT (Partido Revolucionario de Trabajadores), as well as militant non-party ("independent") activists. The most important of the militant groups was Línea Democrática, an organization with a vaguely Maoist ideology, but not directly connected with any political party. Cooperation among the different militant groups was always tenuous, but despite differences the militants did manage to work together on a regular basis between 1976 and 1982.

Already, at the first convention held by the new leadership in July 1976, dissension emerged within the reformists' ranks between those advocating limited reforms and those seeking to lead the union in a more militant direction. The moderates, led by Hernández Juárez, sought to enact a series of limited reforms. These involved such things as regular reporting of information about union accounts and bargaining with the company, the right to speak out at union conventions regarding tactical issues, and greater autonomy from state officials in internal union activities. The militant faction sought more sweeping reforms, including regular biannual elections, the banning of reelection of top officers, and the separation of the union from the ruling PRI and the PRI-dominated Congreso de Trabajo (CT).[12] Another major plank in the militants' platform involved the formation of alliances with "independent" unions and movements—particularly, the Tendencia Democrática in the SUTERM (Sindicato Unico de Trabajadores Electricistas de la República de México), one of Mexico's two main electrical workers' unions—which were fighting for the democratization of the Mexican labor movement as a whole. While a compromise was reached at the first convention—in which the union pulled out of the PRI, but stayed in the CT—the battle lines were drawn.

The STRM's position regarding technological change has evolved over the years. First, the union opposition clamored for the leadership to champion the fight for protections against technological change, while the union leadership denied the problem, focusing instead on wage, benefit, and local workplace issues. After the union leadership successfully defeated the union opposition (in the process, denying union benefits and voting rights to thousands of union members) in 1982, the leadership began to develop a response to technological change. A third period ensued from 1985 to 1988, in which the union used a combination of work stoppages and top-level negotiations to try to gain greater protections regarding technological change for the union membership. Finally, in 1989, the government and company management counter-attacked, forcing the union to cede many of its recently-won rights and to yield on many other contractual clauses. These changes set the stage for a reduced, though not insignificant, union role in the introduction of new technology.

In the first six years of Hernández Juárez's tenure (1976-1982), most of the technology remained mechanical, but installation of computer technology began. Computerized technology was introduced in the form of digital switches for central telephone exchanges and as record-keeping devices for certain clerical functions (Interview S-94-8). While the introduction of computer equipment to carry out clerical functions was limited, the introduction of new switching equipment would have dramatic effects in Mexico, just as it had in Canada. Also, the role played by the technicians or *técnicos* was key. Though less numerous (roughly 10% of the union membership; 15% if one includes technical departments other than *centrales mantenimiento* or switch maintenance) than the operators (roughly 30%) or outside plant workers (roughly 40%), technicians played a central role in both of the union's political factions. The leader of the union, Hernández Juárez, was himself a former *técnico*, though he drew his political support from the more numerous outside plant and operator workers. The union's dissident movement was led by the *técnicos*, especially in Mexico City, where roughly half of all Mexican telephone workers were located. Much of the conflict between Hernández Juárez and the union dissidents was ideological in nature. But sectoral divisions between the *técnico*-dominated dissident coalition and the operator-dependent[13] leadership shaped both the debates over technological change and the course of the conflict between Hernández Juárez and the dissidents.

In this respect, it's important to note the difference between the four formal strikes that occurred between 1978 and 1980 and the internal[14] union conflict of 1982. The first wave of protests and strikes centered on three issues: 1) wages, 2) regulating working conditions, and 3) union relations vis a vis the government. Hernández Juárez and his allies sought to achieve a modus operandi with the PRI government and the labor establishment, forging especially close links with CTM (Confederación de Trabajadores Mexicanos) leader Fidel Velázquez. The STRM union opposition sought to build strong links with Mexico's fledgling "independent" movement and form alliances with opposition movements in the SUTERM (electricians) and other unions. The opposition tried to encourage strikes as a way to gain rank-and-file support and championed the wage and working conditions demands raised by those workers. Hernández Juárez and his supporters sought to settle the strikes as quickly as possible in order to sell workers on the idea that top-level negotiations—not rank-and-file, opposition-led, militant action—was the best path to improving wages and working conditions. In some areas, the opposition was successful in promoting its militant views, while in others Hernández Juárez and his supporters adopted rank-and-file demands as their own and thereby gained considerable support. This can be seen in the history of the four strike conflicts.

In April 1978, the STRM went on strike for the first time in 16 years. The government and telephone company management were taken by surprise.[15] Apparently, the union leadership had assured the government that the strike threat would be lifted, but the membership refused to go along (Martinez Lira 1986: 220-221). Service was cut off nationwide and remained off for 16 hours. In the end, the workers were unable to break the government-imposed salary cap, but they did get additional benefits, including an extra day of vacation and a year's reduction in the age required to retire with a full pension (Martinez Lira 1986: 224). This was the beginning of a pattern that has been followed by the STRM to this day, in which government wage and price guidelines are formally adhered to, but in which alternative mechanisms such as benefit increases, *retabulaciones* (wage increases for workers in specific departments) and, more recently, productivity bonuses, are deployed so that telephone workers receive benefits and increases beyond that which most Mexican workers, even in the unionized sector, are able to achieve.

Important in the settlement to the April 1978 strike was a commitment by the company to negotiate a *convenio departamental* (department-level work conditions agreement) with the operators, which would include a *retabulación*—or across-the-board wage increase—for all members of the operator division of the company. But management dragged its feet. As of March 1979, no resolution had been reached. The entire union then struck on the basis that the company had violated the provision of the 1978 Collective Agreement ensuring that a *convenio departamental* would be signed for the operators. The faction led by Hernández Juárez sought to delay strike action (Martinez de Ita 1982:146), but ultimately led the strike when it became clear that the patience of the operators had worn thin.

The strike was launched at 10 p.m. on March 12. Ten minutes after the strike began, government troops entered the telephone facilities and partial service was restored within two hours with the help of management personnel (Xelhuantzi López 1988: 105). But the strikers caught the public's imagination. Strikes over management's contract violations, though permitted in Mexico, are extremely rare. Furthermore, the show of solidarity displayed by 15,000 workers from other Telmex departments who struck in solidarity alongside the 9,000 operators was impressive.

After twenty-four hours, the strike was lifted, as the operators succeeded in forcing the company to honor its previous agreement (Xelhuantzi López 1988: 106). Though Hernández Juárez was a reluctant leader of this strike, the successful resolution of the dispute did much to consolidate his support among the operators. This base of support would prove key to his ability to overcome later challenges to his leadership.

A month later, the union struck again—this time over the annual salary revision. Again, the telephone facilities were occupied by troops in a *requisa*. This time, the strike continued for an entire week. With the strike still unsettled on May 1 (Labor Day), the telephone workers marched in the Mexico City Labor Day parade dressed in red and black. The following day, the strike was lifted. Telephone workers failed to break the government's wage and price controls, but did make some gains, such as the conversion of some temporary positions (*eventuales*) into permanent positions (*planta*) and an agreement by the company to enter into negotiations on the revision of three other department-level contracts. This ensured that there would be further *retabulaciones*, or wage increases that circumvent the government's wage and price controls (Martínez de Ita et al. 1982: 148-150).

The last of the four strikes occurred in April 1980. Again, the union leadership was opposed to going on strike, but acceded to rank-and-file pressure. The key issues were wages and pensions (Domínguez Cruz 1982: 120). In this confrontation, the government and Telmex management chose harsher tactics, bringing in troops to begin the *requisa* three hours *before* the scheduled strike outbreak and making active efforts to encourage telephone workers to become *esquirroles* (scabs). All told, 317 workers returned to work before the strike was lifted (Xelhuantzi López 1988: 135). While well under 2% of the total STRM membership, the number was high enough to cause significant disruption. The strike ended with minimal union gains. Hernández Juárez led the retreat, arguing that, "The retreats when they are obligatory due to the correlation of forces are achievements of the same importance as when we come out victorious" (Xelhuantzi López 1988: 137).

In addition to the conflicts with management, the period of 1976 to 1980 had been a period of intense internal union conflict. Major battles included the 1978 union convention decision to extend the term of Hernández Juárez and the union leadership for an additional two years and the application of the exclusion clause to 79 members of the leftist opposition in 1979 (Martínez Lira 1986: 259-260, Xelhuantzi López 1988: 113, Rangel Pérez 1989: 42). In 1979, Hernández Juárez also struck a deal with a Maoist group called Línea Proletaria (Workers' Line),[16] in which the group would support Hernández Juárez in exchange for his permitting the group's activists to enter the union and implement their own small assembly (*asambleas chicas*) model of political organization. This move allowed Hernández Juárez to gain more access to the shop floor and made sure his allies got credit for workplace gains, rather than the leftist dissidents. In 1980, Hernández Juárez broke his "no reelection" pledge and was returned to office in an election tainted with allegations of fraud. More than half of the members of the union's election commission resigned in protest (8 of 14), but Hernández Juárez and his allies had clear majority control over the union's convention which certified the election tally as valid (Martínez Lira 1986: 268). So it is possible that a clash similar to the one that occurred in 1982 might have taken place without the threat posed by technological change. But it is doubtful that dissidents would have been able to pull off a full-scale revolt, involving thousands of telephone workers protesting in the streets, if the rank-and-file hadn't felt threatened by the new technology and hadn't felt that the union's response to this threat was inadequate.

As one worker stated, "Beginning in 1980, we began to know the plans of the company regarding the new technology. We began to mobilize ourselves against the company's plans. This mobilization started to gain a lot of strength" (Interview S-90-15). By 1982, the movement had taken off, fueled by workers' desire, particularly among the inside plant workers whose jobs were most threatened, to negotiate with management regarding the new technology. As the digitalization of the switch technology became imminent, the political conflict became much more acute. This problem was exacerbated by management, which sought to remove union activists, particularly those who opposed Hernández Juárez, through mass dismissals. The problem is stated concisely below by one STRM opposition member:

> Management had already decided to modernize the telephone system. Here the company was faced with a problem ... There was an opposition, that, at least, responded ... They wanted to fire the entire opposition movement. They fired many union brothers and sisters, up to 500. The people became discontented. And the March 8th movement was born (Interview S-90-17).

While Hernández Juárez and his group had achieved a measure of support among the operators and among outside plant workers,[17] among inside plant workers, it was very clear that he did not enjoy a significant level of support. And it was these workers who were most directly impacted by the technological change. As one technician explained, "The company wanted to digitalize the entire telephone system. We did not oppose ourselves to this project. What we wanted is that they respect some gains we had made in working conditions, that they not weaken the union, and that this modernization benefit us, that we be trained" (Interview S-94-6). Throughout 1981, the *técnicos* led a series of slowdowns and other on-the-job actions to put pressure on the company to agree to a revision of their department work agreement (*convenio departmental*). In response, management began to fire workers. The technicians sought support from the central union office. But the leadership refused to back the workers, who were largely Línea Democrática supporters. As a result, "The movement became a political movement once again. It was accompanied by work stoppages. This time not all of the workers walked out, only a majority" (Interview S-90-15). On March 8, a work stoppage broke out, involving roughly half of the telephone workers. The union leadership abandoned its central Mexico City headquarters, which was occupied by union dissidents. When Hernández Juárez and roughly 2,000 of his supporters tried to reoccupy the building, they were repelled by an even greater number of dissidents.

Due to their conditions at work, technicians or *técnicos* were especially close-knit. As one *técnico* explains, "The work was difficult . . . that was a reason that required that the telephone worker be well paid, among other things. And one more thing, it required better maintenance of the workforce. This created conditions of sympathy and friendship and solidarity" (Interview S-94-6). But this close-knit nature also led to insularity, which made it difficult for technicians to gain the support of other sectors of the union, such as operators. Although technicians attempted to build an alliance with operators sympathetic to their cause, enough operator shop stewards stood by Hernández Juárez to frustrate these efforts. Other groups of inside plant workers, such as private switchboard workers and workers in the marketing and sales department (*comercial*), were also active in the movement. Not coincidentally, they were among the other groups to be most directly hit by the first wave of the new technology.

Dissidents also sought the support of outside plant workers, but such support was limited. While outside plant workers in some Mexico City compounds and some key large provincial (outside of Mexico City) sections, such as Puebla, Hermosillo, Guadalajara, Guaymas, Jalapa, Veracruz and Monterrey (Interview S-94-8) lent their support to the opposition movement, other outside plant workers workers either avoided involvement in the dispute or supported the union leadership. Also missing from the opposition movement was solid support from the Mexico City operators, who, due to the nature of their jobs, were at the nerve center of national communications. As one opposition activist said, "A grave error of ours was with the operators. When Juárez left the union building, he stayed with the operators in the work centers to obligate them to stay and we did not analyze the situation correctly. This permitted Juárez to spread the idea that it [the wildcat strike] was nothing more than a few crazies among the workers outside Mexico City . . . operators outside Mexico City always call Mexico City operators to find out if there is a work stoppage. They [Mexico City operators] answered and gave false information" (Interview S-94-25). This struggle is analyzed in detail elsewhere (Dubb 1992). But there are key aspects worth mentioning. First, it would appear that both the opposition and Hernández Juárez had cut "deals" with members of Telmex management and, in the case of Hernández Juárez, with state labor officials as well. Despite the wild cats, at no point did the company cut off dues payments to Hernández Juárez. The labor bureaucracy, especially Fidel Velázquez, strongly backed Hernández Juárez, allowing his team to set up office in the Congreso del Trabajo offices (Interview S-94-9). Furthermore, the government and Telmex management were more cooperative, agreeing to contract concessions in the 1982 round of negotiations. Whether this was an effort to calm down the situation generally or an explicit strategy to assist Hernández Juárez, Hernández Juárez clearly benefitted. The denouement came when police removed opposition activists from the union's Mexico City headquarters in June, after the strength of the opposition movement had dissipated (Interview S-90-1).

It would appear that the opposition had more than sufficient opportunity to win the conflict, but in-fighting thinned their ranks and facilitated Hernández Juárez's rebuilding efforts. An added obstacle to the opposition's success was that a minority within the opposition movement accepted help from factions within Telmex management, which in the end helped discredit the movement (Interview S-94-9).

When the movement was finally defeated, Hernández Juárez imposed severe punishments upon opposition supporters to discourage future internal strife and secure his political future. These included sanctioning entire departments of workers. For example, all Mexico City technician and private switchboard workers were deprived of access to union benefits. The fired workers were rehired in August 1982, but only after each signed individual contracts that amounted to loyalty oaths to the leadership of Hernández Juárez. Moreover, due to the sanctions applied by Hernández Juárez, most opposition members were prohibited from running for union office. While the opposition remained in disarray, elections were moved up a year to make sure that Hernández Juárez was reelected for four more years. No pretense was made of applying union bylaws in the levelling of these sanctions; rather, these were strictly penalties for being on the wrong side of a political dispute.[18] This would lead to the period of union governance called by union advisor Xelhuantzi (1988: 299) the "useful democracy"—or, perhaps more accurately, "the dominance of Hernández Juárez." Despite the fact that Hernández Juárez had triumphed, the strength of the revolt demanded a union leadership response on technological change issues. Slowly, this response took shape. In the 1982 and 1984 negotiations, the union once again concentrated on economic issues, such as wages and pensions, though minor gains were made in that a national training commission was established in the 1982 contract and a clause requiring that department-level contracts be updated if significant technological change occurs was strengthened in the 1984 contract (Solís Granados 1992a: 264). Meanwhile, management also responded by slowing the pace of the introduction of technological change. In part, the company had slowed the implementation of digital technology because of delays in the shipment of the Alcatel digital switches for which it had contracted, in part because of the Mexican debt crisis and the depression-like conditions that followed the Mexican government's declaration of insolvency in August 1982, and in part because of an attempt to buy union peace.

"Union policy was to attend to [undertake the work involved in] new services in exchange for increased wages" (Solís Granados 1992a: 264). Because there were 63 different departments where such *retabulaciones* could potentially be granted, there were widespread possibilities for workers to become active in seeking localized benefits. But the amount of union leadership support given to particular departments was uneven. Departments supported by Hernández Juárez received much greater support from the central union. This support included Hernández Juárez holding union meetings at the workplace on company time, which was tantamount to engaging in temporary work stoppages. Some of these meetings could last all morning. The government responded by seizing the telephone company facilities on Sept. 8, 1984, *four days* before a strike action was scheduled to begin. This *requisa* lasted until October 30, when the immediate revisions to department-level contracts were worked out. As well, work began on developing a less conflictual means of negotiating technological change (Martinez Lira 1986: 311-316).

The introduction of technological change again accelerated when, in September 1985, Mexico City was struck by a pair of major earthquakes, causing extensive damage to the old electro-mechanical exchanges and significant structural damage in one telephone tower leaving 15 telephone workers dead (Vásquez Rubio 1986, Xelhuantzi

1988: 281-282) and 4,000 telephone workers—mostly operators—without work (Telmex 1991: 166).[19] This led to a significant increase in the pace of technological change. In response, the union developed its "modernization program." As explained by one union staffer, "The first thing that we saw was that there was going to be unemployment and the second that there were going to be profound workplace changes, because we were no longer going to be telephone workers, but rather telecommunications workers" (Interview S-94-27). According to this union staffer, it was not until 1987 that the union had developed a comprehensive modernization project.

The STRM's modernization program was an attempt to establish a joint union-management framework in which technological change issues could be discussed prior to implementation. It was based on a type of "codetermination" model. It significantly differed from the European case, however, in that the union argued in favor of the proposal by suggesting that such codetermination was necessary because the union and the company have a joint interest in modernizing. Though a fairly ambitious program, in many respects it suffered because of the limited differences between the STRM modernization project and that of Telmex. The similarities created a lack of confidence among the rank-and-file. Nevertheless, the STRM's efforts between 1985 and 1988 to establish a union presence in the technology sphere was one of the most ambitious of such projects in Mexico. Examining its successes, as well as the reasons why it was stymied in 1989, is important in understanding the present framework in which the Mexican telephone workers' union operates and how that differs from the situation faced by the TWU in British Columbia.

In 1985, a general union assembly resolved that the union would fight for greater control over the company's contracting-out of work and to defend the principle of majority government ownership of the telephone company (Solís Granados 1992a: 264-265). In 1986, the collective agreement established a new clause, Clause 193, which contained a commitment from the company that the STRM would have access to the jobs created by the new technology; that the union would have a limited role in the implementation of new technology; that union members would not be laid off due to the implementation of the new technology; that a joint union-management technological change committee would be created; and that the union would be regularly consulted regarding health & safety and training issues related to technological change (Solís Granados 1992a: 265).

In 1987, the STRM went on strike to gain *retabulaciones* for outside plant and operator workers, but it was a *huelga de derecho* or "legal strike" (derisively referred to as a "paper strike" by frustrated workers) in which the union members stayed on the job. The "strike" consisted of on-the-job slowdowns, the wearing of red and black strike colors, and other similar protest actions. In spite of the fact that workers did not leave their jobs, troops occupied telephone facilities two hours before the "strike" was to begin on April 8 and remained there until a settlement was reached on April 16 (Solís Granados 1992a: 268, Vásquez Rubio 1987). The strike was mainly political; Hernández Juárez had won a 6-month term as President of the Congreso del Trabajo and was seeking to prove his mettle (Corro 1987).

Though not reflective of technological change per se, the 1987 strike was indicative of the liberalization of the union that occurred around this time. Opposition activists, through the exercise of pressure at the shop floor, in large part created their own opening. But it would appear that union leaders also realized that they needed pressure to be placed on management if the union was to make progress in negotiations over technological change. In any case, the union leadership incorporated some opposition members onto the executive committee of the union. So, for the first time since 1980, there was a significant opposition presence on the union executive committee. This liberalization was only partial, which would lead to problems in 1989. But it marked, nonetheless, a significant shift from union policy.[20] In 1987, the union formed two commissions to negotiate the terms of the introduction of new technology—a modernization commission and a worker-owner dispute resolution commission (Interview S-94-27). In the 1988 negotiations, the union succeeded in making gains in collective bargaining, as a precise bargaining procedure was established regarding the implementation of technological change (clause 193), and clauses regarding the national training (clause 185) and health & safety commissions (clause 136) were strengthened. On paper, at least, these clauses allowed the "union practically to achieve codetermination in the administration of technological change and work organization" (Solís Granados 1992a: 275).

At the STRM's September 1988 Convention, union leaders distributed a 40-page glossy brochure extolling the virtues of their modernization program. The program involved the establishment of five joint committees—a productivity committee, a technological change committee, a health and safety committee, a training committee, and a recreation and culture committee. Despite the upbeat tone of the brochure, however, there were indications that future conflict was fast approaching. Included in the "project" of the STRM Modernization Committee was the consolidation of 63 departments into six areas. While there are some potential benefits from such a centralization, centralization would provide a manner for the central union leadership to increase its power at the expense of union counsellors and shop stewards (STRM 1988: 9, 31-33).

In March 1989, the government and Telmex management presented an ultimatum to the union that it sign an agreement to prepare the way for the privatization of the telephone company. Central among the demands was the elimination of *all* department-level contracts and their replacement by "job description" documents which would be much less restrictive and need not be renegotiated when technological change occured. Acceptance of this demand would eliminate a key "veto" right that the union had previously used as a lever to extract economic and working condition concessions from management.

In the month of negotiations that followed, which culminated in a document known as the *convenio de concertación*,[21] the union leadership, the union counsellor and shop steward network, the government, and company management became involved. The goals of the four parties were unusually transparent. The union leadership wanted an agreement that would ensure the union's survival and that would strengthen its control over the union itself. The union shop steward and counsellor network wanted to preserve the union's recent gains and their departmental rights. The government wanted to be able to sell the company at the highest possible price. The company management wanted to get rid of anything that encumbered its "right to manage"—i.e., all the joint commissions and all the work rules that gave the union a say in the implementation of technological change.

The hard line of company management might seem surprising, given that it had just signed a collective agreement the previous year that outlined a power-sharing framework regarding the implementation of technological change, in a manner not unlike the role played by the Contracting-Out and Technological Change Committee in British Columbia. But Telmex management was very divided on the issue. As one union activist said, "There are the hard-liners, such as Pérez de Mendoza and Luis Casco and the moderates, like Guillermo del Hoyo. When the *concertación* comes down, del Hoyo is out" (Interview S-90-2; see also Ortiz Magallón 1993: 64-65). This debate was evident in management ranks for some time, as can be seen in the following excerpt from a round-table discussion that occurred in 1987 (Telmex 1987a: 205-206):

> C.P. Manuel Romero A: Sir, more than a question, a reflection. From what we have heard today, I think that we are at the proper time to review everything that has happened, because the deterioration in labor relations does not occur overnight; then, perhaps, this review would serve us, for one thing, to not fall into the same errors of the past ... There are things that the union does not need, but by agreement, one has to contract with them, then there are things that in this moment I do not want you to respond to me and explain why, but there are things that come to my mind in this moment and I believe they shouldn't occur.

> Lic. Guillermo del Hoyo: I am going to tell you why ... Human Resources is not only labor relations; Labor Relations has other areas as you know, in which there are consultants and advisors; surely there are areas of Human Relations you will have to work on; if I have a vacancy that has remained unfilled for two or three years, instead of looking to fill it, perhaps I sit down ... with the union to convince them that if they have been able to work ably with that number of people for three years, perhaps it is no longer necessary to hire to fill the vacancy, but better to train those we already have. But that requires a labor of leadership and of convincing that the area of selection of incoming personnel will have to be done with you and with the union.

In the 1989 negotiations, one of the most important demands of corporate management was to have full authority to decide whether or not a vacancy was to be filled, so as to enable the company to use attrition to reduce the size of the workforce. The union leadership, for its part, saw privatization as inevitable and thus sought to strike the best deal it could.

Two weapons in the government's arsenal were its ability to permit or deny Telmex entry into new services and its ability to set the date when long distance competition would begin. As one union advisor explained, "We opted to accept the privatization and in that way defend our work. If we did not accept, open competition was going to come [immediately]" (Interview S-94-0). Whether privatization was inevitable seems doubtful, but it is clear that the Mexican government wanted it. One indication that privatization might not have been inevitable was that six years later, many other Latin American and European countries continued to run their telephone systems as government-owned enterprises (Petrazzini 1995).[22] Once the union leadership accepted the "necessity" or desirability of privatization, however, it was limited in the level of resistance it could offer.

While the government and the union leadership were in agreement about the desirability of privatization, the workers, and particularly the hundreds of STRM shop stewards and counsellors, were not convinced. Indeed, one tactic used by the union leadership to get members to accept the *concertación*, a document designed to pave the way for privatization, was to argue that the agreement was the only way to keep the company under public control! As one union activist said, "When the *concertación* came, Hernández Juárez was already prepared. They said that it was so they wouldn't have to sell the business. So we wouldn't be fired" (Interview S-90-5).

The opposition had not fully recovered from the post-1982 internal repression, but was in the ascendency. But it was unable to offer an alternative proposal. There was a lot of pressure from the government and the union leadership to get in line. There also was not a lot of time to formulate alternatives. One union activist contends that, "The *concertación* was imposed by the (union) executive committee in a terroristic manner" (Interview S-90-6). Nonetheless, when the initial document was circulated, the shop stewards complained loudly enough that negotiations were extended two weeks, through the Holy Week holiday. As this same activist said, "We in the opposition succeeded in getting the shop stewards to enter to negotiate. There was a lack of access. We succeeded in rescuing some things . . . In reality, the executive committee was rescued by the membership" (Interview S-90-6).

There are very different opinions regarding the degree of danger the union faced. While some believed that Hernández Juárez's statements were nothing more than scare tactics, others believed that the government's threat to eliminate the union if it did not cooperate was real. One union executive council member at the time explained that, "At the beginning of the negotiations a part of the union was very frightened because the threat was there. I don't think it was a demagogic harangue of Hernández Juárez, the threat was that they would take away the union's registration" (Interview S-94-15).

Negotiations were tense. According to one outside observer, President Salinas not only set the general parameters of the negotiations, but played a direct role in them. According to this observer, "at one point, negotiations between the Director General of Telmex and the head of the STRM reached an 'irreconcilable' impasse. They were called into the president's office. *El presidente* said, 'unless you resolve it between the two of you now, if you don't fix it, you'll have a problem'" (Interview U-94-1).

At the center of the negotiations was the conversion of the department-level contracts (*convenios departamentales*) into job descriptions. As one executive council member said, "One thing that saved Hernández Juárez was the participation of 600 shop stewards in direct negotiation with the company. Because in this manner the majority of the departments was able to defend a good part of their department-level contracts (and get them converted) in the job descriptions [*perfiles de puestos*]" (Interview S-94-15). The provisions of these *convenios* varied widely by department, but the table below makes clear the breadth of items that they covered:

Table 5-1: Main Features of *Convenios Departamentales*

1. Definition of work. Protections against contracting-out of work.

2. Union workplace representation rights.

3. Training obligations of the company.

4. Company provision of tools and work clothes.

5. Extra payment for workers who act as supervisors ("in charge" payment).

6. Holiday pay bonus in addition to that required by main contract.

7. Setting of salary-levels.

8. Extra payment for working on new technology (typically 8%).

9. Extra-pay provisions for a variety of items such as out-of-town work, transportation costs, weekend work, use of English on the job, etc.

10. Overtime payment provisions.

11. Health-and-safety provisions.

12. Provisions regarding petitions for a paid or unpaid leave of absence.

13. Establishment of joint committees to monitor exams used for promotions.

14. Seniority rights provisions.

15. Provisions regarding the creation of new job categories.[23]

Not surprisingly, many disputes centered on which of the above provisions would be carried over from the old *convenios departamentales* into the new *perfiles de puesto.* For instance, one disputed item was whether the assignment of operators' shifts would continue to be done by strict seniority. According to one union negotiator, "The company considered that this [involved] intervention in the administration of the company, and in reality, it did. We considered that it was something that fundamentally betters our working conditions according to our seniority and we defended it" (Interview S-94-15).

While many workplace rules were salvaged and the threat of the government to decertify the union was averted, the *concertación* nonetheless meant a substantial change in the balance of power at Telmex, weakening the union and strengthening management. Among the changes in the *concertación* agreement were the elimination of the company's obligation to fill vacancies; the elimination of the company's obligation to get union agreement before transferring employees; the elimination of department-level contracts and their replacement by less restrictive job description documents or *perfiles de puestos* which permitted much greater management flexibility in the workplace regarding the assignment and organization of work; a dramatic reduction in the influence of the union over technological change with only advance notice requirements remaining; the agreement of the union to participate in a 45-day study designed to increase productivity (Telmex 1989); an increase in management discretion regarding who it must train; and restrictions on shop stewards holding meetings at the workplace. In exchange, salaries of workers outside Mexico City were increased to equal those earned by workers in the capital (STRM and Telmex 1989a, 1989b).

There were also some unwritten "agreements" that sweetened the deal for the union considerably. While there would be few new hires due to the elimination of the company's contractual obligation to fill vacancies, union leaders were assured that no current union members would be laid off (Interview S-94-0). As well, the union was promised that it would receive stock options when the company was sold in exchange for easing the way for privatization. In the end, the stock option the union received was valued, before the December 1994 devaluation of the peso, at roughly U.S.$20,000 per telephone worker.

Overall, it is clear that the *convenio de concertación* was a defeat for the union and a triumph for hard-line Telmex managers (de la Garza 1989). Within the union, the leadership improved its position, however, in that there was, as a result of the contractual changes, a more centralized negotiation structure (Interviews S-94-3, S-94-30), while the union shop stewards and counsellors lost influence, although not as much as would have been the case in the original government proposal. The government got what it wanted, which was to have the path to privatization cleared. Privatization plans were made public five months later, in September 1989. Finally, though it paid financially, management got most of what it wanted—a vastly restored "right to manage" technological change at Telmex. There has been a lot of discussion as to whether the *concertación* agreement provides the basis for a new model of Mexican unionism.[24] While it is true that the STRM is an unusual union in the Mexican context in some respects, there is nothing unusual about a union being forced to make work rule concessions and being compensated with shares in a privatized company.[25]

Just as the conclusion of the 1981 strike in British Columbia marked the consolidation of a particular division of power between management and the union, so too did the 1989 *concertación*, albeit with the scales being tipped decidedly in favor of management. Of course, the STRM had maintained its basic structure. The shop floor organization of the STRM, despite being weakened by the *concertación*, remains stronger than that of most telecommunications unions, including the TWU. It is certainly stronger than most unions in Mexico, many of which don't have a shop steward organization at all (de la Garza 1992). But the *concertación* did successfully restrain the union's attempt to influence technological-change control issues. In essence, the *concertación* meant that the union had accepted that it would not grow, while the company would. Current membership would be more or less protected, but the union's relative strength is destined to gradually, but surely, decline.

TECHNOLOGICAL CHANGE AND OPERATOR SERVICES IN BRITISH COLUMBIA

The modernization of operator services provides a good case to study in both the TWU and the STRM, since it largely came after the consolidation of their respective technological change negotiating frameworks (1981 in the TWU, 1989 in the STRM). In both cases, the formal contractual framework proved inadequate to the task, which meant that shop steward action would be key. The Mexican operators were able to use their political clout to ensure the establishment of relatively favorable transfer rules. The Canadian operators had much less political clout and were also less well organized than their Mexican counterparts. The TWU did spend considerable resources in developing community campaigns to limit the number of closures of small town operator offices and the union filed grievances regarding the lay-offs that did occur. Unlike the issue of contracting-out of plant work, however, the operators' issues were never taken to the bargaining table. While the Contracting-Out and Technological Change Committee worked fairly well for TWU plant and clerical workers, it worked less well for small town operators, whose numbers were declining too quickly to be easily accommodated by transfers to other job categories.[26]

In British Columbia, the switch-over to computerized operator services began in 1976 (Mather 1980), with the first office installation of a system known as TSPS (Traffic Service Position System). In the old cord board system, operators had to plug in their jack to answer the call and had to record the cost of the phone call manually. This was replaced by a system in which both call routing and billing occurred automatically, reducing substantially the control that operators had over the pace of their work (Bernard 1982: 167). Of course, this system also resulted in an increase in operator productivity, which allowed the company to save money by closing offices.

The first closure of an operator office in a small British Columbian city was announced in 1979 when the Penticton office was closed. The TWU sought to form community coalitions to prevent further office closures, arguing that as a company receiving a monopoly license from the state to operate, BC Tel had a social responsibility not to damage the economies of small communities. As Bill Clark put it in a presentation to a Cranbrook coalition meeting, the TWU's position "is simply that the people who are affected by change—the customers and the people who work with the equipment—should be the ones who make the decisions about the implementation of technological innovation. If these decisions are left in the hands of privately-held corporations, there is a real danger that the pursuit of profit will endanger the public interest" (Feb. 26, 1980 speech, in Hiebert 1986a). Moreover, while management claimed that it could save up to C$400,000 a year by closing an operator office (Cregan 1986, Kelleher 1989), the TWU disputed that charge, contending that the same computerization equipment that could centralize all calls to one location in the province (or outside the province, for that matter), could easily distribute calls to multiple locations.[27] As a TWU video put it, "None of this is necessary. Technology has an equal capacity to decentralize work" (TWU 1986). Indeed, the TWU cited a 1984 Northwest Tel (which serves Canada's Yukon Territory) annual report, which stated that, "The installation of a computer system in 1983 has allowed the Corporation to decentralize [clerical service representative offices from Yukon's capital Whitehorse to] each of the five business offices" (TWU 1986). As a result of the success of the TWU public campaign, the closure of the Cranbrook operator office was postponed. But other offices were closed in Vernon and Nelson (Kelleher 1989). Also closed were operator offices in Williams Lake and Terrace (Hiebert 1986b). And in 1986, after a three-year reprieve, the Cranbrook office itself was closed.

When its public campaigns were unsuccessful, the union tried to challenge the company by arguing that the transferring of operators to cities hundreds of miles away amounted to a "constructive lay-off": that is, management anticipated that most operators would not be willing to move and would be forced to quit. Because the collective agreement forbade lay-offs due to the introduction of new technology for all employees with greater than two years' seniority, the union argued that the company's move to force operators to transfer to a new site hundreds of miles away from their homes or quit violated the collective agreement.

In the arbitration procedure, each party selects a nominee to an arbitration board and the two nominees then select a mutually acceptable third person. In a 1983 arbitration decision (Munroe 1983), the arbitration board held that a constructive lay-off could be said to have occurred when " . . . the employee is unwilling to move, and reasonable grounds exist for such an unwillingness; and the employee would in any case be redundant at the new location." In the Cranbrook case, it was anticipated that roughly half of the 80 operators would be compelled to quit and accept the contract's indemnification, rather than transfer (Aldridge 1989).[28] In a 1989 decision (Kelleher 1989; see also Hoey 1990: 7), however, the arbitration board ruled that while there had been a technological change in 1983, the fact the company did not close the office until three years later, after growth in customer demand for operator services had failed to meet company projections, meant that the lay-offs had not been caused by the technological change.

The union's political/legal approach was partially successful. As one union executive council member explained, though the union was unable to prevent the lay-off of Cranbrook operators who weren't wiling or able to move elsewhere, "They haven't told people to 'quit or move' since" (Interview T-93-60). And some of the operator offices that remain in smaller cities, such as Campbell River on Vancouver Island, may have been saved as a result of the union's pressure (Interview T-94-80).

Despite the TWU's partial success in its campaign to fight centralization, there are some contrasts with the plant workers that are worth emphasizing. Little effort was made to take demands on behalf of the operators regarding the office closures to the bargaining table. This contrasts with the degree to which the union sought to prevent lay-offs of plant workers in 1982. Then, the union used the courts as well as the bargaining process to protect the workers. In the end, the union signed a highly controversial accord with the company to allow the temporary relocation of 292 plant workers affected into clerical and operator positions and agreed to special recall procedures to ensure the plant workers' ability to return to the plant division, as soon as positions became available.[29] Regarding these workers, one union executive committee member of the time said, "We went to the Court [to prevent the lay-off] and won. BC Tel took it to the Court of Appeal and they won there. But we were at the bargaining table by then and we said, 'no lay-offs.' We got a letter of agreement that said there would be no lay-offs" (Interview T-93-12).

Of course, the number of operators who were facing lay-off was smaller, and they did have the option to move a few hundred miles to retain their jobs. But no major walk-outs occurred. In the absence of significant shop floor militancy and given the limited political clout of operators in the union, the leadership did what it could to protect its members. Most of these tactics, even much of the work behind the "public" campaigns, required the labor of very few people. Many of the operators remained on the sidelines. Unlike the outside plant campaigns of the seventies, there was little effort to mobilize the membership as a whole. The political and legal tactics used by the union leadership eventually did stop the closures of a few remaining provincial operator offices. Closures of operator offices since that time have involved offices in the Vancouver area, where transfer to another position is much easier on the workers involved. Furthermore, the union had already achieved a strong baseline, through the contractual provisions governing technological change. These made it difficult for the company to lay-off employees with more than two years' seniority, since doing so required the company to demonstrate that the lay-offs were not due to technological change. As will be seen, though, the amount of energy expending in defending operators in British Columbia, though not insignificant, pales when compared with that displayed by the STRM in the newly privatized Telmex.

OPERATOR SERVICES MODERNIZATION IN MEXICO

"The operators as a group are possibly one of the most critical of the union leadership. Right now, they support it . . . but they are not unconditional supporters of Francisco Hernández Juárez . . . If the union leadership does not clarify its line of action or rectify its errors, it is most likely that it would be among the operators where the most uncompromising opposition would arise" (Dominguez Cruz 1982: 190).

"Operator services gave Hernández Juárez power and operator services is going to take it away. Operator services is already very discontented with Hernández Juárez" (Interview S-90-16).

The support of operators has been a key factor in Hernández Juárez's ability to remain secretary general of the union from 1976 to the present, but that support has consistently been conditional. Because the operators can easily contact each other throughout the country via the telephone network they operate, they have significant ability to organize politically. While a majority of operators has stayed clear of aligning themselves with the opposition, they have used their position to pressure both the company and the union leadership. At times, some operators have formed oppositional groups, such as "04" (named after the Mexican number for information) or allied with small outside groups, such as MAS (Movimiento de Acción Sindical or Union Action Movement), thereby gaining the ability to work with other opposition groups, but operating independently of them (S-94-5). At the same time, operators have been able to play their hand fairly well, using the threat of defection to extract concessions from the union leadership.

After the 1985 Mexico City earthquake, rumors began to spread about the likelihood of the installation of computerized technology, as had already occurred in British Columbia and indeed throughout the industrialized world. The earthquake had put 3,500 operators—nearly a third of the total operator work force—temporarily out of work. The company realized that it was able to operate without them, but "the telephone workers were able to get the union to coordinate an emergency plan" (Vásquez Rubio 1986: 6). After much struggle, the union won full payment of wages and benefits for the operators who were unable to come to work because of the earthquake damage.

In the 1986 collective agreement, there was a special clause that established a "manual traffic commission."[30] In negotiations, some hard-line company officials advocated full automation of telephony and the elimination of the operator department entirely (Interview S-94-15). This attitude generated great concern within the union. National assemblies of operators were held, at which solidarity actions were designed. These involved modest actions, such as wearing buttons to work demanding a resolution to the conflict, but signalled that operators were alert to the perils of their situation (STRM 1987).

The union's executive committee, led by Hernández Juárez, strived to calm operator fears, promising, in a paternalistic fashion, that they would all be taken care of. But many operators were not convinced. As one said, "Hernández Juárez says to give a dial tone to the entire world. No one believes this. There could be 3,000 early retirements" (Interview S-90-16). There were also threats from the company of mass dismissals.[31]

The operators were able to respond. First, the operators successfully resisted management attempts, in the wake of the *concertación*, to roll back gains in informal work rules that the operators had achieved over the previous decade. As one operator said, "There were a series of customs that were unwritten. The company tried to change them. It did not succeed. There was a frightening battle over it." (Interview S-94-9). These "customs" included such things as the right to switch shifts with fellow operators and the right to unpaid leave to deal with family matters (Interview S-94-9).

For a long time, many operators did their best to ignore the threats. "At first, the operators did not think the modernization was so important. In 1991, 1992, when I would say, 'It's coming now,' the union sisters understood [its importance]" (Interview S-94-11). Some activists visited the United States and Canada to collect information regarding the technological change. As one operator stated:

> The effects of the restructuring are the same in the United States, Canada, and Mexico . . . they are reducing the number of operators from 12,700 to 5,700 in the STRM. The operators visited Canada and the U.S. to prepare themselves. The necessities of the restructuring are the company's, not the workers'; the company has the obligation to guarantee posts and to train the operators. This was achieved by a shop-floor campaign. The collective agreement is not strong, but the operators have gotten the right to be retrained and have preserved their jobs (TIE, 1994).

A combination of shop-floor tactics and the ability of operators to put pressure on union leaders (STRM 1991b, 1991c, 1992a) led to a final agreement on the modernization of operator services in April 1992. In the agreement, 5,700 workers would remain in operator services. 500 operators (instead of the feared 3,000) who were nearing retirement would receive an early retirement, but they would receive a pension equal to their current salary. According to the agreement, roughly 4,500 would be transferred (STRM 1993a).[32] But the union did succeed in gaining operators the ability to select by seniority if they would be transferred and, if so, where. This was not easy to achieve, given that the collective agreement offered no such protection. As one operator said, "They have permitted us to go to the department that we want. There has been a great struggle over this" (Interview S-94-11). Among other things, this meant that the high-paying, male-dominated, outside plant jobs have been opened to women for the first time in Telmex history (Interview 94-S-0).

Of course, the solution is not ideal. Thousands of operators had to transfer and nearly 40% of these transferees had to move to a new city. Those who remain in operator positions suffer the negative effects of the technology—namely, an increase in the intensity of work and in the intensity of supervision (Interviews S-94-11, S-94-16, S-94-23, S-94-26). As one operator put it, "The people work like mules—and what's more, without providing quality service. Operator service has stopped being a quality service" (Interview S-94-16). As another operator noted, "The supervision becomes more intense and sophisticated. We have practically three levels of supervision, one who is a union sister (chief's assistant), the second is the control by management . . . and the third is the control of the machine" (Interview S-94-23). In addition, there is a continuing battle over whether or not operators who are pregnant will be granted leave from working on the computers (Interview S-94-26).

Still, the operators' achievements are not inconsiderable. When the union leadership was prepared to make work rule concessions in the *concertación*, the operators' shop stewards were able to resist many of the changes. When the management of the newly-privatized company, attacked informal operator work rules, it had only limited success, as operators used work stoppages and other tactics to ensure informal work rules continued to be respected. In the end, despite work rule concessions made in the *concertación*, which gave management, on paper, virtually complete freedom to transfer workers as it saw fit, the operators were able to win many significant protections.

CONCLUSION

In examining the struggles of the TWU and the STRM with respect to technological change, many similarities emerge. In the 1970s, both unions, in the context of the threat posed by automation both to the skill content and the existence of technicians' jobs, rebelled against company paternalistic work relations. Yet there were nonetheless major differences in how that rebellion was resolved by union leaders.

At BC Tel, the TWU leadership organized an occupation of telephone facilities province wide as part of its ultimately successful effort to ensure that union jurisdiction would not be eroded as new technology changed the nature of telephone work. Indeed, from this struggle emerged the TWU's social unionist strategy. That strategy, as well as the political clout of the technicians, made a difference.

Importantly, because of the TWU's successes in maintaining union jurisdiction, the union was able to protect its position vis a vis management. Erosion in the union density ratio stopped. By contrast, STRM coverage declined from 69.7% of all Telmex workers in 1977[33] to 64% in 1990 (Corona 1992: 162).[34] Figures for the TWU are shown in the table below:

Table 5-2: Union-Management Ratios at BC Tel, 1981-1990

	TWU coverage at BC Tel[35]
1981	65.5%[36]
1983	79.7%
1985	76.2%
1987	77.6%
1990	83.1%

As well, the TWU's success in 1981 clearly discouraged management attempts to seek contract concessions from the union on workplace issues. Instead, as is covered in the following chapter, management has sought, with limited success, to work outside the collective bargaining process to impose changes in workplace organization.

The STRM's story is different. Initially, in 1976 technicians were united and succeeded in overthrowing the state-supported leadership of Salustio Salgado. But such unity did not last long. After six years of bitter internal struggle, opposition technicians revolted again in 1982 against a union leadership which they felt was not meeting their needs. Despite state intervention, the failure of the opposition to oust Hernández Juárez was largely the result of internal divisions and tactical errors. The opposition's defeat ensured the consolidation of the more "bread and butter" unionist strategy backed by Hernández Juárez; it was also one of the factors that made possible the 1989 *convenio de concertación*, which weakened the STRM's overall contractual protections regarding technological change considerably.

In comparing the performance of the two unions with respect to the operators, it is clear that the resolution in the two cases was similar, though the way they achieved that solution was fundamentally different. The TWU, due to its successes in the digitalization battle, was well placed to ensure operators the right to transfer to another city. Not satisfied with this, the union leadership pressed for more. But in the absence of militant rank-and-file action and given the relatively weak position of operators within the union vis a vis their plant brothers, the TWU was able to stop the shutdowns only after a majority of the operator centers in small cities had already been closed. In the case of the STRM, the digitalization battle left the union in a weaker condition. There were unwritten guarantees that there would be no lay-offs, but many of the contractual protections giving the union a say in who was transferred and how were eradicated by the *concertación*. Under these conditions, the operators were nonetheless able to battle supervisors on the shop floor to maintain the privileges they had won in the previous decade and to pressure the union leadership into lending the support necessary to conclude a successful transfer agreement.

The successful conclusion of a transfer agreement at Telmex for operators demonstrates, of course, that the *concertación* was not an unmitigated disaster for the STRM. But the STRM is a union that remains vulnerable on many fronts. Unlike the TWU, the STRM has been unable to gain significant protection against the subcontracting of work. The STRM union leaders' choice to ally themselves with Mexican state officials has also had its price, as was evident in the concessions the union was compelled to make in the 1989 *convenio de concertación.*

Meanwhile, the structure of work at both Telmex and BC Tel is changing rapidly. As computerization is introduced into clerical parts of the business, the number of job functions shifted to clerical workers grows. At the same time, operator services shrinks dramatically. As well, the numbers of inside and outside plant workers also decline, albeit at a slower rate than operators. These shifts have led to tremendous changes in the types of jobs telephone workers perform. The resulting reorganization of production both alters the distribution of workers among the different telephone company departments and facilitates management attempts to change the organization of production *within* specific departments. These issues pose severe challenges to both unions, as shall be seen in the following chapter.

NOTES

1. Note that there was an intermediate technology, the electronic switch, also known sometimes as a crossbar switch, which still used cabling but had a computerized central processing unit. These electronic switches were used in much of the rest of Canada and in Mexico, but not in British Columbia. The reason, according to Elaine Bernard, was that GTE—the parent company of BC Tel—did not produce an electronic switch, and thus switched directly from step-by-step switches to digital switches (Bernard 1982: 163).

2. As Elaine Bernard (1982: 152) points out, "The seventies heralded the computer age at BC Telephone. This massive wave of technological advance was part of a second industrial revolution which continues today."

3. As discussed in the next chapter, though the union had functioned as a single organization on paper since the 1940s, the plant, clerical, and traffic divisions maintained a large degree of autonomy until the union was restructured in 1977; as president of the union during this period, Donnelly played a central role in promoting these changes.

4. Outside corporate pressure on BC Tel management was evident at the time. As one newspaper reporter wrote, "Unofficially, BC Tel engaged in this fight for phone companies everywhere. The 6-year old contracting-out clause had to go or telephone unions everywhere would be seeking the same terms with their employers" (Dobie 1978). However, BC Tel's rejection of the conciliator's report did help the TWU in its efforts to garner public support, as did the fact that the dispute centered on preventing lay-offs due to technological change, an issue that evoked considerable public sympathy. See Persky 1978, Phillips 1978, Smith 1978, Thurlow 1978.

5. This work has since been taken over by Centrex equipment, in which a local operating switchboard is operated via remote control from the telephone company's central switchboard exchange.

6. The ratio of unionized employees to management had fallen from 19:1 in 1949, to 3.7:1 by 1979, permitting management to maintain most normal service despite the fact that few unionized workers crossed union picket lines (Bernard 1982: 168). This ratio of 3.7:1 is not unusual. In many companies in North America, the ratio of union to management employees is even lower. In the eighties, Telmex management succeeded in implementing a similar system of increasing management classifications, largely as a means to reduce union influence. By 1990, the time of Telmex's privatization, only 64% of Telmex employees were STRM union members.

7. The convention minutes do not indicate the exact vote tally. But throughout the eighties, the margin of elections between the "Clark faction" and the "Donnelly faction" would remain close. In 1986, for instance, Clark won reelection when the Chair of Convention broke a 46-46 tie in Clark's favor (TWU 1986a).

8. This theme is echoed in press accounts at the time. For instance, a September 1980 newspaper article noted that "Middle management numbers have swelled to more than 2,000 people." Jurisdiction was rightly seen by outside observers as a "contentious . . . issue, which would give the union some control over management's move to increase staff" (The Province 1980).

9. By vacating the premises when they did, the union leadership avoided the filing of criminal charges, but the union did end up having to pay a fine of C$60,000 for its illegal occupation of the telephone company buildings (Bernard 1982: 223).

10. Indeed, BC Tel won accolades in the business press for the decline in acrimony. See Twigg 1987.

11. The term *charro* has a long history in Mexican labor. Originally referring to a style of rural clothing, the term became associated with government-controlled unionism in 1948 when the Mexican government under President Miguel Alemán violently imposed its favored union leader, who frequently wore a *charro* outfit, on rail workers while jailing the rail workers' elected leadership. Technically, a *charro* union leader is one whose modus operandi is marked by violence and extreme corruption. However, the word is frequently used to refer to any union leader or union which maintains an unswervingly pro-government stance. Regarding the usage of the term *charro*, see also de la Garza (1988, 1993).

12. The Congreso de Trabajo (Labor Congress) or CT is Mexico's largest federation, whose members include most major labor unions and federations in Mexico, including the CTM. The CT's role corresponds to the role played by the CLC (Canadian Labour Congress) in Canada. That is, both groups act primarily as coordinating bodies and have relatively few powers that they can exercise over their individual members.

13. The wording "operator-dependent" is not coincidental. Though more progressive in this respect than most Mexican unions (or many U.S. or Canadian unions, for that matter), there is no question that Hernández Juárez and his group is male (mostly outside plant) dominated. The female operators (there are no male operators at Telmex, still) have been very capable at using shop-floor pressure tactics to ensure that the leadership is responsive to their demands, but only a few women have made it to high leadership positions in the union. An informal "glass ceiling" at the STRM most definitely continues to exist and certainly existed during the period (1976-1982) discussed here.

14. However, external parties, such as Telmex management, did seek to use the internal union conflict to their advantage, as explained below.

15. The government has not allowed itself to be caught by surprise again, at least not when an official strike date (*emplazamiento de huelga*) has been announced. As a rule, the government will seize the telephone facilities with troops *before* the time a strike is scheduled to begin, regardless of assurances from the union that no actual work stoppage will occur. Such *requisas*, as they are known, have occurred in 1979 (twice), 1980, 1982, 1984, and 1987. The legality of these state actions is questionable. The government uses World War II-era legislation giving it the right to seize communication facilities when national security requires it to justify intervening.

16. Línea Proletaria's strategy involved using a *política de dos caras* (two-faced policy) in which it was willing to make deals with government officials in

exchange for gaining space for organizing (Interview S-94-9). As such, it often worked to undermine other leftist movements, earning these groups' enmity. To their credit, Línea Proletaria's focus on workplace issues often earned them popular shop floor support, in contrast with other leftist groups that sometimes focused too much energy on fighting ideological battles against the capitalist state. Línea Proletaria, in addition to its activity in the telephone workers' union, was also active among various mine workers' union sections in northern Mexico and in organizing peasants and teachers in Chiapas. The Zapatistas, among other groups, have some Línea Proletaria roots (Ross 1995: 276-277).

17. Unlike the situation in British Columbia, the STRM did not actively pursue limits to the contracting-out of work, though preserving union jurisdiction over work was an important opposition demand. One key reason why union leaders were not under as much pressure to fight for union jurisdiction is that there has always been a waiting list for new telephone service in Mexico. In short, there was no scarcity of union work and no threat of lay-offs among outside plant workers. At times, the wait has been over two years to get new service. This gives outside plant workers the ability to earn additional income by charging a "gratuity" to those telephone customers who wish to jump the queue. Until recently, the union (and management) turned a blind eye to such practices (Interview S-94-18c).

18. Union by-laws, for instance, require that charges be specified in writing. But no written indications of violations of union bylaws were ever presented. As one opposition worker said, "I was fired. I don't know for which reasons. They paid me my liquidation. From 1979 to 1984, I didn't work in Telmex because of the (union-initiated) firing" (Interview S-94-6). As another worker who had union rights suspended for ten years put it, "The union penalties never arrive to you in writing. They don't leave written (evidence)" (Interview S-94-8). In interviews with Juárez supporters, the discriminatory treatment is acknowledged, albeit reluctantly. One Hernández Juárez supporter explained the union leadership's practices this way: "One has to understand that Hernández Juárez and his people are people that were forged in struggle . . . The process was of confrontation, totally. It is in their roots. It is very difficult for there to be much sensibility in the treatment of the people who are not in agreement with their ideas. I do not say that it is right or that it is wrong. It is a bit of an explanation of this situation and the reason of the conduct of certain of our union brothers and sisters" (Interview S-94-22).

19. Restoring work to normal conditions took about two years. As one former Telmex operator explained, "After the earthquake, there were nine months without work. Later, there were daily shifts of four hours. Then, alternating weeks with and without work" (Interview S-94-9).

20. Regarding opposition demands, see Salinas and Barba 1987 and Línea Democrática 1987 for the viewpoint of those who were excluded from this "liberalization." See also Cano Miramontes et al. 1994 for a more recent statement of Línea Democrática views. Regarding the views of the "loyal" opposition, see Vivares Torres 1988 and CILAS 1992. See Coordinadora Democrática de Trabajadores 1991 for a thorough overview of both groups' concerns.

21. There is no adequate precise English translation of the term. Literally, it means a "concerted agreement" or an "agreement to agree." Terms used in labor negotiations in the United States and Canada for such documents include "Memorandum of Understanding" and "Letter of Agreement."

22. Two prominent examples in Latin America are Brazil and Colombia. (On the latter, see Díaz and Salazar 1991). In Europe, most countries continue to have publicly-owned telephone systems, including France, whose France Telecom now owns 24.5% of the voting shares of Telmex stock. The arguments raised in favor and against the privatization are covered in greater detail in chapter 7, which looks at the role of the state in Mexican and Canadian labor relations.

23. Telmex-STRM, *Convenios departamentales*, various years.

24. See Coparmex 1990 and Sánchez y García 1994 for a business perspective celebrating business' gains in the agreement; see Pazos 1991 for a right-wing argument that the agreement went too easy on the STRM. See de Buen 1989, Rueda 1989, Xelhuantzi López 1992, Medina Nuñez 1993, Mercado Maldonado 1993, and Jones Tamayo 1993 for arguments that the *convenio de concertación* provides the basis for a new Mexican unionism. For analyses that see the *convenio de concertación* as a more clear-cut defeat of the STRM, see de la Garza 1989, Dubb 1992, Sánchez Daza 1992, Solís Granados 1992a and 1992b, Aguilar Mares et al 1993, Bothello and Addis 1994, and Modragón Perez 1994. See Rodriguez Reyna (1989) for a journalistic account that focuses on the restrictions the agreement places on the STRM.

25. The pattern of giving shares to workers in newly privatized companies had been followed in 1984 in Britain when Margaret Thatcher privatized British Telecom. Workers at the Argentine and Venezuelan telephone workers also received shares when their companies were privatized shortly after the Telmex privatization (Petrazzini 1995).

26. Though not covered here, other technological changes have been addressed reasonably well by the joint BC Tel-TWU Contracting Out and Technological Change committee. These issues include the installation of fibre optic cabling, the installation of new computer inventory and tracking systems,

and the installation of a provincial network operations center (the next step of the digitalization process, not yet implemented in Mexico).

27. Furthermore, the TWU argued that the economic impact of removing the telephone company positions on smaller BC communities totalled millions of dollars a year. According to the union, the loss of 68 full-time jobs and 22 seasonal jobs in Cranbrook would directly reduce the income of that community by $1.13 million a year, with an additional $2.6 million lost due to multiplier effects; in Vernon, the union contended that the loss of 86 jobs would reduce that community's income directly by $1.23 million a year, with an additional $2.6 million due to multiplier effects (TWU 1979, 1980b).

28. This was in line with the number of lay-offs there were when the Nelson office closed. In that case, only 32 of 66 operators transferred. Of the rest, 15 either quit or were fired, while 19 more took a one-year unpaid leave of absence, mostly to keep their options open, in case they decided they could move. But most of these effectively also quit (BC Tel and TWU 1983).

29. This agreement, covered in greater detail in the following chapter, was highly controversial both because of the contents of the agreement—neither suspending seniority job bidding provisions nor transferring junior plant workers into operator services and clerical were popular—and because by cutting a deal that protected the membership in the short run, it reduced the incentive to bargain changes to the collective bargaining agreement that would protect the membership in the long run. As one opponent of the "292" agreement said, if challenging the lay-offs by using the arbitration process had failed, "We would have then known that our clauses were not the envy of all and could have attempted to negotiate safeguards for future changes that our membership would face" (Interview T-93-73).

30. Traffic or *tráfico* is the term used in Mexico to refer to "operator services"; since the word "traffic" is still often used to refer to operators in North America, the term is translated directly here. Regarding the special clause establishing the commission, such interim clauses or *transitorios* are a common feature of Mexican collective bargaining agreements. These clauses last only for the duration of the agreement and subsequently expire, unless a new interim clause is placed in the following contract. In the case of the operators, the specific clause referred to in the text was Transitorio 15.

31. See, for instance, Cooper Tory (1988: 159) for a table showing early management plans to reduce the number of operators by 10,000. See also Lovera (1990) for an article demonstrating the threat that 5,000 operators be dismissed *en masse*.

32. To be precise, 1745 transferred to another city while 2686 transferred to a different job but in the same city (STRM 1993a).

33. Figure calculated based on figures contained in Solís Granados 1992a: 176 and Lara Sánchez 1992b: 13. See also STRM 1994b.

34. More dramatic is the contrast with U.S. unions. In 1990, union density ratios for the seven Baby Bells ranged from 60% to 71% (Bolton 1993: 132). At AT&T, between 1984 and 1990, the number of unionized employees fell from 261,568 to 137,920 while the number of managers actually increased slightly, from 111,432 to 115,851. When non-union employees at NCR (an AT&T subsidiary) are factored in, overall union density fell in six years from 67% of total employees to 46% (Keefe and Boroff 1994: Tables 2 and 3).

35. Calculations for BC Tel are based on union membership figures from Labour Canada 1994, which maintains figures only for years in which collective bargaining agreements are renewed, and overall employee numbers (including management employees) from Statistics Canada (various years). Because the union membership and total membership figures come from different sources, the above percentages are not precise—for instance, it is likely that the figures were measured by Labour Canada and Statistics Canada during different months. Nonetheless, the chart clearly demonstrates the TWU's ability to arrest the shift in work from unionized to management employees that had occurred at BC Tel between 1945 and 1979.

36. The percentage of management employees is likely inflated for 1981 due to what were surely temporary management hires during the 1980-81 strike and lock-out. However, part of the increase between 1981 and 1983 is real. BC Tel hired many workers after the strike, increasing the number of TWU members from 10,000 in 1981 to 11,400 in 1983 (Labour Canada 1994).

CHAPTER SIX

Work Organization and Union Response

Technological change in the telecommunications industry has had dramatic impacts on workers and the unions representing them in both Mexico and British Columbia. In particular, labor-saving technological change can threaten both individual workers' jobs and, more broadly, a union's ability to maintain its influence in the workplace. But in addition to the direct threats that technological change can pose to union and job security, technological change can have other, more indirect effects. Not only does technology create new services and increase the speed of service provision, but technological change can also create new possibilities in the way the work itself is organized. As one BC Tel manager explained, "Technology has created some enablers that will change the game. Technology is a driver" (Interview T-94-71).

In some cases, management seeks to take advantage of technological change to implement a Taylorization of the work. That is, management acts to exploit the new possibilities arising from a change in machinery to implement a more specific division of labor. In a Taylorist system, work is segmented. An individual worker in a Taylorist system is responsible for performing a very narrow segment of the production or service delivery process. What is central to the work is the worker's ability to perform a single, repetitive task mechanically. Individual initiative is discouraged. In the telephone industry, the job of an operator provides a typical example of the Taylorist production system. For instance, the operator is supposed to answer every call with exactly the same phrase. Little room for worker creativity is permitted. In organizing work in this manner, management seeks to maximize the replaceability of the worker and to simplify surveillance by homogenizing worker behavior, thereby making non-standard behavior easier to identify.

As a system of work organization, Taylorism first emerged around the turn of the century. Taylorism was an attempt to enable management to exercise greater control over the production process, by breaking the work process into its component parts, thereby enabling managers to better monitor the workforce and increasing work efficiency. Prior to Taylorism, the dominant form of work production was craft production. Craft production involved giving workers a greater number of tasks, but also greater authority to determine the best manner in which to perform the work. Though Taylorism has been the dominant form of mass production in both Canada and Mexico for decades, its presence does not extend to all work functions. For instance, outside plant work still operates along craft production lines. Due to the number of tasks involved in the repair and installation of telephone cable, it has proven impossible to break down cable splicing and related work into distinct tasks, each to be performed by a separate person. As a result, outside plant workers in the telephone company retain far greater on-the-job autonomy and work variety than their operator counterparts.

More recently, there has developed a third model form of work organization, known either as "flexible specialization" (Piore and Sabel 1984) or "team production" (Parker and Slaughter 1988). In team production, management seeks to organize the work process among groups, in which different groups or "teams" each handle a segment of production that is broader than that which would be handled by a worker in a Taylorist work process but narrower than that which a worker would perform in a craft production process. In some cases, such as in automobile manufacturing, team production has resulted in tremendous gains in production efficiency.[1]

Team production involves a mix of elements from craft and Taylorist production. Like craft production, team production involves giving workers responsibility for more than one task, but unlike craft production, team production retains the Taylorist emphasis on centering responsibilities on easily identifiable tasks as a means to permit managers to accurately assess and monitor performance. While the monitoring may be less visible in team production than it is on the assembly line, it is frequently more pervasive. The all-encompassing nature of team production surveillance includes such features as the systemization of peer pressure and the use of computer monitoring, and often incorporates aspects of the design of the jobs themselves. Though a "team member" may be given a greater number (and hence, to at least a limited degree, variety) of tasks to perform, the way those tasks are performed is quite structured. For the clerical members on work teams in the TWU, for instance, the time spent per call was still monitored and workers were still expected to use set phrases. The number of different types of calls increases, but worker autonomy on the job remains limited (Rojot 1992, Parker and Slaughter 1988, Müller 1993, Watanabe 1993, Nomura 1993, Interview T-93-50).

In the telecommunications industry, historically both Taylorism and craft production have been used. While operator jobs have been fully Taylorized for decades, not only outside plant, but many inside plant and clerical jobs, were not easily susceptible to the Taylorist process of breaking the production process up into its component parts. Thus, both in Mexico and British Columbia, large numbers of telephone workers enjoyed considerable on-the-job autonomy. And while computerization has changed things a lot, it is still the case that many telephone workers retain a considerable degree of control over the timing and pacing of their work. As a result, company management must mix coercive means of control with more cooptive methods by which they actively seek worker consent. This is why, historically, telephone companies have tended toward paternalism, providing special non-wage benefits to workers (such as sick benefit and life insurance plans) and attempting to influence workers off the job through company-sponsored sports clubs, social events, and self-help programs (Bernard 1982: 82).

In the last two decades, technological change in telecommunications has increased management's ability to regulate the timing and pacing of work. In addition, there has been a proliferation of attempts to create joint union-management programs to implement "team work" proposals in which workers are given a greater "say" on the shop floor in exchange for an implicit agreement to increase productivity, frequently through speed-up, though sometimes via changes in the organization of production. At Telmex, for instance, there has been a productivity program in place since 1993 which is designed to meet those ends. The STRM, together with management, has pursued workplace restructuring in the hope that doing so will lead to higher wages for union members, but not without facing considerable dissent at the workplace from workers who feel managers' shop floor actions do not match management's cooperative rhetoric. At BC Tel, on the other hand, while there have been a proliferation of company cooperation programs, these programs have largely floundered due to TWU opposition.

But in analyzing the differences of responses of the TWU and the STRM to the question of work organization, I wish to focus on two specific questions: 1) How do unions deal with reorganization of the workforce when this occurs, whether the cause be a reduction in a department's size or the transferring of workers into an expanding department? 2) How do the unions deal with programs, such as quality circles or work teams, that are primarily intended either to bypass the union to resolve grievances or to increase productivity?

Central to the question of reorganizations that create or eliminate particular lines of work is the issue of union jurisdiction. While jurisdictional issues are more pressing in British Columbia—due to BC Tel's greater utilization of advanced computing technology—the STRM at Telmex must deal with many of the same problems. Moreover, because there were stricter jurisdictional lines and transfer rules to begin with at Telmex, in some respects the STRM has been more affected by this matter. Here the decision the union must make is whether to accommodate change or to impede it. While the TWU's general position is to slow the change, the STRM has adopted a policy of encouraging and pushing change forward, in the hope that this will make it better prepared for further changes to come. Both the TWU and the STRM have had limited success in getting their respective companies to maintain job categories that management has wanted to phase out, but the TWU has been significantly more successful in maintaining union control over new and emerging jobs, effectively raising the cost to the company of introducing them. This area does seem to be one where unions are, to a large degree, obliged to accommodate changes in the industry, stemming in part from the pressures of globalization.

The other question concerns cooperation programs with management. Here the difference between the two unions is stark. In both cases, management has tried to introduce quality circles and other similar programs. But while the STRM leadership has favored such programs, the TWU has successfully opposed them. The stark difference in these two unions' responses is indicative of overall differences in the two organizations' strategies. Here, clearly, no imperative to accommodate globalization exists and the impact of the state labor regime is also limited.

By analyzing the two unions' responses to different cooperation programs, one gains an appreciation of the distinctive nature of each union's approach. While the STRM has become a trend-setter in the signing of company-union cooperation agreements in Mexico, the TWU has resisted the continental industry trend toward joint union-management productivity programs. As will be seen, the TWU's resistance is a product of the union's history and, in particular, its successes in gaining contractual protections against subcontracting and the shifting of work from union to management.

These differences are clearly seen by examining union responses to specific job cooperation programs. At BC Tel, there have been over a half dozen company attempts to implement work cooperation programs, both of the "quality circle" grievance resolution type and, more recently, elaborate work teams and productivity programs. While management has had some partial successes, overall the impact has been quite limited. While the union's tactics change case by case, its strategy of non-cooperation remains a constant throughout.

In the case of the STRM, there is a split between the leadership and the membership. The leadership has signed several agreements signalling its willingness to cooperate with management, but on the shop floor a different attitude prevails. Although varying compound by compound, the level of real change is far less than what one would gather from reading reorganization and productivity agreements.

Finally, regardless of whether management promotes specific cooperation programs, there is a continuing struggle over workplace practices and norms and the level of worker or management control over the work process. Here implementation of productivity and work team programs at both BC Tel and Telmex are examined, focusing on Telmex's attempt to reshape workplace relations among traditionally autonomous outside plant workers and BC Tel's attempt to restructure its clerical operations. While clerical workers have traditionally been inactive in both unions, this has changed quickly in the last few years in British Columbia, due both to feminist social pressures and the changing nature of the work, which increases both the skill level required and the strategic importance of the work done by clerical workers in the company.[2]

DRAWING LINES IN SHIFTING SAND—CHANGING TELEPHONE WORK BOUNDARIES

Prior to the wave of technological change in the telecommunications industry that began in the seventies, there had developed two very distinct systems of work organization at BC Telephone and Telmex. At Telmex, the STRM had fought for and had established a separate department-level contract or *convenio departamental* for each of Telmex's 63 departments. As a result of this system of departmental contracts, union political action was organized very much along departmental lines. Within these classifications, workers were able to secure significant protections. Arbitrary transfers and the like were prohibited, but there was also a downside for workers, since transfer at a worker's own choosing was also difficult, as workers who transferred forfeited many seniority rights and had to begin at the bottom of the pay scale in their new departments. For management, this system often served to keep workers isolated from workers in other departments, thereby increasing its leverage in the workplace, but also led to an increasingly cumbersome set of rules, with essentially 63 separate contracts, each governing a portion of the company's workforce and many of them quite detailed in their regulation of what work the employees in a specific department could do.

At BC Telephone, the TWU developed along three different tracks, based on the three main divisions of the company—plant, clerical, and operator services (then called traffic). These divisions functioned like the 63 Telmex departments; instead of having department-level work contracts, each of the three BC Tel divisions had separate appendices to the collective bargaining agreement which governed most issues related to working conditions. This divisional structure resulted in political activity within the union being focused on the plant, clerical, and traffic divisional councils. In plant, where the TWU was strongest, the union fought for and established a single "craft" classification covering most outside and inside plant workers. This arrangement gave management greater flexibility in assigning work, but carried with it parallel management obligations to allow free transfer among craft jobs, to provide retraining to workers who successfully bid by seniority into new jobs, and to pay most of workers' moving expenses, regardless of whether such retraining and transfering were cost-effective. In the clerical division, by contrast, a system of narrow job classifications existed, making this much more similar to the situation within the

STRM. Operator services at BC Tel fell in an intermediate category, more similar to plant in that it had a single classification, but without concomitant management retraining obligations (BC Tel and TWU, *Collective Agreement*, various years).

In both the TWU and the STRM, the onslaught of technological change which began in the 1970s created a need for a more coordinated response among the different divisions (TWU) or departments (STRM). Jurisdictional boundaries that once clearly separated one job task from another began to disintegrate. On the management side, the sweeping nature of the changes made it desirable to have a single bargaining agent for the workforce, one which could be held accountable for agreements made, even though such a change would reduce management's ability to play one union division off against another. On the union side, the rapidity of the changes created rank-and-file pressure for rapid, coordinated union responses. In addition, the rise of more activist leadership in both unions in the mid-seventies meant that local union shop stewards and union members made more demands on their leadership. This created contradictory pressures: on the one hand, there were increasing demands on the union leadership to "do something," but at the same time, local activists often felt compelled to take action on their own, without central union approval. In both unions, this led to conflict, though in the Mexican case this conflict was much more severe. In the TWU, these pressures helped push the union to create a single union structure in 1977, which included the formal elimination of the divisional structure. In the STRM, the union leadership responded to the demands for change by creating the coordinator position in 1979 (roughly equivalent in role to the business agent in Canadian and U.S. unions). These union officials served as intermediaries between shop stewards and the union executive board. Their existence, effectively, increased the level of control exercised by the central union leadership over the STRM's 500-plus shop stewards (Martinez de Ita 1982, Martinez Lira 1986).

TWU AND WORK ORGANIZATION

In examining the issues involved in intra-union jurisdictional lines and the conflicts that arise, one key issue is the response of unions to the elimination or contraction of lines of business. In British Columbia, the creation of phone repair stores located in major shopping centers (Phone Marts) in the mid-seventies shifted parts of the phone repair

function from outside plant workers who before had to go door-to-door
to service phones to clerical workers, who were now responsible for
staffing the new stores and completing all of the processing information
of the customers' repair orders. Coupled with severe recession in the
early 1980s, the shift in work resulted in the emergence of the outside
plant "surplus" issue which lasted from 1983 to 1986, since now the
company's operations demanded fewer plant workers and more clerical
workers. As a result, plant workers were temporarily placed in clerical
or operator positions to avoid lay-offs (Interview T-93-68).

In Mexico, similar disruption was caused by the phasing out of
mechanical private branch exchanges (PBXs). This eventually led to
the shifting of these workers inside plant positions. More recently,
mechanics have been shifted outside plant positions, due to Telmex's
contracting-out of telephone truck repair work. Despite their efforts to
stop company downsizing, both unions have been unsuccessful in
getting management to alter its business plans. However, the two
unions have succeeded in avoiding permanent lay-offs through
negotiated transfer arrangements.

A different issue is raised regarding union jurisdiction when a
telephone company expands into a new line of business. In the case of
Mexico, the STRM has been cut out of new technologies and new lines
of business, as Telmex's mainly non-union subsidiaries are the primary
source of growth (Solís Granados 1992b: 62, Vásquez 1994). The
TWU, on the other hand, has managed to hold on to succession rights
and maintains its hold on representing workers in almost every sector
of the business.[3]

The Phone Mart issue provides an early instance in which
management sought to shift work in order to reduce costs. The first
Phone Mart opened in 1974. In these telephone stores, telephone
customers would bring the phone to the center for repair, instead of
calling for a repair worker to come to their homes. Creation of the
Phone Marts had two effects. First, it shifted some tasks from telephone
workers to the customers, who no longer had the convenience of free
home pick-up of damaged telephones. Of course, the customer
benefitted in that it was now possible to drop off a phone for repair,
rather than having to wait for a repair worker to come and pick it up.
Second, it shifted some of the work from outside plant telephone
workers to clerical telephone workers, since it was clerical workers who
staffed the stores and collected the telephones. The union tried to resist
the change, both by filing a policy grievance against the change and

through protest actions. The union also encouraged its members to paste bumper stickers on their backs protesting the creation of the Phone Marts. When 67 union members were suspended by the company for wearing the bumper stickers, 2,000 workers walked out in sympathy (Bernard 1982: 159-160). The union feared that the Phone Marts would lead to lay-offs, but it turned out that management threatened lay-offs primarily to pressure Canadian regulatory authorities to grant the company a rate increase. Although 170 workers, 160 of whom were from plant, were laid off, they were quickly rehired once the company had received the rate increase it was seeking (Bernard 182: 165-167).

That the union failed to stop the shift of work from home repair visits to repair centers is not surprising. But the change illustrates the nature of many problems that were beginning to appear in the early seventies with the increasing rapidity of both technological change and related changes in work organization. At the same time that this shift resulted in the phasing-out of some installation-and-repair (I&R) jobs, it also involved the creation of the position of Phone Mart representative. These workers would soon gain a significant presence in the company, as the switch-over to Phone Marts was completed province-wide.

As Bernard explains, "Changes introduced in one work area generally had repercussions in others" (Bernard 1982: 174). These changes led to a shift in the structure of the union which went from having three autonomous divisions to a unified structure in 1977. The three divisional councils were eliminated two years afterward (Bernard 1982: 176, 194). According to Bernard, "The need to respond immediately to company-initiated changes made it absolutely necessary that the three divisions work in close cooperation" (Bernard 1982: 174) and was a key factor leading to the change in union structure.

The new central union structure helped the union ensure that workers in new company subsidiaries remained part of the union. In 1981, the CRTC decided to allow competition in "terminal" equipment—that is, telephone sets, private switchboards, and anything else that can be connected to a telephone jack (The Province 1981). As a result of the decision, BC Tel aimed to develop an accounting mechanism to separate the "competitive" side of the business (terminal equipment) from the monopoly side of the business (local and long distance calling). Under the three-division structure, the TWU would have been hard-pressed to deal with the situation of a management demand to separate out an entire section of both clerical and plant workers and place them under a separate contract. But since the new structure included both clerical and plant workers, the TWU was able to keep the new competitive sector within the same collective bargaining agreement, by creating a separate appendix for people working in the competitive areas of the business. In essence, this created a fourth division (known as BTE or Business Terminal Equipment), but ensured that new operations of BC Tel remained within the union's jurisdiction (Interview T-93-68).

While the TWU made some work rule concessions for the competitive branch of the company, it was able to maintain most contractual safeguards for the transferred workers. This didn't always prevent management from treating the workers in the competitive branch differently, though. As one BTE worker says:

> If I didn't take any coffee breaks and only took lunch, I could finish Thursday at noon. Normally, I'd work at my own pace and take all my coffee breaks. When BTE came in and we started selling sets, people didn't want to admit they weren't getting their job done. They figured, "maybe it was me." For a long time, guys wouldn't say anything. Then, the crews started talking, gradually. Sometimes people were a whole week behind. Guys were working through their lunch breaks. Then, they started giving their work back. But it was still difficult (Interview T-93-23).

As this worker explains, "At BC Tel, what they do when they form these departments, they make them out to be hot shots [as if] they were better than everyone else. The company is very good at splitting off people like that" (Interview T-93-23). In general, the union was less well organized on the shop floor in the competitive sections of the company, but eventually a backlash developed against the speed-up.

In 1992, the company folded the terminal equipment group back into the rest of the company, including the workers in such high-growth areas of the business as cellular telephones. The re-integration of BTE workers created its own problems. In January 1992, nearly 1,000 BC Tel clerical and inside plant workers walked out over the company's failure to respect seniority during the merger (Interview T-93-34). Although formally part of the company and controlled by the terms of the collective agreement, BC Tel management still treats its subsidiary "diversified" operations differently than its long distance and local telephone operations. This is a continuing source of tension. As one shop steward complains, "Sometimes we'll have 16 grievances from our temp [temporary worker] committees. It's absolutely ridiculous. In the two years that I've been here I'm just starting to get a foothold on what's going on" (Interview T-93-57).

Despite the union's continuing difficulties at the shop floor level, the TWU's unified union structure has been reasonably successful in ensuring the maintenance of union jurisdiction over BC Tel's newer operations. But the resulting problems have often increased strife among the union's divisions. Indeed, while strengthening the union's organizational capacity, the ability to act in a unified fashion across the three divisions has also also led to open divisional and gender conflict. Under the tri-divisional structure, such conflict had been present, but was less visible.

The plant surplus issue of 1983-1986 demonstrates the manner in which the different divisions had became more integrated, as well as the continuing inter-divisional tensions. The conflict also illustrates the limited options available to a union facing threats of company cutbacks. In 1982, BC Tel threatened to lay-off 2,100 of its roughly 12,000 unionized employees, 1365 from plant and 735 from clerical (Bernard 1982: 225), but was temporarily prevented from doing so, when the TWU took the issue to Court (Interview T-93-12).[4] There were multiple reasons for the attempted lay-off. Partly, it was a management effort to pressure the union during contract negotiations. But there was also an economic recession that reduced new service orders and line construction. As well, technological and organizational work changes resulting from computerization were shifting some tasks, such as cable pair assignment, from plant workers to clerical workers. This is why plant workers were disproportionately targeted in the lay-off notice. Eventually, after negotiations, the company and union agreed that no one would be laid off, but that 292 plant workers would be "temporarily" shifted into clerical and operator positions, where the need for labor was greater.

This issue, referred to by union activists to this day as the "292" issue, split union activists into two sharply divergent camps—those who supported President Bill Clark and the majority of the union leadership versus those who supported the position of the Secretary-Treasurer Don Bremner, former President Bob Donnelly, and the minority of the union's central executive committee. In examining the difference between the positions of these two groups, one can see more clearly the different possible responses to management's reorganization of the workforce. The union's new centralized structure made it easier to prevent lay-offs while avoiding another knock-down confrontation with BC Tel management. At the same time, however, the settlement involved challenging the traditional prerogatives of the three union divisions which, though formally eliminated, still carried significant weight in the union decision-making process.

The union was caught in a bind in dealing with management claims that there was a labor "surplus" at the telephone company. Either the union agreed to shift workers or it would have yet another major fight with the company, this time acting to defend against lay-offs or involuntary transfers of its members. As one union executive member put it, the union agreed to transfer the workers "to lower-paying jobs— at current pay, [they were] red circled—with first rights back into the craft section" (Interview T-93-68). As one former union official explained, "Here's where those [contracting out and technological change lay-off protection] provisions started rolling in. They couldn't lay-off, but they could move people, transfer people, etc. The best we could do was negotiate administrative letters to mitigate damages" (Interview T-93-12).

But the above view was not unanimous. As another former union official argues, "We had what was considered to be a first rate technological change and lay-off clause that we believed was going to see us through any and all change, but in the after-light, I don't believe that the clause or the clauses were as strong at defending the members as we originally believed" (Interview T-93-73). The key problem, according to this former union official, was that the agreement "provided the company the ability to identify surpluses—not by seniority—in areas and move them through some minor selection process to other work functions" (Interview T-93-73). Defenders of the agreement note that the company's right to reassign and/or transfer employees outside of seniority order is provided in the Collective Agreement[5] (Interview T-93-68). But opponents of the agreement believed that "with our overtime bans, super service [work to rule] and other tactical maneuvers, the company would have to hire back those workers that may have been laid off" (Interview T-93-73). Moreover, agreement opponents argued that by cutting deals, the long-term strength of the union was sapped. According to this view, even if the union tactics to prevent lay-offs failed, this would have enabled the union to more clearly identify the shortfalls in the Collective

Agreement and "We would've then known that our clauses were not the envy of all and could've attempted to negotiate safeguards" (Interview T-93-73).

Although accepted by the membership, the agreement was very unpopular. First, it required junior plant workers to transfer into clerical and operator positions, preventing more senior clerical workers and operators from bidding into those slots. In addition, this forced men to do what was considered to be "women's work," which many of the men resented, even though they liked the alternative of being laid off even less. As one plant worker explained, "It [preserving jobs] sounds good on the surface, but the guys couldn't type, wouldn't type, and wouldn't learn, but were getting top wages, while the clerks were getting low wages and doing the work" (Interview T-93-15). The women in the operator and clerical positions were not impressed. As one operator said, "They [the male transferees from plant] showed up late. They tinkered around" (Interview T-93-31). Or, as one clerical shop steward put it, "The 292 period was grievance city. The 292s didn't want to be there . . . Then other people were upset, because they [the plant transferees] were getting the big bucks. It was a very unsettling time" (Interview T-93-43). Resentment increased even further when, during certain periods, there would be some plant workers logging overtime work, while other plant workers remained in their clerical or operator slots. As one plant worker said, "I was dissatisfied . . . because they let the rest of the company work overtime. You would see the people in craft working overtime and think, 'Why can't I do these jobs?'" (Interview T-93-21).

Second, the surplus agreement allowed plant workers to bid back into the first jobs available, taking prime work opportunities from more senior plant workers. This provision in the agreement was known as "super seniority," because those workers who had been transferred out of plant were placed at the top of the plant posting list for any jobs that became available, ahead of workers who had greater seniority. This caused resentment among those who were unable to transfer into jobs in more desirable locations, as a result of the transferring of junior employees back into plant division posts (Interview T-93-15).

At the January 1984 union convention, President Bill Clark asked for a vote of confidence, one year into his second three-year term as union president. In his speech, Clark made clear both his support of strong workplace rights and his moderation on wage issues, a position that has remained central to the TWU's general social unionist orientation both before and since. Clark staked out his position as follows:

> My background is that of a supporter of Socialist Trade Unionism. I still believe that Socialism and Trade Unionism go hand in hand. I am convinced that the wage increases we bargain every couple of years are determined within a percent or two by community pressures more than any other factor and therefore are not our main reason for being. However, that which we (all unions) have gained over the years makes our movement a very special and important social instrument. Unions cannot, in a Capitalist economy, create jobs . . . our most important role is to protect workers from unemployment to the best of our ability and to protect the conditions we have gained (Clark 1984).

Clark's position prevailed, though by a relatively narrow margin.[6] Two years later, Clark would be reelected for a third term after a 46-46 tie was broken by the Convention Chair.[7] But the 292 issue, besides dominating union political factional conflict for years to come, had other important effects. First, for over a decade, it effectively pushed company lay-off threats to the background. There was a kind of unwritten agreement that the company would work out the necessary transfer arrangements with the union rather than resort to lay-offs and that the union would show the necessary flexibility to make this work. Second, it marked the union's acceptance of a much slower pace of resolution of "rights" issues. The TWU held on to its seventies' gains, but made far less progress in the eighties. In part, this reflected larger trends in the economy and the election of a Conservative government in Canada in 1984, which made labor gains harder to achieve. But it was also a conscious decision by the union to go slow: the loose ends of the work jurisdiction issue were tied up, but little other progress was made on major issues and no changes were made to either the assignment of work or transfer areas of the Collective Agreement. Third, the 292 agreement illustrates the rather extraordinary lengths the union leadership was willing to go to protect plant workers, suspending seniority rules and transferring them across divisional lines to clerical and traffic jobs, rather than accept a single plant lay-off. This contrasts starkly with the extent of the union's efforts in the clerical and operator services divisions, where the union has accepted much greater use of temporary employees, who can be "laid off" much more easily or, more accurately, whose contracts the company can simply choose not to extend beyond their expiration dates. Finally, an unintended consequence of the handling of the 292 issue was to wake up the union's sleeping giant—the clerical division. This was true both because the 292 transferees highlighted the difference between female and male wage scales and because male workers refused to abide by the more authoritarian working conditions that many of the female workers had been forced to accept. As one of the "292" transferees explained:

> They put 50 men in with 200 women [at a telephone manufacturing assembly plant]. I could not believe the way the women were handled. They were numbered at stations. They would yell out, "37, you're not working hard enough." I was told that if I didn't shape up, they'd ship me out. I said, "I'm not a number. Don't talk to me like that. I believe you owe me two warnings." I guess no one had ever said this ... From then on, the women started smartening up (Interview T-93-11).

While other factors, such as the rise of feminism in Canadian society, also played a role in the rise of clerical women's activism, the 292 transfers accelerated the process by breaking down the union's divisional structure and the tradition of plant dominance.[8] These changes would play a major role in determining the approach the TWU would take when BC Tel sought to implement work teams in its Business Division in the 1990s.

Still, the fault lines of conflict arising from the 292 conflict have carried over into other work reorganization disputes. This can be seen in two labor conflicts, one rooted in the transfer of women into outside plant ("craft") positions, made possible by a letter of agreement negotiated by the union leadership in 1990, and the other a series of surplus worker transfers negotiated by the union in 1993. In both cases, the tensions among the three occupational divisions and between male and female workers have been evident, as has been the continuing dominance, albeit at a reduced level, of the male plant workers. Indeed, these differences have often been exploited by company management as a means of sowing discord within the union.

The 1990 letter of agreement negotiated between the TWU and BC Tel management was signed in a period of economic recovery, following a prolonged economic recession that had prevailed in British Columbia during much of the 1980s. All of the "292" workers had returned to their craft [plant] positions by 1986. Back in the early eighties, the union had offered training to non-craft workers in the craft prerequisites. As a result, hundreds of non-craft workers were craft-qualified, but without craft jobs. Under the collective agreement posting procedure, 5 out of 6 plant vacancies had to be filled by the internal job posting procedure, while 1 out of 6 could be hired from the outside; new positions could be filled internally or externally, at the company's discretion. As a practical matter, since the early eighties, there had been little hiring and nearly all positions had been filled internally.[9] Workers outside of the craft classifications who were craft-qualified had the right to bid on open positions, but successful applicants had to take a drop in pay, until they reached the top of the higher craft salary scale four years later. In most cases, the reality of the situation was that clerical women applicants were not considered. As one union activist put it, "The old boys' network didn't want women" (Interview T-93-50).

Under pressure from women members, the union sought to negotiate changes. A union committee with two plant members and two clerical members negotiated with management a letter of agreement to permit easier entry of craft-qualified women into craft. The final draft of the letter of agreement satisfied almost no one. The two clerical representatives both resigned from their committee posts in protest, because "they wanted it [the job bidding] done strictly on a seniority basis" (Interview T-93-50). Instead, the letter of agreement specified that 75% of all posted positions were reserved for current craft applicants, while 15% were open for non-craft applicants. 10% of positions could be filled with outside hires. In exchange for being limited to 15% of the positions, the non-craft applicants were guaranteed that they would not have to take a cut in pay to transfer into craft.

Meanwhile, plant workers were unhappy, since their percentage of replacement postings fell, at a time when craft jobs were finally becoming available, after years of limited job availability. Resentment was widespread (Interviews T-93-15, T-93-16, T-93-23), even though the letter negotiated actually required, for the first time, that management fill most new positions with internal postings (Interview T-93-68, T-93-50). The difference in posting rules before and after the letter of agreement are listed in the table below:

**Table 6-1: Internal Hiring, Minimum Percentage Requirements
BC Tel, Craft Positions**

	Replacements	New positions
Pre-1990	minimum 83% internal (effectively from craft)	No internal hiring requirement
1990-present	minimum 75% from craft, 15% from non-craft	minimum 75% from craft, 15% from non-craft

Exacerbating the situation, the economic recovery allowed the company to begin hiring from the street again. While the company used to be unrestricted in the number of new positions it could fill hiring from the street and now was restricted to only 10%, the appearance, to workers who had grown accustomed to the posting of all positions, was that the new letter had robbed them of their ability to bid into the preferred positions that they had hoped to obtain during the economic expansion. As one union activist noted, under the old hiring procedure, management could have chosen on its own to promote gender equity and didn't need to negotiate with the union. But "when the company has a difficult issue, they'll take it to the union. Where we always used to fight the company, we fight ourselves more" (Interview T-93-50).

The economic expansion was short-lived. By 1993, a combination of slower economic growth and competitive pressures resulting from the 1992 Canadian regulatory decision to deregulate the industry led to renewed threats by management to reduce the number of workers. Again, the union responded by negotiating a letter of agreement to prevent lay-offs. Again, this letter of agreement was supported by a narrow margin (40 in favor and 38 against) at the union convention (TWU 1993a). Faced by conflicting pressures within the union and a general stagnation in the number of jobs available, the union leadership remains locked in a dilemma. The limits on opportunities for promotion and mobility within the company exacerbate strains between different work groups. Moreover, as the industry changes through such developments as competition in long distance service provision, the union's ability to influence the direction of the industry is reduced. As a result, the TWU leadership is increasingly squeezed between the demands of members seeking immediate benefits and its desire to maintain the TWU's traditional social unionist strategy.

STRM AND WORK ORGANIZATION

Because of Mexico's significantly lower level of telephone penetration, the pressure to reduce the size of the workforce is far lower than in Canada, where telephone penetration rates are among the highest in the world.[10] Nonetheless, technological change still involves a shifting of the workforce from some departments to others—and many similar issues do emerge. Indeed, to a certain extent, the logic of expansion, which requires more rapid changes in the company's structure, placed added pressure on the STRM to adapt to changes in the company's business organization. Two organizational changes were particularly important. First, the *convenio de concertación*, discussed in the previous chapter, both eased the implementation of technological change and formally eliminated the departmental structure of the company. Second, there have been more active efforts, pursued jointly by the union leadership and management, to gradually combine job categories. Just as pressures to modernize in British Columbia led the TWU to take a more flexible stance toward worker transfers, similar pressure in Mexico has led the union to adopt a more flexible stance. It should be noted, however, that the union's position in Mexico has been much more enthusiastic in its accommodation to the company than the TWU, whose response has been both reluctant and measured.

Beginning in the fifties and reaching its full-blown development in the late seventies and early eighties, the STRM had managed to force Telmex to adopt a set of very specific work rules that governed the relationship between the union and management in 63 different departments of the company. Conflict, when it did erupt, tended to take place along department lines.[11] This is true of both internal union and union-management conflicts.

Sometimes, as was the case with the operators in the late 1970s, department-level identity and action could work to the benefit of the workers. Even after the department structure was formally abolished, the operator shop stewards were able to use pressure tactics to make substantial gains for their members. The system also ensured a significant degree of decentralized authority, which served as a check on the central union executive's ability to impose its views on the entire membership. Indeed, the department system and the hundreds of union activists this system spawned is probably the prime limiting factor on arbitrary central union authority. This legacy serves, to a large degree, to explain why internal union authority relations at the STRM, though less than fully democratic, are significantly less authoritarian than is the case in many Mexican unions.

But the department system did have drawbacks. One was that it tended to generate demands that were narrowly focused on department-level issues, sometimes in ways that blinded members to larger issues that were having an impact on all telephone workers. Second, the department system made it easy for the central union leadership to punish its opponents in certain circumstances. In this respect, the fate of the 2,000 private switchboard workers provides an extreme, but not entirely atypical, example of the manner in which the department-level structure served to isolate departments from one another, particularly after the post-1982 demobilization of the union. Especially in smaller departments, where shop floor organization was limited, and in those departments that were opposed to the union leadership, this division and isolation led to an increased focus on wage and local union issues, while working conditions issues that affected several departments simultaneously often received minimal attention.

Under the pre-1989 system, workers had a partial veto over the implementation of technological change in that the Collective Agreement required the company to reach an agreement with the workers before implementing new technology if this new technology would substantially alter the nature of their work (Interview S-94-3). Normally, workers used these negotiations to earn a *retabulación*, or salary increase, in addition to the general wage increase. Typically, it took a year or two to reach such an agreement. Generally, workers would agree to work under the old wage scale, with the understanding that they would receive back pay to cover the period between the time the technological change was introduced and a written agreement was reached.[12]

Occasionally, however, the entire system of negotiations would break down, as happened with the private switchboard workers. In such circumstances, management had an alternative route it could pursue. If workers refused to work on the new equipment, the company could create a non-union subsidiary or contract the work out to another company. Although this was costly to the company in the short run (since they still had to pay the workers even if they did not do the work), it reduced management's dependence on union labor.

The switchboard workers' inability to reach an agreement was a major reason for their support of the 1982 rank and file revolt against Hernández Juárez. When this revolt failed, however, they were left isolated and unsupported by the union leadership. Cut off from union leadership backing, the workers found that management was not eager to negotiate. The result was some resistance by the affected switchboard workers, but greater passivity as time wore on with no resolution in sight. Telmex management took advantage of the union in-fighting to contract out the work on the new digital private switchboards, which are similar to the Centrex systems used in the United States. As manual switchboards were replaced by digital ones, Telmex's employees had less work, but since the union contract protected the workers' wages, many of the private switchboard workers resigned themselves to the situation. As one opposition activist said:

> There have been certain outbreaks of protest . . . but this has been minimal and has been a consequence of the following: the workers— during the process of technological substitution, not only because they require fewer workers, but under this pretext of technological change—have been displaced by other [non-union] workers. The union leadership has not been interested in this. The subsidiaries are started and the worker is displaced. The worker, if well paid and well treated, does nothing (Interview S-94-6).

After 1989, the rules of the game changed. Now, the formal barriers between departments had been eliminated, and management— having transferred the work to subcontractors and wishing to place workers where the work was, liquidated the department and transferred the workers to outside plant jobs. The switchboard workers sought instead to be transferred to higher-paying and more skilled central office maintenance (inside plant) jobs and staged demonstrations at the company headquarters building in Mexico City to back this demand. Management compromised by agreeing to put the workers on a waiting list for the preferred central office maintenance jobs. As central office maintenance is itself being downsized due to modernization, however, it is not likely that the private switchboard workers will gain access to many central office jobs. This state of affairs was reluctantly accepted by most of the protesting workers, but roughly 200 of the former 2000 workers in this department have carried on the battle and have filed a claim in Court against the company and the union for failing to respect their department work contract that had in their view guaranteed their work prior to 1989 (Interviews S-94-1, S-94-27).

This court case appears to have little chance of succeeding, but it is indicative of how political conflicts within the union—and the strong department divisions in the union—have affected workers at Telmex. On the one hand, prior to 1989, STRM workers enjoyed great protections, since they were guaranteed the right not only to a job, but to a job in their given department. On the other hand, the rigidity of the department lines at times served to divide the workers, rather than unite them. The relative lack of cross-departmental linkages within the company provided space for the rise of opposition to the union leadership, but also facilitated the union leadership's ability to direct repression at specific departments and keep members from different departments isolated from each other. Because every department had its own protections prior to 1989, members in one department were not directly threatened by the union's willingness to acquiesce in the creation of non-union subsidiaries or the transfer of work to other firms. Indeed, if the union leadership withdrew its backing and a worker's labor became redundant, as was the case of the manual switchboard workers, it was still possible for that worker to accept his or her pay and not worry about not having work. When the protective departmental clauses were dropped in 1989, union members in the private switchboard department saw that their position was precarious, but now it was too late to act. Indeed, though some workers from other departments are sympathetic toward their plight, there is also a great deal of resentment of the fact that many of these workers were "collecting a pay check for years without working" (Interview S-94-1). Even obvious and crude tactics of repression by the union leadership, such as withholding $20,000 in shares owed to the workers, didn't spark widespread sympathy.[13] Instead, the struggles that do occur remain largely localized in the different departments. So while the system of departments did (and, to a large extent, still does) encourage the taking of militant action to consolidate local demands, it has also served to isolate departments from each other, particularly in the period since the failed opposition revolt of 1982.

In the post-*concertación* industrial relations world at Telmex, the STRM leadership has had to adjust. While the leadership failed in its attempt to extend the union's influence over technological change—in fact, a key element of the union's traditional control, the department-level contracts, was lost—the leadership has had greater success in its proposal to increase work retraining and the consolidation and grouping of job categories in a manner that broadens the work performed and allows greater worker mobility among departments. As one union staff member explains, while the union has "very little" influence over technological change, "in the organization of work, our influence has been decisive" (Interview S-94-0).[14] While it is arguable whether the influence of the union has been as dominant in the organization of work as the above statement implies, the changes in the organization of work have been substantial. These changes have begun to alter not only the way telecommunications work is organized at Telmex, but also the way the union itself functions.

The STRM leadership began to confront the problem of the changes in work organization in 1985. A formal union strategy was worked out in the next couple of years. "At first," says one union staffer, "we saw [the industrial changes] as a process of technological modernization; we did not have a handle on the whole modernization process. But by 1987, yes [the union had developed an approach]. On training, etc. It was by then sensible to speak of a union project" (S-94-27). On the issue of work organization in particular, the union's approach has been to embrace change while seeking to take advantage of the uncertainty in the transformative process to strike a deal pledging labor peace in exchange for a greater say in work organization. *In particular, the union has agreed to assist management in promoting productivity-enhancing speed-up and to reorganize work through the combining of job categories; in exchange, the union has sought increased pay, a greater company commitment to retraining, and a larger say for the union in the administration of work organization programs.* In many respects, this is a classic business unionist response of exchanging pay for productivity, but with an important difference: instead of letting management "take care of" the productivity side of the equation, the union actively seeks to boost productivity so that wages will rise more rapidly.

In outside plant, the plans to combine jobs involve three stages. First, in 1989, the *convenio de concertación* created job profile documents, which were much more flexible than the former department-level contracts. Second, there is supposed to be a period of training in the different job categories. And third, this is supposed to be followed by a subsequent levelling of the salary levels. (Interview S-94-2). This process has progressed at different rates in different compounds. In some, the old department structure remains fully intact, while some of the newer compounds were established with the new system already implemented. But overall, most outside plant workers continue to work their jobs much as they did before the 1989 *convenio* officially changed their job titles and descriptions.

Prior to 1989, there were five principle *convenios* in outside plant. These included *convenios* covering repair workers, installation workers, line workers, cable splicers, and underground cable workers. On paper, the 1989 *convenio de concertación* merged all five groups into a single job category and consolidated pay rates across department lines, though the jobs themselves remained largely separate. In 1991 and 1992, management began to train workers in work areas beyond those covered by their own department. In 1993, Telmex managers began to implement a new structure which subsumes all five work areas in one category. But there was significant worker resistance to this. While those with the harder work (such as underground cable laying) didn't mind being given the easier work (home installations), the reverse, not surprisingly, was not so easily accepted. As one outside plant worker explained:

> My coworkers in underground cables, their work is very dirty and very tiring. And if they have the ability of going to do installation and they let them take their truck home, they are enthusiastic about being "universal workers". But if you ask an installation & repair worker if he wants to be a worker who does cable splicing or underground cable installation, well, you've got to be kidding if you think he wants to go. These jobs are considered punishment, since their [installation and repair] work is much cleaner (Interview S-94-25).

As a result of such resistance, the combining of job categories and the creation of multifunctional workers, though well mapped-out in union and management documents, is largely non-existent in plant compounds. As one outside plant worker explains, "Each department has certain qualities that have not been written down. These remain intact. The job descriptions [included in the *concertación*] have not thoroughly affected the departments" (Interview S-94-13). But as some job categories are eliminated or downsized, a gradual assimilation of workers is taking place. Workers who are transferred are placed on parallel seniority tracks and, if their former salaries were higher, then they have their salaries "red-circled" (Interview S-94-13).[15]

A greater, if unintended, change has come about in the level of supervision in outside plant work. As a result of a government-mandated telephone line expansion rate of 12% a year, union workers who served as first-line supervisors have been put to work in installation and connection. Quality has suffered as a result.[16] As one of these workers explains, "Now there is no longer supervision. For example, according to the company's instructions, I should make sure the wire reaches to the upper corner. If the wire is too low, there is the possibility of line faults. It is within the reach of children" (Interview S-94-18c). In addition to poorly-done connections, mapping also suffers. According to this same worker, "Some 90-95% of the orders that they give us we have to modify so that it's all right—the technical data, especially" (Interview S-94-18c).

While the merging of job categories has progressed slowly, some departments, such as those of private switchboard workers and automobile workers, have been eliminated entirely. The resulting transfer of workers from downsized or eliminated departments has created a cross-over of workers from one department to another to an extent never before seen in the STRM. While the effects will only become clear in the years to come, it is apparent that the transfers will affect workplace dynamics. This is especially true for the operators, some of whom are entering what were exclusively male jobs at Telmex for the first time. As one former Telmex worker notes, "The more conservative workers stayed, while the risk-takers moved" (Interview S-94-9).

In general, those operators who have transferred to plant jobs are glad to be done with operator work. As one former operator relates, "Now that I am in outside plant, I like it. You don't have the pressure of the supervisor. It's more relaxed. Of course, in the street there is more danger. But you're not so controlled" (Interview S-94-11). In terms of the politics of the union, the transfers will likely reduce the militancy of the operators, as it is the militants who have tended to transfer out, but they may also increase the militancy of the outside plant workers. In many cases, the workers who choose to transfer are being moved from Mexico City, where many of the operators were concentrated, to mid-sized Mexican cities, such as Mérida or Veracruz, where there is a high demand for new telephone line installations. There are also many transfers from small cities where operator centers are being closed to mid-sized cities where Telmex has installed modern, computerized equipment. The transfer of Mexico City activists may alter the traditional regional political dynamic of the STRM, where the more militant Federal District sections have been counterbalanced by the more conservative smaller sections (Interviews S-94-9, S-94-11).

In the meantime, however, the centralization of union leadership authority has been dramatic. In many respects, Hernández Juárez has sought to centralize control since he assumed the leadership of the union in 1976. In 1978, he formed an alliance with a group known as Línea Proletaria (Interview S-94-9),[17] which advocated action based on rank-and-file discussion of the issues and recommended the establishment of small assemblies (*asambleas chicas*), as well as the creation of union coordinators who would collect information from the rank and file and communicate their views to the union leadership (STRM 1979). While ostensibly bringing decisions "down to the masses," the new structure served to limit the power and influence of shop stewards (*delegados departamentales*) by creating a parallel structure for transmitting information. By 1983, Hernández Juárez had broken his alliance with Línea Proletaria. Workplace assemblies declined in number, but the system of coordinators remained. In September 1988, six months before the *concertación*, the union leadership tried to further centralize operations by seeking to channel the negotiations of the 63 department work contracts into six areas—transmission, switching, outside plant, clerical and administrative, operator services and general services (STRM 1988: 9). As the union leadership explains in this same document:

> To date the [department level work agreement] revisions have been characterized by their encouragement of wage competition between departments, causing a permanent spiral of contract revision demands, which allows the company to feed the permanent economic expectations, accentuating division in the struggle and fighting among departments . . . with this we run the risk of arriving at a situation in which the union is seen solely as having economic goals, showing ourselves before public opinion to be a union that does not take into account the present economic conditions (STRM 1988: 31).

According to the Modernization Commission of the STRM union leadership, centralization was necessary to "establish an equilibrium between the economic issues that are a priority for the workers and the new work conditions that generate modernization" (STRM 1988: 32). In April 1989, the *convenio de concertación* went much further, doing away with department-level contracts entirely.

This has had precisely the centralizing effect in negotiations that one would expect from such a change. As one telephone worker explains, "The [national executive] committee, well, Hernández Juárez and his team, are the filter through which all the important labor negotiations pass" (Interview S-94-31). One particular effect is that local commissions (or task forces) are no longer named by departments to solve problems, which was previously the case. As one worker notes, "There are no longer commissions named among the workers, constituted by workers, to do union work. This [process] has been centralized. We depend now on what the National Executive Committee wants or is able to obtain" (Interview S-94-29). In addition, shop steward authority to solve local problems has declined. "Before," explains another union activist, "shop stewards could negotiate directly with the company and now they no longer can" (Interview S-94-25).

The centralization process, despite its costs in terms of reducing the ability of shop stewards to resolve workplace grievances and the parallel reduction in shop floor militancy, has had beneficial effects in some areas, notably in facilitating the transfer of operators to other departments. Indeed, as was the case with the TWU, the rapidity of change in the industry, beginning in the late seventies, was an important factor for greater centralization, political concerns aside. While the union has failed to alter the balance between working conditions and wage issues, in one key respect there has been limited progress. Namely, the STRM has started to address the hemorrhaging of work to non-union contractors and Telmex non-union subsidiaries in a more forthright manner. In particular, as part of the Concession Title privatizing the enterprise, the STRM received a guarantee that it would have representation rights in any new subsidiaries formed by Telmex (Interview S-94-22). This guarantee was formalized in the first Collective Agreement signed between the newly-privatized Telmex and the STRM in April 1992. This concession to the union is only of limited value, since there are already 18 Telmex subsidiaries in which the STRM does not have representation and these have accelerated their growth since 1990, when the concession was written.[18] But the agreement marks an important change in the attitude of the union, in that the STRM has begun to place greater emphasis on securing the union's jurisdiction, after 14 years of largely neglecting this issue (STRM 1992b).

NEW WORK ORGANIZATION AND UNION-MANAGEMENT RELATIONS

In addition to the changes in the organization of work discussed above, through the contraction, expansion, or combination of different work areas or transfers of workers among different job tasks, management at both BC Tel and Telmex has attempted to institute programs that seek either to 1) reorganize mechanisms of conflict mediation between workers and management or 2) reorganize the production process itself. Included in the first set of programs are such efforts as Telmex's "Quality Model" and BC Tel's attempts to establish quality circles. Despite management protests to the contrary, these programs tend to be ideological in nature (see, for instance, Parker 1985; see also Verma 1991: 54). That is, they seek to alter workers' perception of the nature of their work and their relation with the company to encourage workers to perceive the worker-company relationship as one of mutual benefit, rather than one involving conflicting interests. At Telmex and BC Tel, management has had limited success in these endeavors.

The second set of programs, however, are far more daring in their scope and in their potential impact on telecommunications work and workers.[19] At Telmex, these efforts have focused on the institution of a "productivity program" in which workers receive bonus payments for meeting company service targets. In this program, workers and managers participate in "analysis groups" to verify the achievement of targeted production levels and to organize production jointly in order to speed up the cable replacement process in districts with antiquated telephone cabling. At BC Tel, the efforts have focused on reorganizing clerical and plant workers in the business division into work teams as a means of speeding up service delivery.

In both cases, management has used language stressing company-union cooperation and the restructuring of the workplace in a less fragmented manner so that workers have a greater say in the production process. However, these surface similarities mask larger differences. For the STRM, the union leadership's strategy has been to cooperate with, and indeed encourage, company speed up efforts in exchange for increased financial compensation for its members through incentive payments. While workers may gain control over the work process in the sense of gaining a say in how to better speed-up their work, they do not gain greater control over health and safety matters, or other aspects of the work process. While some of the membership support this policy, others remain skeptical and there is significant workplace resistance to the increased productivity norms that are being instituted. Some increase in productivity has occurred, but there has been no transformation in the relationship between the union and company management, or between workers and managers; rather, what has been put in place is a classic pay-for-productivity bargain. Still, while the pay-for-productivity exchange is similar, the components on each side of the bargain have changed. Management's provision of a guaranteed salary has been replaced by a combination of a base salary plus productivity bonus payments. The union, instead of pledging to cooperate with management's unilateral organization of work, pledges instead to provide input to better the work process and thereby further increase productivity. That is, while management retains control over the work process, workers are supposed to actively contribute to increase productivity. These changes remain more limited in reality than theory would suggest. But limited though the actual changes may be, the STRM's response reflects one way in which unions that focus on "bread and butter" concerns are likely to respond to competition and globalization in the telecommunications industry.

The story of the TWU's response to workplace change is fundamentally different. Unlike the STRM, and unlike other North American unions such as the Communications Workers of Canada (now part of the Communications, Energy and Paperworkers union), which represents telecommunications workers at Bell Canada and the Communications Workers of America, which represents telecommunications workers in most of the United States, the TWU remained actively opposed to management efforts to reorganize the workplace. While the union has worked with management to ensure the successful implementation of technological changes that effectively increase worker productivity, through its cooperation on the Contracting-Out and Technological Change Committee—and as noted earlier, to facilitate management transfers of workers—the TWU has consistently opposed management efforts to "reengineer" service provisioning in ways that union leaders and members see as reducing worker control over the work process. As shall be seen below, however, the union's resistance has not dissuaded management from trying, as one program after another has come and gone in the past decade.

WORK REORGANIZATION AND UNION RESISTANCE AT BC TEL

> I haven't seen anything like this in years. Getting jobs that put you dealing with customers you've never dealt with before. A situation where management did not tell customers that, due to reorganization, orders were going to be late. Net result: people are being screamed at, yelled at, insulted on the phone by customers. From the perspective of the customer, rightly so. When you know they're right, it does not help. You do work that used to be done by four other people, because the others are not "ready to take it on." There's a huge disparity in the workload. Some people here basically go to work and read the newspaper. Other people are drowning.
>
> TWU counsellor (Interview T-93-32)

In 1993 and 1994, BC Tel instituted its grand experiment in the latest of its new work process program—work teams. As the above quote should make clear, this particular attempt at work re-organization would prove disastrous. Ever since the 1981 strike, the introduction of new work reorganization programs have been a constant at BC Tel. The programs change, but the effort to reorganize does not. Still, there has been a major change in focus over time. While the early programs focused on boosting workplace morale while trying to weaken the union, the latter programs, like similar attempts in Mexico, seek to actively alter the organization of the work process itself (see BC Tel 1992b and 1993a, Gemini 1992a and 1992b, Evans 1992a and 1992b, Dumanceau 1992, McIntyre and Evans 1992, Pilgrim 1992, Wilson 1994).

While "human relations" programs had been tried at BC Tel before,[20] the first major effort came in September 1981, six months after the end of the bitter 1980-81 dispute which was resolved only after B.C. unions began a series of rotating general strikes in response to BC Tel management's intransigence. After that struggle, heads rolled at BC Tel management. A new industrial relations chief, Don Champion, was brought in, to replace the more combative Frank Tucker. This change ushered in a period in which significant union-management conflict persisted, but at a much lower level than in the 1969-1981 period.

In September 1981, Don Champion spoke to a specially-called union convention to present management's quality circle program. The response to his presentation by union delegates was highly skeptical.

One delegate asked if the program was "another smoke screen." Another complained that "We can't even get cooperation on safety problems." A third delegate stated, "You can't have participation with employees when a boss is there—it just doesn't work" (TWU 1981d). The union did not reject the proposal outright, but set conditions that it suspected the company would not accept. As one union official says, "The union took the position that it wanted to pick the [quality circle] participants, have equal participation in the steering committee, and train them [the participants]. The company said flat out 'No'" (Interview T-93-1). A former union executive member confirms that the union fully expected management to reject their conditions (Interview T-93-73). The company tried to implement the program anyway, backed off, and then resumed the program again in 1983 (TWU 1983b). Despite fierce union opposition, a significant minority of the membership did participate in the program. As one union counsellor explains, "A lot of the people went into it for their personal enrichment. It does teach some skills—running a meeting, brainstorming . . . motives for participating were time off [of work], to seek a promotion, or to make things around them work better" (Interview T-93-2). In these groups, typically about 10 to 20 workers would meet, on company time, with a manager present, and discuss work-related problems. The union ran a major campaign against the quality circles, including frequent articles denouncing the program in the union's periodical, the *Transmitter*.[21] The union effort, though not sufficient to entirely shut down the program, was successful enough so that the overall impact was limited. One operator who did attend quality circles meetings claimed the main benefit was that "[they] take us off the board to attend the meeting . . . Half the time I was sleeping" (Interview T-93-31). According to one union counsellor, "They had no clout at all. It was a wonderful way to feel good" (Interview T-93-18).

In some workplaces, particularly in operator services, some changes resulted from the quality circles program, but these charges were pretty limited. As one operator said, "I think there were a few things around the office that changed because of quality circles, but I can't remember what they were. There were a few changes made. Half the lunchroom was [made] smoking and half non-smoking" (Interview T-93-61). Or, as another operator said, "We got a stereo system. We got a food machine which has gone down. There were no changes in our work per se. Just cosmetic changes" (Interview T-93-62). As one union counsellor commented, "The company's idea behind quality circles is to make employees feel like they really had an effect on the workplace. It was an alternative to union meetings. Obviously, it wasn't effective, because they cancelled quality circles" (Interview T-93-30).

But quality circles had an indirect effect. As one union executive member noted, "The workers who stayed behind picked up the slack and worked harder for those who were off the job . . . If you do that long enough, and quality circles went on informally for six to seven years, the majority of people who participated were people with very low seniority and people who didn't like to work . . . It would be interesting to see what impact it had on our members. Well, we know what effect it had—it speeded up their production" (Interview T-93-64).

More important in strengthening the company's hand was its new, more humane approach to labor relations in general. Even though the mid-1980s was the period of the "292" transfers and the shutting down of small city operator offices, overall tension levels at BC Tel dropped markedly. As one union counsellor noted, "They manage smarter. They don't suspend [as often]. They write more reprimands. [They leave] more gray areas" (Interview T-93-10). As another union counsellor explained, "After the '81 strike, the company decided it really didn't want to fight anymore, so it began to be real nice to us . . . And they spent a lot of years trying to convince us they cared about quality . . . Kind of odd that we also had our worst contracts, in terms of pay" (Interview T-93-32). Or, as another union counsellor put it, "Although GTE [BC Tel's parent company] would like to break us, they try to break us with kindness" (Interview T-93-50). The effect, over the course of the eighties, was not so much to reduce worker allegiance to the union, but rather to create an attitude in which workers were more reluctant to trust the more critical appraisal of management activities frequently made by union activists. As one union executive member lamented, "The company gets these slick programs. If we tell the members, 'Don't participate—it's not in your best interests,' they don't even listen to us" (Interview T-93-60). As another member of the union's central executive put it:

> People are not prepared to accept "no" anymore, without rational reasons . . . in 1982, it was different, with quality circles. The best quote at a meeting in Prince George was, management said to one of our delegates, "We have a really bad reputation in the community these days," and the delegate said, "No, *you* have a really bad

reputation in the community these days. *We* don't" (Interview T-93-64).

The company's less caustic approach to human relations at the shop floor also extended to its relations with the union. In particular, management began to take advantage of the joint union-management Committee on Contracting-Out and Technological Change established in 1978 and strengthened somewhat in the 1981 contract. By using the committee process, management was able to sooth the disruptions in the workforce caused by technological change, particularly among central office maintenance workers, in sharp contrast with how such issues would have been handled in the seventies.[22] Since 1980, test work has been centralized twice. First, it was centralized to five regional centers (Aissa 1991). Then, in 1993, it was further centralized into a single provincial network operations center or PNOC (BC Tel 1992c). At both stages, the number of workers employed in testing declined, but all workers retained their employment. As one worker notes, "The technological and contracting-out clause has kept us employed. I'm glad they did [go on strike in the late seventies to get the clause], because I'm still employed because of it" (Interview T-93-45). Enhanced job security has paved the way for tremendous changes in work organization in high-technology areas with a minimum of conflict. As this same worker explains, "To put this place [PNOC] together, half of it was done against the collective agreement" (Interview T-93-45).

There is a fear, however, that if the company's earnings decline as a result of competitive pressures, lay-offs may ensue. Though the Collective Agreement forbids lay-offs caused by technological change, it permits lay-offs for economic reasons. As one union counsellor notes, "I was over in Victoria two months ago. I was talking to people who work in the RNOC [Regional Network Operations Centre] whose work had been transferred to PNOC and they were basically doing nothing. The boss would have odd programs and they'd be fighting over who'd get to do it" (Interview T-93-2). As this union counsellor says, "We know it [the existence of surplus workers] is due to technology, but if the economic impact [hits], they're just riding surplus. Now they're bottom line drops. [Management will say] 'Oh, it's economic.'" (Interview T-93-2).

But while work organization directly related to technological change has been implemented with relatively little conflict, such is not the case with management's attempts to restructure clerical and inside plant work in its business services division. The difference is rooted in two primary factors. First, the restructuring of work that is not directly tied to the introduction of new technology falls outside the purview of the joint union-management Contracting-Out and Technology Committee. Second, management's restructuring plan in the business service division challenged authority relations on the shop floor, by homogenizing and automating much of the work.

Management efforts to undertake this restructuring began in earnest in the late eighties with the Office Efficiency Program (OEP), in which BC Tel managers sought to systematically evaluate and streamline the overall work process. As one union activist noted, "I think OEP was more to be feared than any quality circle. I think the union really overreacted to it [quality circles]. But there's no question that OEP: they represent the choppers. Cutting here, cutting there" (Interview T-93-24).

The union responded to the new program by distributing thousands of pamphlets urging non-participation at worksites (TWU 1988b). The union dubbed OEP "office elimination program" to emphasize the program's focus on reducing office size and hence eliminating jobs, a clear move by management back to Taylorism (Interview T-93-64; TWU 1987, TWU 1989). A key part of the program involved what was, in essence, refined time-and-motion studies by BC Tel managers. To counter management's efforts, the union engaged in a variety of harassment tactics:

> For inside clerical workers, we suggested that when the manager sat with them [to find out what union members' jobs involved], we told them to give them their job description . . . when we discovered that members had a manager sitting with them, we made arrangements for other union members to phone them and tie them up for hours with bullshit orders . . . everywhere they [managers conducting the OEP study] went, the departments ground to a full stop . . . One particular incident—it was the middle of winter—the installation and repair person wore really warm winter clothes and kept the [truck] windows open while the manager froze to death all day long (Interview T-93-64).

According to this union executive member, a key reason why OEP was unsuccessful was that "first-level management was also feeling threatened" (Interview T-93-64) and, consequently, did not crack down on such workplace antics as described above. Upper level management, however, has persisted in its restructuring efforts by trying other programs in rapid-fire succession. These carried such names as Operation '95, Competitive Improvement Project, and Gemini.

In the fall of 1992, management tried another tactic. Firing its consultant who suggested that the way to implement work teams was to get rid of the union, the company agreed to what were, in essence, the union's terms for cooperation, set out at its convention in September 1981! That is, a joint program was established in which the union had equal representation on the steering committee. The union also had the right to appoint at least one shop steward to each team. And training needs of team members were to be determined by the joint union-management committee (BC Tel and TWU 1993). The agreement, which established the union as an equal partner in the pilot program, did not prohibit management from setting up work teams unilaterally elsewhere in the company. However, the union leadership went to its membership and said, "We are involved under [certain] conditions and these are the conditions, and [since] you are not covered under these conditions, we suggest you don't participate . . . And that proved effective" (Interview T-93-64; see also TWU 1993b).

The trial covered the business division, which contains roughly 700 workers. Roughly 200 of these 700 had to change work locations in order to implement the reorganization project (Interview T-93-64). The importance of the trial, however, extended beyond these workers because, had it succeeded, it would surely have been extended to other departments. In addition, because the telecommunications business is driven by services provided to large users, this department is a primary source of revenue for the company. With deregulation, it is anticipated that the share of company resources devoted to large business customers will increase even more.

For some workers in the business division, particularly those involved in residential or small business sales, the effect of the work teams was peripheral. As one clerical worker explained:

> Really, there's only so many things you can do with a service order, so many ways to take a telephone call. You usually get a new boss out of it. I've never seen the work become more efficient or less tedious. There was a program called "inverting the pyramid." They give you mugs, change the stationery. We're still doing the same

things. [But now] I guess the customer is on top. We're on the bottom (Interview T-93-34).

But for others, the work teams represented an important shift in the way their work was done. The goal of the team process was to separate customer orders into two tracks: a "fast track" for small business orders and a "customized track" for larger businesses which have more complicated service orders. As one union counsellor attests, "The outcome the company wants is to industrialize the process, build an assembly line process with fast-track and customized orders" (Interview T-93-32). According to one union executive member, "60-70 percent of the people are under extreme stress . . . [Some have even gotten to the level where] you shut down completely—staring at screens. You don't care. If you keep caring, you crack" (Interview T-93-64). The two sets of processes were outlined by BC Tel management as follows (BC Tel 1992b):

	Fast Track Order Process	Customized Order Process
Type of Customer Order:	Modified "off the shelf"	Uniquely created
Objective	Fast, accurate execution	Get order right first time
Key accountability	One-stop-shop	Quote through billing
Organizational alignment	Centralized, geographical	Decentralized, product-based

In other words, the "fast track" process was designed to speed-up service delivery on small orders. The number of tasks the individual clerical worker had responsibility for increased, but the work pace increased and dead time, during which time a worker may rest, fell dramatically, leading to heightened stress levels. The ideal for this "track" was for orders to be distributed through a computerized call distribution system so that a worker need not pick up the phone. Instead, as iwith operators and residential service clerks, calls would be directly piped into the worker's headphones.

It is in the area of customized orders where worker discretion is required and where the work team's role was most important. A team was supposed to consist of a technician, an engineer, a coordinator, a clerk, a senior marketing service rep, a commercial rep, a system support rep, a business support rep, a special accounts rep [billing], and a computer account rep. But, as one union counsellor described, "They don't have enough people for the workload . . . [for instance] some have one commercial rep for three teams" (Interview T-93-47), instead of one rep per team, as the teams were designed to have on paper.

In theory, the rearrangement was supposed to generate increased efficiencies. Sometimes it did. For instance, a clerk, upon receiving a technical order, could refer it to the technician in her own work group, or if there was a billing question, could refer it to the billing rep of his/her work group (Interview T-93-47). But problems arose in the implementation of these changes, particularly in the breakdown of the informal, team-like work practices that existed prior to the initiation of the new team program. As one union executive member argued:

> What [work teams] destroyed is informal procedures. Give any work
> group a specific task and they do it long enough, over time they build
> up an informal network that exists. They discover ways to short
> circuit the job—to get it done faster. They develop their own informal
> procedures. It's not written down anywhere. It something that's
> internal. They changed people's phone numbers. They broke down
> that underground infrastructure. They destroyed that completely.
>
> (Interview T-93-64)

Breaking down informal procedures is a standard technique for management to gain greater control over the work process. Indeed, there are some important parallels between the informal work practices of telephone workers described here and the informal work practices, described by Harley Shaiken, of machine tool workers prior to automation (Shaiken 1986). As Shaiken writes, "Any self-respecting senior machinist has a legendary 'black book' that records the problems encountered and the shortcuts discovered on previous jobs, usually in some indecipherable shorthand" (Shaiken 1986: 54). The analytical skills acquired on the job by some of the specialized business service workers are equally complex. By more clearly defining the tasks to be performed and making greater use of computerized supervision, upper management seeks to increase its control over the work force. What is different about the resulting changes in telecommunications work, though, is the degree to which lower-level management work is threatened. The work teams were designed to be largely self-supervised, which obviously meant a reduced role for supervisors. As one union counsellor explained, "There were probably six or seven managers managing the different groups of people we have in the team, where there is one manager now" (Interview T-93-47). While resistance from lower-level management wasn't immediately visible, there were tell-tale signs; essentially, the program was allowed to founder. The same union counsellor described the ambivalence, "I'm really glad I don't have a manager all the time, but there is a time when a customer wants to go to a manager and hopefully a manager will be available. They are never around. Even if we needed the support, we couldn't get it" (Interview T-93-47).

In the end, the work team program folded in the fall of 1994, when the union announced that it would pull out, slightly less than two years after the experiment began. Presumably, management will try other forms of work reorganization. Whether the union will be able to negotiate a long-term resolution to the issue of workplace control—or, more realistically, a framework, such as a joint committee, within which such issues can be negotiated—remains to be seen. As will be seen below, the contrast with the Mexican STRM couldn't be more stark. Though effective at blocking certain forms of workplace changes that are generating high stress levels in the workplace, the TWU's response to date is, in the words of its own activists, "ad hoc" (Interview T-93-32).

What is clear is that the main effect of BC Tel management's workplace reorganization programs, other than achieving limited workplace changes, has been to create an atmosphere of widespread cynicism. As one union executive member suggests, however, management is presumably able to use the information gained through such programs to refine the future implementation of technological change, especially the implementation of software systems that will enable the same work group to perform a greater number of tasks (Interview T-93-64). The cynicism that pervades in the workplace is perhaps best summed up in a paper presented by one union delegate at the TWU's January 1994 convention:

> We have seen corporate philosophies declared with much solemnity and then promptly forgotten. Department goals set and forgotten. We have been competitively improved. And now, after nearly two years of gestation, we have been teamed (Wilson 1994: 1).

Though negative sentiments regarding team programs are common among telephone workers wherever such programs have been tried, the TWU's stance is highly unusual. Unlike the unions at Bell Canada and AT&T, the TWU's union leadership has not only refused to endorse work teams, but has actively resisted them. This has not prevented the union from cooperating with the company, as has been done on numerous occasions regarding technological change, but has served to preserve a much more traditional, confrontational attitude.[23] Conventional wisdom holds that unions must cooperate with management in redesigning the workplace in the era of global competition (Hoerr 1991). So far, at least, the TWU's ability to hold its own in resisting work teams and quality circles suggests that this is, at best, true to a limited extent.[24]

WORK REORGANIZATION AND UNION RESPONSE AT TELMEX

In the STRM, efforts at cooperation have a different genesis and a different trajectory. Here the union has, at least in part, sought to use the language of cooperation as a technique to establish a new path for unions in a hostile Mexican labor environment. The union has also used work process restructuring as a means to skirt government wage and price controls (STRM 1993b). Prior to 1989, this end-run of government wage controls was done by revising department work contracts, but the *concertación* eliminated these contracts, and hence sharply restricted the ability of individual departments to earn *retabulaciones* or department-specific wage increases. In exchange for the STRM's agreement to raise overall productivity, however, the government has been willing to concede additional wage gains to union workers.[25]

The STRM first proposed the installation of a "Quality Model" in 1988. Based on quality circle programs, the union sought to demonstrate its commitment to raising productivity in exchange for higher pay for its members and the right to influence in the implementation of new technology. As noted in the last chapter, this effort failed when the union leadership was pressured by the government to sign the *convenio de concertación*. Nonetheless, it is important to examine the "quality model" the union proposed, as it served as a forerunner to the Productivity Program established between the privatized Telmex and the STRM in 1993.

In the STRM's vision of the quality model, the goal is to actively encourage management to adopt a high-wage, high-productivity model of development. While this model is adorned with lots of philosophical nonsense,[26] the central notion that the union must focus on "productivity with quality" (Sandoval Cavazos 1988: 23) is defensible, given that Telmex is the high-wage service provider in Mexico's telecommunications market. After the 1989 *concertación*, the union sought to resuscitate this idea, getting the company to commit to negotiations concerning a new Program of Quality and Productivity as part of the 1992 Collective Bargaining Agreement (Telmex and STRM 1992).

Based on this agreement, Telmex and the STRM established a Productivity Program, initially in outside plant and later extended to the company as a whole (Telmex and STRM 1993a). The key elements of the plan were: 1) the curtailment of overtime payments and their conversion into bonus payments, tied to the achievement of corporate service goals, many of which were already set by the privatized company's concession agreement with the government in 1990, and 2) the establishment of joint union-management analysis groups to monitor the fulfillment of these service targets and, in outside plant, to plan the rehabilitation of districts with antiquated cabling.

In terms of the STRM's high-wage, high-productivity approach, the results are mixed. Work intensity has increased, but the productivity gains, especially in outside plant, have fallen short of projected goals, requiring that additional piece work rates be set for priority jobs done outside the normal 8-to-4 work schedule (Lovera 1994, Telmex and STRM 1993b; see also Telmex and STRM 1994a, 1994b). As far as wages are concerned, these climbed somewhat prior to the December 1994 peso devaluation. But for many workers, especially those in outside plant, the incentive wage payments were less remunerative than the amount they earned through overtime payments before the program began. The productivity agreement thus proved to be of limited effectiveness in circumventing government wage guidelines. Over all, the union's productivity push has trapped it in an impossible game. With the company providing expanding service, but with no increase in the size of the unionized workforce since 1988, the union is losing leverage, as more and more the company can send its work to contractors and non-union affiliates if the union is recalcitrant. Through its productivity program, the union has sought to boost its production so that management will not wish to avail itself of its contracting options.

But acting in this manner actually reduces the need for management to hire new workers. As long as the process continues, the union's position will be increasingly tenuous.

Moreover, the union's promotion of higher productivity is proving disorienting for many workers; instead of the analysis groups balancing working conditions and wages, often these groups contribute to the speed-up. Often such speed-up focuses purely on increasing quantity, leading in some cases to a decline in service quality.

The productivity program was introduced in two stages. The first stage applied only to outside plant and was implemented in November 1992 (Interview S-94-3). In this stage, productivity bonuses were paid in direct connection with the amount produced, but the lack of quality controls made it possible for some workers to earn a lot of money by doing high-quantity, low-quality work (TIE 1994). As one worker explained, "They put a price on each job. They constructed a table of prices. One worker earned 20 million pesos [U.S. $6,500] . . . The process began to cost management a lot of money" (TIE 1994). Or, as another worker stated, "At first, they did it as the union proposed. They paid the incentive according to each individual's productivity. Three months later, they changed the program and now the payment's given in proportion to the compound's productivity. In the first stage, some earned a whole lot of money" (Interview S-94-7a).

The second stage was initiated in June 1993 and was implemented company-wide. This time, management made sure to put a cap on the incentive payment. Receipt of these incentives was contingent on workers reaching production goals jointly determined by management and the union. Overtime payments were to be curtailed and the money that management had dedicated to overtime was to be converted into a fund, equal to 40% of workers' salaries, to be paid out in the form of productivity incentive payments, except for outside plant workers, whose bonus was a slightly higher 50% (Interview S-94-24).

This program has major effects on the distribution of income *among* work groups. According to one union executive member, previously 70% of the pool of overtime money went to outside plant workers, with operators and *técnicos* each getting roughly 15%, and clerical and administrative workers receiving almost nothing. Under the new system, plant workers only get 47%.[27] Not surprisingly, this was not popular with outside plant workers. But there are more problems.

Indeed, problems with the incentive program abound. Payments of incentives often are delayed. Work stoppages have often proved necessary to get management to make the agreed-upon incentive payments (Interviews S-94-11, S-94-15, S-94-17, S-94-18b, S-94-18e, S-94-26, S-94-32). In addition, there are enormous administrative problems. Each work "area" (operator services, outside plant, central office, transmission, and clerical) has its own targets. For operator services, the key target is to answer 91% of all inbound calls within 10 seconds. For central office, there is a set of transmission indicators. For outside plant, there is a separate set of indicators, designed to encourage workers to keep a high percentage of telephone booths in service, respond rapidly to repair and service orders, and to keep line faults at a low level. Clerical incentives are tied to achieving a sufficient number of new orders. Transmission incentives are based on expanding the number of lines in operation. Beyond such obvious problems as the fact that a decline in service orders may result from an economic downturn, rather than poor performance by clerical workers, there is the problem that many jobs are hard to measure in quantifiable terms at all. For instance, administrative workers receive, per capita, the average of everyone else's incentive payment. Workers in some specialities are paid bonuses on the basis of the per capita average of the performance of their work area, such as outside plant or transmission (STRM 1993b, 1993c, 1993d, and 1994d).

Assuming a given work group has reached its target, the group must split the incentive fund. But this fund is not split equally. Workers who have missed work have their absent days discounted from their incentive payment. In operator services, workers have part of the bonus payment discounted if they are late too frequently. In some areas, such as outside plant, part of the incentive payment is also individually calculated. As one union coordinator explains, this is an incredibly complicated process:

> The individual payment is determined by dividing the individual increase in productivity—which is the percentage of increase in individual productivity times the number of days worked times the salary—by the sum of all the individual productivity increases in the department. The administrative workers, as one cannot measure their productivity directly, receive a bonus percentage equal to the highest individual increase in productivity of the department. In that way, those with the highest productivity and the administrative workers receive the great majority of the bonus fund. Of course, if the compound doesn't reach the target, there's nothing to distribute. Also,

one should note, if I increase my productivity, but all the coworkers in my department also increase their productivity, the incentive payment stays the same, since the bonus fund is capped (Interview S-94-24).

As one plant worker notes more succinctly, "How much we earn is variable; we don't all have the same bonus payment" (Interview S-94-17). In outside plant, where the discord over the incentive program has been the greatest—since the program resulted in a significant pay cut for them—additional money has been offered for weekend and evening installations. In essence, this is a resurrected form of overtime, except that the company, instead of paying overtime (as is required by Mexican labor law), pays workers a set amount of money for each installation. These payments include 70 pesos (roughly U.S. $20 before the 1994 devaluation) per installation, 70 pesos for every 3-4 repair orders, and piece work rates for reconstructing districts with antiquated cable, where the payment varies according to the amount of work performed. According to a union coordinator, roughly 20% of the outside plant workers "work every day until 8 o'clock [in the evening] and even on Saturday and Sunday," while the other 80% settle for the reduced pay levels caused by the productivity program (Interview S-94-24).

The analysis groups are supposed to oversee the incentive process and prevent abuses. Some union activists even see these groups as instruments for increasing the union's control over the work process. Indeed, given that the analysis groups give a small set of workers at each office the chance to meet on company time to discuss work-related issues, this is not an unrealistic expectation. But so far the record of the analysis groups, like that of the productivity program itself, has been decidedly mixed. In some places, members of the analysis group spend 40 hours a week in their group activities. In many other worksites, the analysis groups exist on paper only. Where these groups are fully functioning, their work is rather extensive. As a member of one such group explains, the analysis groups aim:

First, to detect the knots—the bottlenecks—of the production process. The analysis group, together with the union coordinator has to get together with management in order to arrive at an agreement over how to reach these productivity goals. The other thing is that there is a quality goal. One has to have fewer than 8% of complaints in the

170,000 lines we have [in our district]. We are around about 24%.
That is the problem—these percentages (Interview S-94-25).

The analysis groups constantly double-check management figures, make sure cable work is done well, order equipment to prepare the reconstruction of districts with damaged cables, and at times go into the field to conduct electrical tests or lend a helping hand on troublesome orders (Interview S-94-25). As an analysis group member explains, "You have to look to make sure the data are not falsified. You talk with clerical workers; while they have 80 to 100 complaints a day, management says there are 250" (Interview S-94-25).

Fault finding is also an extensive process, involving the checking of hundreds of points in the telephone service network. As the same analysis group member says, "We have to see if these 250 complaints are in the switching or in the cables, and see if subcontractors are harming the cables they open . . . in the analysis groups, you have to be attentive" (Interview S-94-25).

The size of the analysis group varies from 4 to 12 members (Interview S-94-18e). There is a management component to the analysis group that meets with the union members 3 to 4 times a week; the rest of the time the unionized members of the analysis group work without direct management participation (Interview S-94-18e). Another analysis group member explains that the group has to do line fault and cable checking, communicate with other analysis groups, work with facility workers to plan the reconstruction of districts, keep an eye on subcontractors and Telmex non-union subsidiaries which compete with the union for telephone construction and maintenance work, and search for available distributor boxes[28] so as to give attention to backlogged orders (Interview S-94-18e).

Some activists, particularly among those who are in the union opposition, attempt to use the analysis groups "as a place where the workers can recover control over the work process and make decisions about the company's programs" (Interview S-94-32). According to one worker, in some of these groups, "They have begun to recuperate work material [away from subcontractor firms]" (Interview S-94-5b). But there are significant problems. As one worker notes, the idea is that "these groups analyze the problems within the work area and propose solutions . . . [We want them to have the] authority to really be able to implement the solutions that they believe to be suitable. And this management has rejected" (Interview S-94-5e). While worker participation has been high in some analysis groups (Interview S-94-5b), "The groups that are well formed are rare. Before, there used to be more participation of the rank-and-file—there was greater worker decision-making authority" (Interview S-94-25).

The attitude of members outside the analysis groups is generally, though not universally, negative. While one worker says they are functioning well (Interview S-94-17), most contend this is not the case. As one administrative worker says "there is a personal reticence, on the part of both the union and management to accept this new model" (Interview S-94-8). An outside plant worker contends that "If they were really legitimized, it would permit us to advance [but] decision-making authority remains with management" (Interview S-94-11). According to an outside plant repair worker, the analysis groups' effectiveness have been "very, very limited" (Interview S-94-13). According to an operator, the analysis group at her work site "seems to have serious deficiencies . . . they focus on immediate questions. There is no planning" (Interview S-94-15). Among central office workers, the analysis groups are administrative creations only, existing on paper, but never meeting (Interview S-94-20). And, as an installation worker notes, although the analysis group at his work site has "influence in the decision making of the compound managers . . . Management rejects or opposes the suggestions in order to not lose control . . . [especially] when it costs money" (Interview S-94-28). Another problem, one that may be endemic to any political organization, is that the selection of analysis group participants has become enmeshed in the union's politics. According to one opposition member, "Instead of being a structure to control the production process, they are being converted into quotas [fiefdoms] of [political] power" (Interview S-94-24).

As another opposition member notes, "The analysis groups have had an uneven application. Where they have had a more concrete application is in the Federal District [Mexico City] . . . in outside plant . . . It is here where they have really disputed with management control over the work process" (Interview S-94-32). In those cases where analysis groups have been established, with full time participation of union members, the union has been able to give workers a sense of greater control over how their work is carried out. But the analysis group's advisory authority is limited to making suggestions on how to increase productivity. As noted by an analysis group *supporter*, worker suggestions that overtime pay may be needed to get certain jobs done, for example, are summarily rejected by management (Interview S-94-28). As another worker sympathetic to the analysis group idea notes, "Effectively, [increasing] productivity is seen as increasing work intensity. Obviously, the function [of the analysis groups] ought to be totally different" (Interview S-94-5b). In some cases, according to one clerical worker, "These groups, what they have done, is to dedicate themselves to be new supervisors of our co-workers" (Interview S-94-5c).

In short, in those places where the analysis groups have been established, they do provide a space for worker involvement in the production process. The clear mandate of the groups is to increase productivity, but workers participating in the groups gain access to company data and are able to suggest methods of increasing productivity that may be less harmful to union members. Moreover, there is the potential to use the groups as a means to demand better working conditions as a quid pro quo for higher productivity. But this potential is not pursued, except by a few opposition activists. Instead, while checking some arbitrary local management decisions, analysis groups have mainly served as another mechanism to speed up production. To the extent that the union is able to get wage gains from the productivity program as a whole, this might be a fair exchange. But here, too, the record is mixed: outside plant pay has fallen, while pay in other areas has increased (at least prior to the December 1994 devaluation).

The other problem, of course, is that due to the *concertación*, there has been a reduction in the union's overall ability to influence the direction of the company, particularly in terms of the implementation of technological change and work organization company-wide (TIE 1994). The fact that management saw itself compelled to negotiate an agreement with the union in 1992 and 1993 *does* speak to the union's continuing ability to influence, through shop floor resistance and other tactics, the direction of the company, but the *terms* of the productivity agreement and the actual performance of the analysis groups show that the union has a long way to go to make up the ground lost in 1989.

CONCLUSION

In comparing the two unions' responses to work organization issues, some interesting similarities emerge. Both the TWU and the STRM have had to confront and accommodate a tremendous shift in where work is performed in the telephone industry. Both unions have had to face declines in the percentage of operators among their membership. Both have seen work expand in some areas and contract in others. And both unions have centralized their decision-making structures, due to a combination of perceived organizational needs and political positioning.

In the TWU, the most notable shift has been that the clerical section of the company has grown tremendously, as computerization allows many functions previously preformed by outside plant workers to be done by clerical staff. The TWU at times has fought this shift, but ultimately has had to accommodate the company, as the TWU's collective bargaining agreement placed few restrictions on company reassignment of work. The shifting of workers, most dramatically in the case of the 292 plant workers who were temporarily transferred into clerical posts, shook up internal union politics considerably, leading to a rise in political consciousness by the largely female, clerical workforce. Plant-clerical conflicts have risen on various occasions since then, notably in 1990 when a letter of agreement was negotiated allowing clerical workers with the proper prerequisites to bid into plant posts and, again in 1993, when a series of letters of agreement were signed by the union and management to facilitate worker transfers and avert lay-offs.

The STRM has not faced the same dramatic shift of work to clerical workers as has the TWU, largely because the computerization of clerical functions at Telmex has not proceeded at the same pace as at BC Tel, though it is certain that clerical workers will become more important in the STRM as computerization proceeds. But the STRM has also had its share of problems regarding shifting organizational boundaries. Indeed, in some respects, the STRM's problems have been more severe, since Telmex's organizational structure has traditionally been more fragmented. In place of the TWU's 3 divisions, the STRM had 63 separate departments.

The mass transfers of operators has been the greatest challenge for the STRM, but it has also had to deal with the liquidation of other departments, such as private switchboard workers and automotive workers. The example of the private switchboard workers provides a stark reminder of the continued existence of sharp factional splits within the STRM, a legacy of the bitter battle for political control that took place in the union in 1982. A difference with the TWU has been the STRM's promotion of the merging of distinct job categories. While the TWU has also had to accommodate to organizational change of this type, it has done so reluctantly. By contrast, the STRM enthusiastically embraces the creation of multi-task jobs, which it sees as part of its overall strategy of pursuing high-wage, high-productivity work, by working with management to boost worker productivity.

The differences of the two unions are much clearer, however, when one compares their approaches to work teams and quality circles. Here a union's ability to respond appears relatively unimpeded by an imperative to accommodate globalization, nor is the state labor regime much of a factor. Rather, the differences in the positions of the leadership of the two unions appear to be decisive. While the STRM union leadership has advocating work teams, analysis groups, and productivity incentive payments, the TWU has fiercely resisted all cooperation programs. Although the TWU has been willing to cooperate with BC Tel management in the managing of technological change, through the contractual mechanism of the Contracting-Out and Technological Change committee, the TWU has not been willing to cooperate with management attempts to boost productivity by reorganizing the workplace. Instead, though the TWU's tactics change according to the program presented, its position has been remarkably consistent for the past two decades. So far, the TWU's resistance has been successful and there is, in fact, little reason to anticipate a change in this respect.

The STRM's accommodationist stance and the TWU's resistance are, of course, emblematic of broader attitudes of the two unions, consistent with their distinctive overall strategic approaches. These differences are even more evident in the next topic of this study—the relationship of the union to the state. For while the STRM cooperated with the state, the TWU provides a rather different example, seeking to swim against the tide of globalization and greater competition in the industry.

NOTES

1. According to GM calculations, during one week of May 1986, a car being produced using team production at the GM-Toyota joint venture Nummi factory in Fremont, California, required 21.2 hours of labor to be produced, compared to an average of 37 hours at other GM plants, which were still organized along more traditional Taylorist lines (Parker and Slaughter 1988: 10).

2. Interestingly, according to a recent study, at AT&T, "The transformation of white-collar work has done remarkably little to alter clerical workers' consciousness" (Vallas 1993: 169). Leaving aside the question of whether clerical work can be accurately characterized as "white collar,"—feminist labor writers tend to refer to such workers as "pink collar" (Freeman 1983)—it would appear that the long-predicted upswing in clerical militancy is beginning to occur, as illustrated by clerical workers' resistance to work teams at BC Tel in the past few years.

3. As one TWU counsellor stated, "BC Tel is splintering off a lot of companies. But so far we've been relatively successful in keeping them under the TWU banner" (Interview T-93-2).

4. The union won in Court on the ground that the lay-off violated the Canada Labour Code. This ruling was, however, overturned on appeal. But by the time the appeal ruling was issued, the union was in bargaining with management over the terms of the collective bargaining agreement for 1983-1984 and was able to get a no lay-off pledge from the company, prior to signing the new Collective Agreement (Interview T-93-12).

5. As is the case with any legal document, a collective agreement is subject to different interpretations. The exact meaning of the TWU's transfer and assignment of work clauses is not clear; it is particularly unclear whether assignment of work across divisional lines is permissible. Otherwise. it seems that the more conservative reading of the contract by the union leadership majority is correct. Nothing in the transfer clause indicates the requirement for the company to go by seniority. Furthermore, the assignment of work clauses don't limit the length of the time for reassignment, though it is implied that this should be done only for short periods of time.

6. As in Clark's 1980 election, exact figures are not available in the Convention minutes. From conversations that I held with various attendees, it would appear that Clark won a vote of confidence by roughly a 60% to 40% split. An indication of the level of hard-core opposition would be that 32 of the 93 delegates asked that their names be recorded in the minutes supporting the immediate implementation of an overtime ban, against the recommendation of the union leadership majority (TWU 1984b).

7. However, Clark would retire one year later, being replaced in a special Convention election by Larry Armstrong, a business agent who was a long-time Clark supporter.

8. This difference is seen in various ways. Besides the increase in wildcats seen among clerical workers in the 1990s, the number of women members on the executive council has doubled from 3 as late as 1986 to 6 of 14 in 1988. In that year, for the first time in the union's history, a female candidate was

elected as Secretary-Treasurer, one of the union's three "table officer" positions. (The others are President and Vice President). While progress by women has stalled at roughly the same level since (in 1995, women held 6 of 15 executive board slots) and the "old boys' network" still dominates TWU politics, its dominance is less pronounced than that visible in other telecommunications unions in Canada. At a tri-national conference of telephone workers from Canada, the United States, and Mexico held in February 1994, the TWU was the only organization present in which more than one-third of its executive board positions were held by women.

9. As one former union business agent explained, "The additions to staff weren't under the job posting procedure. But having said that, the company usually posted them. The reason they posted them was because they could get trained people into the jobs" (Interview T-93-50).

10. From 1976 to 1988, the size of the Telmex unionized workforce doubled from approximately 20,000 to 40,000. However, since 1988, it has remained roughly the same, much as has been the case in BC Tel, where unionized workforce levels have remained roughly constant in the 11,000-12,000 range for the past 15 years. One key difference is that the ratio of management to union employees at BC Tel has levelled out since 1980, while at Telmex the management:union ratio rose from 9% to 19%; as well, the size of non-union subsidiaries has increased at Telmex, as has the extent of work contracted out.

11. As shown elsewhere (Dubb 1992), the four main internal union conflicts of 1958, 1967, 1975-76, and 1982, all originated in department-level grievances that shop stewards felt had not been adequately addressed by the central union leadership. The 1975-76 conflict stemmed from a dispute over the renegotiation of a *convenio departamental* in the central office maintenance department; one of the key actors in the *convenio* negotiations was Francisco Hernández Juárez.

12. Prior to the 1989 convenio de concertación, Clause 189 of the Collective Agreement stated that, "Management and union agree to revise the department-level work agreements of those Departments in which there are introduced substantial administrative or technical changes." In most department-level work agreements, "substantial" was defined as affecting 50% of more of the department's workforce.

13. The union leadership withheld the shares in the privatized company owed to these workers in an escrow account until such time as the workers drop their claim or a court orders the union to relinquish the shares. Union leaders feel that such actions are an acceptable, albeit illegal, response. As one union advisor explained, "It's a tactic. The shares are set aside for them . . . But it will cost them work [to file a claim against the union and receive their shares]. If we

hadn't done anything, we could have had many more people filing grievances against the union" (Interview S-94-27).

14. In particular, the union has successfully promoted "the creation of a general system of training at Telmex," which has included the creation of new training school, known as Inttelmex; the construction of new classrooms; the creation of new courses; the conducting of surveys to assess training needs; and the creation of training profiles in 13 of the larger work groups. Overseen by a joint committee with 18 union and 18 management representatives, training has so far focused on the 4,000 operators who are transferring to other specialities (Interview S-94-21). Union leader Francisco Hernández Juárez represents the union on the committee overseeing the new Inttelmex training school. The impact of these changes on workers other than transferring operators has been limited (Interviews S-94-7a, S-94-7c, S-94-10c, S-94-11, S-94-17, S-94-28) though there has been a limited increase in course availability (Interviews S-94-10b, S-94-25, S-94-31). Perhaps there will be a greater impact in the level of training after the operator transfer process is completed.

15. Red-circling is a common practice in industrial relations when a worker who is transferred from a high-paying job to a lower-paying job continues to receive the higher salary, until such a point where increases in the salary of the new job exceeds the salary the worker received at the former job. At that time the worker simply is paid the same as other workers in the same job category.

16. This is one area where the STRM has been successful in maintaining work under its jurisdiction that in other telephone companies would be a management function. In most other Telmex departments, by contrast, the union-management dividing lines are similar to those that exist in the TWU.

17. Though of little importance here, Línea Proletaria considered itself to be a Maoist group. Its "revolutionary" program is unclear, but the basic idea was that the installation of base-driven structures such as the small assemblies would lead to an eventual transformation of the union itself.

18. For instance, the number of workers in the small union representing workers at one Telmex subsidiary, Impulsora, which hires facilities design specialists, has increased from 362 in 1988 to 482 in 1992. This increase is larger than it seems, however, when one considers that most of the 362 workers in 1988 have passed on to management positions. 143 of the 482 people covered by the Collective Agreement at Impulsora were hired in 1990 and 155 more were hired in 1991—all at a time when the number of STRM members remained stagnant (Impulsora and SINATIMEL 1992).

19. For a general overview of work team programs, see Kochan et al 1986: 146-177. For a critique of team production see Parker and Slaughter 1988 and Parker 1985. For critiques based on individual country studies, see Cooper

1993 (Australia); Watanabe 1993 (Japan); and Müller 1993 and Müller-Jentsch et al. 1992 (Germany).

20. The first such program was known as the Challenge of '72. As one union executive member explains, "Basically, it was a 'Royal Commission' to investigate the state of industrial relations at BC Tel—more like a 'group hug' session and summarily dismissed by the members, who were cynical" (Interview T-93-64).

21. See, for instance, TWU 1983b, TWU 1985a, Shniad 1986, Hiebert 1987, Hiebert 1988, TWU 1988a, and TWU 1988b.

22. The dramatic nature of this change was commented upon by one arbitrator: "I used to have a lot of arbitration work [from BC Tel and the TWU]. I don't see it anymore" (Canada Notes: Misc1).

23. An example of the union's willingness to compromise and accommodate management was the executive's decision to enter into a Letter of Agreement to permit the company to contract out residential long distance sales work (i.e., telemarketing sales of long-distance discount programs to heavy telephone users) in exchange for a guarantee that union members will be given all the work related to the processing of the orders. In this highly controversial case, the union leadership decided that, given long distance competition and the fact that competitors were using door-to-door sales to gain residential customers from BC Tel, the number of sales jobs lost would be offset by the increase in the number of BC Tel customers and hence the amount of work for BC Tel workers.

24. Indeed, compared to the CWC/CEP at Bell Canada or the STRM at Telmex, the TWU has done a better job of preserving jobs for its membership than unions that have participated in workplace restructuring. The number of employees per 10,000 lines at BC Tel is 84, at Bell Canada 67, and at Telmex 68.9 (BC Tel 1992b, STRM 1994c).

25. Indeed, in the past few years, it has been government policy to encourage pay-for-productivity, though no one has gone as far as implementing this principle as have the STRM and Telmex. See STyPS 1991.

26. An example: "This reflection has its antecedents, as is to be expected, in the Greek world: Parmenides, Archimides in the first place, giving place to a school of thought in the West that has been continually updated: from St. Anselmo to Heidigger, passing through Lagrange" (Sandoval Cavazos 1988: 25). Trying to portray these philosophers as advocates of a high-wage, high-productivity production model is, to put it kindly, a stretch.

27. Calculation based on the fact that plant workers make up 37.34% of the Telmex workforce, but receive incentive payments that are 25% than other Telmex workers (50% v. 40% of the base salary). Though plant workers'

earnings (due to higher overtime) have traditionally been high, their base salary is very close to the average for all Telmex workers. In Feb. 1994, the average outside plant worker salary was N$79.66, only 52 centavos greater than the salary of the average STRM member (STRM 1994c).

28. A distributor box is a metal cabinet in which neighborhood telephone lines are connected to a single T-3 cable, which carries the calls from the distributor box to the local switching exchange.

CHAPTER SEVEN

Telecommunications Unions and the State

In analyses of Mexican labor, it is common to see unions described as creatures of the state, but rarely is a similar description applied to unions in Canada. While there are differences in the relationship between the state and labor in Mexico and Canada, these changes are not as profound as is commonly believed. Moreover, the nature of the telecommunications sector reduces even those differences that do exist. This occurs for two reasons. First of all, dealing with the shop-floor issues that inevitably emerge regarding technological change in the industry requires localized expertise; as a result, telecommunications is less amenable than many other industrial sectors to being run by state-selected political operatives in a top-down fashion. Additionally, telecommunications, because it is an increasingly important element of infrastructure for a range of other industries, tends to be heavily regulated by the state, even if state officials adopt "free market" principles elsewhere. In Canada, the state interacts with the TWU not only through the Department of Labour's mediation of labor disputes, but also through the decisions of the CRTC, Canada's main telecommunications regulatory decision-making body. Today, deregulation is being pursued in both Canada and Mexico, but such "deregulation" would more accurately be characterized as a restructuring of government regulation (Horwitz 1988). As a result, the STRM and the TWU operate in an environment in which state intervention plays an important role in influencing union decisions indirectly through regulation, but in which union officials enjoy a fair degree of autonomy from direct state intervention in internal union affairs.

Two main aspects of the state-union relationship are examined in this chapter: 1) the relationships among the state, unions, and political parties in the two countries both prior to and following the onset of the wave of technological change that began in the 1970s, 2) the manner in which state policy decisions in the area of telecommunications (particularly privatization and deregulation in Mexico and deregulation in Canada) have altered these traditional relationships, as well as the tactics used by the two unions in their interaction with state authorities. As discussed in greater detail in Chapters 3 and 4, the thesis of Mexican labor exceptionalism does not hold up well to scrutiny, particularly in the telecommunications industry. Indeed, in many respects, as shall be seen below, the role of the state in telecommunications is becoming more similar in the two countries. Nevertheless, while state policy in the two countries is converging rapidly, the unions' responses have been rather different, a difference that stems in large measure from the unions' distinct strategic goals.

UNION, PARTY, AND STATE: THE TENUOUS RELATIONSHIP

Both the TWU and the STRM maintain nominal political independence in that neither union is affiliated with any political party. Nonetheless, both provide consistent support to a single political party, often to a greater degree than other unions that do have party affiliations. The reason for this support is clear: given the central role the state plays in regulation of the industry, it is to the union's advantage to build favorable ties with government officials. But this superficial similarity masks important differences. In the case of the British Columbian TWU, the union's alliance is with the New Democratic Party (NDP), a social-democratic party whose primary organizational and financial backing comes from English-Canadian labor unions in British Columbia, Manitoba, Saskatchewan, and Ontario.[1] In the case of the Mexican STRM, the union's alliance is with the Partido Revolucionario Institucional (Institutional Revolutionary Party, hereafter PRI), whose current financial backing comes primarily from Mexico's business elite, even though the PRI was initially founded by unions, peasant federations, military officers, and government bureaucrats. A second important difference is that the Canadian NDP has been in power at the provincial level in British Columbia only twice (1972-1975 and 1991-present) and has never governed at the federal level, where most telecommunications regulatory issues in Canada are decided. By contrast, the PRI has maintained near-total control over Mexican politics since 1929. A final important difference is in the structure of the two country's political systems. The Mexican political system is highly authoritarian, dominated by a single political party (the PRI) that uses electoral fraud, intimidation, and control over the media to ensure its permanence in power. Canada's political system, on the other hand, is more pluralist, in which often dramatic shifts in power occur via electoral competition, encouraged by minimal voter party loyalty and its first-past-the-post parliamentary voting system.[2] These differences in a) the nature of the party's platforms, b) the degree of power wielded by the party backed by the union, and c) the regime itself greatly influence how unions in the two countries interact with the state.

To put it bluntly, electoral democracy does make a difference. Because Mexico has had an authoritarian political system, the ability of Mexican unions to publicly challenge the government's economic policy has been reduced.[3] The existence of electoral democracy in Canada allows unions there to fund an independent political party, the NDP, that promotes their public policy views regarding macroeconomic policy and enables them to push for laws that facilitate union organizing. Mexico's more authoritarian political system has resulted in labor leaders there being forced to confront much greater repression and greater state interference in internal union affairs (such as the election of union officers) than their Canadian counterparts (see, for instance, La Botz 1992).

Nonetheless, in terms of labor's daily interaction with the state, the impact of these differences can be easily exaggerated. Moreover, the differences in the role played by the state in telecommunications in the two countries has decreased as technological change accelerated. Despite the important differences in politics in the two countries, the dynamic of union-party, and ultimately, union-state relations exhibit some important similarities. While at one time the role of the state in the STRM was clearly greater than the role of the state in the TWU, in recent decades the role of the state has increased in Canada and decreased in Mexico. As a result, the difference is much less than it once was.

To analyze these issues, I focus first on the state's role in the TWU and STRM digitalization disputes, discussed previously in Chapter 5.

Returning to examine these disputes allows for more careful study of the role of the state in industrial relations conflicts. From this analysis, it is clear that Mexican state labor officials have been active in STRM politics in a way that has not occurred within the TWU, although, even here, differences are not as great as what is commonly argued. Moreover, Canadian state officials, through Canadian Labour Relations Board (CLRB) injunctions and Department of Labour mediation, also exercise considerable influence. Unlike what the corporatist model would predict, the Mexican state and the PRI[4] are not able to run the STRM in a top-down manner, although they exercise considerable influence.

Because the STRM maintains relative independence from the state and the PRI in setting collective bargaining goals and in managing internal union affairs, more and more the STRM's interaction with the PRI and the Mexican state parallels that of the TWU's interaction with the NDP and the Canadian state. That is, the Mexican state acts as a mediator of conflicts and an industry regulator and the STRM acts as a pressure group within the PRI, seeking to use its political ties within the party and with state officials to pressure management or the state to make concessions. The shifting nature of the state's role in the telecommunications industry and the contrasting responses of the TWU and the STRM to state deregulatory and privatizing efforts are the focus of the second half of this chapter.

MEXICO: TECHNOLOGICAL CHANGE AND THE DEMISE OF TRADITIONAL "CORPORATISM"

Much has been written about the STRM's relationship with the state. Different terms have been used to describe the STRM including "modernizing union" (Hernández Juárez y Xelhuantzi López 1993), *neocharrismo* (Cano Miramontes et al. 1994),[5] and neocorporatism (Ortega 1992). But these epithets often obscure as much as they enlighten. Part of the problem comes from the common myth that modernization and relative independence from the state leads to greater union democracy, a claim made frequently by STRM union leaders (Hernández Juárez and Xelhuantzi López 1993). Thus, some union opposition members argue that the union has not changed (Cano Miramontes et al. 1994), since if it had changed there would be more internal union democracy. By contrast, the union leadership argues

(Xelhuantzi López 1988) that the STRM is an exemplary case of union democracy.

In fact, there is little evidence to suggest that a flowering of union democracy has occurred under Hernández Juárez. While there has been a change in the structure of union power, both the old structure and the new structure are based on largely non-competitive elections and systemic hierarchical, patron-client power relationships. Modernization in the case of the telephone workers' union in Mexico has not led to democratization. What *does* change is that the technical nature of the information required to bargain collectively on workplace issues requires some ceding of authority by state bureaucrats to rank-and-file union members who are knowledgeable about industrial issues. While state policy decisions actually become *more* important on the regulatory end, on the industrial relations end the union's monopoly over the technical skills required to operate a telephone system gives it significant leverage.

The extent and limits of state authority in the Mexican telecommunications sector are demonstrated by the *convenio de concertación*. Through that document, state officials succeeded in imposing changes in workplace rules granting managers broad authority. Thus, at one level, this would have to be considered the demonstration *par excellence* of state control over labor. At the same time, however, there would have been no need for the agreement at all, if the STRM hadn't been operating as an autonomous agent in the workplace, contrary to what corporatist theory would predict. The existence of the *convenio de concertación* is thus not simply an indication of the Mexican state's power, but also an indication of the increasing difficulty Mexican state officials have had in exercising control in the increasingly technologically-complex telecommunications industry.

The telecommunications industry, not only in Mexico, but also in Canada and the United States (Zureik and Mosco 1989: 508), has been marked by a high degree of company paternalism, a system which combines the carrot of company-provided benefits with the stick of rigid workplace control. As Vallas mentions in his study of telephone workers at AT&T, the telecommunications industry is particularly prone to paternalistic control because telecommunications workers are "dependent on a given employer, have lost command over important production skills, and are employed by a firm that enjoys a monopolistic economic position" (Vallas 1993: 66). In other words, although many telecommunications workers are skilled, these skills are not easily transferable outside the telephone industry. Because within a given region, a single telephone company had a monopoly, without a strong union to protect them, workers were in a very vulnerable position. Moreover, because the company had a monopoly, it was able to spend the necessary funds to "co-opt" workers by offering company-paid benefits in an attempt to forestall independent union organization. In the case of Telmex, this has included company sports and recreation clubs, dormitory facilities for operators who work the night shift, and a company-run pension plan. In the absence of a strong union, such benefits can be and are withheld discretionally, thus giving supervisors considerable leverage over workers' behavior.

Though telephone workers in Mexico have been unionized since the Mexican Revolution (1910-1917), paternalistic control of the workplace was largely maintained, sometimes by direct Labor Ministry intervention. For instance, in 1962, the Mexican government removed the union's elected leaders and imposed a slate of union officers who had been defeated in the union's elections earlier that year. During this period of government-imposed union leadership, paternalism reigned and worker discipline was maintained, especially among female operators. As one current union advisor explains:

> This company was characterized as being one of the businesses most distinguished for its aggressive treatment [of its employees]. It is a rigid inheritance. Beckman, the first CEO, established a command structure, a structure of domination and of control . . . even corruption was used by management as a control mechanism (Interview S-94-14).

The union leadership's role was to negotiate generous wage and benefit packages,[6] while otherwise remaining largely invisible in the workplace. The union leadership's aloofness was deeply resented by union members. Regarding Hernández Juárez's predecessor, Salustio Salgado, one union activist comments, "In his office, he would never attend to you. He never had the time. He never felt like it. He always delegated. That is fundamentally the difference [with Hernández Juárez]" (Interview S-94-28; see also del Valle Sánchez 1978).

By examining Salustio Salgado's rule, one can discern some important features of the STRM at that time. First, the union was directly affiliated to the PRI. The secretary general was more a party official than a union official. There is no clearer sign of this than the fact that at the time of the rank-and-file revolt in 1976, Salgado was busy running for a seat in the Mexican Senate as a PRI member. Second, the fact that the union leadership was more involved in PRI affairs than union affairs created a power vacuum.[7] This vacuum was filled by shop stewards, particularly in those departments where the use of modern technology and the education level of the workforce was greatest, such as among witch maintenance (*centrales mantenimiento*) workers. Third, as this power vacuum was filled by shop stewards, state labor bureaucrats lost control over the union. It was this power vacuum that was filled when the government-supported union leadership was overthrown in 1976 and Salustio Salgado replaced with Francisco Hernández Juárez.

The fact that a power vacuum existed in 1976 meant that there was an opportunity for union leaders and union shop stewards to push for a restructuring of union-state-PRI relations Indeed, a key element of the conflict between the different factions of the union between 1976 and 1982 centered on this question. On the one hand, Hernández Juárez and his supporters favored reestablishing an "alliance" with the state and PRI, adjusting the relationship to give the union greater internal autonomy, but remaining supportive of government economic policies and cooperating with management in the implementation of new technology. On the other hand, many union shop stewards, particularly those in Monterrey, Puebla, Guadalajara, and Mexico City and especially among inside plant departments, sought to permanently sever their ties to the PRI. Some sought to shape the union in an oppositional mold, in which the STRM would join with other unions in opposing government economic austerity policies. Others were less ambitious, seeking to maintain a "non-aligned" stance in which the union would interact with the state-managed company in a collective bargaining context only, while severing all ties to PRI and state politics. These different opposition currents formed a loose alliance, in conjunction with a group known as Línea Democrática (Democratic Line). It was in this process of the clash between two opposing blocs—the pro-PRI *juaristas*[8] and the anti-PRI *democráticos* (who received some support from Mexico's communist and socialist parties)—that the present relationship among the STRM, the state, and the PRI was forged.

During the struggle between Hernández Juárez and the Línea Democrática,[9] there are three main points at which key decisions were made by the union or union officials: the 1976 convention, the 1979 convention, and the 1982 rank-and-file revolt against Hernández Juárez's leadership. The union decisions made during these these conflicts would prove decisive in the building of a new state-party-union relationship. At the STRM's 1976 Convention, held two months after the rank-and-file revolt that had led to the change in leadership, differences that had emerged between leftists and PRI reformists were temporarily smoothed over, with the union staying in the Congreso de Trabajo (Labor Congress, hereafter referred to as CT). Later, at the STRM's 1979 Convention, an extended debate was held, which led to the narrow approval of an internal restructuring of the union which permitted Hernández Juárez and the rest of the union leadership to limit the influence of union shop stewards. Finally, during the 1982 rank-and-file revolt, Hernández Juárez survived largely because of the support received by the PRI-dominated CTM (Confederación de Trabajadores Mexicanos, or Mexican Workers Confederation), the largest single union in Mexico. After this conflict, the STRM remained much closer to—and more dependent on—state officials and the PRI than it had been in the previous six years. However, as explained below, there do remain some important differences compared to the pre-1976 STRM.

The first STRM convention following the certification of the victorious insurgent slate by the Labor Ministry in 1976 set the parameters of the future debate. Events to that point had proceeded rapidly. The union rank-and-file revolt began on April 22. In May, there was a Labor Ministry-supervised special election in which the insurgent slate, headed by Hernández Juárez, trounced the slate led by incumbent secretary general Salustio Salgado by an 8-1 margin.[10] In July, just two months later, delegates from across Mexico were called together in Mexico City to hold the union's first convention under Hernández Juárez's leadership.

By this time, fissures within the insurgent union executive committee had already begun to develop. On one level, the battle could be seen as yet another partisan struggle among supporters of the PRI and various leftist parties.[11] But most union shop stewards were not affiliated with any political party and the dynamic of competition between the two groups had more to do with internal labor issues than external partisan ones.

Labor Ministry officials did not remain neutral in the dispute, but instead demanded that the STRM 1) remove the "most radical" members from the national executive committee, 2) reinstall 24 supporters of Salustio Salgado who had been expelled by the new leadership, 3) stop "attacking" the company, and 4) publicly condemn the activities of an opposition movement in the electricians' union—the single most important opposition movement to arise in the Mexican labor movement since the late 1950s.[12] In case the union refused to go along, managers of the state-owned telephone company were sponsoring parallel conventions of the recently-deposed union leadership (Martínez Lira 1984: 187-195).

After much give-and-take, a compromise of sorts was worked out, in which the STRM acceded to some, but not all, Labor Ministry demands. The Línea Democrática was limited to four slots on the executive, 20% of the total executive (Martinez Lira 1984: 194, Xelhuantzi 1988: 355). The union disaffiliated from the PRI but reaffirmed its membership in the CT, the main state-sponsored labor federation. The STRM did not issue official pronouncements either supporting or opposing the Tendencia Democrática (Democratic Tendency) in the electricians' union.[13] The expulsions were carried forward in name, but the state company's management refused to act on them.[14] And finally, the union leadership under Hernández Juárez gave informal assurances to management that workplace unrest would be discouraged.

Differences were thus papered over for the moment, but not for long. Towards the end of 1977, arguing that holding elections would threaten "democratic continuity" at a time when Telmex managers were seeking to restore the former union leadership (Martinez Lira 1984: 217), Hernández Juárez called a special convention to approve an amendment to the union's bylaws extending his term of office by two years. At the same time, Hernández Juárez shut down production of the union periodical, which was edited by a member of the Línea Democrática opposition, after it printed an editorial opposing the postponement of union elections (See STRM 1977 and Martinez Lira 1984: 216).[15] Over the fierce objections of union opposition activists, the bylaw change was approved.

The sharp differences in the positions held by Hernández Juárez supporters and opposition activists were most evident at the STRM's Fall 1979 Convention. At that convention, Hernández Juárez presented a document, called *Democratización sindical* (Union Democratization) which proposed restructuring the union away from its department structure (STRM 1979). This document placed emphasis on "small assemblies" (*asambleas chicas*), a sub-divisional structure which, opponents feared, could be used by Hernández Juárez and his supporters to more effectively isolate "radicals." Línea Democrática and other independent telephone worker union activists in Monterrey, Puebla, and Guadalajara responded with an alternative proposal, denominated *Documento resolutivo* (Document of Resolutions), which called for stricter adherence to the goals of the 1976 revolt, including the prohibition against the reelection of union officials.

This debate ended in a 115-113 victory for Hernández Juárez and his supporters.[16] The debate clearly illustrated the two sides' different conceptions of the proper relationship between the state, PRI, and the union. The opponents of Hernández Juárez characterized the union leadership's position as follows (STRM 1980:9):

1. The principle enemy of the workers is the Línea Democrática.

2. Strikes are negative for workers.

3. An alliance is necessary with our class enemy, the state.

4. It is necessary to change union structures for others which permit greater control over the worker rank-and-file.

5. It is necessary to reelect the national representatives.

The language is harsh, but when casting the rhetoric aside, this is a fair explanation of the position of Hernández Juárez and his adherents. Indeed, union leaders did seek to centralize authority and to resolve matters where possible through negotiation with state officials.[17] By contrast, opposition activists placed a premium on strike action and shop steward authority and sought to maintain a much greater distance from the state and the PRI.

During this period, neither Hernández Juárez nor the opposition had full control over the union. Despite the internal strife at the time, it was during this period that the greatest working conditions gains were won. The reason for these gains was clear: each side in the conflict was willing to advocate militant actions in pursuit of workplace rights as a way to gain more adherents, though the Línea Democrática advocated union-wide strikes, while Hernández Juárez argued against strikes, preferring to instead focus on more localized shop floor actions.

After 1982, when Hernández Juárez gained greater control over the union, such militancy began to decline. This occurred for two reasons. First, in order to prevail in the 1982 conflict, Hernández Juárez had to rely on Laabor Ministry support. This action led him to subsequently become more dependent on the support of state labor officials, as support among the rank and file was no longer as high. Furthermore, the opposition's strength was always greatest at the shop steward level. The reduction of its prominence, therefore, translated into a reduced ability of the union to generate pressure against company management and state labor officials at the shop floor.

The dynamic of this interaction among state, union, and party can be seen in the way that the relationship functioned in the years between 1978, when the tacit cooperation between Hernández Juárez and Línea Democrática broke down, and 1983, by which time Hernández Juárez had succeeded in excluding Línea Democrática and similar opposition groups from open participation in STRM politics through the suspension of the union rights of hundreds, even thousands, of union members.[18] During this period, the Línea Democrática and other opposition groups pressed for strike action and campaigned in their departments for workers to vote in favor of striking, while Hernández Juárez and his supporters resisted these strike movements. These strikes were discussed in Chapter 5, but it's important to examine these strikes here to understand how they relate specifically to the question of union-state-PRI relations.

One thing to note is the unique nature of the 1978-1980 Telmex strikes in the Mexican context. That is, these were strikes which were initially opposed by the union leadership, but in which they agreed to support the rank-and-file's decision. As a result, in 1978, for the first time in 16 years, telephone workers in Mexico went out on a formal strike, in a work stoppage approved by a vote of the union membership. In 1962, when the last telephone strike had occurred, Labor Ministry officials responded by ousting the union's leadership and imposing the losing electoral slate as the new union leadership. But in 1978, state officials faced a dilemma. Since the union leadership actually opposed the strike, replacing the union leadership wouldn't have solved the problem! At the same time, while Hernández Juárez *personally* opposed the strike, he refused to commit political suicide by opposing the union rank-and-file. As a result, he accepted the will of the membership and led the strike. The state labor officials, accustomed to dealing with leaders of unions with a demobilized membership, were taken completely by surprise, and for the first and only time since World War II, the government permitted a telephone strike without intervening with troops to restore service. Making the best of a "bad" situation (from the standpoint of labor control), state officials mediated a settlement between the STRM and state Telmex managers in which it was agreed that operators would get a salary increase and that a department-level workplace agreement (*convenio departamental*) would be negotiated. The agreement stipulated that the amount of the salary adjustment would be determined later and applied retroactively to the date the collective agreement was signed. When the parties failed to negotiate these details, telephone workers struck again in March 1979, with the important difference that this time state labor officials were better prepared. This time, the Communications and Transport Ministry (Secretaría de Comunicaciones y Transportes, hereafter SCT) called on special troops under its jurisdiction to restore telephone service once interrupted. Despite this action, however, the union succeeding in compelling management to settle the details of the agreement and to pay the back wages owed.

This dynamic of opposition-led strikes, supported reluctantly by a union leadership with limited control over rank-and-file workers and fearful of losing rank-and-file support, was a major departure from the top-down unionism of the 1962-1976 period. State officials who had control over the management of the company and the SCT could call in troops to maintain service, but their ability to intervene in union affairs was sharply diminished. Hernández Juárez and his supporters could, to a significant extent, use the militancy generated by opponents to negotiate better deals for the rank-and-file, but feared that success in strikes would strengthen the opposition at the expense of the union leadership. The opposition could militate, but was subject to suspension by union leaders, which meant denial of union benefits, such as loans, requests for unpaid leave, and access to promotions. In some cases, the union leadership expelled members, which would mean that the member would be out of a job.

To the extent that members of the opposition could maintain rank-and-file support in their departments, they were partially shielded from repressive measures. Nonetheless, the opposition's position was tenuous, since Hernández Juárez and many of his supporters refused to accept the legitimacy of opposition and would act to squelch opponents when possible. While Hernández Juárez did not act to repress those who merely challenged him on specific issues, he did act to suspend union participation rights and benefits of those who were seeking to promote the election of new leadership.

To break the logjam, the opposition needed to successfully challenge the suspension and expulsion of its militants. This could be done either by reaching an accommodation with Hernández Juárez or by replacing him. On the other hand, Hernández Juárez had the choice of reaching an accommodation with the opposition as he had during the 1976-77 period or seeking to destroy its organization. State labor officials could support the opposition, they could support Hernández Juárez, or they could promote Salustio Salgado and his supporters (Rosina Salinas et al.). In essence, they were divided between those who supported Hernández Juárez and those who supported the return of the old guard. The influential Fidel Velázquez, head of the PRI's labor sector since the late 1940s, lent his personal support to Hernández Juárez.[19]

Hernández Juárez sought to break the logjam by 1) suspending the union rights of opposition supporters, 2) making adept use of the patronage benefits that a leader of a Mexican union enjoys, and 3) working to undermine the opposition's base of support by altering the union structure to reduce the power of opposition union activists. This involved forming an alliance with an outside "Maoist" group, Línea Proletaria (Proletarian Line) and providing Línea Proletaria members with jobs in the union. These Línea Proletaria members would then seek to win local union offices and run the subdepartmental assemblies set up by the union in 1979 (Interview S-94-9, Velásquez 1993). Through local action—i.e., work stoppages at specific work sites, but not wider strikes—Hernández Juárez sought to show to rank-and-file that workers who supported the union leadership would receive greater benefits than those who opposed it.

From 1978 to 1982, Hernández Juárez's strategy was largely, but not completely, successful. In departments which required significant technical skill, it was difficult to hire political allies from the street. On the other hand, in departments where training time was less extensive, such as traffic, Hernández Juárez was able to generate support among the rank-and-file. His supporters were able to challenege successfully long-time workplace practices that were particularly objectionable to operators, such as management's policy of requiring operators to ask permission before going to the bathroom. Hernández Juárez pressured Telmex managers to allow him to hold union meetings on company time, increasing the presence of the union, and Hernández Juárez himself, in the workplace (Interview S-94-9).

This set the scene for the 1982 conflict. In January 1982, as another round of contract negotiations was approaching, opposition members and Hernández Juárez supporters arrived at an informal truce. But neither side honored the agreement. Telmex managers, likely with Hernández Juárez's support, began to fire union activists, the great majority of whom were opposition supporters. Opposition activists responded by leading a work stoppage, in an attempt to get the dismissed workers hired back. But the walk-out quickly became a struggle against Hernández Juárez, as it was felt that he was not devoting sufficient union attention to fighting the dismissals. Calls were made for Hernández Juárez to step down as secretary general and for the secretary general of the Monterrey section to serve as an interim leader until elections could be held (Interview S-94-25).[20] On March 8, the opposition seized the union headquarters building and Hernández Juárez, after failing to force his way back in, moved his headquarters to the CT offices, where Fidel Velázquez provided him with an office. Unlike 1976, where everyone was united in the walk-out, there was no breakthrough. Instead, rank-and-file workers gradually gave up and went back to work. Also, the fact that some opposition members sought to form a united front with "old guard" opponents of Hernández Juárez served to discredit the opposition (Interview S-94-9). With the opposition divided against itself, police in June acted to storm the opposition-occupied union headquarters, enabling the union leadership to move back into the central union building. In August, the dismissed workers, who by this time numbered more than 500, were allowed back to Telmex, after signing a loyalty oath to the union leadership. While factions remain in the STRM to this day, the nature of internal STRM politics changed, as did the union's relation to the state.

Internally, of course, Hernández Juárez prevailed. After a period in which the opposition was excluded (1983-1987), opposition participation in union bodies was permitted, but only to the extent that opposition members who participated accepted the permanency of Hernández Juárez as the union's secretary general. As Hernández Juárez put it in the union's 1979 debate, disagreement over issues is fine; disagreement over who leads the union is not (STRM 1980: 33).

Hernández Juárez's successful effort to reduce the opposition's base of support meant that the state's problem of having to fight opposition-led strikes would be a matter relegated to the past. But because Hernández Juárez's strategy had involved not simply disorganizing the opposition, but organizing his own mass base of support, he enjoyed greater leverage than many other union leaders in Mexico. That is, there was a *mobilizational* aspect to Hernández Juárez's strategy, which distinguishes him from many other Mexican labor leaders.[21] Especially among the operators, a majority of whom supported Hernández Juárez, there remained a significant capacity to mobilize. After the 1982 rank-and-file revolt, Hernández Juárez tried to demobilize some of his *supporters*. In particular, with the opposition largely debilitated, it was unnecessary to share power with Línea Proletaria. In parting company with his former allies, Hernández Juárez charged, among other things, that Línea Proletaria was tied to then-Budget and Planning Minister, Carlos Salinas de Gortari, and thus should be purged from the union (Interview S-94-9).[22] But Hernández Juárez was not terribly successful in demobilizing his supporters, which, as shown in Chapter 5, helps explain the ability of operators to have a degree of success in pressing their demands about the need for worker involvement in the carrying out of technological change in operator services.

Where Hernández Juárez's consolidation of power has had the greatest impact is in the relationship between the union and the PRI. This impacts the union's relationship with the state since the PRI and the state are intertwined. Since 1976, there has been no formal link between the union and the party. However, subsequent to the defeat of the 1982 rank-and-file revolt, there was a significant *rapprochement*. The first sign of change came in September 1982, when Mexican President José López Portillo gave the opening address at the STRM's annual convention. This ritual has since been repeated annually by subsequent Mexican presidents. The second change was that Hernández Juárez was elected President of the CT in 1987 for a 6-month term (Corro 1987). This appointment is largely symbolic. However, given that the CTM membership is roughly equal to 50% of the total CT membership, reaching the presidency of the CT meant having the support of CTM-leader Fidel Velázquez, then the main leader of the PRI labor sector. Upon taking office, Hernández Juárez announced publicly that he had always been a PRI member and urged the STRM to affiliate with the PRI (Guzmán 1987b). The union did not do so, but union activists were given union paid time off to campaign on the PRI's behalf in the 1988 presidential election.[23]

The third change was the creation of a new union federation in 1989, known as the Fesebes (Federación Sindical de Empresas de Bienes y Servicios or Federation of Unions in Goods and Services Business). Founding members of the Fesebes were the Central Mexico electricians union (SME), the streetcar workers' union, the cinematographers' union, the air pilots' union, the airline groundworkers' union, and the STRM. Essentially, the Fesebes sought to formalize the relationship of these unions, which represent workers in the high technology niche of the Mexican labor market, with Mexican *técnicos* (economist wing of the PRI) and against the Mexican *políticos* (machine-politics wing of the PRI). The latter include most high-ranking Labor Ministry officials. In this arrangement, the *técnicos* served as a bulwark against the *políticos* in the Labor Ministry, giving Fesebes union leaders freer reign internally in exchange for their unquestioning support of *técnico*-supported macroeconomic policies and the promotion of modernization programs in high-technology or high-prestige industries. This enabled member unions to pursue shop floor and collective bargaining gains, but constrained their ability to change overall macroeconomic policies that harm their membership.

Obviously, such an arrangement is a far cry from union independence from the state. However, it did provide space, within the context of overall union support of modernization, for relatively autonomous collective bargaining relationships. As such, with Telmex privatized, the state has kept out of the negotiations between Telmex management and the STRM. The Labor Minister remains present at the time of the contract's signing and is sometimes involved in mediation, but otherwise takes a hands-off approach.

While this strategy has had some important successes, it does have some important costs, not the least of which was that such a strategy tended to isolate the STRM from other unions and limited its ability to influence government macroeconomic policy. These disadvantages became more pressing in light of the December 1994 devaluation, which resulted in renewed inflation in Mexico and decreases in Mexican worker wages. As a result, the Fesebes became more active in working with other Mexican unions, becoming part of a 21-union alliance known as the Foro (La Botz 1996).[24] In August 1997, some of the "Foro" member unions, including the STRM, formed a new union federation, the National Union of Workers (Unión Nacional de Trabajadores or UNT). The National Union of Workers has issued many pronouncements and led demonstrations calling for changes in Mexican labor relations, but actual changes in industrial relations behavior to date remain limited (Payne 1998).

Potentially, the STRM's participation in the UNT could signal a major shift in union strategy. Certainly, the STRM has become much more willing to denounce Mexican government policy initiatives with which it disagrees. But while the UNT's formation may lead to a strengthened social unionism in Mexico, such a result is far from assured. Indeed, a more likely scenario for the STRM would be the further consolidation of a relationship between the telephone company and the union that is similar to that of business unions in the United States and Canada. While such an arrangement would give the STRM greater autonomy from the state, it will not necessarily address other problems, such as the decline in union density and of overall union strength in the Mexican telecommunications industry.

TECHNOLOGICAL CHANGE AND STATE INTERVENTION IN CANADIAN UNIONISM

As in Mexico, Canada has also experienced some major changes in relations between the state and labor over the past two decades. Initially, the state played a relatively minor role vis a vis the TWU. In the 1970s, however, state intervention increased as union-management conflict escalated. In the 1980s, as union-management conflict subsided, the role of the state Labor Ministry also receded somewhat. However, while active intervention by the Department of Labour has fallen, changes in the industry have created an increasingly important role for another state agency, the CRTC (Canadian Radio-television and Telecommunications Commission), the Canadian regulatory commission which oversees telecommunications.

Despite Canada's "pluralist" tradition, telecommunications work relations have always been subject to substantial state influence. Indeed, according to Dwayne Winseck, labor relations in the telecommunications industry can best be characterized as "semi-corporatist" (Winseck 1993: 118). In particular, Winseck argues that "corporatist" features in Canadian telecommunications labor relations include measures such as federal labor legislation which emphasize state mediation of disputes,[25] federal regulation of the industry through the CRTC and its predecessors the BRC (Board of Railway Commissioners) and later the CTC (Canadian Transport Commission), and a history of quasi-representation of workers through company-sponsored employee associations. At some companies, particularly Bell Canada, these associations were not replaced by independent trade unions until the 1970s (Winseck 1993: 101-102).

It is arguable whether corporatism, or even semi-corporatism, is really the correct term to describe these arrangements. Generally speaking, corporatism involves centralized bargaining and three-party (state, business, and labor) negotiations. Neither of these conditions have ever existed in Canadian telecommunications. What is certain is that after a period marked by a high degree of labor-management conflict, a labor relations system in Canadian telecommunications did emerge. In this system, the state, while establishing the overall economic and political framework in which both company managers and unions (or company-sponsored employee associations) operated, was largely passive. "Corporatist" features, such as they were, entailed the understanding that employers granted a monopoly by the state were to pass some benefits on to their employees. As a result, Canadian telephone company workers earned higher wages and benefits and had greater employment security than workers in less protected sectors of the economy. Though the state had formal mechanisms, such as the labor ministry or the telecommunications regulatory commission, with which to intervene, it rarely did so. Because state regulation didn't change and because the level of labor militancy was low, the daily practice of labor relations involved interaction between management and worker representatives, with state representatives barely entering the picture. This situation began to change, however, in the early 1960s, as labor militancy in the TWU began to increase and as technological change in the industry began to accelerate.

The first sign of change was the increased intervention of state officials in the negotiation process, as negotiations regularly reached an impasse and state conciliators had to be brought in to resolve labor-management disputes. As Bernard notes, "From 1959 through the sixties not a single contract between the company and the union was concluded without the intervention of federal government conciliation services . . . Before 1959, there had been only one instance in conciliation in over 30 years of bargaining" (Bernard 1982: 127). Bernard suggests that an important factor in the change of relations was the purchase of a majority share of BC Telephone by the American multinational General Telephone in 1956 (Bernard 1982: 125-127).[26] These disputes largely focused on wage issues, though other items addressed in the negotiations included a reduction in work hours for operators to seven hours a day (1963), increases in vacation time (1965, 1967), group health insurance (1967), and the institution of the Rand formula or modified closed shop dues check-off provision (1967) (DOL 1980).[27]

In 1969, for the first time in fifty years, BC Tel workers voted to strike (Bernard 1982: 132-151). Though the main focus of the strike was the demand for higher wages, the strike accelerated changes in the outlook of both rank-and-file members and union activists—in particular, fueling a greater desire for worker authority on the job. As Bernard puts it, "While the dispute centred on wages, long-standing grievances were at the root of the new militancy . . . There was a widespread feeling that a strike was necessary to change the company's attitude toward the union and the workers. The union's position was that only a strike could establish its authority in the workplace" (Bernard 1982: 133). Management's disdain for the union was illustrated in a debate between a union representative and the company president, J. Ernest Richardson, held at the University of British Columbia in Vancouver during the strike. As one union activist explains, "Richardson—he demanded that he go first and then leave" (Interview T-93-12).

The strike settlement was not a defeat for the union, but neither was it a tremendous victory. The strike lasted six weeks and resulted in an additional 2.84% increase in wages over the state conciliation officer's pre-strike recommendation of 17% over two years. At that rate, it would take workers four years to make up the money in higher wages lost during the six weeks of the strike (Vancouver Sun 1969). Though the union's financial gains were modest, the strike did yield many of the results anticipated by union activists. These included a greater sense of unity among the union's often-fractious divisions (plant, operator services, and clerical) and a new level of workplace influence and respect from management officials. Additionally, the strike placed the creation of a jointly-trusteed pension fund squarely on the negotiating agenda. As one union activist noted, "In closed meetings, we hammered away—myself and another plant member. MacKassey, the federal labor minister, elicited a promise from the employer that we would talk about pensions. That was all he elicited" (Interview T-93-12).

At the same time, the strike illustrated the tenuous nature of the union's position. In particular, it was clear that the telephone company could continue operating, with difficulty, but operating nonetheless, with 1,500 management employees filling in for 6,600 striking workers.[28] This issue brought squarely to the union's attention the increasing importance of automation in the industry and the crucial need for a union response (Bernard 1982: 140-142; see also Bernard 1982: 94-111).[29]

Finally, the strike was also important in that it shifted union-management relations from the "business" to the "political" realm. Because the union went on strike and because the business could operate without union workers, at least for a number of weeks, the union had to rely on sympathetic actions by other unions and groups to create economic and political pressure on management to settle. "Flying pickets" followed BC Tel supervisors. Whenever these supervisors entered another company's premises to do telephone work, TWU pickets were set up. These were honored by construction unions and effectively shut construction sites down. Other groups, such as the BC Union of Students, supported the strike and condemned management's use of students as strikebreakers. Most importantly, the New Democratic Party (NDP) also supported the strike and issued a call for nationalization of the telephone company, making this a central issue in its election campaign (Bernard 1982: 138-139).[30] The strike and the solidarity actions that the strike engendered broke the TWU's traditional political isolation, resulting in much closer ties with the NDP. As one union leader of the period explained, two years after the strike, "In 1971, for the first time, I got our council to agree to put an amount equivalent to $1/member to a labor political action committee that everyone knew was going to the NDP" (Interview T-93-12). During the decade that followed, NDP-TWU relations would become stronger, as industrial relations at BC Tel moved farther and farther from conventional bargaining and as both state and NDP interventions in the conflicts became more and more significant.

    In 1971, for the first time since 1957, an agreement was reached between management and the union without recourse to government mediation. According to Bernard, this was the result of a conscious company decision to improve labor relations and involved the hiring of a new director of industrial relations, J.H. Bruce. The previous industrial relations head, D.M. Carter, was transferred to Florida (Bernard 1982: 145-146). Although the 1971 agreement included wage and benefit gains, the two most important items were non-wage issues. First, the agreement explicitly delayed (again) resolution of the pension issue; the terms of the present pension plan were written into the Collective Agreement and made a negotiable item. Second, a new article was added dealing with contracting out.

    The Labour Department didn't mention the contracting-out clause in its summary of the terms of settlement (DOL 1980: 12-14). In fact, it would appear that the company gave—and the union got—a bit more than each had bargained for. According to one union steward, "The contracting out [provision] was more by luck than by design. It was not really the way it was intended" (Interview T-93-41). Whether the union got the contracting-out clause by luck or design, it is clear that management thought it was giving much less. In essence, the contracting-out clause did three things: 1) it listed a group of jobs, such as snow clearing, that the company could contract out without negotiations with the union; 2) it stipulated that "the Company shall not contract out any other work preformed by the classifications set out in the Agreement without negotiation with the Union prior to the contract being let" (and in the event the contract is let, it must be given to a unionized company if such a company is available to do the work); and 3) in the event employees are laid off, the company is obligated to avoid contracting out wherever possible. In the event of a dispute, the contract called for a single arbitrator to make a binding decision within 72 hours of hearing the complaint (BC Tel and FTW 1971).

The clause provided significant protection from union work currently being performed being contracted out to non-union companies. The protection turned out to be even greater than initially anticipated. As was ruled in repeated arbitrations,[31] the second part of the agreement was taken to mean not only the *actual* work performed by the classifications was protected, but the *potential* work as well. For instance, not only must management get union permission to let out current warehousing jobs, but it must obtain union permission to contract out any future warehousing work that is of the same type as that done by union members. As a result, the contracting-out provision not only preserved jobs, but created jobs as well. Management responded to this situation by trying to contract out some jobs surreptitiously. But whenever management was caught, the union responded with wildcat actions.

This constant battle over contracting-out set the tone for relations between TWU and BC Tel for the rest of the decade. The first casualty of this battle was BC Tel's Industrial Relations chief, J.H. Bruce, who resigned in 1973, allegedly in protest over the company's return to hard-line tactics after company management rejected a federal government conciliation report in the following round of negotiations (Bernard 1982: 146). Bruce's replacement, Frank Tucker, accentuated the hard-line tone in the company's approach to the union. According to one union officer, Tucker's goal was simply to destroy the union:

Gen Tel was clearly on a union-busting campaign in telephony. They destroy small bargaining units in the U.S. The resolve to the strike [typical in the U.S.] was [that] the people who went on strike were put on a preferential hiring list for two years, especially in right-to-work states. They [management] just trampled them [workers]. Frank Tucker, the Vice President of Industrial Relations, had more power in the BC Tel executive than the President or Chairperson. He was absolutely brutal, that man. I believe he was Gen Tel's hit man.

(Interview T-93-68)

Initially, Tucker moved slowly. At times, management under Tucker would single out individual workers for discipline or violate the contract in an egregious manner, which typically provoked large-scale walk-outs in response (Bernard 1982: 160-161). At the bargaining table, Tucker would pounds his fists on the table (Interview T-93-68). But when the federal government intervened, BC Tel management accepted the government's "conciliation" reports in both 1973 and 1975 (Ladner 1973, 1975). These reports provided for substantial gains in wages and the creation of a jointly-trusteed union-management pension fund.[32]

The return of more conflictual labor relations inevitably led to state mediators playing an ever increasing role in BC Tel industrial relations, an intervention resented by BC Tel management. Indeed, perhaps because of this resentment, Tucker was also notable for what he did not do. Seeking to restore traditional BC Tel paternalism, which had been undermined by the 1969 strike, Tucker rarely called on the federal government for aid. As one union executive committee member noted, Tucker "didn't believe anybody had the right to tell the company how to run the business . . . He believed nobody had any business interfering in BC Tel labor disputes, so when there was a strike, he would never call on a third party" (Interview T-93-68).

Due to management's reluctance to call on the state to repress the union, the union grew bolder in its tactics. In June 1974, for instance, the union staged a province-wide walk-out involving all 10,000 unionized workers in a protest over the suspension of a clerical employee and in response to what the union viewed as a series of contractual violations by management (Bernard 1982: 162, Cull 1974, Fan 1974). The union also grew more vigilant in its enforcement of the contracting-out provisions of the collective agreement, staging walk-outs when violations were spotted as its arbitration victories on the issue continued to accumulate (Bernard 1982: 179). Management, in turn, began to harden its position, seeking to remove the contracting-out clause from the contract.

Accelerating technological change made the union unwilling to cooperate. As then-Plant Council General Secretary Bill Clark said at the time, "We are faced now with an accelerated program, introducing dedicated plant, electronic offices (local switching), computer type toll operations, communications satellites, various types of carrier systems imposed on local and trunk cables, and faster and cheaper methods of placing and splicing cable" (quoted in Bernard 1982: 158-159).

As explained in Chapter 5, the dispute over technological change was ultimately resolved through the 1977-78 strike and lock-out and then the 1981 sit-down strike and lock-out. These two disputes brought to an end the last traces of the old BC Tel paternalistic labor regime and solidified union rights regarding contracting-out, union security, and technological change.

In addition to the conflicts' direct impact on union-management relations, the role of the state in BC Tel industrial relations changed substantially. On the one hand, the struggle cemented the TWU's alliance with the NDP, as the TWU had relied on both NDP support in Parliament, and the support of the British Columbian labor movement in particular, in order to prevail. As one observer noted, central to the TWU's response to automation was its effort to "raise the struggle out of the economic plane, where the union was losing, and elevate it to a political plane where the union thought it might have a better chance" (La Botz 1991: 110).

At the same time, however, management's relationship to the state also changed. In particular, BC Tel management learned that there were limits to TWU militancy; the TWU leadership had pulled back from the sit-down strike when ordered by a judge to do so. According to Bernard's account, the reason for this decision was simple: a majority of union executive council members felt there was no alternative. As Bernard writes:

> Discussion within the union leadership turned to whether or not the tactic of passive resistance should be followed . . . A second tactic—defiance of the court order—was discussed but the majority view was that this would lead to the smashing of the union . . . Neither of these alternatives was considered realistic (Bernard 1982: 216).

As set forth in Chapter 5, the union did prevail in the conflict by complying with the Court order to vacate and relying on the support of other unions to carry out rotating general strikes. But however necessary obedience to the Court might have been, the union's decision to obey the Court's order was a signal to the company that it could gain leverage over the union by using the state, instead of seeking to keep state involvement at a minimum to preserve management discretion. Subsequent to the 1981 dispute, BC Tel gave up on its attempts to reestablish its 1960s paternalism. The company was no longer reluctant to use the legal system as a way to moderate union behavior. Management's position was strengthened when a Conservative government was elected to govern Canada in 1984 for the first time in 21 years.[33] As one union officer explains:

> The Conservatives come on board in '84. [After that election] the CLRB (Canadian Labour Relations Board) would be out here in six-and-a-half hours from Ottawa and issue a cease-and-desist order back to work. The Liberal Government wasn't near that quick. A week later they'd come to town; they seemed to take an approach—unless there was a threat to public safety—of "let 'em have a go at it" (Interview T-93-68).

Chastened by the state's increased intervention, not only in negotiations, but now in local walk-outs, the union took a more conciliatory approach. At the same time, management had its own reasons to become more responsive, not the least of which was its desire to restore employee morale (Interview T-93-32). Furthermore, for the first time since the monopoly system in telephony had been instituted in the late 1910s, competition was introduced in the terminal equipment market (telephones and private electronic switchboards). This meant that labor-management disputes might now result in a loss of business to competing firms.

The introduction of competition inserted yet another factor into the equation: the fact that the CRTC now would regulate the terms and conditions of the industrial restructuring process. This meant that it would be the CRTC which would set the rules of competition in ways that would either facilitate or hinder corporate profit-making, and not coincidentally, in ways that would affect unions' abilities to promote the interests of their members. This change made a second actor, the labor-backed NDP, even more important than it had previously been in publicly supporting the TWU in industriaal disputes, as political negotiations became as important as collective bargaining in determining workplace relationships. The CRTC and its predecessors had always played an important role, but the regulatory rules of the game were largely "background" information. Since the rules had remained constant for so long, unions felt little need to intervene in regulatory proceedings. As a result, the interaction between the company and the regulatory body was limited to such matters as the setting of rates and the monitoring of service delivery. By the late 1970s, however, this was no longer the case. More and more frequently, important decisions in the telecommunications industry began to be made at the CRTC and the Department of Communications. This, in turn, impacted union tactics and changed the way it interacted with both management and the state. Unwilling to cooperate in the deregulation of the industry, which was seen as a threat to union members' jobs, and faced with matters that clearly fell outside the scope of collective bargaining, the union had to devise new tactics to deal with the new threats to its members' welfare.

In comparing the TWU's situation with the STRM, it is clear that there remain important differences. The greatest difference is in the nature of their relationships with political parties. While the TWU maintains a close alliance with the NDP, the NDP is only rarely in power at the provincial level and has never been in power at the federal level. As a result, the TWU is usually not bound to act "responsibly" by the NDP in the way that the STRM is with respect to the PRI and the Mexican state. For example, the STRM is expected to sign corporatist wage and price control pacts. In Canada, wage and price controls, when put in place, are typically imposed directly via government legislation, without either seeking or demanding union consent. The enforcement of such wage and price control pacts in Canada occurs largely through state mediation of disputes.[34]

A second difference is that in Canada, there is a multi-party state and an expectation that public debate take place even within a particular party. In Mexico, debate is still restricted largely to different factions of the PRI and is largely held behind closed doors. Unions are expected to show deference to the ruling PRI and the state and to dissent quietly, if they dissent at all. A corollary to this is that the Mexican state actively seeks to prevent the formation of a social democratic party comparable to the Canadian NDP, as is demonstrated by the fact that the government is responsible for the murder of more than 200 PRD members. While the PRD is clearly the party that comes closest to representing a social democratic viewpoint in Mexico, its economic positions are more moderate than the moderately social democratic Canadian NDP.[35]

A third important difference is the form of interaction among union, state and party. In Mexico, since the PRI and the state have been historically intertwined, relations with the state are more "political" in character, as opposed to the more legal or administrative character of Canadian union-state relations. End-runs by the STRM around the Labor Ministry by appeal to its *técnico* allies in the government cabinet are the rule, not the exception. When the Mexican state wants to discipline the STRM, the instrument of choice is discretionary refusal to apply federal labor laws that benefit workers, such as the law that requires 10% of a company's net earnings to be remitted to its employees. The TWU, on the other hand, interacts with state officials through specific bureaucratic channels that are more institutionally defined, such as Labour Ministry mediators, arbitrators, or the courts. However, the TWU is not adverse to using its links with the NDP to get around resistant state officials, particularly on regulatory issues (Personal correspondence: 1996).

Indeed, despite the above differences, there are important similarities in how the TWU and the STRM interact with state authorities. In both cases, staate officials play an important role in mediating disputes, while refraining from direct involvement in the negotiations themselves. Thus, both the STRM and the TWU have partial autonomy from the state. The state stays out of internal union affairs and is not directly involved in industrial disputes, but state officials stand by, ready to act should either of the parties request assistance, as is often done by both unions. In addition, both the STRM and the TWU maintain strong relationships with political actors, but at the same time seek to avoid excessive dependency on political parties. Both refuse to formally affiliate with these political parties. This relationship of arms-length support has served both unions well, enabling them to reap the benefits of close links with an external political organization, while limiting the negative fall-out that can come with being associated with policies with which many members disagree. Finally, both unions are finding their interactions with the state to be shifting from labor to communications officials, as regulatory change becomes more rapid and more far-reaching in its effects on telephone workers' jobs.

With Mexico, in particular, the shift began as the Salinas faction gained ascendancy within the PRI gained ascendency. An important part of Salinas' platform was to accelerate the privatization of state enterprises that had begun under Salinas' predecessor, President Miguel de la Madrid.[36] Near the top of the list was the privatization of the telephone company.

PRIVATIZATION, THE STRM AND THE NEW MEXICAN REGULATORY ARENA

Unlike Canada, where a tradition of state regulation of telecommunications dates back to 1905, in Mexico state regulation of telecommunications really only began after Telmex was privatized in 1990. Even in the period before nationalization in 1972, government regulation was minimal. The government monitored the company directly, becoming a minority stockholder in the 1950s and a majority stockholder in 1972. As part of the conditions of sale of Telmex in 1990, a new system of regulation was created. In doing so, Mexico followed an international trend within public and private telephone systems known as *corporatization* (Caby and Steinfield 1994: 45). When corporatization occurs, either a state-run company is restructured and set up at "arm's length" from the government and a separate regulatory authority is established, or a newly-privatized company is placed under the jurisdiction of a specific government regulatory agency. In Mexico's case, the regulatory authority for the newly privatized Telmex rests mainly with the SCT, but the Treasury Ministry plays a major role in the setting of telephone rates. While Telmex has never been directly run by a government ministry, during the period of public ownership it was never run at arm's length, as government ministers frequently intervened in the company's operations and no independent regulatory agency existed. To date, the STRM has not made submissions to government regulators in the same manner as has the TWU to Canada's CRTC. But Mexico's 1990 creation of a regulatory framework is another sign, in addition to privatization and the Mexican government's active pursuit of foreign investment in telecommunications, of the impact of globalization on the industry in Mexico. Not surprisingly, national differences are becoming less marked. As a result of both privatization and the creation of a new regulatory regime, the nature of the STRM's interaction with the Mexican state has shifted. In particular, the importance of its interaction with the SCT has increased, while its interaction with the Labor Ministry has become less important.

The privatization process began this transformation, so it is necessary to review briefly the privatization process and the union's role in it. Alhough the STRM was initially opposed to privatizing the company (Llamas Salvador 1988), once union leaders saw that government leaders supported privatization, they did a 180-degree turn and supported the privatization wholeheartedly (Hernández Juárez 1990).[37] According to union officials, the union backed privatization as a way to preserve jobs and delay the onset of full competition in long distance service. As one union staffer stated, "The government had a deficit . . . if we did not let Telmex grow, in a short time, 2 or 3 years, the very necessities of the transnational companies were going to begin to put on pressure for a more efficient service. The entrance of other businesses was imminent" (Interview S-94-0). At its September 1989 Convention, the union formally endorsed privatization on the condition that there be no lay-offs, that the Collective Agreement be honored by whomever bought the company, and that the union itself would be maintained (Interview S-94-0). At this same convention, President Salinas made a public announcement that the government's majority share in the company would be sold.

While the government announcement and the union's formal approval of the sale occurred in September 1989, an extended process of secret negotiations between the union and the government had preceded the public announcement. As early as 1986, union officials traveled to Europe to assess industry developments. This trip "confirmed the assumptions that we had from reading the information that there were well identified tendencies in telecommunications— deregulations, privatizations, mergers, new technology, new services" (Interview S-94-27). As a result, union staffers "did an analysis and we arrived at the conclusion that it was more viable for the business to privatize" (Interview S-94-0).

The threat posed by the privatization was complex. In Mexico, nothing even remotely approaching universal telephone service existed. This situation made privatization distinct from countries such as Japan or Great Britain, where the same process had occurred a few years earlier. In Mexico, the privatization dynamic was explicitly linked to technological modernization and internal business restructuring, as set forth in the Concession Title (SCT 1990) that was attached to the sale of the company.

According to union officials, the union itself held veto power over the decision to privatize. As one union staffer put it, "We provided the key, the possibility [of privatization] with our agreement" (Interview S-94-0). Once the STRM publicly endorsed privatization, there were two main issues: 1) worker ownership of stock; 2) the union's response to the new regulatory regime, both in terms of protecting its jurisdiction over telecommunications work and negotiating service targets. On these issues, the STRM's record is mixed. The union did succeed in obtaaining for workers a large number of shares in the newly privatized company. Additionally, the service targets provide some assurance that the company engages in labor-intensive projects that should employ STRM workers. There is also a recognition that the STRM will be the representative of the employees at any new company subsidiaries that are formed. However, workers quickly cashed in their shares and the privatized Telmex has spread most of the expansion work to already-existing subsidiaries that are either non-union or have much weaker unions than the STRM. Moreover, while making some progress, the STRM has yet to fully adjust to the new institutional framework. Although the regulatory regime has the potential to provide the STRM with new ways to influence the business, to date it has made minimal use of these avenues.

The STRM had the most success in obtaining stock shares for its membership. This trend began in Great Britain in 1984, where workers were given shares in British Telecom over the opposition of the union (BTUC 1990, BTUC 1991). Workers received 8% of British Telecom stock. In the case of the STRM, however, it was the union leadership which was behind the push to gain the shares. This approach has since been used in Venezuela and Argentina, where workers have received 11% and 10% of the shares of the privatized companies, respectively (Benítez 1992: 13). The STRM's stock ownership as a percentage of total capital was small (4.4% initially, reduced to 3.1% after a low-interest loan from the government used to buy the shares was repaid in 1992). Nor did stock ownership afford the union the opportunity to have a single seat on Telmex's Board of Directors. The amount of money involved was, nonetheless, substantial. After the loans were repaid, the value of the shares peaked in 1993 at just over U.S. $20,000 per worker, roughly twice the average annual income of telephone workers at the company.

Nonetheless, the stock deal was highly controversial within the union. There were two key reasons for this. One was the method of purchasing the shares. The union initially bought the shares as a block. The goal, according to union officials, was to gain leverage over the company. As one union official stated, "From the beginning, we thought about the possibility of growing as a stockholder and having access to the Board of Directors" (Interview S-94-0). But opposition activists worried that the union leadership would use its control over U.S. $800,000,000[38] worth of shares as a weapon against its opponents. Since shares were later withheld from 200 private switchboard workers for filing a claim against the union, it would appear these fears were not unfounded. A second reason for controversy was that union officials sought to make use of the share purchase ideologically to suggest, albeit rather implausibly, that the union's ownership of 4.4% of the shares of the company meant that the union and the company now shared common interests.[39] STRM leader Hernández Juárez took the position that, "Stock ownership will contribute to the consolidation of common objectives between management and workers which need to be made deeper and stronger" (Hernández Juárez 1992: 6).

Opposition activists responded by arguing that the union's cooperation was being bought by the company, resulting in less vigorous enforcement of Collective Agreement language. As one union opposition activist explained:

> Look. What happens is that the stock shares have served the executive committee a lot ideologically. It is treated like winning the lottery without buying a ticket. [They say] while other workers are fighting to avoid being laid off, you have a secure job, they aren't taking away your benefits . . . thanks to the union that has worried for you. Because of that, it has benefitted ideologically and that has convinced many people that there's no reason to complain about Collective Agreement violations, since we are 100 times better off than other unions (Interview S-94-25).

Other opposition activists see the ideological impact of the shares as less dramatic, but still important. As one installation and repair worker put it, "At the beginning, it had a political importance, because the union discourse justified the privatization in that way. They bought our acceptance of the privatization, no more" (Interview S-94-29).

While union leadership supporters argued for the need to cooperate more closely with the company now that the members of the union were stockholders and while some union opposition activists argued against becoming owners, the main objection to the union holding the shares as a block came from rank-and-file workers who simply wanted to own the shares themselves so they could cash in and use the money for the purchase of homes and cars. While most union delegates were willing to tolerate speeches from the union leadership about the need to cooperate with management because they were now shareholders, there were limits. Turning over the cash to the union members was one of these. As one operator explained:

> Hernández Juárez wanted control [over the shares] in order to win a position on the Board of Directors . . . The idea of Juárez was to have control, when he sticks his foot in his mouth and says if we were to give the shares to the workers, they'd be worth 60 million (pesos or U.S. \$20,000) per worker. Well everyone says, "We want our money." Juárez cried crocodile tears, but finally gave up the money. The attitude was, "We know Hernández Juárez has a luxury car and house. That's fine. We've tolerated it. But give me my slice of the pie. Hernández Juárez wants everything." It was a very difficult moment for Juárez. It was a trial by fire for him and he had to concede to distributing the shares (Interview S-94-23).

After gaining access to their shares in 1992 following the union's repayment of the government-financed loan and the union convention decision to divide the shares up among the workers, most workers sold the shares to purchase homes or automobiles. By the spring of 1994, fewer than 9,000 workers out of the more than 40,000 STRM members still held shares in the company (Interview S-94-30). This situation is similar to what occurred at privatized telephone companies in Venezuela, Argentina, and Great Britain. In every case, the overwhelming majority of the workers have shown a greater interest in cashing out than in being part-owners of the newly-privatized company. As one union official argued, "The fundamental problem is that of all workers in the world. We live on a fixed salary. We don't have savings. That's why the people demanded the money" (Interview S-94-0).

Despite all of the difficulties, the payment of a \$20,000 benefit per worker, even though it was a one-time deal, has to be considered a major union victory. The union clearly achieved a good price for cooperating with the privatization, albeit at a significant cost in terms of control in the workplace. The union has been less successful, however, on the issues of union security and adjusting to the regulatory regime.

While the STRM has accomplished some things, particularly the provision in the Concession Title which prohibits the creation of new non-union subsidiaries, it has failed on the larger issue of maintaining its jurisdiction over work. Existing non-union subsidiaries are simply expanding, as is the contracting out of work (Vásquez 1994, Solís Granados 1992b: 62). As well, the union has failed to articulate an independent position on the social responsibility of the company. Instead, the union has sought to ensure mechanical compliance with the targets and is still subjected to public wrath at the inadequate quality of telephone service.

The document that governs the regulatory process in Mexico today is the Concession Title (*Título de Concesión*), which sets forth a series of conditions which the newly-privatized Telmex must meet. The Concession Title is interesting, as it is in some respects a departure from other privatizations in Mexico. Obviously, the reason for this is the unique nature of telecommunications. Rhetoric aside, telecommunications, especially in countries such as Mexico where universal service has yet to be achieved, is not a commodity like any other. Rather, it is a vital part of a nation's economic infrastructure. As a result, special considerations must be made to ensure that these basic economic development needs are met. In addition, there are legacies of Mexico's economic nationalism in the requirement that Mexican capitalists retain 51% of the voting stock and in the fact that the agreement maintains ultimate telecommunications authority with the state.[40] Since the Concession is made for 50 years, back-dated to 1976, with the possibility of a 15 year extension, the government is entitled to take over Telmex in 2026 or 2041 without compensation (SCT 1990).

The Concession includes a number of provisions to ensure the meeting of national infrastructure needs. For instance, it contains price guidelines which ensure the private owners a high rate of profit for a six-year monopoly period. From these profits, they are obliged to finance expansion of the network and improvements in sound quality, under threat of fines should service or expansion targets specified in the Concesión not be met. The Concession requires 12% annual growth in the number of lines for the first three years of the Concession. In 1997, Telmex is permitted to reduce prices somewhat to meet the theat of competition. In 1999, the introduction of marginal cost pricing, which favors business over residential customers, is permitted. Cellular and other new telecommunications services are to be provided by Telmex subsidiaries, in order to separate accounting for competitive and non-competitive segments of the business. The Concession also allowed the government to keep one representative on the Board of Directors for the first three years after privatization. Afterward, the company remains obliged to send regular reports to the Communications and Transportation Ministry (SCT 1990).

The union's role in all of this is rather limited. The union's primary achievement was to specify that the STRM will be able to organize any future subsidiaries in the company. However, as pointed out by one observer, there is nothing in the Concession Title to suggest that workers in other subsidiaries will be covered under the same terms and conditions as workers in the main Telmex company (Mondragón Pérez 1994: 191). In any event, the usefulness of this provision has been limited, since 17 subsidiaries of Telmex already exist and their employees are not represented by the STRM. Many of these subsidiaries have no union at all. Telmex management policy has simply been to expand these subsidiaries and increase the contracting-out of work. Despite increased union pressure in the 1990s to restrict contracting-out, union progress in this area has so far been limited.

More importantly, the union was constrained by its allegiance to the state and the PRI. STRM policy until the December 1994 devaluation had been to give unquestioning support to government macroeconomic policies, seeking to work out industrial relations concerns on its own. While the acceptance of government macroeconomic policy creates its own long-term problems, the union's willingness to yield to the government on issues outside the industrial relations realm is particularly harmful in the regulatory arena where government decisions can directly impact union members. The union's limited scope of action has also set back efforts to organize other workers. The union already finds itself entirely excluded from the rapidly growing cellular market, as the STRM has no members in either Telmex's cellular subsidiary or in any of the competing cellular companies.

By the summer of 1994, union officials were beginning to realize that the union was being held hostage to service targets and that these targets, more than any independent union modernization strategy, were really driving union action.[41] While the service targets include high-profile rural telephone and urban residential telephone line expansion, which are clearly highly labor intensive and which one would anticipate the union would support, the Concession requirements emphasize projects which use little labor and are designed to improve service quality for business lines. Thus, old switching equipment is modernized rapidly, since the new digital equipment is needed for fax and data transmission, but progress on residential line service is slower. The union's quandary is especially evident in the productivity program, in which the union is pledged to dedicate its efforts toward goals which are either specified in a Concession Title in which the union had relatively little say or, which are set unilaterally by company management. Belatedly, the STRM sought to devise a response. One union staffer explained the union's proposal as follows:

> We are working on a proposal that, without rejecting the opening [of the market], without rejecting competition, seeks two conditions in order to make coherent the deregulation: 1) There should be a national telecommunications project and 2) within this project, there must be assigned specific responsibilities to the business Teléfonos de México. What does this mean? It means that we are certain that competition in itself does not resolve all our problems. We think that Teléfonos de México should compete but in conditions in which it is the principal business responsible for this national project and in which other businesses will be complementary (Interview S-94-27).

Evidently, for the union to negotiate such an agreement would be a major achievement. Unfortunately, it has been unsuccessful in achieving such an accord. The exclusion of the union from the setting of telecommunications policy did, belatedly however, have an effect, being at least partially responsible for Hernández Juárez and the STRM's recent turn toward more open questioning of Mexican state policies.

THE TWU AND STATE REGULATION (I): THE DEREGULATION BATTLE

As Winseck notes, interventions by the TWU and other Canadian telecommunications unions in regulatory proceedings "coincided with a substantial departure from traditional regulatory conventions as more and more areas of the telecommunication industry were opened to competition" (Winseck 1993: 201). In 1974, the first such intervention occurred as the TWU and CWC jointly made submissions to the CRTC's predecessor, the CTC (Canadian Transport Commission) to oppose directory assistance charges, the use of retail outlets to sell customer equipment, and the implementation of installation charges (Bernard 1982: 160, Winseck 1993: 108). Despite the unions' joint opposition, the CTC implemented these changes. In 1979, the TWU and CWC again intervened, with a similar lack of success, when an application was filed by CNCP Telecommunications to have full interconnection with Bell Canada's network in order to provide competitive data exchange and private line services (Winseck 1993: 110). The CRTC ruled in favor of the company's application and against the unions, thus permitting full competition in the provision of terminal equipment.

In both cases, the unions' primary goal was to preserve the jobs of the membership.[42] Charging for long distance information or for installations reduced the demand for those services and hence the number of operator and outside plant jobs. Using retail outlets to sell customer equipment created new clerical positions, but reduced the required number of repair and installation workers. Opening the terminal equipment market to competition might not significantly alter the total number of jobs, but would reduce the number of terminal equipment jobs remaining within the traditional telephone companies where the unions' members were. As such changes began to be made by the CTRC, the unions found themselves fighting more and more of their battles at the CRTC, rather than on the shop floor or at the negotiating table.

Still, the first significant breakthrough in the regulatory arena came not in opposition to regulatory change, but as part of the 1980-1981 dispute between the TWU and BC Tel management. In this case, the item being considered by the CRTC was a request for a rate increase by BC Tel. Unfortunately for BC Tel management, they had submitted their rate increase request at a time when contract negotiations with the union had reached an impasse. For the first time ever, the union intervened in a rate hearing in order to point out service deficiencies at BC Tel and otherwise embarrass company management. As one union official explained:

> What is normally a two week pro forma procedure was turned into a tutorial on how screwed up the priorities of the phone company were. We got a very, very positive response from the public . . . The culmination of these hearings was a video we prepared. Bill Mitchell, a lineman at the time, we had him do a 12-to-15 minute video tour of the outside plant of the Lower Mainland [Vancouver area],

demonstrating the devastating shape of the outside plant . . . The
company qualified Mitchell as an expert in Western Canada. He gave
a "down home" narrative. I'd seen the video. I watched the row of
[company management in] suits getting into a fetal position . . . We
made it [the hearing] into a circus (Interview T-93-1).

The rate case intervention assisted the union tactically, since the
union's deliberate prolongation of the hearing limited management's
ability to retaliate against its selective strike action, which was aimed at
the high-end business customers of the company. The hearing
intervention was also consistent with the TWU's traditional emphasis
on job preservation and creation. Here it pressed the need to hire more
employees to meet service obligations. But the union's efforts were
also important in altering how it viewed the state and its relationship to
the company. At the same time as the TWU had been confronted with
limitations in the collective bargaining arena—illustrated by the court
order to vacate the BC Tel buildings—the union saw the regulatory
arena as an area where further progress could be made. As one union
officer put it, "We've changed our approach . . . we learned how to
effectively deal and apply pressure through the CRTC" (Interview T-
93-60).

In assessing the TWU's efforts, one must examine the union's
attempt to involve itself in efforts to resist deregulation of the industry.
In its efforts to fight deregulation, the TWU used a variety of tactics,
including submissions to CRTC hearings, advertising on television, and
forming alliances with a wide array of community groups who also
opposed deregulation. Throughout the 1980s, the TWU also
strengthened its ties with the NDP, making substantial financial
contributions and at one point dedicating an entire edition of the union
newspaper, the Transmitter, in support of a successful NDP provincial
campaign (TWU 1991b). In all of these respects, the TWU followed a
classic social unionist strategy. It refused to be confined to collective
bargaining and sought, in the words of one union official, to "break
down the division between consumers and workers and show that
workers are consumers" (Interview T-93-1). The TWU's efforts were,
to a significant extent, effective. Ultimately, however, the TWU's
efforts to defend the principle of telephony as a public-regulated utility
service—a single network, operated in the public interest—were
unsuccessful. Canadian long distance telephony was redefined by the
CRTC as a commodity and this sector was opened up to competition.

Reviewing the history of this deregulation struggle reveals both strengths and weaknesses in the TWU's social unionist strategy. As well, it shows how the social unionist approach can be impacted by the pressures of globalization.

In Canada, the first attempt to deregulate came in 1984, on the heels of a similar decision to deregulate telephony in the United States. According to the terms of a 1982 settlement of a U.S. anti-trust suit, AT&T was forced to divest itself of holdings in its 22 local telephone operating companies, which were consolidated into seven "Baby Bells."[43] In addition, competition was encouraged by forcing AT&T to subsidize the newly-formed Baby Bells for a five-year period, while competing companies, such as MCI and Sprint were allowed to operate without being required to pay this subsidy. In exchange, AT&T was granted the right to enter the computer market, from which it had previously been banned. The effects of these decisions were clear: costs would be shifted from long-distance customers (mainly business) to local customers (mainly residential). Indeed, by 1991, the distribution of costs between local and long distance revenues had shifted from 40:60 to 73:27 (Winseck 1993: 128). Such cost-shifting was clearly inegalitarian, but it was argued that opening long distance to competition would foster greater operating efficiencies and technological innovation and thus, in the long run, benefit all telecommunications customers.

In Canada, the same arguments were made, but there were substantial differences in the political arena in which the debate took place. First, in Canada, the issue of whether or not to deregulate was handled by a regulatory body, not the courts. This meant that unions, consumer groups, and others had the opportunity to intervene in a manner that had not been available to such groups in the United States. Second, the Canadian market was more fragmented than the U.S. market, both in terms of ownership of telephone lines and in terms of the regulatory authority. In the United States, AT&T controlled over 80% of the market and the Federal Communications Commission (FCC) had undisputed authority over the regulation of telecommunications, despite frequent turf battles with state regulatory commissions. In Canada, while Bell Canada controlled half the market, the remainder was made up of an assortment of private and publicly-owned telephone companies. In fact, Canada's telephone companies fell into three categories: 1) publicly-owned, provincially regulated (AGT of Alberta, Manitoba Tel of Manitoba, and SaskTel of

Saskatchewan); 2) privately-owned, provincially regulated (eastern
Canada); and 3) privately-owned, federally-regulated (BC Tel in British
Columbia, Bell Canada in Ontario and Quebec). The division of
regulatory authority left it unclear whether anyone had the *authority* to
deregulate, never mind whether or not it was desirable to do so.

For these reasons, it was not possible to ram through deregulation.
In 1985, the CTRC held hearings on the request by one company,
CNCP, to be allowed to link up to (interconnect with) the existing
public telephone networks in order to provide competing long distance
service. In these hearings, there were 1700 written responses and
presentations by 43 delegations, making these the most contested
telecommunications hearings since the 1905 proceedings that had led to
the establishment of federal regulation (Winseck 1993: 225). Unions
joined forces with provincial governments which owned telephone
companies, particularly in Manitoba and Saskatchewan, to oppose the
changes.

The response from the public was much greater than either the
CRTC or the recently-elected Conservative government had
anticipated. This was largely a result of reports that local phone rates
were rising in the United States due to deregulation. Ralph Nader came
up and joined the campaign against deregulation in Canada (Interview
T-93-12). A deluge of organizations from Saskatchewan and Manitoba,
especially, voiced their opposition to the deregulation proposal
(Winseck 1993: 226). The TWU, in conjunction with the CWC,
launched a C$500,000 publicity campaign,[44] involving local television
appearances (Webster 1985) and advertisements in which a man
dressed up like Alexander Graham Bell urged customers to call in and
voice their disapproval (TWU 1985b). The publicity campaign worked.
As one union representative explained:

> We hired a communications firm . . . It was [their] opinion that if we
> told the people of BC the truth and explained the situation, we would
> win. It worked. We had a massive response. From that we developed
> quite a fight-back [campaign] (Interview T-93-12).

As a result of the public opposition generated, the CRTC backed
off and denied CNCP's application to compete in long distance
telephony (CRTC Decision 85-19). The CRTC tried to mitigate
damages for those who had sought deregulation by rejecting the
application on business grounds, while upholding the principle of

competition (Winseck 1993: 226-228). Nonetheless, the decision did bring about a considerable delay in the deregulation process. The Conservative government, the CRTC, and telecommunications "user groups" (largely banks) had to begin anew, this time working methodically to remove the obstacles opposing deregulation, rather than seek to rush deregulation, as had been attempted in 1984-85.

The pay-off to the Canadian unions' resistance can be seen by contrasting the effects of maintaining monopoly provision of services in Canada with the implementation of deregulation in the United States. Between 1978 and 1987, the number of telecommunications jobs rose 3% in Canada, compared to a 23% drop in the United States, where large work force cuts followed the advent of deregulation in 1984 (Winseck 1993: 200).[45] Nor is it the case that Canadian companies avoided firing workers simply because Canada had yet to catch up with the United States in its level of service provision. To the contrary, jobs in Canada were maintained despite the fact that Canada had already established universal service, with telephones reaching 96.5% of all homes by 1976 (Mosco 1990: 3). By 1992, this figure had increased slightly to 98.7% of all homes (Stentor 1993). By contrast, only 93% of all homes in the United States had telephone service (Mosco 1990: 3). Being regulated monopolies, Canadian companies were forced to hold on to labor-intensive, low-profit parts of the business, thereby protecting union members from lay-offs. Being a regulated industry also meant that large telecommunications consumers, such as banks, had to pay higher rates for service than they would in a competitive regime. Perhaps more importantly, they were limited in their ability to exert market pressure on the telephone companies to emphasize their needs over those of the general public.[46]

Subsequent to the 1985 CRTC decision (CRTC 1985), government planners began to analyze why their efforts to introduce deregulation had been stymied. In response, a new game plan was drawn up to properly prepare Canada for deregulation. In a May 1985 confidential memo, the Department of Communications recommended spending C$1,000,000 on surveys and a "public information" campaign to "prepare the public for the debate."[47] In particular, the report argued that the debate "should not use American statistics."[48] Although the report acknowledged that "most Canadians are satisfied with the telephone system," it also stated that "opinions are volatile and subject to being influenced by the first one to clearly explain the situation to them." The Communications Ministry further recommended that big business lend only "selective" support, since otherwise "support by big business could trigger [opposition by] a common front." Such a common front was to be prevented "at all costs," since "a common front would create the biggest threat to the Government's ability to manage the changes" (DOC 1985; see also TWU 1988c).

Although the memo was later leaked to the press, the Conservative government largely stuck to its game plan, which, in addition to using cynical public relations language, also entailed the shifting of costs from large business users to residential users and on consolidating federal jurisdiction in telecommunications. While the TWU was ultimately unable to stop the business-backed government onslaught, it did succeed in slowing the process considerably. For instance, in 1987, the CRTC sought to give a competitive edge to a "reseller"[49]—that is, a company which buys a block of long distance circuits and resells to at a discount rate—by waiving the requirement that the company file a tariff for the services. When BC Tel and Bell Canada asked for similar waivers, the TWU responded by suing the CRTC, forcing the CRTC to rescind its decision (Winseck 1993: 232-233, Richardson 1991).

Nonetheless, despite the TWU's and others' efforts, the different pieces of the deregulation puzzle came together, albeit a bit "behind schedule." In 1988, after the Conservatives won an electoral battle in a campaign which focused primarily on whether or not Canada should enter into a free trade agreement with the United States, the pace of telecommunications deregulation began to quicken.[50] In 1989, the federal government's deregulation efforts received a boost when the Canadian Supreme Court ruled that the federal government's regulatory authority extended to all privately-owned telephone companies (AGT v. CRTC and CNCP; see Hogg 1990). As a result, telephone companies previously under provincial regulation in eastern Canada came under the jurisdiction of the federal CRTC. Shortly afterward, the Conservative provincial government privatized AGT. In Manitoba, the Conservative provincial government signed a Memorandum of Understanding with the federal government, agreeing to accept CRTC jurisdiction. This meant that only SaskTel in Saskatchewan remained outside of the CRTC's regulatory oversight. When a second proposal to introduce long distance competition came before the CRTC (CRTC 1990), this time from a partnership between the Canadian cable company Rogers Communication and CNCP Telecommunications, the TWU and the CWC again responded with a major campaign, using advertising (TWU 1990b), op/ed articles (see, for instance, Shniad

1989), submissions to the regulatory agency (TWU 1991c) and community presentations (Interview T-93-60).[51] The TWU alone dedicated C\$270,000, over 5% of its annual budget, to the "fight-back" campaign (TWU 1991d). While the response to the campaign from the public was again favorable (Interview T-93-60) and many town councils and neighborhood organizations passed resolutions of support, opposition from provincial governments was sufficiently muted and some consumer groups were mollified by promises that local rates would not be allowed to rise.[52] This left the unions much more isolated in their opposition. In June 1992, the CRTC published Decision 92-12, which introduced long distance telephone competition in Canada (CRTC 1992). Shortly afterward, this new regime was consolidated in legislation (Urlocker 1992, Winseck 1993: 248-256), by passing a new Telecommunications Act in June 1993 (TWU 1993c).

THE TWU AND STATE REGULATION (II): THE UNION RESPONSE TO COMPETITION

> Regulation reform stayed constant in the eighties. There was major success in 1984 . . . the problem comes now that the dike is bust, people are much confused as to the position to take. The company wants no social obligations, nothing (Interview T-93-1).

While the TWU's social unionist strategy was highly successful in the 1980s, preserving union jobs by delaying deregulation in Canada by seven years and making some contractual gains on jurisdictional issues, the deregulation decision in 1992 left the union in a quandary. As one union executive committee member put it, "We fought our battle on deregulation, gave a great fight, possibly delayed deregulation by close to a decade up in Canada, but we never had a plan for when we would ultimately lose. We all fought the battle confident that we would win, but we should've been preparing for the worst-case scenario. So we've been in a very reactive mode for the last year-and-a-half" (Interview T-94-74).

Union efforts to respond have taken three different forms. One approach has been something called service enhancement, in which the union works on business proposals to expand service in labor-intensive areas to increase the number of jobs available to union members. The second is to undertake aggressive organizing and work more closely with other Canadian telecommunications unions. A third option is to stand pat and continue to fight what's left of the deregulation battle, which primarily entails seeking to dissuade the provincial government from entering the industry as a competitor, thereby reducing the total number of competitors in British Columbia, and preserving the company's obligation to provide inside wire service at no cost to the customer. So far, the union has taken half-steps in each of these directions, but has had difficulty in adapting to the new industrial environment created by deregulation. Coming into question in this process is the union's relationship with the NDP and the viability of its social unionist approach.

The first option pursued by the TWU was to push the company to expand aggressively the scope of its business, so as to employ more, rather than fewer, workers. This proposal was presented to union delegates at the TWU's convention in January 1993 and received widespread, though far from unanimous, support (TWU 1993d). The proposal followed within the traditional TWU emphasis on job promotion, but could be viewed in two different ways. Some within the union saw service enhancement in a social democratic codetermination vein as a way to change the terrain of struggle with the company to include the development of business plans: that is, they saw service enhancement as a means to force the company to address service issues, even in a competitive business environment. As one union rep put it, "I want people to fight the company and work with the public" (Interview T-93-1). However, other people in the union have supported the idea of service enhancement more from the standpoint that, in the post-deregulation environment, the union and the company had to work together more closely. As one union executive member explained, service enhancement "is a series of ways and methods of assisting the company to generate money so we can keep work" (Interview T-94-6). This latter position was also evident in a consultant's report to the union, which stated that "the members' success and company success are mutually dependent" (Flanders and Cohen 1991: 12). For the same reason, many others opposed the proposal since to them it meant working *too closely* with the company in developing business plans for specific service enhancement proposals. As one worker protested, "I think the company will use what we give them to fuck us, not to give us more jobs" (Interview T-93-10).

While those who supported the latter type of service enhancement emphasized working together with the company, those who supported the former version of service enhancement placed greater emphasis on working with the provincial NDP (which won the provincial elections in British Columbia in 1991, leading to the formation of the first NDP government in the province in 16 years) to pressure the company into paying increased attention to service. These two visions have clashed on repeated occasions and are part of a larger debate not only within the TWU, but within the Canadian labor movement as a whole about the appropriate relationship among unions, the state, and the NDP, in the post-Free Trade Agreement world.

Full pursuit of either path was complicated by TWU internal politics. The end of the 1980s saw the breakdown of an old pattern in TWU politics. Traditionally, the TWU had been divided into two factions. One faction, led by President Bill Clark (1980-1987), was characterized by a social unionist outlook, but was also less confrontational, seeking to resolve most disputes via negotiation. The other grouping was more militant but also had a somewhat more business unionist outlook and was led by Bob Donnelly, the TWU president between 1977 and 1980. Later, this faction was led by Don Bremner, Secretary-Treasurer of the union from 1978 to 1988. But it should be noted that the differences between the factions were much less than the differences between the union leadership and opposition in the STRM. Both factions have operated within an overall consensus of moderately militant social unionism when compared to most other North American telecommunications unions.

The internal politics of the union, however, was altered by the TWU's 1988 elections, in which five business agents from the Donnelly/Bremner camp were defeated at Convention, leading Bremner himself to resign (TWU 1988d). This election result, combined with Clark's retirement the year before (Clark took early retirement in 1987) led to a reconfiguration of internal union politics (Interviews T-93-16, T-93-19).

The January 1988 elections had left the Clark camp triumphant, but without a program. This result was in-fighting within the Clark camp and the division of the union again into two factions. One faction led by former Donnelly supporter Cathy Henderson (Secretary Treasurer, 1990-1993) and Clark supporter Linda Hebert (Business Agent, 1983-1995) moved toward the traditional Bremner/Donnelly position of militant business unionism, but, as the effects of deregulation began to impact the membership, began to appear more and more similar in its advocacy of cooperation with management to the position adopted by the STRM. The other faction, led by two former Clark supporters—Rod

Hiebert (Vice President, 1987-1992, President 1992-present) and Neil Morrison (Business Agent, 1987-1992, Vice President 1992-present)— was arguably more faithful to social unionist philosophy than Clark, but was also even more inclined than Clark was to work things out with management, rather than cause disruption in the workplace. By the early 1990s, shop floor militancy at the TWU had dropped to low levels not seen at BC Tel in decades. The union leadership's tendency to want to resolve disputes by negotiation with company officials galled many old-time union activists (Interviews T-93-8, T-93-11, T-93-16, T-93-22, T-93-27, T-93-72).

Larry Armstrong, a Clark supporter, had succeeded Bill Clark as president, defeating Bremner at a specially held TWU convention in November 1986. While Clark was highly partisan in his running of the union, creating many opponents among union activists in the process, Clark did succeed in maintaining widespread rank-and-file support. Armstrong did not. In March 1990, the first contract negotiated by the new union leadership was voted down by the membership by a narrow 51% margin (TWU 1990a). This contrasted to the routine 80%-plus approval that contracts negotiated by Clark had received. The initial contract rejection was interpreted by union leaders and activists alike as a no confidence vote by the rank-and-file in the new leadership.

The contract rejection led to Labour Ministry intervention. After slight revisions, a second contract vote was held. This time, the membership overwhelmingly approved. After the election, the union leadership held a retreat at which decisions were made to rebuild relationships with the rank-and-file and temporarily mend fences among themselves. This included the decision to make use of focus groups to tap into members' feelings and views (TWU 1990b). Many delegates resented the use of focus groups which were often seen by union counsellors and shop stewards as an attempt to shift the blame for the decline in rank-and-file activism from the union leadership to them.

For a short while, though, it appeared as if the 1990 contract vote were just a blip in an otherwise smooth transition. President Larry Armstrong, after surviving a motion of no confidence at the TWU's June 1990 Convention, took early retirement in January 1992. Vice President Rod Hiebert easily defeated Don Bremner on a 60-to-39 vote to assume the presidency (TWU 1991d). The 1992 contract was approved by an 82% margin (TWU 1992a).

But the union's internal affairs deteriorated when it was discovered that a planned $500,000 central union office renovation cost over

$1,000,000. As a result of this incident, Secretary-Treasurer Cathy Henderson was defeated in her January 1993 reelection effort by a 51-50 Convention vote, illustrating the sharp division between union factions (TWU 1993a). Given that the revelations about the cost overrun surfaced simultaneously with the issuance of focus group reports backing the adoption of a union service enhancement strategy, enthusiasm for service enhancement was minimal.

The result was stalemate, with a formal meeting between company and union officials not occurring until December 1993. This meeting was full of pleasantries and friendly speeches, but produced little of substance beyond an agreement to hold four meetings a year between top management and top union officials on "strategic issues."

Despite the slow movement along this path, however, some steps have been taken. One project initiated under the rubric of service enhancement was the contracting-in of collections work, which allowed the business to save money by doing the work in-house, thereby providing the union with more jobs (Osing and Silvester 1992). Eleven jobs were created in the Vancouver billing department, where the program was implemented in 1993 (Interview T-93-43).

More important was the union's pursuit of an agreement with the NDP government to develop a provincial telecommunications infrastructure project. In October 1995, the BC government and the TWU announced the initiation of an "Accord" in which the BC government pledged to use its purchasing power as the largest consumer of BC Tel telecommunications services as leverage to ensure that the benefits of the information age will be extended to rural, as well as urban, customers (British Columbia 1995). Though it remains to be seen how successful efforts in this direction will be, the agreement itself is clearly the biggest success that the union has had in its service enhancement efforts, compelling BC Tel to maintain some degree of social obligation even in a competitive marketplace.

A final tactic followed by the TWU in the post-deregulation era has been to organize competing companies. The TWU helped organize other telephone companies in the past, but such organizing efforts have been traditionally arms-length efforts. For instance, in the 1970s, the TWU lent money and business agents to help the fledgling CWC organize Bell Canada. The TWU also assisted unsuccessful organizing efforts by an independent group known as TEMPO (Telecommunications Employees' Management and Professional Organization) to organize BC Tel's managers. In 1978, TEMPO lost a certification vote by a margin of 975 to 896 (Bernard 1982:172, Dobie 1980). Organizing is a traditional social unionist activity in that it provides a means to strengthen the union movement as a whole by increasing the size of the unionized sector. By contrast, more traditional business unionism has traditionally eschewed organizing, focusing on the economic interests of current members.[53] However, the TWU, protected by the monopoly status of its industry, had never organized aggressively.

In October 1993, President Hiebert moved forward gingerly, putting forth a union organizing policy. After much initial skepticism on the part of some union activists, the TWU overwhelmingly endorsed the policy at its Convention in January 1994. As a result, an organizer was hired and an attempt was made to organize a non-union subsidiary of BC Tel that employed roughly 200 in the production of telephone directories. The attempt ultimately failed (Personal correspondence, 1996). The TWU did succeed in picking up a few dozen workers who were disaffected with their representation under the IBEW. However, attempts to organize beyond the scope of BC Tel to date remain limited and BC Tel workers still constitute roughly 98% of the union's total membership. As with service enhancement, the success of the organizing effort has, to date, been limited.

The TWU has had significantly more success in increasing the level of cooperation among Canadian telecommunication workers' unions. Formal meetings organized among Canadian telecommunications unions were reinitiated in February 1994 in Halifax and meetings have been held roughly twice annually since. This development creates the first formal channel of cross-union cooperation since the Canadian Federation of Communications Workers (CFCW), a loose TWU-CWC confederation, collapsed in 1986. Such cross-union communication has the potential to lead to more concerted union action in telecommunications in Canada, and possibly mergers among some of the unions, thereby addressing the onset of competition by a pooling of their resources.

In the meantime, the TWU has continued to fight in the regulatory arena to keep the scope of deregulation as limited as possible, to limit the extent of competition, and to maximize the influence of social considerations in the setting of telecommunications policy. Though not completely successful in these efforts, the TWU has enjoyed a measure of success here, particularly in the case of inside wire. BC Tel had tried to "give away" the residential inside wire that it owned to its customers, in the hope that this would end its obligation to conduct costly maintenance work. Customers could then choose whether they wanted to buy a maintenance contract from BC Tel or contract a local electrician to deal with it. The TWU took on this issue legally, under an old common law principle that you can't force someone to accept an unwanted "gift." In the end, the union won. As a result, inside wire installation was preserved as TWU work (Canada Notes: Misc 8). Since close to 10% of all TWU members do installation and repair work, a significant portion of which involves inside wire, this action preserved hundreds of TWU jobs, at least for a time. According to one installation and repair worker, roughly 30% of his work involves inside wire and for new workers, inside wire work can constitute 80% of the installation and repair work load (Interview T-94-78).

Another issue has been created by the provincial government's entry into the field of telephone competition. This situation contains many ironies. On the one hand, a socialist union is in the position of arguing against government provision of telephone service. This is ironic given that for decades it has been TWU policy that BC Tel itself should be bought out by the province! On the other hand, the socialist (NDP) government's position is equally ironic, since the company it sought to build, named Westel, would have served the high-end business niche market, thereby forcing BC Tel to devote more resources to this same market and neglect service to rural communities (Canada Notes: Misc. 11). While, in 1995, the TWU and the NDP finally reached an accommodation on this issue, the dispute created a major strain in their relationship for the two years that it lasted.

To date, the TWU has been able to hold on to members' jobs and continue to pursue a social unionist strategy. Nonetheless, whether the TWU can continue to hold on through sheer tenacity is unclear. But it is certainly the case that so far the TWU's greatest successes have come in areas of its traditional expertise, namely its tenacious battles in the courts and with regulatory bodies. On Westel and inside wire, the TWU used its ties to the NDP, built up over the past two decades, and its 20-year experience in the use of regulatory and court obstruction tactics, to maintain control over union work. Surely the use of such tactics will continue to be important for the union in the years ahead, as indeed many union successes are more the work of perseverance than brilliantly conceived tactics. Nonetheless, while sticking to its guns will continue to be important, the challenges posed by globalization will undoubtedly require substantial changes in TWU tactics and strategy in the years to come. Just as the STRM's strategy has not adequately addressed the threats posed by deregulation in Mexico, the TWU's strategy faces its own shortcomings. Efforts to organize workers in other companies have had limited success and the development of the service enhancement program has faltered. The Accord and greater cooperation with other telecommunications unions provide signs of promise, but it would be hardly correct to argue that the TWU has thus successfully traversed the crisis brought about by deregulation. The TWU union factions and activists have yet to resolve where cooperation is appropriate and where resistance is necessary in the newly-restructured telecommunications industry. Answering this question is important for any union, but is particularly key for social unions like the TWU which seek to use their organizations to promote social reform in conjunction with community groups within a capitalist economic framework.

CONCLUSION

One of the most important changes in telecommunications during the 1980s and 1990s has been the change in the role of the state. Previously, both in Mexico and Canada, as elsewhere, the dominant form of organization in the industry was the monopoly. This was governed either directly through majority stock ownership, as was the case in Mexico from 1972 to 1990 (with a minority government share before that going back to 1958) or through strict regulation as occurred under the auspices of the BRC, then the CTC, and then the CRTC in Canada. But globalization in telecommunications has altered the role of the state in the industry and has led to a reduction in differences among nation states.

Now both Canada and Mexico are in the midst of implementing regimes that permit broad competition and significant additional entry of foreign capital. Regulatory efforts and state intervention are focused more on creating competitive conditions, rather than on monitoring the industry, as was the case in Canada, or direct management of the business as was the case of Mexico. Even the Mexican Concession Title, with its extensive service targets, is nonetheless a document first and foremost designed to create the necessary conditions for full telecommunications competition. The problems faced by the STRM and the TWU, then, are often similar. Yet the responses given by these two unions have differed sharply.

For the STRM, its efforts to date involves recourse to a Mexican version of American business unionism. But this orientation poses particular difficulties, as it is no longer sufficient for the STRM to address the issues which confront its membership by acting solely at the level of collective bargaining and negotiations with the PRI.

The TWU, on the other hand, is working to build upon its social unionist tradition. Beginning in the late 1960s, the TWU began to carve out a path that placed particular emphasis on job control and union security. In this effort, in the 1970s and 1980s, the TWU had notable successes in creating a joint union-company pension plan, in securing union jurisdiction over work within the company, and in placing strict limits on the company's ability to lay-off due to technological change or contract-out telephone work. Due to its different strategy, the TWU's tactics are different than the STRM's. The TWU has been and remains adept at operating at multiple levels—in the Courts, in regulatory agency decisions and in community campaigns, as well as within the NDP or a collective bargaining framework. But the very nature of the changes that globalization has brought to the telecommunications industry threaten the core of the social unionist vision. As competition becomes more intense in the industry, notions of telecommunication companies' social responsibility are increasingly cast aside.

As a result, both the STRM's strategy of "bread and butter" business unionism and the TWU's broader social unionist strategy are confronted with significant difficulties. In the next chapter, the problems faced by both unions are exaamined in greater detail as are their attempts to deal with the dilemmas posed by the increasing globalization of the industry.

NOTES

1. French-Canadian unions generally support the Parti Quebecois (PQ), a Quebecois nationalist party. The PQ's politics are sometimes considered social democratic and sometimes not (see Lipsig-Mummé 1990). One clear difference with the NDP, however, is that NDP bans donations from large corporations, while the PQ does not; thus, business interests play a much greater role in funding the PQ and, not surprisingly, French-nationalist business interests have a significant say in the formation of PQ policy.

2. A recent example of the often-dramatic shifts that occur can be seen in the 1993 Canadian federal elections. In that election, the ruling Conservatives' share of parliamentary districts fell from 157 seats to two. The main opposition

Liberal Party's number of Parliamentary seats doubled from 86 to 178. The New Democrats fell from 43 seats to nine. The Bloc Quebecois (the federal branch of the PQ), rose from eight to 54 and the upstart right-wing Reform Party rose from one seat to 52 seats.

3. The 1997 elections in Mexico provide some evidence of a shift in Mexico's political system in a more democratic direction. In these elections, the PRI lost its lower house congressional majority for the first time in the party's history. This result has led to much more vociferous public debates in economic policy, though actual changes to those policies have been limited.

4. In Mexico, the state and the PRI are clearly linked. Indeed, at times in this study, the two together are denominated the *PRI-state* because of this intersection. When addressed separately, however, the PRI refers to the political party organization (including its corporatist structure) while the state refers to Labor Ministry and other government officials. In these terms, the STRM's relationship with the state is more important than its relationship to the PRI. This is typical of unions in high-technology industries in Mexico.

5. *Charrismo* is a Mexican term referring to government-bought and controlled union leadership. While the term *neocharrismo* is difficult to translate into English, it could be translated as "corruption of a new type."

6. The union has never done as well financially (in terms of real wage and benefit increases) as during the 1962-1976 of "corporatist" rule. On the other hand, in terms of its relative position, the STRM has performed better financially since, as real wages have fallen less at Telmex than at most other companies in Mexico.

7. If nothing else, Hernández Juárez has endeavored to make sure this situation is not repeated. As the same union activist comments, "Brother Francisco has had a constant closeness with the whole guild [*gremio*]. He does this with visits to every compound, without exception. Sections in the interior as well, even the most distant one. And this closeness with the people has also been of attending to them, of listening to them. He waits for one of them to chat about a particular problem; he is expected to attend to it or channel it to the Executive Committee for them to attend to the problems. This is one of the great differences with the previous Secretary General. Brother Francisco holds these sessions every week, be they individual or of a work group. He has always shown a disposition to attend to them" (Interview S-94-28).

8. Among STRM union activists, supporters of Hernández Juárez are known as *juaristas*.

9. For a more complete historical description of these events, see Martinez Lira (1984) for an analysis sympathetic to Línea Democrática and Xelhuantzi López (1988) for the union leadership's position. See also Dubb 1992.

10. The exact vote total was Hernández Juárez 14,888 (86.3%), Salustio Salgado 1,813 (10.5%) and 549 (3.2%) voted for "new elections," a "none of the above" option that was also on the ballot (Martinez de Ita 1982: 126).

11. By 1982, all of the Mexican leftist parties except for the Trotskyists merged to form the PSUM—Partido Socialista Unificado de México (Unified Socialist Party of Mexico). After the 1988 elections, the PSUM, the Trotskyists (PRT) and PRI dissidents who had favored the presidential candidacy of Cuauhtémoc Cárdenas combined forces to form a new center-left electoral party in Mexico, the PRD (Partido de la Revolución Democrática) or Democratic Revolutionary Party.

12. As one opposition activist explained, the movement of the electrical workers, led by Rafael Galván, formerly a stalwart of the "left wing" of the labor sector of the PRI, was particularly important, precisely because Galván came from the PRI. "It worries them more when they are attacked by those who are within, rather than from outside of the house [of labor]" (Interview S-94-6). Regarding the Tendencia Democrática, see Trejo Delarbre 1990 and Gamboa González 1985.

13. The vote to affiliate with the CT was 171 in favor and 45 against. However, this vote was clearly *not* indicative of the much greater split among union shop stewards over this issue. Rather, as part of the general compromise, many in the opposition agreed to a pragmatic truce with the state and the PRI (Martinez de Ita 1982: 132).

14. As explained in Chapter 4, in a closed shop, such as that operated by the STRM with Telmex, being a member of the STRM was a condition of employment by Telmex. However, Telmex managers consistently refused to recognize the expulsions of the 24 supporters of Salustio Salgado and thus none of the 24 lost their employment as a result of the union's actions.

15. As covered in Chapter 5, the Línea Democrática responded to this and other repressive measures by stepping up shop floor activism and promoting strikes among the membership.

16. Technically, the vote involved a choice between 3 positions: 115 voted that solely the Hernández Juárez-supported document be distributed, 107 voted that both be distributed, 6 voted that solely the opposition document be distributed (Martinez de Ita 1982: 152). The result was an endorsement, albeit a narrow one, of the position adopted by Hernández Juárez and the union leadership majority.

17. Hernández Juárez is currently serving his sixth four-year term as secretary general of the union. The importance of permanent reelection for the current leadership and their hostility to internal opposition is made clear by the following statement made by Hernández Juárez in the debate: "We are not

against those workers who have different ideas, with those we want to discuss the ideas, analyze them . . . But that is one thing and it is something else that the Executive Committee have to put up with a group of unionists who want to take us out of the union leadership" (Hernández Juárez, quoted in STRM 1980: 33).

18. Numbers are imprecise, as there were overlapping individual and collective union suspensions. The former were aimed at union activists, while the latter served to punish entire departments that had opposed Hernández Juárez's leadership. Roughly 500 were subjected to individual sanctions and more than 2,000 to collective sanctions.

19. To quote from one STRM official, "Fidel Velázquez was able to accept Hernández Juárez .. Fidel Velázquez supported the [1978-1980] strikes and later established a very profound relationship" (Interview S-94-27).

20. According to STRM by-laws, when the position of national Secretary General is vacated, this position must be filled by the Secretary General of the largest section outside of Mexico City, which is Monterrey (STRM 1990).

21. Note that similar distinctions are made among regimes in the Latin American literature. If one were to classify the STRM in the same manner as Latin American political regimes are, then the STRM under Hernández Juárez would best be described as an example of "inclusionary" authoritarianism. For a discussion of inclusionary authoritarianism as it applies to labor regimes, see Collier 1995.

22. It is possible this allegation is true. Of course, Hernández Juárez was himself "tied" to Salinas and would be the most important Salinas ally within the labor movement during Salinas' government of 1988-94.

23. In both Canada and Mexico, it is common practice for unions to give some union members paid leave to work on the campaigns of candidates supported by the union.

24. "Foro" is short for "Foro: El Sindicalismo frente a la Crisis y ante la Nación" (The Forum: Unionism Addressing the Crisis before the Nation).

25. Of particular importance is the Industrial Disputes Investigation Act (IDIA), passed in 1907, and described in more detail in Chapter 4. Federal regulation in telecommunications began the following year, when the Board of Railway Commissioner's charge was extended by legislation to include the regulation of the telephone system (Winseck 1993: 53).

26. Three years later, in 1959, General Telephone merged with Sylvania Electronics to form the General Telephone and Electronics Corporation (GTE).

27. The Rand formula, first used by Canadian Judge Ivan Rand to settle an auto industry dispute in Ontario in 1945, specifies that all workers in the bargaining unit must pay union dues and the union must represent all workers in the bargaining unit, but workers are not required to become union members

(Bernard 1982: 128, Carter and McIntosh 1990: 32). The use of this form of a modified closed shop is common throughout Canadian industry.

28. Not surprisingly, BC Tel managers and managers at BC Tel's parent company, GTE, also took note of the company's ability to run without union workers for six weeks, albeit with a resulting backlog of installation and repair orders. As well, both BC Tel management and GTE management in the United States took a hard line towards telephone workers in the 1970s. As mentioned briefly below, GTE was able to use new technology to debilitate U.S. telephone union locals. However, unions too have been able to adjust, by focusing on shutting down specialized business services, and, as demonstrated below, by using the state as a lever to pressure company management. See also Bayko and Schiller (1984) regarding the CWA's ability to impact AT&T during a 1983 U.S. strike.

29. Interestingly, there is evidence of direct involvement of BC Tel's parent company, GTE, in the dispute. According to the Canadian government conciliator, BC Tel imported GTE supervisors from the United States to act as strike-breakers. See Kelly 1969.

30. The NDP lost the 1969 BC provincial election, which took place shortly after the strike's settlement. However, it won the 1972 provincial elections. After the election, the NDP government backtracked from its promise to buy out the company, citing cost considerations, and instead bought 3% of the company's stock equity, to increase the provincial government's influence over the company. The NDP government hoped to gain a seat on the Board of Directors, but did not succeed in doing so. To this day, the BC government remains the second largest stockholder in the company, after GTE (Bernard 1982: 163).

31. Between 1971 and 1977, the union won 9 of 11 arbitration rulings on the issue (Clark 1984: 3). Though the union lost on two occasions the issue was always whether the work being contracted out was the *type* of work "regularly performed" (Interviews T-93-12, T-93-68) by TWU members, rather than whether work of current employees was being outsourced.

32. As covered in Chapter 5, however, BC Tel only acceded to the creation of the pension fund, after losing a five month strike at its much smaller OK Tel subsidiary, which was consolidated with BC Tel operations after the strike.

33. It should be noted that there was a six month period of a minority Conservative government in 1979-1980. The Conservative government fell when its first annual budget resolution was rejected by Parliament on a vote of confidence.

34. Interestingly, when an NDP government was elected in Ontario in 1991, it attempted to work out a corporatist deal with the province's public sector

unions (Ehring and Roberts 1993: 324-325). When these unions balked at the deal offered, however, the government turned around and legislated a so-called "social contract" (an odd sort of contract where only one party signs), thereby assuring the demise of the NDP government at the following election in 1995.

35. The PRD's "radical" image is more a result of its intransigent stance vis a vis electoral fraud than its economic policy. The PRD did (unsuccessfully) seek to maintain national control over banking and telephony and has also favored maintaining Mexico's community-based *ejido* agricultural sector. But on NAFTA, the PRD agreed that a continental trade pact would be beneficial, objecting only to the terms of the agreement, unlike the NDP, which strictly opposed "free trade." In terms of macroeconomic policy, in 1994 PRD presidential candidate Cuauhtémoc Cárdenas ran on a "balanced budget" platform (Caballero et al. 1994), while the NDP has favored running a deficit to fund social spending (NDP 1993).

36. Between 1988 and 1992, $20 billion in revenue was raised in privatizations in Mexico, primarily through the sale of state-owned airlines, banks, and the telephone company (The Economist 1993).

37. As explained in Chapter 5, getting membership support for this about-face was not easy, as is illustrated by union officials' resort to deceptive claims that work rule concessions of the April 1989 *convenio de concertación* were needed to keep the company public, when in reality the document was designed to make the purchase of Telmex more attractive to private investors.

38. The original purchase price for the 186.6 million shares was U.S. $324,900,000 (Mondragón Pérez 1994: 196-197). However, within 18 months of the initial privatization, the value of the shares had more than doubled (Nacional Financiera 1992).

39. Obviously, unions and companies do sometimes share common interests, but receiving 4.4% of the shares did not appear to noticeably alter workers' views of the company or their relationship to it. One reason for this might be that the union was specifically excluded from having any control over decisions made by the company. The union never gained a seat on the Board of Directors and when decisions are made, they are made according to a pyramid scheme detailed in the original sale offer. Though Grupo Carso, Southwestern Bell, and France Telecom combined own just 20% of Telmex stock, they have 51% of the voting stock. The Board of Directors is constituted by 18 representatives of the three companies, with only two representatives for the other 80% of the stockholders. Moreover, though it could be argued that workers who own stock share a commonality of interest since their stock value increases if the company's profits go up, Mexican labor law requires profit sharing even for workers who don't own stock (Fuentes 1994: 141, see also

Chapter VIII of the *Ley Federal de Trabajo* (Federal Labor Law), reprinted in Trueba and Trueba 1993: 72-80).

40. Mexican control was ensured by requiring that groups bidding on the 20% controlling share of Telmex stock be at least 51% controlled by Mexican nationals. Thus, the controlling Mexican capitalist group, Grupo Carso owns only 10.2% of Telmex stock, but has effective voting control over the company.

41. An important characteristic of the STRM leadership is that it rarely admits mistakes, even when it changes tactics to correct for its mistakes. For instance, STRM leaders take the position that it was appropriate for Telmex to be publicly owned when the union supported a publicly-owned telephone company and that it was appropriate for Telmex to be privately-owned when the union changed its position to favor a privately owned telephone company. According to union officials, the union's position has always been correct on this matter (Interviews S-94-0, S-94-27).

42. While it is not surprising that unions look out for the jobs of their membership, it should be noted that a strong case for maintaining monopoly provision of many telecommunications services can be made, as this has proved to be a successful strategy of national telecommunications development (see Weber 1989). As one analyst explains, "A strong government role [in telecommunications] could permit rapid infrastructure upgrades and/or the offering of new services not likely to provide a return in the short term, if deemed a national priority" (Steinfield 1994: 6-7). France, the industrialized country which opened up to competition *least* in the 1980s, is frequently cited as being particularly successful in the pursuit of a such a strategy (Steinfield 1994, Winseck 1993). During the 1980s, the French telecommunications equipment supplier Alcatel grew rapidly to become the industry's second largest company, with sales exceeding even AT&T outside of North America (Sánchez Daza 1992).

43. These "Baby Bells" were only "babies" in comparison with the giant AT&T. For instance, even before it purchased Pacific Telesis and Aamertech, Southwestern Bell was more than twice as large as the Mexican national telephone monopoly Telmex (Based on figures in Pitta 1996 and Telmex 1993a). For a general overview of the investment portfolios of the seven Baby Bells at the start of the 1990s, see Andrews 1990.

44. The meeting minutes don't specify the TWU's share, but as the TWU represented at the time roughly 12,000 telephone workers in comparison with the CWC's 25,000 (the CWC's total membership was higher due to the presence of a significant number of electrical and telephone manufacturing workers in the union), the TWU's proportion would have been about $150,000,

an amount equivalent to roughly 5% of its annual budget at that time (TWU 1984c).

45. The contrast between Canada and the United States fits a larger pattern. According to a 1990 OECD study, between 1978 and 1987, the UK and Japan, where deregulation took place, also suffered job losses while in Germany and France, where deregulation did not occur, employment increased by 18% and 9%, respectively (Winseck 1993: 154). While some of the job growth in France and Germany was likely due to the fact that they did not achieve universal service until 1990 (Noam 1992: 45), deregulated Britain experienced a job decline during the same period, despite having an even lower telephone penetration rate than either Germany or France (Mosco 1990: 5).

46. Much is made in the industry press about the rising cost of telecommunications, especially for banks. But in 1990, telecommunications costs were less than 3% of the banks' revenues. Even if the $470 million spent on telecommunications by the six largest banks in Canada in 1990 was cut in half, this would increase their $3.7 billion in profits by less than 7% (Winseck 1993: 171). While cutting costs is surely a factor, the banks' main benefit from deregulation seems to be that they gain leverage over the telephone companies. As one BC Tel worker said, "Some of the big companies, they are threatening, always threatening, to go to the competition. They're using that as a threat to get better service. Some of the big customers are even threatening to set up a telecommunications system of their own. Who wins? The big customers. Your basic customer doesn't" (Interview T-93-39).

47. This "preparation" was particularly important, given that survey data showed 92% of Canadians already considered their telephone service to be either good or very good (Blackwell 1989).

48. In Canadian communications policy, as in Mexico, nationalism has always played a large role at the rhetorical level (see, for instance, Clyne Commission 1979), though, again as in Mexico, in reality the sector has always been fairly open to international—i.e., primarily U.S.—investment (Babe 1990: 5-8).

49. Reselling is a phenomenon created by regulation. Essentially, regulations created bulk-volume usage discounts. But many medium-sized companies aren't large enough to buy a WATS line or similar service, so they buy a portion of a circuit from the reseller who does buy the WATS line. The reseller earns a mark-up on the sale and the purchasing company pays less than it would have if it used the regular public long-distance network (Interview T-93-71).

50. In 1988, voters opposing free trade split between the Liberals, who won 32% of the vote and the New Democrats, who received 20% of the votes. As a

result of Canada's first-past-the-post parliamentary political system, the Conservatives' 43% was sufficient to triumph, even though a majority of the population had voted for parties which stood in opposition to the U.S.-Canada Free Trade Agreement (Colombo 1993: 153-154). Consistent with its history of financial support of the NDP, the TWU donated C$50,000 plus the wages of four campaign workers to the campaign (TWU 1988d).

51. BC Tel management, on the other hand, began planning for the onset of deregulation (BC Tel 1990).

52. This promise was broken in 1994, when the CRTC issued Decision 94-19 which allowed telephone companies to raise local monthly fees by $2 in 1995, 1996, and 1997 (for a total of a $6 rate increase) in order to compensate for the reduction in their long distance charges (TWU 1994d, Shniad 1995).

53. This is detailed in Freeman and Magdoff 1984. American unions spent roughly half as much per capita on organizing as their Canadian counterparts. However, in the 1980s, as traditional unionized sectors declined, even business unionists have come to appreciate the imperative to organize in order to avoid further declines in their membership.

The Globalization Dilemma

Both the British Columbian TWU and the Mexican STRM have some unique qualities. The TWU, both in terms of tactics (such as the occupation of telephone facilities in 1981) and in terms of contractual gains (such as its technological change and contracting-out provisions) has at times been a trailblazer among Canadian unions. Though the STRM's contractual achievements are less spectacular, relative to the situation of the Mexican labor movement as a whole, the STRM does stand out. Due to the high visibility of both the Mexican telephone company and of STRM union leader Francisco Hernández Juárez, the STRM is among the most praised and criticized of Mexican unions.

The massive changes brought about by globalization in telecommunications have posed a major challenge to both unions. If indeed it is the case, as many have argued,[1] that the telecommunications industry will be as important to the 21st century as the automobile industry has been to the 20th, then the way globalization is confronted by telecommunications workers' unions will have an important impact on the development of the overall economy. This chapter will draw out key aspects of the two unions' responses to the issues raised by globalization and assess the impact of the choices that they have made to date. In particular, I shall review a) the nature of the challenge posed to unions by globalization, b) the degree to which variation in union response is feasible, c) the way in which union responses are formed within this feasible range of responses (i.e., the unions' internal decision-making process), and d) the distinct challenges confronting each union in the face of globalization and in light of the tactical and strategic routes each union has taken.

GLOBALIZATION AND THE TELECOMMUNICATIONS INDUSTRY

As a term, globalization is often a code word used to justify the transfer of wealth from labor to capital. However, this does not mean that it is solely an ideological phenomenon. There have been major changes in the international organization of production. Telecommunications is central to these changes, functioning as a key industry in the new economic environment. Furthermore, it is itself heavily influenced by these organizational changes. Where telecommunications was once characterized as a highly-bureaucratized environment of government-owned or regulated monopolies, the onset of globalization has generated a new oligopolistic market structure in which the scope of the telecommunications industry has been widened—subsuming what have traditionally been separate fields, such as computer technology, cable television, and telephony. A new, albeit unstable, equilibrium of economic power among suppliers and buyers has been established, permitting privately-owned multinational corporations (frequently referred to in the literature as "users") to exercise considerably more influence vis a vis the traditional telephone companies. As well, on the supplier side, the industry has been marked by more frequent formation of strategic alliances between corporations in different sectors of the widening telecommunications field as well as an increase in mergers and acquisitions. The alliance between MCI and Banamex to provide phone service in competition with Telmex in 1997 is one example of the strategic alliance trend (Aguilar and Hernández 1994, Rebollo Pinal 1994). This alliance is notable for another reason, namely that a major "consumer" of telecommunications services is now also a provider of those services. The Stentor alliance of Canadian telephone companies, headed by Bell Canada, is another example of the increasing coordination of telecommunications through corporate alliances. The sale of part of Telmex's shares to the U.S. telephone company Southwestern Bell and another part to France Telecom itself provides one example of how the number of telephone companies functioning is decreasing internationally. There have also been a number of mergers and acquisitions among telecommunications manufacturing firms (Rosablanda Rojas 1994).

The role of the state has been transformed simultaneously. Although the state still plays an important role in setting the rules and regulations by which telecommunications companies operate, the state's regulatory role serves a different function than it did prior to the wave of globalization. Before the state telephone regulatory board was apt to be "captured" by the regulated telecommunications *supplier* (or "carrier") companies. Now it has instead been "captured" by large corporate *consumers* of telecommunication services, especially large banking and other financial institutions. This change is visible, albeit to a lesser degree, even in countries where state monopoly ownership and control over the public long distance telephone network continues. This shift has occurred because, even in those countries that have maintained a more traditional model of telephone service provision, the proliferation of computer technology has led to the establishment of "value added" services outside this monopoly sphere. In addition, some large business have been able to set up private telecommunications systems to meet their internal telecommunications needs. Governments can mitigate the effects of this shift in market power, as has been done in some European countries, or accentuate it, as has been done in Canada and Mexico. While some governments have sought to limit the negative aspects of this shift in market power, none have sought to reverse it (Winseck 1993).

These changes—the improved market position of large corporate telecommunications users vis a vis supplier firms, the widening scope of the industry, and the changing role of the state—all have important effects on the telecommunications workforce, and, by extension, on the unions which represent those workers. While not all of these effects are negative, these rapid and profound changes create major stresses on the workforce, which leads workers to demand that their unions respond.

First, the new market structure forces telephone companies (suppliers) to alter their business strategy. Typically, telephone companies have had an "engineering" focus. Because they had a guaranteed customer base and had sole responsibility for maintaining the network, telephone company managers could place great emphasis on addressing the system's needs as a whole, rather than the needs of individual customers (Horwitz 1988: 278). Digital technology, however, made it feasible for large corporate customers to create their own internal private telecommunications networks (Mosco 1990). Even without deregulation, this change gave large corporate customers the ability to extract concessions for themselves, some of which detract from the maintenance of an efficient telephone network. As a result, telephone companies place less attention on network maintenance than previously, while giving considerably more attention to the marketing of specialized services to large corporate customers.

The industry's widening scope has created an entirely new set of problems. Three separate industries—computing, cable and telephony—increasingly are becoming integrated with each other. In some countries, both cable and telephony were owned by the state, so the issue of convergence of cable and telephone is less difficult to administer. Such is the case in France, for instance. Indeed, technically, the French state company that owns a quarter of the voting shares of Telmex is not France Telecom, but rather France Cable et Radio, though the latter is a wholly-owned subsidiary of France Telecom. In Mexico, where the introduction of cable television is very recent, cable has been set up separately from telephony and is privately owned. In Canada, the country with the world's highest level of cable penetration, the issue of cable-telephone convergence is extremely pressing.[2] Unionization rates in cable are significantly lower than in telephony, which poses a major organizing challenge for the Canadian telecommunications unions if they are to maintain their relative strength (TIE 1994).

Finally, the elimination of telephone company monopolies strongly impacts the workforce. In Mexico, the state sector was a protected environment for workers, who received higher wages and benefits than most other workers, even those fortunate enough to be represented by unions in the private sector. As explained by Winseck (1993), a similar "semicorporatist" pattern of labor relations developed in Canada's regulated monopoly industrial structure. In the telephone sector, state-owned enterprises and regulated monopolies encompassed expectations of corporate obligations, in terms of providing well-paying jobs for workers, and, in Canada, high quality service.

As well, such enterprises were characterized by a structure of bureaucratic organization of the workplace, with a rule-defined separation of job functions. The TWU outside plant and technician workers, grouped as they were in a single "craft" category," are an important exception to this trend. This was an area in which the union had successfully resisted the Taylorization of job function. However, clerical and operator work at BC Tel was very much divided up in this fashion. At Telmex, telephone workers were divided into over 60 departments, each with their own specific work rules, making it an almost perfect example of bureaucratic, rule-defined management and union resistance to the same. At the same time, although job functions were strictly divided at Telmex, plant and technician workers (and some clerical workers) at both BC Tel and Telmex enjoyed considerable on-the-job autonomy, as supervision was limited by the individualized nature of the work.

The introduction of competition, coupled with privatization in Mexico, reopens questions on such issues as company social obligations, work organization, and control over technology. These questions are invariably reopened by management, which sees competition as an opportunity to increase profits and reduce social obligations. The reasons for this are obvious: with the changing telecommunications market structure, the focus of state regulatory action shifts from ensuring the maintenance of service quality to providing a "level playing field" for competition (Crandall 1993, CRTC 1993, Mosco 1990, Winseck 1993). Thus, corporations are given the green light to initiate changes in labor relations and service provision to respond to competitive pressures. Moreover, with the increasing formation of alliances and growing concentration of capital in the industry, management practices that are tried out at one firm in one country spread rapidly throughout the industry and across national borders.

Of course, service obligations and labor conditions cannot be disregarded entirely. State regulatory agencies still set minimum standards, and, in specific cases, may establish elaborate service targets, as was the case in Mexico in the 1990-1997 transitional period immediately following privatization (SCT 1990). However, the underlying theory holds that it is the market which will now ensure service quality, as poor quality providers will lose out in the competitive marketplace. But since a large percentage of telecommunications traffic serves a very small number of corporate customers, the competitive marketplace focuses on servicing these big users' needs, while the needs of residential customers are often neglected.[3] Fierce competition for high-volume customers may result in innovations in the types of services offered, which may later work its way down to smaller customers. Nonetheless, absent state regulation, a shift in industry priorities does occur.

Residential customer service is more labor intensive than large corporate customer service. As a result, the shift in industry priorities, leads to a declining demand for labor. In Mexico, workforce levels have remained frozen at Telmex since 1989, despite a marked increase in the number of lines, averaging 12% a year since 1991 (Telmex 1993b,

1993c, 1993d). In Canada, workforce levels have remained largely the same since 1982, when terminal equipment competition began. With the remaining workers, corporate management may opt either for a "high wage, high value-added" strategy or a "low wage, mass production" strategy.[4]

It has been suggested that the only viable union response is to push management to adopt a "high-wage, high-value-added" strategy by cooperating with management to boost productivity in exchange for wage gains (Kochan and Osterman 1994). Such a suggestion implies that globalization in telecommunications will generate a largely uniform union response. Since industrial change often leads to the establishment of a dominant model of production, it might seem logical to suggest that in industrial relations, there likewise would emerge a new dominant model of production. Or perhaps there could be a dual market division in telecommunications, with unionized firms pursuing the "high-wage, high-value-added" strategy, while nonunion firms follow the low-wage, mass-production approach. But in fact unions' responses to globalization, as seen through the comparison of the British Columbian TWU and the Mexican STRM throughout this work, can be far more distinct than such analysts would predict. While the STRM has acted in the cooperative pattern that observers such as Hoerr or Heckscher would predict, the TWU has continued to operate within a much more militant, social unionist frame. Of course, this does not mean that there are not many similarities that the two unions share by virtue of operating within the same industry. But the differences are substantial. While the TWU's social unionist strategy has moderated somewhat, there would appear to be little likelihood of a convergence between industrial relations at BC Tel and those at Telmex.

NATIONAL LABOR REGIME AND FEASIBLE UNION RESPONSE

It could be argued that the differences between the TWU and the STRM are primarily the result of differences in national labor law, or what might be termed a national labor regime—the set of rules and practices that define de facto labor relations in a given country. Indeed, there are some important differences in Mexican and Canadian labor law and practices which impact a union's ability to act. Not surprisingly, the authoritarian nature of the Mexican state leads the Mexican labor regime to be less permissive than the Canadian labor regime. This means that Mexican union leaders have less decision-making freedom and hence, a lesser degree of strategic choice, than their Canadian counterparts. In the STRM in particular, though internal divisions were more decisive, Mexican state labor officials did act to oppose the ascension of a group of more militant trade unionists to union leadership in 1982 (see Chapter 7).

But the fact that STRM leaders have a more limited set of choices than their Canadian counterparts does not mean that they are forced to embrace the cooperative path favored by the Mexican government. Nor does the less authoritarian nature of the Canadian regime automatically lead to more militant trade union strategy. This can be seen by contrasting the STRM and TWU briefly with two other unions—the SME (Sindicato Mexicano de Electricistas), which represents electrical workers in Mexico's Light and Power (Luz y Fuerzas) Company, one of Mexico's two state-owned electricity companies; and the CEP (Communications, Energy & Paperworkers union), which represents a wide array of workers, including telephone workers at Sask Tel and Bell Canada. The Mexican SME follows a moderate social unionist strategy more similar in many respects to that of the Canadian TWU than the SME's erstwhile STRM ally. Conversely, the CEP despite paying lip service to social unionism, is in many ways closer in strategy to the STRM than it is to the TWU, with whom it has maintained a cooperative, but strained, relationship.

This paper has sought to demonstrate that while the TWU and the STRM face similar issues, the decisions they make are often different and that these differences are frequently the result of internal factors, not externally-imposed imperatives. In looking at unions such as the SME in Mexico and the CEP in Canada, which go moderately against the grain of their labor regimes, however, one can better see the extent and limits of union variation in the two countries. The SME and CEP are important for other reasons as well. The TWU and the CEP (then the CWC) worked jointly on anti-deregulation campaigns in both 1984-85 and 1990-92 and are currently the leading actors in a new, informal, all-Canada alliance of telecommunications unions. The SME and STRM have signed "alliance pacts" twice—in 1960 and 1978—and were the two leading unions in the Fesebes confederation of unions, founded in 1989. As well, the CEP and the STRM, in conjunction with the CWA in the United States, signed a solidarity pact for the purposes of exchanging information and encouraging cross-national cooperation in 1992 (Benítez 1992). In short, the SME and CEP are not just any two unions, but in fact the two unions which most frequently interact with the STRM and the TWU, respectively.

SOCIAL UNIONISM IN MEXICO: THE MEXICAN ELECTRICAL WORKERS' UNION

The SME was formed in 1915, in the midst of the Mexican Revolution. Originally, workers at the Mexicana telephone company were part of the SME.[5] This situation did not persist for long, as workers at the Mexicana telephone company soon formed a separate union. Still, there has continued to be significant communication between electrical and telephone workers ever since. During the 1930s, the SME was a major player in the growing Mexican labor movement. In 1936, the SME held a nine-day strike from July 16 to July 25, successfully shutting down electricity generation and winning nearly all of its demands (Thompson 1966: 171-173). Since 1936, the SME has only gone on strike once, in 1987. On this latter occasion, the Mexican government used troops to ensure continuity of service. Despite the infrequency of its strikes, the SME has been successful in making headway by using other mobilizational tactics, including wildcat actions and street demonstrations. In the face of major challenges over the years, the SME has maintained its prominence in the Mexican union movement and currently has more than 35,000 members. Though its strategy has varied over the years, over all it has pursued a remarkably consistent strategy embodying moderate social unionism.

The first thing to note about the SME is that it has maintained an unusually high degree of internal union democracy. Central executiveposts are subject to election by the rank-and-file every two years, with half the membership turning over every year. Voter turn-out has consistently been greater than 65% and occasionally surpassed 75% (Barrera Barrera 1992). As a result of the annual elections, the SME is a very politicized union, with organized factions running candidate slates. Incumbent candidates are frequently defeated when the rank-and-file become disaffected. In 1993, for example, incumbent secretary general Jorge Sánchez, who was blamed for signing a modernization agreement with the government that members opposed, was defeated by insurgent candidate Pedro Castillo (Interview S-94-1, Almazán González 1993).

In addition to holding regular and frequent elections, power is dispersed within the SME, with authority split among three boards—the central executive committee, an autonomous treasury committee, and an autonomous judicial committee. Because of frequent split-ticket voting among the rank-and-file, it is rarely the case that one slate has control over all of the key boards simultaneously. As a result, a political equilibrium is maintained (de la Garza 1989b, Estrada Medina et al. 1993). While there have been secretary generals who have engaged in corruption or who have ruled in an autocratic manner, no SME leader has ever concentrated as much power as STRM secretaries general traditionally have.

Second, although the SME is heavily involved in ruling party PRI politics, it has succeeded in maintaining an arm's-length relationship with the party. The STRM under Hernández Juárez has tried to follow the SME model. What remains distinctive about the SME, however, is that because of the existence of regular competition between organized factions, the union has never become dependent on any specific sector of the PRI in the way that the STRM had with PRI technocrats by the late 1980s. One group of the SME does support PRI technocrats and was in power in the SME from 1987 to 1993. But the other main SME faction maintains a greater distance from the PRI and flirts with support of independent groups and the PRD.

It is important to emphasize, however, that despite its occasional flirtation with anti-PRI groups, the SME is not a union with a revolutionary agenda. This is true even though the SME has, on occasion, engaged in much greater coalition building with popular movements than the STRM. Thus, for instance, the SME provided clandestine financial support to striking railroad workers in the late 1950s and participated in a brief popular mobilization effort known as the Mesa de Concertación Sindical (Table of Allied Unions) in 1987 (Valdes Vega 1990). Indeed, the SME's reformist orientation is often criticized by those looking for a more radical stance. According to one observer, the SME only discusses immediate workplace issues and is characterized by a "guild-like" structure (Benítez Chávez 1991: 114-115). Nonetheless, although the SME has focused largely on workplace issues, its strategy on workplace issues is distinct from that of the STRM. Like the TWU—and unlike the STRM—the SME has focused much more on maintaining union jurisdiction over work and maintaining strict control over the workplace, in the face of modernization "imperatives."

As a result of the SME's tenacity on jurisdiction, over 98% of all electrical jobs at Luz y Fuerzas are unionized, a percentage far higher than the 64% coverage of the STRM at Telmex. More recently, the

1994 Modernization Agreement, negotiated by the Castillo-led slate after the membership rejected an agreement negotiated the year before by Jorge Sánchez, provides a marked contrast with the STRM's 1989 *convenio de concertación* (Romo 1994; STRM 1994e).

While in the *convenio de concertación*, the STRM agreed to accept privatization and to make work-rule concessions in exchange for monetary compensation, the 1994 Modernization Agreement of the SME illustrates a different approach. In essence, in order to keep the electrical company in public hands and maintain union control in the workplace, the SME has moderated its wage demands. Luz y Fuerzas was originally owned by private investors, but was taken over by the government in the 1960s. Nonetheless, the sale was never fully closed. As a result, the business was not formally incorporated and the government frequently threatened either to privatize or to "liquidate" it and merge Luz y Fuerzas with the larger Federal Electricity Commission as a lever in negotiations with the union. This would mean, among other things, merging the union with the much larger pro-government SUTERM electricians' union. In 1985, the de la Madrid government began a wave of privatizations that continued throughout the Salinas government (1988-1994) period. By 1988, the SME felt sufficiently threatened to take the long-standing privatization threat more seriously. As a result, the union formulateed a specific strategy. As one SME central committee member explained:

> The key problem is to protect the work material. We have to fight for the survival of our own business. It had been 15 years that the business has been in liquidation. Six years ago, a strategy was established. The sole strategy has been that Luz y Fuerzas would end the process of nationalization as a regional state-owned business. It would mean [that the union would need] to force a change in state policy (Romo 1994).

In the productivity agreement that was reached with the government in February 1994, the union agreed to work with government managers to increase productivity and accepted a five-year "no hire, no fire" arrangement similar to the understanding in the STRM-Telmex *convenio*. But the framework in which this cooperation took place was different. Instead of weakening clauses regarding the presence of joint union-management committees, their importance was acknowledged and their authority extended. Indeed, the union gained three seats on the Board of Directors of Luz y Fuerzas as part of the agreement. In contrast to the dozens of changes in the Telmex-STRM collective agreement that were made in 1989, there was not a single change in the collective agreement that resulted from the 1994 SME-Luz y Fuerzas modernization agreement, except for those changes that were proposed by the union and accepted by management (Romo 1994).

In short, while the SME has not been as successful in achieving wage gains as the STRM[6]—partially because of trade-offs for improvements on other issues and partially because of the electrical company's more precarious financial position—it has been more successful in maintaining its jurisdiction and control in the workplace. The SME has also had moderate success in forming links not just with the PRI, but with non-PRI popular organizations. Most notably, the SME has been successful in getting the federal government to formally create a newly nationalized enterprise in the midst of an era of massive privatization (Romo 1994).

In comparison with the TWU, the SME's achievements are more extensive in some areas and less extensive in others. The TWU has never come close to achieving its goal of creating a state-owned telephone company. Nor has the TWU succeeded in organizing lower-level management in the same manner as has the SME (Dobie 1980). On the other hand, the TWU has been more successful in its community organizing campaigns and has won some important contractual provisions regarding technological change lay-off protection and contracting-out of work that the SME has not been able to obtain. While there are many differences in the two labor regimes and industries, it is nonetheless the case that the Mexican SME is, in many respects, more similar to the Canadian TWU than to the Mexican STRM. This fact casts doubt on the view that identifies national regime as the key factor in explaining differences between unions generally and between the TWU and the STRM in particular.

LABOR-MANAGEMENT COOPERATION IN CANADA: THE COMMUNICATIONS, ENERGY & PAPERWORKERS (CEP) UNION

What we found was that the dynamics are different in different parts of the country, and it was very hard to reconcile priorities when one wanted to be making one issue a priority at a given time and some other part of the country had a different demand on them (Pomeroy 1988: 213-214).

Just as the SME is, in many respects, more similar to the Canadian TWU than its Mexican counterpart and sometimes-ally, the STRM, the CEP is, in many respects. more similar to the Mexican STRM than its Canadian counterpart and sometimes-ally, the TWU. Indeed, as the statement from CEP President Fred Pomeroy[7] indicates, despite the fact that the TWU and CEP (formerly CWC) have been able to work together on many issues of mutual concern, relations between the two unions have often been strained. Like the TWU, the CEP (and its CWC predecessor) has been an active union and has not been reluctant to go on strike when necessary. The CWC went on strike at Bell Canada twice in 1979—once for plant workers and a few months later in a separate operator strike—and again in 1988 (Kumar et al. 1991: 339-345). But more like the STRM, the CEP's concerns have focused more on wage rather than non-wage issues. As well, the CEP has been more willing to cooperate with management, endorsing joint productivity programs, and has been more reluctant to aggressively confront government positions. Even on deregulation, the CEP's preferred tactic was to work to soften the blow, rather than seek to stop deregulation altogether, as the TWU sought to do (Hannafin 1992). The CEP is also a signatory to a triple-alliance pact with the STRM and the CWA (Benítez 1992).

Part of the reason for the strain between the TWU and the CEP is historical. The CEP's predecessor, the CWC, began as a much smaller organization than the TWU, originally being a small collection of nine locals that split from the United States-headquartered CWA (Coates 1990: 53). When the CWC left the CWA over such issues as changes in Canadian pension laws, a lack of funds for organizing, political differences with their more conservative U.S. counterparts, and a general wave of Canadian nationalism (Winseck 1993: 99-100), the only major telephone company organized by the CWC was Sask Tel in Saskatchewan. At that time, TWU membership exceeded the CWC's by roughly a 3:1 margin (CFCW 1973:1).

Later in the decade, however, the CWC mounted an organizing drive to unionize Bell Canada (CFCW 1975, 1979). The TWU provided some support, including financing one organizer and extending a low-interest loan, but the CWC took the initiative to organize and did the bulk of the work. Once the CWC successfully organized plant and traffic workers at Bell Canada, the CWC gained nearly 20,000 new members. As a result, the CWC was now by far the larger organization. This created strain for obvious reasons: the CWC desired recognition of its overwhelming numerical superiority, while the TWU wanted to make sure that all unions' views were weighted equally so that its voice was not drowned out by the much larger CWC.

But beyond this historical point, there are major differences between the CEP and the TWU in terms of philosophy. While the CEP follows social unionism in comparison to the IBEW—which represents Albertan telephone workers—the CEP's brand of social unionism has been rather tame.[8] Indeed, in terms of both bargaining strategy and interaction with the state and management, the CEP has more in common with the STRM than the TWU.

While the CEP has an internal governance structure that shares some important features with the STRM, there is significantly less clientilism, in part because in the Canadian industrial relations system unions have significantly less control over the distribution of contractual benefits. Like the STRM, the CEP is a national union with relatively autonomous local sections. Although CEP sections are formally autonomous, as one CEP activist explains, "Most of the local people do what the leadership tells them" (TIE 1994). Also, as in the STRM (and unlike the TWU), changes in leadership are infrequent. Indeed, Fred Pomeroy was the only CWC President during the twenty years (1972-1992) of its existence and Pomeroy continues to head the telecommunications section of the newly-created CEP.

Like the STRM and the American CWA, and unlike the TWU, the CEP endorses cooperation with management in relation to workplace reorganization. Indeed, there are similarities in the way the CEP has ceded workplace rights in its 1994 "flexible" collective agreement with Bell Canada and the concessions made by the STRM in its *convenio de concertación* with Telmex and the Mexican government. Included in the CEP agreement was a five-year wage freeze in exchange for a Bell Canada commitment to avoid lay-offs (Personal correspondence, 1996; TIE 1994). As one CEP activist at Bell Canada explains:

> In 1992, the union came out with a policy paper, "Our Agenda for the Future." Essentially, [it envisions] cooperation with management. The union formulated the plan of process engineering. What has happened is that . . . with Bell Canada, there is [now] a letter of agreement on workplace reorganization. The collective agreement is

> wide open. The union has agreed with management that there is a
> need for a flexible collective agreement. Bell technicians lost 2 hours
> a week and work a 4-day work week [36 hours]. Operators' salaries
> were frozen [but] people on the national bargaining committee swear
> that the process worked (CEP local representative at TIE 1994)

Even prior to the approval of the CEP's "Our Agenda for the Future" document, there were numerous differences of opinion and of approach that surfaced between the TWU and the CWC which illustrate the philosophical divide between the two unions. Perhaps most important are their differences on the deregulation fight and how the two unions sought to approach dealing with the state on the issue.

Publicly, the CWC and the TWU were successful in maintaining a "common front" approach on the deregulation struggle, as they both recognized the overwhelming impact that an unfavorable decision would have on their members' job security and wages.[9] This cooperation was important and was by no means automatic, as is illustrated by the fact that the more strictly business-unionist IBEW did not participate in the anti-deregulation telecommunications union coalition at all.[10] Nonetheless, privately, each union expressed serious misgivings about the other's strategy. These differences were also reflected in some of the public tactics taken by each union. Moreover, the dispute between the TWU and the CWC on this issue sheds some important light on the issue of how the two unions relate to the state and their distinct union philosophies.

As Winseck relates in his research, one area of disagreement was over the use of the courts. While the TWU made and continues to make frequent use of the courts to challenge government policy objectives, the CWC has refused to do so. On one occasion, when the TWU mounted a court challenge to force the government to abide by the telecommunications law requiring resellers to file tariffs with the CRTC, the CWC refused to support the action. As Winseck explains, "The CWC feared provoking the wrath of federal state power in the event of a successful court challenge to the government's policy objectives. The TWU, however, lived up to its reputation as the most militant telecommunications labour union by exerting its opposition through the formal legal system" (Winseck 1993: 233). In 1993, four years after the TWU won in court, the Canadian government approved legislation that allowed for resellers to conduct sales without going through the federal regulatory system. Depending on what side of the argument one wishes to take, the TWU's court intervention was either successful because it bought four years of valuable time, or it was counterproductive because the TWU's action resulted in government retaliation which caused the 1993 Telecommunications Act (Bill C-62) to be broader in scope than it otherwise would have been.[11]

More basic than the dispute over the tactics to take with respect to the courts, however, was the broader issue of how to approach the deregulation fight as a whole. While the TWU favored outright rejection of the proposed deregulatory change, the CWC favored a more equivocal opposition. This difference is evidenced by the rhetoric the CWC used to couch its arguments. The CWC saw itself as being more tough-minded and realistic in its reaction to the pressures of "global competitiveness," (see, for instance, Coates 1990) as indicated in a 1991 CWC document titled *Our Niche in the Global Economy* (CWC 1991).[12]

In an October 1991 letter from the TWU to the CWC, the TWU expressed its concern over these differences in approach. In response to a draft submission paper of the CWC regarding the convergence of telephony and cable television, the TWU stated, "While we agree that competition is an important issue, the TWU sees increasing competitive pressures on Canadian society as the problem; the CWC appears to see increased competitiveness as the solution" (Hiebert et al. 1991: 1). Furthermore, the TWU felt that trying to operate within the language of global competitiveness was self-defeating and that a better approach would be to take a strict social unionist approach, seeking common cause with the broader public by emphasizing the social benefit of continued monopoly telephone service provision. According to the TWU, a key failing in the CWC's proposed position was that "Nowhere . . . is there mention of the social dimension of regulation— the need for the regulator to ensure that Canadian investment in telecommunications infrastructure reflects <u>all citizens' right to have access to state of the art communications technology at affordable prices</u>" (Hiebert et al. 1991: 4, emphasis in original).

The dispute did not abate after the CRTC's decision to open long distance telephony to competition in June 1992. On the heels of the pro-competition regulatory decision, the Conservative Government's legislation revising national telecommunications law came under consideration by Parliament. While the TWU sought to maintain outright opposition, labelling the government's legislation "fundamentally flawed" (Hiebert 1992), the CWC favored the tactic of seeking amendments in the legislation to reshape the notion of public interest to include employment protection in the bill, even though the CWC felt that the chance of such amendments passing was slim. However, the CWC adopted a position in favor of delaying consideration of the bill since such a stance "allows the CWC to work with the TWU" (Hannafin 1992).

Since the passage of Bill C-62, the Telecommunications Act, and the merging of the CWC into one of three divisions of the newly-formed CEP, the CEP has continued to pursue building a cooperative relationship with management. The most dramatic development was the January 1994 agreement with Bell Canada, referred to earlier in this section, which established a 4-day, 9-hours a day workweek for technicians, froze operator pay for a period of five years, and, importantly, suspended most Collective Agreement obligations. In these aspects, the CEP's behavior was much closer to the Mexican STRM than to the TWU. Indeed, in some respects the CEP's embrace of management philosophy is even more enthusiastic than that of the STRM. In contrast, it's worth noting that while the TWU has had to agree to early retirement packages, there have been no contract concessions of the magnitude made by both the CEP and the STRM. Like the STRM, the CEP, when it has gone on strike, has placed a greater emphasis on wages. This has resulted in a predictable mix of costs and benefits. Until the 1994 agreement with Bell Canada, CEP wages had gained ground vis a vis TWU wages (which were historically higher due to the fact that the CWC hadn't organized Bell Canada until the mid-1970s), but during the same period the number of CEP telephone worker jobs per 1,000 telephone lines has declined much more rapidly. Indeed, comparing the two unions' performance between 1982 and 1991 demonstrates the significant impact of the two unions' strategies on the number of jobs they are able to preserve or create. While different management priorities or different provincial demand conditions might explain part of the gap, it seems clear that a major reason for the TWU's ability to preserve a greater number of jobs for its members is due to its contractual achievements in the areas of outsourcing and union jurisdiction. Exact figures are in the table below:

Table 8-1: Wages and Jobs, 1982-1991, TWU and CWC Bell Canada[13]
(Daily wage figures are calculated in constant 1981 Canadian dollars).

	TWU/BC Tel			CWC/Bell Canada		
	1982	1991	Change	1982	1991	Change
Total jobs	11400	11074	-2.86%	22900	20000	-12.66%
Operator wage	68.89	70.24	+1.96%	59.18	66.63	+12.59%
Plant wage	104.47	102.42	-1.96%	98.27	100.28	+2.05%

As can be seen from the chart, Bell Canada operators gained ten percentage points on BC Tel operators in nine years, while plant workers gained four percentage points. And this is after discounting for the greater inflation in the Toronto region vis a vis Vancouver. In nominal terms, the difference is even more dramatic as can be seen in Table 8-2.

Table 8-2: Nominal Wages, 1982-1991, TWU and CWC Bell Canada[14]
(Daily wage figures are in Canadian dollars, not adjusted for inflation)

	TWU/BC Tel			CWC/Bell Canada		
	1982	1991	Change	1982	1991	Change
Operator wage	76.12	112.38	+47.64%	65.87	115.21	+74.91%
Plant wage	115.44	163.87	+37.81%	109.37	173.39	+58.54%

Of course, higher inflation rates make higher nominal wage increases more likely. However, if anything, higher inflation makes higher real (after inflation) wage increases less probable. The fact that the CWC was able to close the wage gap with their BC Tel counterparts during the 1982-1991 period is all the more impressive in this regard. However, this achievement came at a cost. First, TWU contracting-out protections kept a number of jobs in-house at BC Tel that were contracted out at Bell Canada; as a result, in 1990, there were 84 workers per 10,000 lines at BC Tel, versus 67 per 10,000 for Bell Canada (BC Tel 1993b).[15] As well, the CWC's failure to obtain job security protections cost the union dearly in 1994 when it was compelled to agree to a five-year wage freeze, providing a stark illustration of the costs associated with a wage maximization strategy (TIE 1994).

UNION DECISION-MAKING PROCESS

Because neither globalization nor national labor regime is a decisive factor in union strategy, understanding union strategy formation requires studying the internal decision-making process within each union. As argued earlier in this work, a variety of factors are at play. Mapping the actual influence of factors in any given policy decision may depend on events that occur at the time the specific decision is made. Nonetheless, as far as the general orientation of union strategy and tactics are concerned, much more can be said. In terms of tactics, such as the question of the level of militancy, it's clear that the key factor is the relationship between shop stewards and the central union leadership. This relationship itself depends on many factors, including the attitude displayed toward shop floor militancy by the central union leadership, the degree to which authority is delegated or centralized, and the variety of behavior in different sectors of the union. In terms of strategy, important issues include the degree of internal union democracy, the sectoral balance of power on the central union executive committee, and the historical legacy of the union, which plays an important role in framing discussion of specific issues as they arise. By looking in more detail at these issues within the TWU and the STRM, one can gain a greater understanding of how they have come to adopt very different responses to the similar problems they face as a result of the globalization of the telecommunications industry.

SHOP FLOOR MILITANCY IN THE STRM

Undoubtedly, shop steward organization is the most important factor in determining the level of union militancy, although it is not necessarily so important in determining the direction that militancy takes. No matter whether the issue involves the implementation of technological change, work teams, or productivity agreements, and regardless of whether we look at the Canadian TWU or the Mexican STRM, workers do best when they are able to organize themselves at the work site and act collectively. Often, this requires minimal assistance from the central union leadership. In both the TWU and the STRM, shop steward and counsellor organization has been relatively high, although over all the STRM's level of shop steward organization is greater.[16] In the STRM, this is particularly true among *técnicos* and *operadoras*. Outside plant workers have a moderately high level of shop steward organization and administrative and clerical workers a low level of organization. In the TWU, steward organization is particularly high among outside plant workers, moderately high among operators and technicians, and low among other workers, although clerical organization has increased markedly in the last few years and for the first time is making its force felt within the union.

Far too little emphasis is placed on analysis of shop steward organization. The literature places tremendous emphasis on the greatness or mendacity of the leadership. Yet, although the leadership does play an important role in concrete workplace struggles over such questions as the implementation of technological change and workplace organization, the role of the central union leadership is an indirect one. Essentially, the central union leadership can discourage militancy, encourage it, take a neutral stance toward it, or be selective in its approach.[17]

Under Francisco Hernández Juárez, the STRM has followed a selective policy. In departments that are politically aligned with the union leadership, the leadership takes a neutral stance towards shop floor action and, in some cases, even encourages it. Thus, departments that politically support Hernández Juárez receive greater support from the central union leadership in workplace disputes and greater backing for their worksite actions, such as slow downs or walk-outs. Hernández Juárez has been fortunate in that there exists a large base of activists who are ready and willing to react to perceived or real management violations of the collective agreement, even, or especially, in those cases where he might have preferred that no action take place. Two cases where this has been especially clear are with the modernization of operator services and the *convenio de concertación*.

As covered in Chapter 5, Hernández Juárez tried to reassure operators that he would "take care of" them so that they did not have to worry about the computerization of operator offices, but the operators did not accept this. Instead, they organized in departmental assemblies and at the workplace, demanding that they be included in any plans for restructuring of their department. It would have been more convenient, perhaps, for the STRM leadership to be able to work something out with management. This, however, was not an option. As a result, operators received far better treatment than that which was required by the Collective Agreement between the STRM and Telmex.

The *convenio de concertación* was another instance where shop stewards played an important role. In this case, shop steward militancy staved off disaster and allowed the union, though defeated, to avoid being demolished. Originally, Hernández Juárez had sought to have the entire *convenio de concertación* submitted directly to the membership, without counsellor or shop steward participation in the negotiations. Rank-and-file activists, even those who generally sided with the union leadership, balked at this suggestion. As a result, 600 shop stewards and counsellors were included in the negotiations with management and government officials and many work rules that were slated to be eliminated were reincorporated into the agreement (Interview S-94-15).

However, as pointed out in Chapter 5 and in Chapter 7, the STRM leadership will seek to repress shop steward activists when their activities pose a threat to the leadership's power. One example of this was provided by the technicians in the STRM. Because these workers were seen as a threat by the union leadership, the STRM leadership took a harsher tack. After the 1982 dispute, the leadership suspended the union benefits of thousands of members and prohibited hundreds of activists from participating in union assemblies and elections. Although the harshness of this repression has since subsided, the union leadership is still capable of acting vindictively. It did so with respect to private switchboard workers, by illegally withholding US$20,000 worth of shares from members of the department as retaliation for their having brought a suit against the union and management for allegedly having failed to protect their work (Interviews S-94-1, S-94-6, S-94-27). Regardless of the merits of the suit, the union's action had a chilling effect on shop floor activism in the affected departments, weakening not only the opposition, but the union's overall presence as well.

Like many Mexican unions, the STRM uses various mechanisms of control, including turning a blind eye to corruption on the part of political supporters, punishing opposition-led departments, and withholding union rights and benefits of political opponents. What makes it distinct, however, compared to the stereotypical government-controlled *charro* unions in Mexico, is neither its modernization rhetoric nor its productivity agreements, but rather the strong work site presence of union shop stewards and counsellors. Although the influence of these union activists has declined substantially since their 1976-1982 heyday, it is still important, especially in comparison to most Mexican unions, where such positions do not even exist (de la Garza 1992).

There are many reasons for this strong shop steward presence. In part, it has to do with the technical complexity of the telecommunications field, which puts a premium on technical expertise. But of course, this is true only in certain sections of the union. There are other sections, such as traffic, where an active shop floor organization exists, even though the work does not demand technical expertise. A more important factor in explaining the emergence of the STRM's shop-floor network of union stewards and counsellors was the absence of leadership under Salustio Salgado in the early 1970s. As described in Chapter 4, a power vacuum during the Salgado period emerged that was filled by shop stewards, especially among technical workers. The existence of this vacuum opened the way to the 1976 rank-and-file revolt that brought Hernández Juárez to power. The filling of this power vacuum limited Hernández Juárez's ability to act unilaterally. Moreover, division within the union executive during the 1976-1982 period led both supporters of the union leadership majority and opponents to seek to mobilize the membership to gain control over the union. After the failure of the 1982 rank-and-file revolt, shop floor activism subsided, but it did not decline to its pre-1976 level.

STRM shop floor activism persists for many reasons. First, it is difficult to erase historical memory: shop floor activists don't stop being activists just because there is no longer a struggle at the top. Furthermore, shop floor activism increases the power that the union— and by extension, the union leadership—can wield. Provided that shop floor activism does not put at risk the central union leadership's authority, Hernández Juárez can have his cake and eat it too. Hernández Juárez can take advantage of shop floor activism to gain bargaining leverage vis a vis state officials and management, while not having to worry too much about such mobilizations endangering his union leadership.

Nevertheless, Hernández Juárez has worked to increase the central union leadership's authority over the shop stewards. This was first done in the 1979-1982 period when, with the assistance of the Línea Proletaria, Hernández Juárez tried to circumvent the departmental assemblies, where shop stewards were most organized, by holding sub-departmental assemblies in which local problems could be addressed and where opposition activists could be identified, and, if necessary, isolated. This tactic was successful in some work groups, especially among operators, but over all, it had limited success. As the 1982 rank-and-file revolt against Hernández Juárez demonstrated, entire departments sometimes functioned as de facto parallel unions, completely independent of the central union leadership. After the 1982 revolt was defeated, Hernández Juárez moved to sever ties with the Línea Proletaria group that had led many of the sub-department assemblies. As a result, the practice of small sub-departmental assemblies was discontinued (Interview S-94-9).

A longer-lasting change in governance was introduced in 1979, with the creation of coordinator positions (Interview S-94-9, Adriano Almilla et al. 1993). These positions, which play a role similar to that performed by union business agents in the United States or Canada, are used to coordinate the efforts of shop stewards and counsellors and to centralize the handling of grievances in the hands of the coordinators, taking them out of the hands of local shop stewards. Further centralization has been accomplished by creating a number of central union staff positions (*comisionados*) and two work commissions—one a Grievance Committee (Comisión de Relaciones Obrero-Patronales) and the other a Technological Change Committee (Comisión de Modernización). The *convenio de concertación* has had the effect of further centralizing authority by eliminating department-level work agreements and reducing the role of shop stewards in resolving local grievances (Interview S-94-30). This centralization of power, particularly the elimination of department-level work agreements, *has* reduced the level of shop floor activism in the STRM, which after falling in the wake of the defeat of the 1982 revolt, had begun to rebound by 1987-88. However, in 1993 and 1994, the attempt of the union and mangement to boost productivity led to renewed shop floor militancy, much to the dismay of the union leadership, due to frequent disputes over the amount of work expected and the amount of productivity bonuses to be paid. In the few areas where analysis groups have been successfully established, these too have become a source of conflict, particularly if they involve a dispute over the contracting-out of union work.

SHOP FLOOR MILITANCY IN THE TWU

Although it has not been as active as its STRM counterpart, the TWU's shop steward network has its own strengths. This network emerged out of the 1970s period of activism, culminating in the province-wide occupation of telephone facilities in February 1981. During this period, the union took a very active role in recruiting and training shop stewards. Management helped this process by managing in a paternalistic fashion which enraged rank-and-file workers. The 1970s was also a period of rising labor activism and power in Canada in general and in British Columbia in particular (Bernard 1982, Robinson 1993).

Following the resolution of the 1981 dispute, however, the TWU leadership began emphasizing negotiation over confrontation (Interviews T-93-1, T-94-74). In part, this was the result of a change in leadership. In 1980, Bill Clark defeated Bob Donnelly to become president of the union. This had two important effects. First, Clark, though supportive of walk-outs at times, was less militant than Donnelly's style had been; Clark was more willing to talk matters over with management before walking-out. Second, Clark, upon assuming the presidency, was no longer directly overseeing education and training and no one assumed the position with the same vigor that Clark had exercised. At first, shop steward training and education languished. Then, towards the end of his presidency, the union allotted $200,000 to fund a four-day shop steward course (TWU 1986a). Though an admirable initiative, this turned out to be an expensive and ineffective way to build a base of rank-and-file activists.

In addition to the change that occurred on the union side after the 1981 dispute, management gave up on its aggressive attacks on the union and instead took a more nuanced approach, seeking to weaken the union through "employee participation" programs and avoiding obvious contract violations that would generate a reaction by rank-and-file workers. As a result, the number of grievances declined and so did the level of shop floor activism (Interview T-93-50).

An additional factor explaining the decline in central union leadership responsiveness to rank-and-file membership demands can be traced to the centralization of the union structure, the result of constitutional changes introduced in 1977 and 1979. These eliminated the three-divisional structure of the union as well as divisional council meetings. Although the creation of a single union structure, as explained in Chapter 6, was necessary to deal with the shifting of work among different divisions, the elimination of the divisional councils removed a key intermediate body that allowed union counsellors to play a more active role in the setting of union policy. Although efforts were made to create new intermediary bodies, including the holding of special regional union conferences, such attempts foundered. As a result a gap developed between the 40 union locals and the central union leadership. Slowly, authority shifted from the union counsellors to the central executive council. This was not immediately a problem, since informal networks persisted for a while. But when a third of the central union leadership retired and another third was voted out in 1987 and 1988, the lack of an intermediary body became a problem. Trust between union counsellors and the central union executive declined and has yet to be fully restored. Larry Armstrong's lackluster leadership (1987-1992) was certainly an important immediate cause of this decline (Interview T-93-34), but the lack of intermediary bodies in the TWU has made it more difficult for trust to be restored, since there was no ready means for divisional counsellors to meet together to collectively communicate concerns. Without trust in the central union executive, shop floor activists become less willing to take risks themselves. Thus, it's not surprising that shop floor militancy has fallen.

As in the STRM, sectoral differences are significant. Although the level of sectional strife is not as great as in the STRM, divisional conflict has been important at times. As covered in Chapter 5, the TWU central union leadership generally does more to back up demands of technicians and outside plant workers than operators. While there has not been the level of vindictiveness toward political opponents illustrated by the STRM leadership, the TWU's efforts to support the operators were more limited than the measures made to support technicians and outside plant workers in 1977-1978 and 1980-1981. While the TWU did its best to halt the centralization of operators, dedicating both legal resources in arbitration battles and political resources in community-based campaigns, stopping the closure of operator offices was never made a bargaining issue, let alone a strike issue. This was the result of many factors, including the lack of initiative on the part of operators, the existence of an "old boys" network that tended to discourage the raising of "women's issues," and the fact that operator representatives on the union executive council were allied with the minority Donnelly/Bremner faction and not the ruling Clark faction.[18]

After Clark's retirement, Larry Armstrong, a Clark ally, became president. During the period of his presidency (1987-1992), the union moved in a much more accommodating direction. More and more frequently, shop stewards were encouraged to let the central union leadership "work out" disputes, rather than walk out to gain a resolution. This trend had begun under Clark, but accelerated greatly under Armstrong (Interview T-94-74). In addition, union backing of activists became more variable, fluctuating according to whether or not the local walking out was allied with or against the union leadership. Again, though Clark himself was hardly impartial, the level of partiality increased markedly. The nadir was reached at the end of January 1992 when nearly 1000 BC Tel workers walked out of a downtown Vancouver BC Tel office building. Because those leading the action were from the opposition faction in the union, the central union leadership refused to back up the walk-out. Union leaders felt that the walk-out was designed to embarrass the union leadership (Interview T-93-60). While the desire of two rebel union locals to get back at the union leadership was clearly a factor, at the core of the dispute were a number of legitimate workplace grievances having to do with management's handling of the merging of two departments in a way that violated the Collective Agreement (Interviews T-93-27, T-94-74). The walk-out and the rank-and-file reaction to the rift between the central union and the union local that the dispute revealed did lead the new central union leadership under Rod Hiebert to begin to take a somewhat less accommodating line in its relations with management. According to one union executive council member, the walk-out "was divisive to the union, but at the same time it was the start of the reawakening of the membership" (Interview T-94-74). By the fall of 1993, there was a marked increase in shop floor activism, as clerical workers organized in response to increasing management workplace demands. For instance, in October 1993, Phone Mart representatives staged a walk-out in several separate locations throughout the province in response to management's failure to conduct a job upgrade review originally scheduled for January 1993. The action succeeded in generating an immediate wage increase to reflect the new ordering duties that had been added to their job descriptions as a result of computerization (TWU 1993e). Of course, as covered in Chapter 6, the TWU's successful resistance to work teams also required building a much more active union presence among downtown Vancouver clerical workers in BC Tel's business account services departments. Indeed, through the course of that struggle, new shop floor leaders emerged and one of them has since become a member of the TWU's central executive council.

UNION STRATEGIC DECISIONS AT THE TWU AND STRM

While shop floor militancy is dependent on the presence of a core of shop floor activists (generally created, unintentionally, by management pressure on the workforce) and then mediated by the amount of authority enjoyed by shop stewards and counsellors and the degree of support given by the central union leadership, the issue of union strategy, or policy-direction, is more complicated. Although the level of union militancy tends to be determined by the rank-and-file, strategic decisions tend to be made mostly by central union governing bodies. Thus, it is not surprising that a union's governance structure plays an important role in influencing the decisions that are made, as does the sectoral composition of the governing central union executive council. Generally, these executive decisions are made within the framework of the dominant ideology or strategic orientation of the union, which is a product of the union's institutional historical experience. In particular, the 1976-1982 period of the STRM and the 1977-1981 period at the TWU were periods of intense conflict both within these organizations and with management. Generally speaking, such a strategic orientation is difficult to change unless a new crisis emerges. The changes being implemented due to globalization in general and deregulation specifically create the possibility of a shift in strategy. So far, however, both unions have continued within the framework established by the conflicts of the late seventies and early eighties, though not without difficulty.

As discussed throughout, a union's strategic orientation helps to define the key problems posed by external events like the globalization of the industry, as well as the way that the union addresses these problems. Because a union's strategic orientation does not arise from issues at any one work site, the process of policy formation of strategic issues is the reverse of policy formation process on tactical issues. That is, it is usually the central union leadership that creates a policy which is then influenced indirectly by the membership, and, depending on the governance structure, subject to either membership approval, or in less democratic unions, only tacit membership acceptance. For this reason, while the union leadership plays only a limited role in determining the level of union militancy, it plays a substantial role in the definition of the problems the union faces and in shaping the manner of their resolution. This contrast is particularly obvious in the two unions' opposite postures on work teams and other union-management cooperation programs.

But it's important to bear in mind that union officers rarely make a conscious decision between one strategy or another. This does happen occasionally, as is evidenced in the 1979 STRM Convention debate described in Chapter 7 or the 1988 Telmex management debate on the proper industrial relations strategy discussed in Chapter 5. Far more commonly, however, debates are issue-specific and don't explicitly involve discussion of strategy. These issues, however, can serve to give rise to a different strategy, much as the TWU's response to automation in the early 1970s ultimately gave rise to the union's adoption of social unionist strategy.

For instance, the debate regarding whether the TWU should enter into a Letter of Agreement with BC Tel suspending job posting rules and allow 292 plant surplus workers to temporarily transfer into clerical positions was not a debate over strategy per se, although analytically certain arguments raised by opponents of the Letter of Agreement reflected a militant business unionist viewpoint. But had the TWU taken the approach favored by the dissenters, overall union strategy would have been impacted. Certainly, the TWU's president at the time, Bill Clark, knew this. When Clark claimed that, "The wage increases we bargain every couple of years are determined within a percent or two by community pressures more than any other factor, and therefore are not our main reason for being" (Clark 1984: 2), Clark was acting out a typical social unionist strategy used to cope with hard times (see also CAW 1993): giving a bit on wages, provided there were no wage cuts (Clark 1988), in exchange for preserving a greater number of jobs. In the event, wages were not cut, but did fall in real terms, since inflation outpaced wage gains during the 1980s. But, contrary to what Clark says, a union *can* push up wages, albeit at a price. As one TWU counsellor explains:

> Years and years ago, BC Hydro (IBEW) used to have substantial crews in all areas. But they did not have any protection for contracting out. Their seniority is regional seniority. What they did was systematically close down whole districts, and then contracted the work out. At Hydro, they are substantially higher paid. Most of the reason for that is the employees bought the jobs with wages. So it may be wonderful getting a 10% increase, but if there's no job to apply for, what's the point? (Interview T-93-25).

Naturally, opponents of the Letter of Agreement didn't challenge the desirability of keeping more people employed. Nor did they argue specifically against social unionism. Rather, they argued that militant action would enable the union to keep more people employed at higher wages. Of course, often militant action does expand the range of wage and non-wage benefits a union may obtain. Whether or not slow-downs and overtime bans (Interview T-94-73) could have forced management to rescind its lay-off threat in the "292" situation is uncertain. What is clear is that the "292" opponents' position challenged the TWU's job creation focus; in exchange for protections regarding technological change and contracting-out of work, the TWU had accepted a considerable amount of management flexibility in assigning workers to where they were needed. At a minimum, the position of opponents with respect to the "292" Letter of Agreement, a measure taken to address the issue of the changing boundaries of work that had been brought about by technological change, put at risk an important component of the TWU's social unionist strategy.

Likewise, in the STRM, the debate over how to implement the productivity program, covered in Chapter 6, is not explicitly a debate about strategy. Indeed, it is worth noting that STRM opponents are not demanding withdrawal of the productivity program. Besides the obvious complaints regarding the numerous late payments and errors in the incentive calculations that the program has spawned (Interview S-94-11), the opposition's main complaint concerns the "lack of participation of telephone workers in the analysis, diagnosis, and formulation of proposals" (Lara Sánchez 1994: 2, Interview S-94-32). As well, opposition activists hope to use the analysis groups to reclaim work from subcontractors (Interview S-94-5b). Nonetheless, implicit in the opposition's critique lies a sharp disagreement with the union leadership's strategy of ceding workplace control in order to pursue higher wages. As of 1996, the productivity program continues, as does the debate over whether the program should be implemented as a union strategy for economic gain or as a means of asserting new forms of workplace control (Personal correspondence 1996).

That debates over specific issues may result in clashes over strategy should come as no surprise. Indeed, this finding is consistent with general regime change theory (Collier and Collier 1991), which stresses the role of dispute resolution during periods of crisis as being key to understanding institutional (in their case, state and national labor movement) behavior. But how does this happen?

Some have argued that there is a connection between "democratic" unions and social unionism, or, in the case of Mexico, independent unionism (Roxborough 1984). While there may be some tendency in that direction, the evidence is mixed. Indeed, Perlman (1928) argues that workers are not revolutionary, but rather prefer "bread and butter" unionism. While Perlman is wrong to suggest that workers are never revolutionary, it is true that sometimes workers prefer to cooperate with management rather than to struggle to achieve some class interest.[19]

As explained in Chapter 3, both social unionist and business unionist approaches are reformist in nature, although social unionism seeks to more actively change relations of power while business unionism seeks to maximize narrowly-defined economic benefits within a given power relationship. Social unionism, because of its broader focus, will tend to provide greater benefits in the long run, but may yield fewer monetary benefits in the short run.[20] Lower-wage workers, in particular, may well be expected to be more leery of making this exchange, even though, historically, social unions' greater organizing zeal has meant that they were the first ones to organize them (see, for instance, Perlman 1928). In the STRM, the social unionist faction consists largely of the higher-wage and/or higher-status workers (*técnicos* and international operators), while the business unionist faction consists of lower-wage and/or lower-status workers (national long distance operators and outside plant in the STRM). The TWU is more mixed, a reflection of the highly personalistic nature of TWU factional politics that results from its parliamentary structure in which 100 counsellors set major policy direction and elect the union executive. Still, there is a weak tendency for a split in the same direction. Higher-wage clerical workers and inside plant and technical workers tend to be supportive of the union's social unionist leadership, operators and outside plant workers less so.

Clearly, it is possible that the workers who identify with the shorter-term monetary goals of a business union orientation would democratically elect leadership that is in favor of cooperation with capital and management in exchange for higher wages and benefits. Indeed, in the case of the SME, a union that almost certainly has the distinction of being the longest-lasting democratic union in an authoritarian country (80 years and counting), one finds roughly equal periods of both tendencies (M. Thompson 1966). Currently, the social unionist group controls a majority of the central executive council, but the business unionist faction was in power from 1987 to 1993.

Empirically, union democracy does appear to make it easier to change strategic direction, as changes in leadership can occur at regular intervals. In an authoritarian union, such shifts occur irregularly. The STRM, despite having a democratic façade, cannot be considered democratic. Major shifts in union orientation or strategy have generally occurred via either rank-and-file revolt (1958, 1976) or government imposition (1962). In a democratic union, it is also more likely that there will be fewer differences between the main factions—that is, they will tend to converge around some "center," particularly if the electoral system involves "first past the post" voting (Downs 1957). In an authoritarian system, opposition will tend to be more radicalized since some of those who, in a democratic system, might form the core of a more "moderate" opposition, will likely be intimidated from engaging in challenging the central union leadership. For instance, while the Clark and Bremner factions within the TWU have certainly differed in their views, these differences pale in comparison with the gap between Línea Democrática and the faction led by Hernández Juárez. But the terms "democratic" and "authoritarian" are themselves imprecise. While it is true that one could call the TWU a democratic union and the STRM an authoritarian union, a more precise description of the TWU political system would be "club democracy" and a more precise description of STRM political system would be that of "machine politics."

Saying the TWU's system of governance is club democracy is to acknowledge that the great majority of decisions are made by 100 counsellors who represent over 10,000 members of the union. Because attendance at union meetings, except for contract votes and other crucial issues, is usually less than 10% of all workers, there is a good deal of abdication. Constitutional amendments in the TWU require membership approval, but turn-out in such elections is routinely below 10%. Only in contract votes does turn-out rise to reasonably high levels, usually around 60% (TWU, *Transmitter*, various issues).

The counsellors in the TWU, who are chief shop stewards for their union locals, meet once or twice a year at convention. At conventions, these counsellors are the ones who vote to establish the union's bargaining policy, elect the membership of the bargaining committee and other standing committees, and elect the 15 members of the central executive committee, which acts on behalf of the union between conventions. Debate at convention is vigorous and incumbent officers are frequently voted out of office, most recently in January 1995 (TWU

1995b). Given that the entire decision-making body consists of only 100 individuals, it should not be surprising that such factors as personalities and the historical political alignment of individual union locals play an important role in determining who votes for whom (Interviews, T-93-30, T-93-82).

The STRM has broader participation, but it is more controlled. The "Workers' Slate" (*Planilla de los Trabajadores*) is determined through a primary system roughly 18 months prior to the actual union elections. Getting on the Workers' Slate is important, since that means a candidate gets to be on the slate that is headed by Hernández Juárez, with the control over resources that this implies. Workers who get selected to be on the Workers' Slate are taken off the job and put in a year-long union training program so that they will be prepared to take over a specific position. Distribution of slots within a slate is done by mutual agreement, but in the event that there is disagreement, Hernández Juárez has the authority to make a binding decision about who shall hold which portfolio (Interviews S-94-4, S-94-22). All of this occurs prior to the actual election.

Opponents of Hernández Juárez have a choice. They can try to become part of the Workers' Slate or they can run an opposition slate against one that has been trained for over a year to take the union positions. In 1988, some chose to run an opposition slate and were overwhelmingly defeated, while some ran on the Workers' Slate (and were hence elected). In both 1992 and 1996, the opposition coordinated its efforts and decide to maximize the number of its positions within Hernández Juárez's slate. However, there are limits to the effectiveness of this strategy. First, only Hernández Juárez can run for reelection. Second, Hernández Juárez is able to ensure that loyalists occupy the most important positions in the union. Third, Hernández Juárez can appoint additional members to the executive council; more than a third of the members of the central executive council are appointed in this manner. As a result, opposition activists are able to have some representation within the central executive committee, but Hernández Juárez is assured of a majority, even if few of his supporters were to make it onto the Workers' slate.[21]

Unlike TWU officers, who can be elected with the votes of 51 counsellors, STRM officers are elected by thousands or even tens of thousands of votes, but these elections are more symbolic than competitive. Unlike the TWU, in the STRM, there is a sharp contrast between the moderate business unionism of the STRM leadership and the more militant social unionism of Hernández Juárez's opponents, although the radicalism of Hernández Juárez's opponents is far less than what it had been in the late 1970s.

In both unions, strategy formation is largely a top-down process, although there is a definite process of give-and-take with the rank-and-file and with opposition movements. In the TWU, the rank-and-file has the greatest influence in setting union bargaining priorities, but less influence in shaping union campaigns or responses to corporate initiatives (Interview T-93-63). In the case of the STRM, the opposition has often spurred the STRM leadership to deal with issues that it otherwise might have avoided for a much longer period of time, especially issues that directly impact an identifiable group of workers, as was the case with the digitalization of switching technology (Sánchez Daza 1993: 77-78; see also Sánchez Daza 1985) and the computerization of operator services (Coordinadora Democrática de Telefonistas 1991, CILAS 1992).

Finally, the way a given strategy is implemented on specific issues is tempered by which occupational groups or factions are involved. Of course, implementation of *any* strategy necessarily involves adjustment to problems as they arise. In the STRM, when operators and outside plant workers protest, their voices get heard, even if they don't always prevail. Thus, in the 1989 negotiations of the *convenio de concertación*, operators were able to salvage in the fine print of their *perfiles de puestos* many rights which were taken away from them in the *convenio de concertación* and, of course, STRM leaders were equally flexible regarding their handling of the computerization of operator services (Interview S-94-15). With plant workers, even though overtime monies have been converted into incentive payments, union leaders have diffused discontent by obtaining for plant workers the ability to supplement their income by carrying out additional orders outside of normal work hours, with payments of up to N$70 per job (Interviews S-94-13, S-94-18e, S-94-24). This enabled roughly 20% of outside plant workers to not only make up, but exceed, their previous earnings (Interview S-94-24).

In the TWU, there are also adjustments made to occupational-based demands. The amount of energy devoted to the "292" conflict is reflective of plant workers' political clout in the union, even though plant workers were split as to the merits of the Letter of Agreement that was signed. As well, the collective bargaining process is rife with instances where union strategy is adjusted to satisfy member demands of different sections of the company. A persistent source of tension in this regard has been the issue of levelling clerical and operator salaries with plant salaries, a social unionist goal that has at times clashed with plant members' economic demands (Interview T-93-60).

TWU AND STRM: COMPARING TWO LOGICS OF UNIONISM

As has been argued throughout, globalization creates a set of common problems for the two unions. State labor laws and practices influence, but do not determine, the direction of union strategy. While the TWU has historically followed a social unionist strategy, the STRM has followed a business unionist strategy, at least since 1982. However, both the TWU and the STRM have had to adjust their tactics to deal with the changing economic environment, especially as this impacts on the telecommunications sector. So far, the changes in the STRM have been more dramatic, as can be seen in the STRM's modernization project in which the union agrees to push up productivity in exchange for financial bonuses. But the TWU is also having to change. Here it is necessary to analyze the logics of the two distinct types of unionism they follow, why they have tried to adjust to the changes as they have, and the unique problems posed by their two distinct types of adjustment.

To reiterate, the environment in which telecommunications unions must adapt and respond has many underlying similarities. However, the STRM and the TWU have different political philosophies, which have an important influence on how they perceive the threats and potential opportunities posed by globalization and how they can respond. To understand this, one must look at the unions' traditional manner of interacting with the state and corporate management.

The TWU has maintained a respectful, but nonetheless antagonistic, relationship with management and an attitude of resistance to state attempts to restructure telecommunications regulations to favor large commercial customers. Emblematic of this resistance was the TWU's intervention at the 1980 CRTC hearings, in which it denounced management's emphasis on technological improvement over the less glamorous tasks of maintenance of line service quality, and the 1981 occupation of telephone facilities, a militant action that demonstrate the TWU's willingness to resist tenaciously management efforts to shift work away from union members. Since then, the TWU has moderated the level of its resistance, but the union continues to dedicate financial resources in both the legal and political realms to pursue a vision of telephony, distinct from the deregulation model that is being pursued by governments and corporations. As part of its efforts, the TWU has maintained an alliance—sometimes strained, often not—with the social democratic NDP in its battles against Conservative and Liberal government initiatives.

The STRM has traditionally maintained a similarly respectful, but antagonistic relationship with management (Interview S-94-14). At the same time, however, it actively cooperated with state initiatives. In particular, until recently, the STRM maintained a strong alliance with Mexico's dominant state-linked party, the PRI. At times, STRM cooperation with the government went so far as to endorse government initiatives that reduced the purchasing power of its membership. With privatization, the STRM began to cooperate with management much more. Workplace disputes still occur, but the level of rancor on both sides has declined substantially. Because of privatization, the STRM's ability to pit state labor officials against telephony company managers has declined, although it can still use its links to state officials to pressure management. However, in general, the STRM's strategy has been to use the strategic position of telecommunications in Mexico's middle industrializing economy[22] to cut a separate deal for its members. In this way, the STRM's strategy fits within the classic "labor aristocracy" mold. While it differs in its choice of tactics, the STRM shares many similarities with the "business unionist" strategy followed by most U.S. unions in the Cold War (1948-1989) period.

Both unions have had their share of successes and failures. For the TWU, the period of both Clark (1970-73, 1980-87) and Donnelly (1973-1980) leadership marked the heyday of the union in terms of its effectiveness. In particular, the 1970s brought tremendous contractual gains. The TWU was a highly combative union during that period, but it was also a union with a specific social vision. The contract gains made during this period speak to that vision of job security and job control: contracting-out protection, technological change lay-off protection, the right to prior information regarding technological change, the creation of a jointly-trusteed union-company pension plan, union jurisdiction protection, and the formation of a union-run health benefit plan. The TWU was even successful in helping to lead the successful opposition to the introduction of deregulation in Canada in

1985, thereby preserving hundreds or even thousands of union member jobs. Wages also went up quickly during the seventies, although in the 1980s the TWU began to lose ground compared to other unions. During the seventies, management had fought the union on control issues and gave on wage issues; the union, however, was more concerned about control issues. The resulting battles led to long strike/lock-out actions in both 1977-78 and 1981. Once management finally acceded to the TWU's demands for greater job control, conflict fell substantially, as the TWU did not press nearly as hard on wage issues as control issues.

The TWU's record was not perfect, however. One key problem that arose during the 1970s and 1980s that has now come back to haunt the TWU is the lack of organizing. In the late 1970s, the TWU sought to assist a sister union to organize middle management, but this effort failed in 1979 by a 55%-45% margin. Bell Canada workers were also unorganized, but the TWU took a parochial view, making limited efforts to organize Bell Canada itself, thereby ceding the field to Fred Pomeroy of the CWC in Saskatchewan. The TWU provided loans and an organizer, but it was the CWC, which was at that time much smaller than the TWU, that ultimately succeeded in gaining union contracts for 20,000 operators and plant workers at Bell Canada. Even in its own backyard, the TWU had little success in organizing, failing twice in the 1980s and again in the 1990s to organize a few hundred workers at Dominion Directories, a wholly-owned subsidiary of BC Tel, which prints BC Tel telephone directories (Personal correspondence: 1996).

This failure to organize is crucial because social unionism relies on using union economic power to shape the nature of the industry and the economy as a whole, ensuring that it is more responsive to working class issues. This is deemed to benefit union members since social unions' actions can seek to alter the shape of the market so that a broader range of needs are met. This in turn ensures more union jobs than does an industry that limits its focus to satisfying the needs of large corporate customers.

A monopoly market provides a unique environment for a union that operates in a social unionist mold. Because a single company controls the industry, the union's use of its economic power ensures worker control of both the company and the industry as a whole. However, with deregulation, this situation changes very rapidly, as now there are many companies in the industry. Conditions gained by the union might be eroded as other companies provide telecommunications services more cheaply or capture profitable niche markets more quickly. In short, the union becomes a market taker, rather than a market maker, unless it succeeds in organizing the entire industry.

Deregulation, in the Canadian context, creates two distinct kinds of pressures. First, there is the pressure created by the entrance of new competitors. For the first time, this creates competition among different long distance telephone companies operating in the province of British Columbia. Deregulation also creates pressure for the harmonization of telephone company practices across the different provinces of Canada. This pressure exists because new competing companies, often backed by U.S. telephone giants such as AT&T and Sprint, operate nationally. As a result, to effectively compete against the new national competitors, "traditional" Canadian telephone companies must also act nationally. This pressure led to the creation of a consortium known as Stentor, that includes all provincial telephone companies and is dominated by Bell Canada. Of course, the TWU has no members at Bell Canada, which means that it has less influence over the direction of the industry as a whole. As well, the TWU's contract is much stronger on job control language than is the CEP's contract. Thus, management at both Bell Canada and BC Tel have an incentive to make Bell Canada's labor conditions the industry standard. While the TWU has been fairly successful in defending its contractual achievements to date, both competition and external national (and implicitly international) pressure have put the TWU's ability to continue to pursue a social unionist vision at risk.

A final problem for the TWU is that the period immediately prior to the onset of deregulation, the 1987-1992 Armstrong period, was largely a period of stagnation in the union and was accompanied by a loss of the TWU's traditionally strong social vision. The union did finally begin to tackle the issue of the gap between male and female wages by getting a "pay-equity" settlement.[23] The TWU made up some lost ground on wage and benefit issues, but the union otherwise acted in a largely reactive and defensive matter. As a result, the TWU was not terribly well prepared for the initial shock of deregulation and was slow to begin organizing efforts even after the decision to deregulate was issued.

Nonetheless, despite the difficulties and an initially slow response, the TWU has begun to adjust its strategy to face the new challenges in the more hostile globalized telecommunications environment. As covered in Chapter 7, these measures have included renewed efforts to organize, renewed efforts to cooperate with other telecommunications unions in Canada, and efforts to encourage both BC Tel management and the provincial British Columbia NDP government to establish a social service commitment for telecommunications service providers. So far organizing success has been limited (a few dozen disaffected IBEW cable workers have joined the TWU) and cooperation with other unions has increased but is still limited. But the TWU has had considerable success in its service enhancement efforts. These culminated in October 1995, with the signing of the BC Electronic Highway Accord. In this document, the provincial government agreed not to enter into long distance telephone service competition and instead to exclusively use BC Tel for its telephone services in exchange for BC Tel's commitment to create universal access to the information highway, including in British Columbia's many isolated rural communities. This effort fits within TWU's emphasis of pushing high labor-intensive service provision work and should, at a minimum, serve as a cushion for job cuts that are likely to come as the process of deregulation and the extension of competition continues.

However, while the Accord negotiated does buy the TWU some time, maintaining a social unionist vision in a competitive industrial situation will almost certainly require far greater organizing efforts within British Columbia and either merger or closer cross-union cooperation throughout the Canadian telecommunications industry. The TWU has been unique among telecommunications unions in North America in its ability to maintain a large degree of union job control in the workplace. Alhough it has been successful in some areas, such as in its resistance to work teams, unless the union is able to build, through organizing and multi-union alliances, a strong countervailing power to BC Tel and other Stentor companies, there are likely to be more and more areas where the TWU will have to cede ground. One area where it has already done this is with sales of telephone service. Although the union contract gave the TWU the right to conduct all sales, the union yielded that right and decided to allow non-union telemarketers to sell BC Tel long distance plans, under the theory that this concession will ensure that the BC Tel customer base is not eroded. In this arrangement, union members are involved only in the processing of the orders after they are brought in by non-union telemarketing firms (BC Tel and TWU 1994). The TWU's actions in this matter are a far cry from its dogged resistance to the contracting-out of work two decades before and demonstrates well the dilemma it currently confronts.

STRM: GLOBALIZATION FOR A COOPERATIVE UNION

In some respects, the STRM has had a lot of job control. Unlike the TWU plant workers, whose job boundaries were quite fluid, job boundaries in the STRM were strictly defined by separate department-level work agreements. But the two unions' work rules are quite different. While the STRM department-level contracts governed local workplace issues, the types of control issues for which the TWU fought so hard involved major incursions into the "rights of management," touching on the host of company-wide issues listed above. Another key difference in the STRM is that there is a greater emphasis placed over all on wage and benefit issues. These differences mean that while the STRM often vigorously challenged management over wages and benefits or over localized job control issues, company-wide job control issues were rarely put on the table, even during the years of fierce struggle between Hernández Juárez and the Línea Democrática prior to 1982, when both sides were eager to exploit new issues to partisan advantage. As a result of the STRM's distinct focus, its response to globalization has been different than that illustrated by the TWU. Simply put, the STRM has viewed the problems posed by globalization differently and thus has responded in a different manner.

As covered in Chapter 6, in 1985 the STRM began to embark upon a new strategic initiative known as "modernization." The modernization project sought to maintain Hernández Juárez's traditional adherence to the political status quo. At the same time, it began to attempt to tackle the problems posed by different aspects of globalization, including rapid technological change and work reorganization, by forming company-wide, union-management joint committees (*comisiones mixtas*) to deal with the issues. As covered in Chapter 5 in particular, the union made considerable gains, in cooperation with a progressive management team, but when that progressive management team was dumped for a more hard-line leadership, the union suffered important losses, as set forth in the clauses of the *convenio de concertación*. Still, despite this major setback, the union has had some success in pursuing joint strategy efforts on worker training (Interview S-94-21). In 1993, the union reached a productivity agreement with management (STRM and Telmex 1993a). These actions are consistent with the traditional wage-oriented approach of the STRM, but differ in a couple of important aspects as far as the way wage and benefit gains are pursued.

First, the new approach requires the union to play an active role in encouraging speed-up. Previously, the union took a hands-off approach to the issue of productivity and sought the best wages that it could get. Now, the union encourages speed-up, but in exchange for higher earnings. A second difference is that the union's relationship with the company involves less state intervention. Prior to 1990, Telmex was a state-owned company, but Telmex management, though officially responsible to the state, acted with considerable autonomy. In many respects, management acted as it would in a private company, responsible to the private shareholders who held nearly half of Telmex stock during the period of state control. Indeed, according to Hernández Juárez, "The structure of the company never was adjusted [to the 1972 nationalization] . . . in such a way that the predominant interests in its planning, operation, and administration were always private and multinational" (Hernández Juárez 1991: 16). Still, privatization removes state officials from oversight responsibility and the new management has been given a freer reign (Petrazzini 1995: 111, Interview S-94-27). A third difference is that the union's relationship with management has become much more centralized; as one union officer stated bluntly, "The greater centralization of negotiations is a fact" (Interview S-94-3). This is utterly contrary to the STRM's rhetoric of decentralization (Interview S-94-27). In addition to the political desire of union leaders to amass more authority, a major cause of this change is, as was the case in the TWU, the need for the union to be able to respond to work shifting from one department to another.

The STRM's approach has had its problems. It has not stemmed the tide of work that is being subcontracted externally or to non-union subsidiaries of Telmex. Nor has the STRM been successful in taking advantage of the increasing amount of work to increase the number of jobs. In 1994, the ratio of jobs to telephone lines fell below that at BC Tel. Still, the STRM has maintained an awareness of the economic changes around it and dedicates an unusual amount of detail to its strategic blueprints, which involves the publishing of 30-page documents at the union's annual September national conventions. The union even had a book published on the matter (Hernández Juárez and Xelhuantzi 1993).

In the STRM's view, the challenge of globalization requires a shift in strategy (Interview S-94-27). Instead of fighting with management over working conditions, wages and benefits, the union seeks to work with management to become more competitive, with the assumption that becoming more competitive will enable the union to continue to obtin good wages, and benefits for its members, albeit with less union control over work conditions. Unlike the TWU, the STRM has largely ceded the ground on determining the direction of the industry, not to mention government economic policy, but, at least until competition comes to directly threaten STRM members' jobs, the STRM's strategy would seem to satisfy at least its the narrow goals of protecting current members. Wages for telephone workers have declined, but less rapidly than has been the case for many other workers in Mexico. While forced transfers and early retirements have occurred, leading some workers to leave the company, no union members have been directly laid off.

But the STRM's achievements must be weighed in light of the problems it still faces. First, it has been unable to explain its own modernization agenda to members, as is admitted by union staffers. As one staff member explains, "We have worked intensively with brochures, with conferences, and directly in work centers. Up until now, we have achieved little in global terms" (Interview S-94-0). Moreover, it leads to confusion among some workers, who come to identify the business' objectives as their own. As one opposition activist stated, "Although it is still not a majority, there are indeed workers that agree that they need to be more productive for the benefit of the company—well, for the benefit of the customer. That is what the company plays on" (Interview S-94-25). Second, to date, the STRM has been unable to confront the coming competition, making limited efforts to organize workers in competing telecommunications firms. Third, the lack of internal democracy hurts the union's ability to collect information and limits its ability to pursue alternative approaches. Finally, the STRM is risking a gradual erosion of its position, as the percentage of telecommunications workers represented by the union declines.

According to one STRM union staffer, what is most important for Mexican telephone workers is "pay for the family" (Interview S-94-14). But how to get "pay for the family" is far from clear. While one can always make short-term financial gains by trading away contract provisions for money, these trade-offs weaken the union's bargaining leverage, and, in extreme cases, can lead to a union's demise.

Traditionally, the STRM has sought to maximize "pay for the family" by fighting Telmex management over work norms, wages, and benefits, while ceding overall company policy decisions to management and agreeing not to challenge government policy decisions. Now the STRM has agreed to cooperate with management to *increase* work norms while seeking a bit more control over training and other company policy issues. At the same time, the union continues to avoid challenging overall management decisions. The difficulty faced by the STRM is different from that faced by the TWU. While some of the TWU's goals are more far-reaching and thus more difficult to reach, should the TWU succeed, it will have succeeded, at least in Canada, in ensuring a strong union presence at the table in the telecommunications industry, which shows clear signs of becoming the single most important industry in the global economy.

The STRM faces a different challenge. Current STRM members, at least, may remain protected from mass lay-offs and wage rates may, relative to other Mexican workers, remain high. However, given current Mexican state policy priorities, it would appear that the STRM risks becoming a bit player in the Mexican telecommunications industry, as non-union competitors grab a significant market share. Because deregulation is occuring before a complete national long distance network is constructed, the opportunities for competitors are greater than those enjoyed by, for instance, MCI in the United States in the early 1980s. Adequately addressing this industry-related threat remains the single most important issue that the STRM must confront.

NOTES

1. See, for instance, Cowhey and Aronson 1989, Angeles 1993, González Aparciazga 1993.

2. As one industry analyst noted, "Canada has the highest level of cable TV penetration of any country, with 73% of Canadian households receiving cable TV in 1991 versus 60.6% in the United States" (Davidson 1993: 43).

3. To quote from a 1993 BC Tel strategic planning document, "In concert with its Stentor partners, BC TEL will pursue rate restructuring in long-distance and local markets necessary to reduce its overall competitive exposure. Long-distance pricing action is selective and aimed primarily at the medium and large business sector" (BC Tel 1993b: 14).

4. On this issue, in the industrial relations field, see Kochan and Osterman 1994, Bluestone and Bluestone 1992, Heckscher 1988, Reich 1992, as well as the discussion of this issue in Chapter 3. For views of this matter within the labor movement, see McPhail 1991, Müller 1993, and Carr 1991. The labor movement itself is definitely ambivalent regarding the validity of the "high-wage, high value-added" strategy. This ambivalence is best demonstrated by

Shirley Carr, former president of the Canadian Labour Congress, who asserts that, "The social democratic countries of Northern Europe have demonstrated that it is indeed possible to reconcile the goals of economic efficiency and social equity," only to caution two pages later that, "The strategy of competing smarter by moving up the value-added ladder has its limits" (Carr 1991: 25, 27).

5. Such a combination is not uncommon. For instance, the IBEW in the United States and Canada continues to represent some telephone workers, as well as electrical workers. In British Columbia, the IBEW represented both electrical and telephone workers until the end of the 1920s, when the IBEW telephone locals fell apart. In Costa Rica, the electrical and telephone company remain a single company under state ownership, although the government is making efforts to separate the two, in order to privatize telephone service while keeping electricity generation in government hands (PTTI 1994).

6. Unfortunately, I do not have wage data for the SME to run a comparison, but the STRM union leaders' claim to have achieved higher wage increases does seem credible, especially given Telmex's greater growth rate (Interview S-94-27). In any event, in February 1994, the average daily STRM base salary was N$79.12 or roughly U.S. $26 a day. One should also take into account the fact that STRM members are paid weekends. Thus, the monthly base salary is close to U.S. $800 per month ($26/day x 30.4 days/month). In addition, the value of benefits is roughly 45% of wages (TIE 1994). Although very low by Canadian standards, this wage is high by Mexican standards, given that the minimum wage at the time was N$13 and the average wage N$26; only heavy manufacturing wages (excluding the maquiladora sector) were higher, averaging N$97.03 (Calva 1994).

Between 1989 and 1993, the STRM experienced some real wage growth. During that period, compounded inflation was 96.75% (Calva 1994), while STRM salary increases during that period ranged from a low of 106.4% to a high of 141.7%, depending on the wage category (STRM 1989, 1993). However, real wage levels—not to mention the U.S.-dollar value of those wages—have fallen substantially since the December 1994 peso devaluation.

7. Before the CEP was created, in which Pomeroy was first named Vice President of the communications section before becoming president, Pomeroy had been the CWC's sole president during the union's 20-year existence as an independent organization from 1972 to 1992.

8. Politically, the Canadian labor movement is divided largely on the basis of Canadian-based unions which follow a more social unionist approach and American-based international unions that follow a more business unionist approach. The CEP, however, is the exception to this rule, siding regularly with

the American internationals against the Canadian national unions such as the Canadian Auto Workers (CAW) and Canadian Union of Public Employees (CUPE).

9. The potential impact of deregulation on wages is most clearly evident in the U.S. airline industry. According to a recent study, U.S. flight attendants' earnings were at least 12% lower by 1985 and 39% lower by 1992 than they would have been if deregulation had not occurred, and the corresponding shortfalls for pilots were 12% and 22% (Crémieux 1996: 223). In telecommunications, however, while labor costs also declined in the United States after deregulation, this has occurred mainly through reducing the number of workers, rather than lower wages.

10. According to Winseck, the IBEW failed to enter the deregulation fights since it saw "deregulation, privatization and competition as inevitable" (Winseck 1993: 181).

11. It is indisputable that the TWU's successful legal challenge led the government to change the Telecommunication Act to allow resellers to sell communications services without going through the CRTC rate-approval process. However, it is not clear that the Canadian Conservative Government would have been more accommodating to telecommunications unions if the TWU had not challenged the government in Court. The TWU intervention likely had no impact one way or the other on the legislation as a whole, other than to ensure the addition of a specific provision ending resellers' obligation to file rate requests with the CRTC for all telecommunications services. For an opposing view, see Winseck 1993.

12. On the CWC's efforts on work teams, see also Coates 1990: 58 and CWC 1992.

13. Data regarding employment are from Labour Canada 1994. Wage figures are from TWU 1992b and represent the top wage rates in the named categories for each union. In terms of TWU/CWC ratios, one can derive from the figures above that while in 1982, TWU operators earned 116.4% of what CWC operators earned, by 1991 this had fallen to 105.4%. With plant workers, the change was less dramatic. While in 1982 TWU linemen earned 106.3% of what CWC linemen earned, by 1991, this had fallen to 102.1%.

14. Wage figures are from TWU 1992b. Again, the ratios of TWU/CWC nominal wages can be derived from the above figures. CWC operators went in nine years from 86.53% of TWU wages in 1982 to 102.5% in 1991 and CWC linemen went from 94.7% of TWU wages in 1982 to 105.8% in 1991.

15. By the end of 1993, the Telmex ratio of workers per 10,000 lines had fallen to 64 (Atterbury III 1994), lower than the comparable figure for BC Tel. However, it should be cautioned that this figure is deceptively low since

subcontractors are not considered "employees" for the purposes of this calculation.

16. Of course, union activists are never satisfied with the level of shop steward organization. There are indeed serious shortfalls in shop steward organization, especially in the TWU. Nonetheless, compared with other unions in the industry, both the TWU and the STRM have an above-average level of shop steward organization, as became clear in a discussion of the issue at a trinational telecommunication union conference held in Oaxtepec, Mexico, in 1994 (TIE 1994).

17. As covered in Chapter 7, state intervention works in a similarly indirect fashion. State labor officials can seek to discourage walk-outs by quickly intervening judicially, as in Canada under the Conservative government of 1984-1993. In Mexico, the Salinas government used high-profile union-busting tactics such as the manufactured bankruptcy of Aeroméxico as a means of invalidating the nationalized airline company's collective agreement. Note too that in the United States, the firing of air traffic controllers in 1981 served a similar purpose.

The fact that state intervention is indirect obviously does not mean it is unimportant. However, frequently neither union leaders nor the state know where outbursts of militant shop floor action will occur; at most, they can seek to either encourage or discourage militant action, as is explained in the analysis of the STRM and TWU leaders' relationship to shop floor leaders below.

18. This is not to say that there was a particular operator-supported plan that was rejected by the union's executive council. However, neither did the central union executive dedicate as much effort to raising rank-and-file awareness as it did, for instance, with the issue of work jurisdiction, an issue that most directly affected plant workers. With the work jurisdiction issue, the union executive put together a video which was shown at locals during contract negotiations throughout the province to promote member support of the union's demands on the issue. The issue of centralization, although fought by the union through arbitration and community campaigns, never became a major collective bargaining issue.

19. The literature on when unionists act or don't act in a revolutionary manner is extensive. For a discussion of Lenin and Luxembourg, see Chapter 3. See also Offe and Wiesenthal 1985.

20. In particular, social unions tend to focus on job expansion issues and democratization of the workplace issues more than does the business union; issues such as contracting-out protection, technological change lay-off protection, and union jurisdiction, which have been major TWU priorities for years, are certainly consistent with social unionist philosophy.

21. An added factor benefitting Hernández Juárez is that he has at his disposal the resources to reward those work groups who support *juarista* candidates or to withhold support from groups which elect *anti-juarista* candidates.

22. Generally, Brazil, Mexico, South Korea, Taiwan, Hong Kong, and Korea are seen as "newly-industrializing countries" or "middle industrializing countries" (Haggard 1990). What this category means is that although these countries have not reached the status of "first world" or "advanced industrialized" economies, these countries are primarily urban and have a large manufacturing base, unlike many other "third world" countries whose economies are dependent on mineral or agricultural exports.

23. Pay equity is the Canadian term for what in the United States is referred to as "comparable worth." Like comparable worth, pay equity seeks to ensure that wage disparities between male-dominated jobs and female-dominated jobs are reduced.

CHAPTER NINE

Conclusion:
The Future of Unionism in an Age of Globalization

"Come, it's pleased so far," thought Alice and she went on. "Would you tell me, please, which way I ought to go from here?"

"That depends a good deal on where you want to get to," said the Cat.

(Carroll 1971: 57)

This book began with a statement that this study was about changes and alternatives—that is, changes in economic structure and alternatives in union strategy vis a vis these changes. Central to the argument of this work is the view that the situation faced by unions is more hopeful than the choice of which lunatic to visit faced by Alice in Wonderland. The strategic orientation adopted by a given union is indeed likely to impact where it gets to. This is true for both the STRM in Mexico and the TWU in Canada, and, more generally, for both the Canadian and Mexican labor movements.

But though unions do have some power—that is, some ability to influence where they get to—it is clear that they have less power than managers and state officials. This work focused on the decisions made by labor for two important reasons: first, because most studies of globalization concentrate nearly exclusively on the decisions made by state and corporate actors and second, because what is being studied here are different logics of resistance, not the logics of domination. There is nothing wrong with studying logics of domination or in

359

studying corporate or state actors. Indeed, much can be learned through such studies. But to conduct an adequate study of unions and their internal functioning requires a very different approach that examines the possibilities of resistance by looking at the obstacles faced by unions and how they confront those difficulties.

Of course, the extent of resistance varies markedly among different unions. Union "resistance" may in fact include very substantial cooperation with management for mutual gains. But even the most collaborationist Mexican state-aligned or *charro* union engages in struggles with management over wage and benefit issues. Indeed, the fact that the level of resistance may vary in level, intensity, and location is the key point. Union strategy ultimately involves a choice about where to offer resistance and how intensely to do so. A union's alternative vision guides its choice of where and how to resist and where and how to cooperate, but no alternative union vision can be generated solely through cooperation with corporate managers.

As explained in the first chapter of this work, this study has focused on the impact of globalization on unions, the changing state-labor relationship, and an examination of how and why unions adopt strategies and tactics to deal with specific globalization-related issues, such as technological change, workplace reorganization, and state telecommunications policy. This chapter, then, takes up each of these themes and summarizes the key findings. I shall then conclude with a discussion of future directions for further research and make some brief comments on the key issues raised by this study.

THE GLOBALIZATION DILEMMA

So much has been written about globalization that there is a danger that the word is becoming nothing more than the ideological mantra of capital. Here, to avoid this, the scope of the analysis was confined to the global telecommunications industry and the actual structure of that industry, which includes a great deal of state intervention, although less than when the dominant industry structure was state-run monopolies. There tends to be a mystical aura around the word "globalization," but there is nothing mystical about the existence of strategic alliances among corporations; the cartel-like division of long distance telephone services overseen by national regulatory agencies such as the CRTC in Canada or more directly by government departments such as the SCT in Mexico; the increased power of large telecommunications' buyers vis a vis the previously dominant suppliers when national telephone monopolies existed in all countries; the redefinition of the state's role in this industrial sector; the implementation of new technology; or attempts to introduce new work organization practices to the industry. These changes are very real. Furthermore, the external environments faced by labor unions have become more similar, both in terms of the nature of the sectoral market and the state's role within that market.

At the same time, it is important to note what globalization is not. Globalization is not the simple denationalization of capital, in which the location of the corporate headquarters ceases to matter. Contrary to the analyses of some (Reich 1992), corporate nationality continues to be important and the state continues to play an important role in promoting the interests of companies based within its borders. The nature of the corporate-state relationship has changed profoundly; this is, of course, especially obvious in telecommunications, where state dominance (and in many countries, direct state ownership) has given way to the dominance of private capital. But the relationships of power that have emerged through the globalization of the industry are not unprecedented. Although the changes that have occurred are substantial, the players are still largely the same. Furthermore, the actors still perform within a capitalist economic framework. Among these players, often ignored in conventional analysis of globalization, are labor unions.

Among those who do analyze the role played by labor unions, three approaches have predominated. These approaches can be labelled convergence theories, national labor regime (or exceptionalist) theories, and strategic choice theories. Each of these contributes something toward a greater understanding of the way unions respond to the changes brought about by globalization. But at the same time, each falls short in some important aspects.

LABOR UNIONS AND GLOBALIZATION

Probably the most popular school of thought posits that globalization of industry will bring about a convergence or increasing similarity in union strategy and tactics. Proponents of this view argue that the evolution of the capitalist economic framework from one built upon strong, semi-independent national Keynesian economies to an international global capitalist monetarist framework reduces the ability of unions to pursue an adversarial approach and that instead unions must learn to cooperate with management. In addition, it is asserted that the range of items for negotiation must be expanded to deal with competitiveness by incorporating such practices as team work and joint productivity committees.

The convergence theorists are right about one thing. Globalization generates a degree of convergence simply because there are more similarities in the approaches taken by management in different internationally-organized firms. Because managers exercise great influence over the nature of industrial development, unions face greater similarities in their industrial environment. Thus, for example, the operating equipment in British Columbia and Mexico is not only similar, it is actually the same, since both BC Tel and Telmex are supplied by the Canadian manufacturer Northern Telecom. As well, both BC Tel and Telmex have digitalized their switching equipment and both are undergoing a continual process of computerization of clerical functions. True, BC Tel is a much more technologically-advanced operation than Telmex—a difference that is especially notable in outside plant (cabling) equipment—but the technological differences between the two companies are narrowing. Again, an example of this can be seen in the deployment of operating equipment. BC Tel's conversion to the current system of TOPS (Traffic Operating Position System) was a two-step, multi-year process, as TOPS combined the functions of the DAISY (directory assistance) and TSPS (operator-assisted calls) first generation computer equipment. The process was completed only in 1994. By contrast, Telmex jumped from manually operating switchboards directly to TOPS, completing the conversion process the same year (Interviews S-94-11, S-94-15, S-94-16).

Another major factor pushing the two countries' industries in a similar direction is that their approaches to regulation of the industry have become more similar. In Canada, active state involvement in the restructuring of the telecommunications industry led the TWU to take a much more active role in the political process and to develop much closer ties with the social democratic NDP. This altered a previous pattern in which most industrial developments were determined bilaterally between management and the union. On the other hand, in Mexico, the government moved to privatize Telmex in 1990 and to establish a regulatory scheme that was more similar to that which has traditionally operated in Canada. As a result, management-union decisions have assumed greater importance in the Mexican telephone industry and the role of the state has been reduced, although it still remains more important than in Canada. Thus, the differences in the influence of the state and political parties on developments in this sector are significantly less than they once were.

Having said this, it must be noted that convergence theorists err in asserting that the logic of capitalist development necessarily generates a specific logic of union response. This error is based on the hidden assumption that all unions are, at rock bottom, interested in what John Commons labelled in the 1920s "pure and simple unionism" (Perlman 1928). This assumption has a certain plausibility in the case of the United States, where so-called "pure and simple" business unionism has indeed predominated. In Mexico, state-aligned "corporatist" unions, though structured differently than U.S. business unions,[1] nonetheless shares a similar focus on the pursuit of immediate wage and benefit gains for current members, while ceding to management the authority to alter work relations as it sees fit, except as restricted by contractual clauses and job classifications. In Canada, business unionism, initially as strong as its United States counterpart, gave way to a more social unionist focus in the 1960s and 1970s, in part due to the Quebecois "Quiet Revolution" and the concurrent upswing in English-Canadian union militancy.

No matter how dominant a "pure and simple" union focus may be, it has always been challenged by alternative forms of unionism. Unlike corporations, which seek to maximize profits for their shareholders,[2] unions are not motivated by a single goal. Some unions seek to maximize earnings of current members, while others seek to expand membership. Still others seek to pursue a broad social agenda, which can include the advocacy of the revolutionary transformation of capitalist social relations, but more often centers on a vision of social reform. The convergence theorists' argument that globalization leads unions to work more closely with management to increase productivity rather than resisting management initiatives fits squarely within the logic of "pure and simple" unionism, but other types of unions will respond differently. In short, globalization presents unions with common problems, but does not dictate common solutions.

THE QUESTION OF EXCEPTIONALISM

A second approach common in the labor literature points, however, not to convergence, but rather to continued divergence due to differences in factors such as national labor regimes, state structures, and levels of nation-state economic development. This study agrees that such factors matter, but contends that they are less decisive than is commonly believed. Despite the significant differences encountered in the course of field research, it was clear many similarities cut across national boundaries and that quite a few of the differences that do exist among union can be better explained by other factors.

Every nation-state incorporates unique factors. In the case of Mexico, there is no doubt that it does have an unusual historical trajectory. Mexico was one of a handful of countries to experience a social revolution in the second decade of the twentieth century (Hart 1989).[3] The Mexican Revolution of the 1910s was largely bourgeois in character, but the labor movement did play a role (Ruiz 1980).[4] This facilitated the labor movement's "incorporation" into the Mexican party-state apparatus under the leadership of Vicente Lombardo Toledano of the CTM and President Lázaro Cárdenas in the 1930s and the later taming of the labor movement into a wage-and-benefits orientation in the late 1940s. Thereafter, many Mexican unions proved willing to sacrifice a large measure of their autonomy in exchange for receiving state support (Collier and Collier 1991). Mexican history is thus "a factor" pushing unions toward the adoption of state-aligned "corporatist" unionism, in which the arena of struggle is limited primarily to wage and benefit issues.

Despite its unique historical legacy, the Mexican labor movement and the situation faced by Mexican workers is not as exceptional as is sometimes suggested. Moreover, the strategic choices faced by unions in Mexico are similar to those faced by unions in Canada and the United States. In particular, the evidence uncovered in this study suggests that it is high time for scholars studying labor to take to heart the late nineteenth-century observation of Mexican President Porfirio Díaz that Mexico is "so far from God and so close to the United States" (quoted in Ruiz 1980: 382). Both in the United States and in Mexico, labor movements have been marked by profoundly conservative ("corporatist" in Mexico; "business unionist" in the United States) strategic orientations since 1920. The period of the Great Depression constituted an exceptional time, as social unionism briefly held sway in both countries in the late 1930s and early 1940s. Both labor movements were then subjected to the purging of communist activists in the late 1940s and early 1950s. Both labor movements are without a political party of their own and, as a result, have aligned with business-dominated political parties. For better or for worse, the Mexican labor movement is much more similar to the U.S. labor movement than either Mexican or U.S. unionists might like to admit.

Mexico's economic underdevelopment vis a vis the United States means that the consequences of pursuing a "bread and butter" unionist strategy for workers are vastly different in the two countries. For most of the postwar period, workers in the United States were the highest paid in the world. Mexican workers, even unionized ones, are much poorer: their wages are far lower, and their working conditions are worse. What is perhaps less obvious is the fact that the gap between union and non-union wages and benefits is greater in Mexico than the United States. That is, in percentage terms, union membership results in a greater increase in wages and benefits in Mexico than in the United States. This is significant given that the United States has the greatest union "wage gap" of any country at a comparable level of development. In particular, the benefits enjoyed by unionized Mexican workers form a greater percentage of their total compensation than do similar benefits for Canadian or U.S. workers. Thus, for instance, telephone workers receive pensions equal to 80% of their former base salary (and tax free!), which is even higher than the TWU pension levels. By contrast, most U.S. telephone workers' pensions are roughly 30-40% of their former base salary (TIE 1994).[5] As a result, unionized workers in Mexico, especially those in national industrial unions, such as the STRM, constitute a kind of "labor aristocracy." This fact is both a cause and effect of Mexican "corporatism" with its focus on wages and benefits, as well as its rejection, to a large degree, of labor solidarity. However, one should not ignore the frequent examples of social unionist or radical unionist behavior in Mexico. The shortage of good jobs typically leads to greater extremes in labor reaction, both in conservative and revolutionary directions. While the conservative tendency has been dominant, both tendencies have been evident. As well, some unions, such as the SME, have embraced a moderate social unionist position, much like the British Columbian TWU studied here.

The Canadian labor movement, too, has its own unique features. One key factor in the history of Canadian unionism has been the dominant role played by U.S. "international" unions.[6] As late as the mid-1960s, 70% of Canadian unionists were members of unions headquartered in the United States. As a result, much of the history of Canadian unionism parallels the history of U.S. unionism. But since the mid-1960s, a combination of growing public sector unions, strengthened French-Canadian unions in Quebec, and breakaways of Canadian sections from U.S.-dominated "international" unions has resulted in the creation of a distinctive Canadian labor movement, in which the dominant tendency has been social unionism. But just as there are social unions in Mexico, there are business unions in Canada. In both countries one finds unions faced with similar options regarding how they wish to confront two major structures of global capitalism: the state and the market.

UNION STRATEGY

One point about strategy bears emphasis: the question is not one of a model of economic development or labor regime per se, but rather the way in which a given union interacts with a given model of economic development and industrial relations and the alternatives which a given union pursues. When speaking of alternatives, it is worth noting that labor rarely has the necessary resources to develop a fully-developed alternative economic model. Even if a given union *does* present a well-developed and well-reasoned alternative, it simply is not within its capacity to impose this alternative on its capitalist counterparts.

On the other hand, without an alternative of their own, it is difficult for labor unions to begin to push the state and the market in directions that are favorable to their members' interests. Labor strategy is thus an important *factor* in determining state-labor relations and economic policy and in influencing corporate decision-making. The actual decisions made, however, will depend not only on the strategy adopted by labor, but on other factors as well, most importantly the relative balance of power between labor and capital in a given nation-state or industrial sector. As well, the choice of tactics and its reflection in the union's overall strategy is important in determining labor's ability to influence the state and the market. State policy that seeks to force unions to narrow their strategic agendas—of which Mexican corporatism is an obvious, but not unique, example—is only sometimes successful. Even when unsuccessful in narrowing union agendas, however, state policy establishes an overall industrial relations structure within which all unions, even oppositional ones, must operate. In saying that business unions in Canada and the United States and state-aligned corporatist unions in Mexico operate according to a similar logic, this does not mean that they employ the same tactics. Though similar in their ideological orientation, Canadian and U.S. business unions operate in a significantly more decentralized labor system than their Mexican state-aligned "corporatist" counterparts. Thus, the former tend to focus their actions on enterprise managers, while the latter focus more on their relations with state labor officials.

A foundational work in the study of labor strategy is that of Kochan, Katz and McKersie (Kochan et al. 1986). Although flawed in some respects, the work of Kochan et al. is nonetheless important in that it begins to look at the question of what unions can do to respond to the challenges posed by globalization. The key insight of Kochan et al. is that unions (and corporate managers as well) can act in ways that in the long run have major effects, not just on collective bargaining, but on the overall economy and the industrial relations system. In terms of this study, this implies that while structures influence unions' choice of tactics, strategies can be employed to change the nature of the structure itself.

Kochan and his colleagues fall short in their analysis in that they focus on the strategic efforts of management and tend to view labor strategy much more as a tactical accommodation to successful management strategy. Ironically, given the focus of this approach on union strategic decision-making, this strategy tends to rule out union strategic planning that is designed to alter state or market structures. Although perhaps understandable as a description of what has been a dominant tendency in U.S. labor strategy, this type of analysis does not adequately address the strategic alternatives available to labor unions in the current "globalized" economic environment.

To begin to answer this question, the theories of different traditional labor movement theorists—notably Lenin, Luxembourg, the Webbs, and Perlman—were examined. Each of these theorists are proponents of different types of unionism, which I labelled as party-led revolutionary unionism, non-party revolutionary unionism, social unionism, and business unionism, respectively. Each alternative involves a distinct logic of unionism, based on different notions of what a union's relationship between itself and outside institutions such as the state or the market can and should be. These strategic orientations affect a given union's agenda and hence indirectly the development of industry itself.

In particular, this study focuses on two different kinds of reformist unionism: social unionism and business unionism. A business union (or its Mexican "corporatist" equivalent) tends to limit its challenges to management primarily to wage and benefit issues. By contrast, a social union tends to focus on a broader array of issues, especially job creation and the defense of community values—in the case of this study, the defense of a company's universal service obligations—and strives both at the workplace and the state level to achieve reforms that will enable it to do so.

MODELLING INTERNAL UNION DECISION-MAKING

This surely is the most difficult problem this study tackles, since there is no more a unified field theory of union decision-making than there is one of corporate decision-making. Indeed, unions are less uniform than their corporate counterparts. Nonetheless, this study is designed to contribute to the understanding of union politics, particularly in the telecommunications sector.

Central to the analysis of union decision-making presented here is the notion that a strategic orientation, which may be implicit or explicit, exists in every union and serves as the filter or lens through which union decisions are made. And unlike corporations, which may adopt very different methods but all share a profit-maximization goal, different types of unions have different goals. The models discussed above are, of course, ideal types and there are varying shades of "social unionist," "revolutionary unionist," or "business unionist" strategic orientations, but these different labels do describe different answers to the question *"What does this union do?"* As discussed throughout, these different types of unions exist across national boundaries and within many different kinds of labor regimes.

As explained in Chapters 4 through 8, one cannot simply "plug in" a response from a given strategic orientation to understand a specific labor response to a specific management action. This is true for many reasons. First, other factors, such as gender and occupational sector, matter. Second, there are often competing groups within a given union which present different answers to the question of *"What should this union do?"* In a democratic union, these different notions are worked out through debate among the factions. In a less democratic union, debate may suppressed. But though less visible, struggles between competing visions do occur, nevertheless.

As pointed out in earlier chapters, certain structural factors tend to lead unions to adopt different strategies, though no one factor is decisive. An autocratic trade union may be more likely to adopt a business unionist strategy than a democratic trade union, since a business union strategy does not require the dispersion of power needed for mobilization that a social union strategy requires. But even so, there are plenty of democratic trade unions that adopt business unionist strategies. To a certain extent, workers in higher status occupational sectors tend to be more supportive of social unionism or even revolutionary unionism than lower status unionists who have more pressing immediate concerns. In the cases studied here, the more "white collar" workers (such as technicians) have tended to dominate in the social unionist TWU while the more "blue collar" workers (such as operators or outside plant) have tended to dominate in the business unionist STRM.

Most important, however, are the historical legacies of the unions themselves. Change in strategic orientation can occur, but even in a highly democratic union, change does not come easily. Generally, some kind of internal or external shock must occur to cause a union to rethink its strategic orientation. Such a shock occurred in the STRM in 1976, when operators initiated a nationwide wildcat strike. Not only did the uprising bring to the fore a new union secretary general, Francisco Hernández Juárez, but more importantly it led to a restructuring of the union, allowing many distinct political currents to operate in an environment where the union's strategic orientation was explicitly opened to debate. A combination of external pressure from the impending implementation of digital switching technology and internal union suppression of dissidents led to a new rank and file rebellion in 1982. Unlike the 1976 rebellion, however, this rebellion was defeated and, as a result, a "corporatist" or business unionist orientation was consolidated in the STRM. When further computerization took place in the mid-eighties, the STRM responded by shifting from traditional wage and job bargaining to negotiating pay-for-productivity agreements. But there is a fundamental continuity in the STRM's approach of the past decade. These pay-for-productivity gains have brought STRM members increased income, but the STRM has achieved this by subsuming union goals into the logic of competitiveness, leaving itself vulnerable to potential downsizing as competition in the industry increases. Some activists in the STRM have sought to push the productivity program in a different direction, using the analysis groups as a mechanism to increase worker control, but with limited success.

The TWU has not experienced the dramatic shifts of the STRM, but there have been significant changes. Most important was the election of Bill Clark as President in 1980, who defeated President Bob

Donnelly. Although the Clark faction was somewhat less militant than the Donnelly group, Clark and his colleagues were successful in institutionalizing a social unionist vision in the TWU, engaging in frequent community campaigns and strengthening ties with the New Democratic Party. Central to this strategy has been a combination of wage moderation with substantial efforts to maximize employment.

In the aftermath of Clark's retirement in 1987, the onslaught of computerized technology has led to a new debate about the strategic orientation of the union. In the environment of the early 1990s, it appeared that the TWU might be veering back toward a more business unionist approach, especially after the 1992 deregulation decision left the TWU temporarily in a state of confusion. Although some social unionist demands, such as pay equity and same sex spousal benefits, were pursued, most demands strictly involved wage and benefit increases. And the demands for pay equity and spousal benefits themselves were hotly contested within the union.[7] Support for the NDP also became more tenuous. At the TWU's January 1993 Convention, delegates voted to de-fund the NDP; the TWU executive subsequently "found" $20,000 in new money to fund four campaign workers in the federal October 1993 elections, a move roundly criticized at the TWU's following convention in January 1994.

Since January 1994, the TWU not only has salvageed its relations with the NDP, but more importantly negotiated an Accord with the provincial government and BC Tel management, seeking to ensure universal access to the "information highway" (British Columbia 1995). Although successful so far, the TWU does face difficulties. Pressures from deregulation and competition are mounting and the ability of Bell Canada to influence BC Tel and other Canadian telephone companies through its dominant position in the Stentor corporate alliance reduces the TWU's ability to defend and extend its social unionist gains. To maintain the market leverage necessary to pursue its social unionist strategy will require that the TWU either organize more workers or that it merge or affiliate with other unions that similar views.

UNION TACTICS: TECHNOLOGY, WORK ORGANIZATION, AND STATE RELATIONS

It is the study of tactics that forms the meat of the empirical part of this study and necessarily so. For despite the importance of strategic orientation in determining when and where labor struggles or cooperates with capital, it is the actual shop-floor and central union tactics that labor unions must rely on to implement their strategies in responding to the specific challenges they confront. In particular, this study focused on the efforts of the STRM and the TWU in the areas of technological change, work organization, and state-union relations to show the extent and limits of the differences that distinct strategic orientations bring to bear on where, when, and how unions confront or cooperate with management and state officials.

In terms of technological change, I focused on two specific changes in technology: the computerization of switching and of operator equipment, the two most important technological changes to occur in the telecommunications sector in the past two decades. As seen in Chapter 5, while the two unions' responses were somewhat similar in the change of operating equipment, their responses were starkly different with respect to changes in switching equipment.

The digitalization of switching created a dramatic shift in the organization of telephone exchanges. While the electro-mechanical and later electronic (semi-computerized) exchanges required substantial maintenance, digital (fully computerized) exchanges required far less maintenance. While some problems do require substantial reprogramming, most problems could be fixed simply by "changing a card." Far fewer workers are required than were on the maintenance of the older systems.

Technical workers in the early 1980s at both BC Tel and Telmex felt threatened by the changes. In the TWU, technological change was at the center of the 1977-78 and 1980-81 strike/lock-out disputes. In part, the TWU's militant response to BC Tel was a reaction to BC Tel management's efforts to bust the union (Interview T-93-68). However, in the course of the dispute, the TWU developed and pursued a social unionist vision. As a result of two bitter disputes with BC Tel management, the TWU was able to obtain agreements that preserved most restrictions on the contracting-out of work, provided a prohibition against lay-offs caused by technological change for all employees with two or more years seniority, and secured new protections against the shifting of union members' work to management. Unlike most other unions in the industry, the TWU has preserved its members' jobs; indeed, during the 1980s, union membership rose slightly, while the number of unionized workers declined slightly at CEP-represented Bell Canada, and fell sharply in the United States due to deregulation.

In the STRM, although technical workers reacted strongly to the changes in technology and staged wildcat strikes, they were not supported by the STRM union leadership. Instead, because the technical workers were important participants in the opposition Línea Democrática faction of the union, their efforts were opposed by union leaders. This internal union dispute erupted in 1982, as dissident members' staged a national walk-out of their own, emulating the 1976 wildcat action that brought Hernández Juárez to the secretary general post. Although thousands of workers participated in the walk-outs, the dissidents' efforts were ultimately unsuccessful. Due to a combination of poor coordination among opposition forces, the existence of a core of workers who remained supportive of the union leadership (particularly among Mexico City operators), and substantial state and internal union repression, including the denial of thousands of union members' union rights, the dissidents were ultimately defeated. This defeat altered the balance of power within the union, permitting greater internal union dominance by Hernández Juárez. At the same time, it reduced the independence of Hernández Juárez vis a vis Mexican state officials, on whom he had depended to defeat the dissidents (see Dubb 1992).

After 1982, the STRM began to deal with some of the technological change issues that the dissidents' rebellion had raised. This led to the addition of an elaborate joint union-management committee procedure for technological change in the 1988 collective bargaining agreement. One year later, however, this clause was eliminated in the *convenio de concertación*. Since then, relations between the STRM and Telmex management have been governed by an implicit, "no hire, no fire" agreement in which the STRM cooperates in increasing automation and productivity in exchange for greater pay for its members. Due to the increase in the number of lines, redeployment of personnel has been fairly easy for management to handle. Indeed, due to the rapid expansion in the number of lines since 1990, by 1995 the number of workers per 10,000 lines in Mexico had fallen below the comparable ratio in British Columbia.

With respect to operators, the differences between the unions are less stark. The TWU, true to its social unionist tradition, engaged in "decentralization" community campaigns, promoting the continued existence of remote operator stations as an alternative to having all operators centralized in big cities. The computer technology, TWU members argued, could be used to either centralize work or decentralize work, and it made sense to bring the work to where the workers were, rather than move the workers to the machines. The TWU members and union activists went to town council meetings in small cities such as Castlegar, Cranbrook, and Nelson to argue their case and got town councils to pass resolutions of support. Advertisements were placed in newspapers. As well, the TWU filed policy grievances in an attempt to stop the forced centralization of work. The TWU's tactics succeeded in slowing the centralization of work and the TWU's contract ensured operators the right to transfer, although transferring might require moving hundreds of miles. The 1989 Cranbrook arbitration decision said that BC Tel could not centralize due to technological change, but that it could centralize, even if it meant lay-offs, if failure to centralize would result in an economic loss. Since 1989, no further centralization of operators has occurred, except for the closure of the suburban North Vancouver office. So the TWU has had some success here. But it's notable that unlike the preservation of the technician job category as union work, the union never made centralization a strike issue, or even an issue at the bargaining table. This is a reflection of the fact that the mostly female operators have had less political clout in the union than their largely male technician counterparts.

In the STRM, on the other hand, although the union could hardly be said to be free of sexism (Cooper Tory 1988, 1989), it is true that the operators have greater political clout. This is true both due to their relatively higher numbers—both because there had been less automation and because the category of "operators" in Mexico is defined more broadly to include many who in the United States or Canada would be classified as clerical workers[8]—and because of the role operators had played in the union's 1976–1982 political struggle. As a result of that struggle, operators in the STRM had developed an efficient network of shop steward activists, especially in Mexico City. Operators were able to organize and pressure the union leadership, which had tended to rely on operator support to maintain itself in leadership positions, to ensure full protections for operators and minimize the adverse impact to operators of the automation of their work. As well, operators engaged in shop floor work stoppages to directly pressure management and publicized their case to the press.[9] The end result—transfer rights and the right to move into some traditionally male-dominated fields—is not unlike the end result in the TWU, but one must bear in the mind that the STRM operators were heavily disadvantaged by their union's weaker contract. In this case, rank-and-file pressure was capable of providing a much better set of options for operators than what would have been the case without that pressure. Among the benefits the operators were able to negotiate were a decrease in the number of positions to be eliminated, the right to refuse or accept transfers by seniority (a right not provided by the STRM's collective bargaining agreement), months-long craft training on company time for those transferring into outside plant jobs, and credit for their operator seniority for those who do transfer.

One can see a similar pattern in looking at the two unions' responses to changes in the organization of work and changes in the role of the state. Again, while the TWU leadership has been willing to confront state officials and corporate managers on a variety of issues, the STRM leadership has sought to cooperate with state officials and telephone company managers, except in those instances where it is faced with significant rank-and-file pressure to resist.

Chapter 6 examined two specific issues: changes in the organization of work *among* different departments or sections and changes in the organization of work *within* different departments or sections. As explained in that chapter, neither the STRM nor the TWU has enjoyed notable success in dealing with shifts of work among departments. In both cases, the shifting of work reinforced already existing pressures in the unions for greater centralization of authority. This centralization at the same time caused a reduction of local activism on which the strength of the unions in part depended. In the STRM, centralization was imposed by management and the state suddenly in the 1989 *convenio de concertación*, although union leaders, for very different reasons, had been seeking greater authority vis a vis STRM shop stewards for many years prior to that change. In the TWU, centralization occurred in several stages: first, in 1977, a unified structure was created and the union's name changed from FTW (Federation of Telephone Workers) to TWU (Telecommunications Workers' Union); second, in 1979, separate sectional (plant, traffic, clerical) councils were eliminated; and finally, through a gradual process[10] real authority shifted to reflect the changes in the structure. This shift was evident in the "292" debate. Much of the debate over the "292" issue involved frustration of local union activists at the central union leadership's unwillingness to take on the larger issue of the organization of work among different departments of the company. This is one area, then, where the TWU leadership explicitly limited its reach. The right of company managers to allocate work among different departments was not contested, so long as workers kept their jobs in the shuffle, even though the shuffling caused significant disruption in the lives of many union members.

While neither the TWU nor the STRM leadership have challenged management's ability to shift work *among* departments, the TWU has challenged changing work organization *within* departments. While the STRM leadership has cooperated with management to reduce the number of work categories and has sought to introduce "analysis groups" in which workers and managers jointly plan the reconstruction of outside plant work, the TWU has fought to maintain the existence of a single "craft" notion of task rotation within that craft organized by workers, rather than by management. Throughout the eighties and nineties, BC Tel management has tried to introduce new work practices, such as quality circles or work teams. These efforts have consistently generated substantial union (and frequently low-level management) resistance, if not outright rejection. The latest attempt to introduce work teams was abandoned by management after the union withdrew from the program in the business services division in the fall of 1994.

With respect to the state, one can see changes that make its role in telecommunications in Mexico and Canada more similar. At the same time, there are substantial differences in how the two unions have responded. In Mexico, the privatization of the company led the STRM to concentrate somewhat less on relations with state officials and to place greater emphasis on relations with the now-privatized company's managers. In British Columbia, the company has always been privately owned, but the importance of decisions made by state regulatory agencies has led the TWU to increase its level of interaction with state officials, particularly those in the CRTC, in an attempt to defend its members' interests. Thus, while previously the two unions had vastly different levels of interaction with the state, these differences have narrowed.

On the other hand, the similar level of interaction with the state, and the convergence of state-industry relationships in Mexico and Canada, does not imply that the unions view the state similarly. Although the level of union-state interaction has converged, the nature of the two unions' interaction with their respective states is quite different. In terms of the regulatory arm of the state, the TWU maintains an aggressively antagonistic relationship vis a vis the CRTC, while the STRM has proceeded very secretively in its relations with the

SCT and Treasury. In terms of governmental relations, while the STRM sought "an alliance" with the state to promote industrialization, the TWU used the state as a lever to promote social democratic reform measures. In this line lies the British Columbian Accord, reached in the fall of 1995, in which the provincial government agreed to use BC Tel as its primary telecommunications supplier in exchange for a BC Tel management commitment to provide universal access to the internet.

IMPLICATIONS FOR FUTURE RESEARCH

This work seeks to grapple with many issues currently affecting labor, and indeed North America as a whole, in a period of rapid economic and political change. When I began research in the summer of 1993, NAFTA was still a possibility, not a certainty. At that time, the word "Zapatista" still referred to a group of peasants led by Emiliano Zapata in Morelos during the Mexican Revolution, not a group of Chiapaneco peasants led by a charismatic, pipe-smoking poet. As for the Mexican economy, while the devaluation of the overvalued "new peso" was not itself surprising, the extent of both the ensuing devaluation and the deepened economic crisis that followed caught just about everyone off guard. While not as dramatic as in Mexico, Canada, too, has experienced considerable upheaval, as Quebec in 1995 came within 50,000 votes of voting to secede from the confederation. In English-speaking Ontario, the Canadian Labour Congress has organized a series of regional general strikes to protest the Conservative provincial government's attempts there to cut back on the province's social safety net.

In other words, the object of analysis in this study—labor's response to globalization—is a moving target. Nonetheless, I believe this work does open up many new avenues for research. Here I shall restrict my comments to three areas which merit further investigation. These are, in no particular rank order, sectoral variability in the possibilities for labor action in the global economy, variability of responses *within* social unionism to globalization, and the question of the future of the Mexican labor movement in a period in which it seems possible that *la muerte anunciada*[11] (death foretold) of Mexico's unique party-state apparatus may finally be taking place, although it should be cautioned that the very frequency of such proclamations in the past leads this author to maintain a healthy skepticism about such claims.

Regarding the issue of sectoral variation, it is worth beginning by stating the obvious: telecommunications is a unique industrial sector. Telecommunications is, of course, a strategic and growing industry. Understanding union action in the telecommunication industry is thus an important part of understanding union action in the economy as a whole. As a sector, telecommunications has three characteristics that have a strong influence on union action: the industry is highly automated, it is highly strategic, and it still requires substantial, albeit declining, fixed investment. The first factor militates against labor influence, while the latter two work in labor's favor. The telecommunications industry, because of its strategic importance, provides a good starting point for analysis, but it's clear that the options available to labor unions will vary according to both the nature of the industry or industries whose workers a given union represents and the degree of exposure each industry has to the international economy. In particular, it would seem likely that, as the internationalization of the economy increases, a growing part of the labor movement will be embracing efforts to restrict capital mobility, much in the way that the TWU's contracting-out clause has. Indeed, there is already evidence that this is happening. For instance, in 1996 outsourcing has proved to be a major source of conflict in the United States in both the aerospace and auto industries (Bernard 1996). How unions deal with outsourcing and the variability that one encounters both across and within industries is one research topic that is clearly in need of further investigation.

A second topic that needs greater research is the question of social unionism itself. Much of this study, of course, focuses on the distinction between social and business unionism. This provided a useful way to distinguish between the strategic outlooks of the STRM and the TWU. However, as with any typology, the distinction drawn here necessarily obscures variation that occurs within modal types. Moreover, this study suggests that social unions (and business unions as well) are having to adjust their tactics to the new economic environment, even as they retain their overall strategic outlooks. For its part, the TWU has renewed efforts, after nearly a decade-long hiatus, to build a cross-Canada alliance of telecommunication unions and has taken advantage of the existence of a provincial NDP government to press BC Tel into expanding the scope of its universal service obligation. Clearly though, while the TWU has made some progress, it has not solved all of the dilemmas inherent in trying to pursue a social unionist vision in an increasingly global economy. Moreover, different social unions are likely to deal with these dilemmas in different ways. If social unionism is going to thrive in a more internationalized economy, then in addition to working at the national level, unions will have to work both "above" the state in the international arena and "below" the state at the community and state or provincial level to compensate for the reduction in the scope of the nation-state's regulatory role. Recent changes in the U.S. labor movement and the prospect of change in the labor movement in Mexico would appear to indicate the likelihood that social unionism will assume more prominence in North America. There have been some good case studies of social unions in Canada (e.g., Lipsig-Mummé 1990) and dissident movements in Mexico (e.g., Cook 1990). But only limited effort has been made to assess how well the different types of tactics that are being tried out by social unions at the local, state or provincial, and international levels are working or whether some means better enable unions to maintain and extend their influence in a global economy than others. What is needed now, then, is comparative analysis that builds on current and previous case studies and works to bridge the gap between labor movement and "new social movement" research.

The last topic addressed here is the future of the labor movement in Mexico. As covered in greater detail in Chapters 3 and 4, this thesis has taken a critical view toward the traditional story told about Mexican labor corporatism. Indeed, while the labor movement in Mexico is more centralized than in the United States or Canada, the term "corporatism" is really a misnomer. Far from being united, feuding within the state-aligned sector of the labor movement in Mexico is common, which is why state labor officials' "divide and rule" tactics have been so effective.[12] Often the line of conflict has been between industrial unions (such as the SME and the STRM) and craft-oriented unions (led by CTM leader Fidel Velázquez). Very briefly, in the late 1940s, there was a split between the industrial unions led by Vicente Lombardo Toledano and the craft unions led by Fidel Velázquez; in the late 1950s and early 1960s, there was a dispute between the industrial unions led by Rafael Galván and the craft unions led by Fidel Velázquez; and in the 1970s, one of the leaders of the "independent" movement was again Rafael Galván (Sánchez Gutiérrez 1987, Trejo Delarbre 1990, Xelhuantzi López 1992). The emergence of the STRM-led Fesebes group, and the STRM's subsequent participation in the UNT is thus not an unprecedented event in the history of Mexican labor. Hence, one implication of this study is that much could be gained by examining in greater detail the divide-and-rule logic of labor control in Mexico, rather than using the lens of the traditional top-down corporatist model.

This study also provides a cautionary note for those who would focus their sights on the leadership struggle among competing labor federations that has emerged in the Mexican labor movement in the wake of long-time CTM leader Fidel Velázquez's death. As seen in this work, there is a signficant amount of variation within the Mexican labor movement. The STRM, for instance, has been operating fairly independently in the collective bargaining sphere from the CTM for the past 20 years, even though Fidel Velázquez and Hernández Juárez were once close allies. Especially in strategic sectors like telecommunications, unions tend to act fairly independently of central labor federations. This is not likely to change no matter who prevails. Moreover, triumph who may, both business unionist ("corporatist") and social unionist ("independent unionist") tendencies will persist in Mexico.

Nevertheless, the overall balance between the two tendencies may change. It is clear that the formation of the UNT is an important development, as it provides evidence of a split among previously allied pro-government union leaders. As the case of the SNTE (Sindicato Nacional de Trabajadores de la Educación, the Mexican teachers' union) shows (Cook 1990), gains for dissident groups tend to be greater when elites are divided. There is evidence that the dynamic that Cook described within the SNTE may now be occurring at the national level in Mexico. Following the line of argument of this work, I would argue that what is key is not only who triumphs, but what vision of unionism triumphs. At present, it is not clear whether what will emerge from the UNT will be just another labor insider power play or a revival of social unionism in Mexico. What is clear is that the December 1994 devaluation and subsequent economic crisis have provided the context for a reevaluation of union strategy within many unions in Mexico. In the event that a more social unionist vision were to gain greater prominence in Mexico, the issues raised in this study about the possibilities for a social unionist response to globalization become all the more important.

GLOBALIZATION IN TELECOMMUNICATIONS AND THE POSSIBILITIES FOR UNION RESISTANCE

If there is no struggle there is no progress. Those who profess to favor freedom and yet deprecate agitation, are men who want crops without plowing up the ground. They want rain without thunder and lightning. They want the ocean without the awful roar of its many waters. This struggle may be a moral one; or it may be a physical one; or it may be both moral and physical, but it must be a struggle. Power concedes nothing without a demand. It never did and it never will .

U.S. abolitionist Frederick Douglas, 1853
(quoted in Syracuse Cultural Workers 1995)

In this study, I have argued, against much of the conventional wisdom, for the continued importance of the role of unions in the era of globalization in general and in the telecommunications sector, seen by many as the single most important industry of the globalized economy, in particular. The findings of this study, moreover, strongly suggest that the differences between the "First World" and the "Third World" are less significant than is often presupposed. The logics by which unions operate in different countries are often similar, though of course the standards of living of workers in these different countries differ markedly. The difficulties faced by the STRM are not a unique product of Mexico's exceptional labor regime. Indeed, its difficulties are quite similar to those faced by its counterparts in the United States and Canada. This is one reason why STRM union leaders and opposition activists themselves have placed greater attention on studying developments in the United States and Canada in recent years.

As this study demonstrates, the TWU and STRM face many similar challenges. Both must confront rapid advances in computer technology, shifts in jurisdictional boundaries, changes in the organization of work, and state actions designed to foster competition in the industry. While telecommunications is less subject to capital flight than many manufacturing industries, such as textiles, telecommunications is becoming increasingly globalized. For instance, it is technologically feasible for line quality in Canada to be checked from a remote testing station in Detroit, Michigan.[13] It is even technologically feasible for operator assistance to be provided by operators who reside in a different country than the callers on both ends of the call. As well, with capital more internationalized, the pace at which new management practices are transferred across national borders has increased. Nevertheless, as a service industry with large sunk capital investment costs, telecommunications unions do have more leverage. This gives them more time to develop a coherent response to the threats posed by globalization. Both because of the size of the impending threat and their still relatively protected position, telecommunications unions have been among the leaders in the labor movement in adjusting to globalization.

The TWU and the STRM demonstrate two distinct responses to the challenge of globalization. The STRM has gone perhaps the farthest of any union in the industry in adjusting a business unionist logic to the new economic environment. Instead of the "pay-for-productivity" implicit bargaining characteristic of U.S. cold war business unionism (Zetka 1995), the STRM has negotiated with Telmex management an explicit program of numerical targets to boost production levels. These boosts, in turn, are tied to incentive payments. The productivity program has been full of problems and may ultimately fail entirely. It nonetheless is a clear extension of business unionist logic to a globalized economy.

The TWU's strategy is not as refined as the STRM's. There are no books published proclaiming the TWU's vision of modernization. But the TWU does nonetheless present the clearest social unionist vision in the industry, at least among North American unions. Best exemplifying the TWU's approach have been its attempts to build an all-Canada coalition of telecommunications trade unions and the October 1995 Accord signed with BC Tel management and the British Columbia NDP government, in which BC Tel pledges to provide universal access to rural British Columbians. This latter achievement in particularly impressive given the general environment in Canada of reducing company social obligations, in the face of the CRTC's 1992 decision to deregulate the industry.

Both the STRM and the TWU face many obstacles. The STRM seems to be in greater danger, because its position in the industry is in danger of rapid deterioration as competition in telecommunications begins. The STRM has made little effort to organize workers in the rapidly growing cellular telephone field or in competing long distance firms. The STRM's position as the key union in the strategic telecommunications industry allows it to extract gains for current members, but this position is becoming undermined.

The TWU's position, however, is not completely secure either. Like the STRM, the TWU faces the threat of having its position in the industry reduced, if it does not either merge or affiliate with a larger union, or begins to organize competing firms, a task with which it has had limited success to date. The TWU's social unionism has enabled it to have more contractual protections and to build more alliances with community groups, but ultimately the success of social unionism, depends heavily not only on a union's ability to articulate a vision, but on the union's capacity to shape the direction of the industry. At a minimum, the latter requires that the TWU continue to represent the majority of workers in the British Columbia telecommunications industry.

The difficulties faced by the TWU and the STRM reflect, albeit with some unique features, the problems faced by unions throughout North America. It is the opinion of this author that the strategies of unions which seek to challenge the rights of capital across a broad front are more likely to bear fruit for unions and the workers they represent than more narrow "corporatist" or "business unionist" strategies. Nonetheless, throughout I have sought to be respectful in my analysis of business unionism and corporatism. Although their authoritarian aspects are deserving of no respect, both business unionist and corporatist unions have achieved real wage and benefit gains. The problem with such narrow strategies is that they allow unions to be outmaneuvered by their corporate adversaries. Indeed, unionization rates are falling and have been falling for some time now in both Mexico and the United States.[14] This is not surprising, given the narrow focus of these unions on the wages, benefits and working conditions of their members; and their corresponding lack of emphasis on wider working class needs.

But, to reiterate, this is not a study of who wears the white hats and who wears the black ones. The challenges faced by social unions are substantial. As pointed out in Chapter 3, social unionism is marked by compromises, despite the fact that the agenda of social unions is broader. Nor does revolutionary unionism necessarily resolve this dilemma. Even the path followed by revolutionary unions must of necessity involve some compromises, in the absence of the conditions in which an actual revolution may be considered presently feasible.[15] Two particular challenges for social unionism are the need to organize unorganized workers and to shorten the work day to spread the available work. Neither of these goals will be easy to achieve, since they both involve sacrifices by current union members. As has been seen throughout this study, sometimes union members are willing to make such sacrifices—because they believe there are long-term benefits which justify the short-term costs—and sometimes they are not.

The path of struggle against the negative effects of globalization is not an easy one. But neither is it impossible. There are, in fact, certain key similarities between the situation faced by workers in the global economy today and the situation of workers in the U.S. and Canadian domestic economies in the 1920s. Then, union membership was declining in many (but not all) U.S. states and Canadian provinces and corporations were able to escape state or provincial government regulation and impose their will on a corporate-dominated federal government. Today, union membership is declining in many industrial countries and corporations are often able to escape national government regulation and impose their will on corporate-dominated world economic institutions. There are different responses to these problems, which may include both "protectionist" measures (like the agricultural subsidies instituted in Western Europe, Japan, and the United States in the Depression) and greater democratization of global or continental institutions, as well as other more radical alternatives (Breecher and Costello 1994). Discussion of such alternatives is beyond the scope of this study, but the point bears emphasis: the current economic relationships are not the only ones possible, and thus it is likely that there will be continued debate and struggle over those relationships and alternatives to them.

Struggle is not pleasant, even when it is non-violent. It is not surprising, therefore, to see the rise of so many prophets of cooperation in a time of great economic dislocation. Whether it is called "mutual gains," the "enterprise compact" or the "new unionism," underlying these proposals is an attractive vision of workers and corporate managers who can "get along." In fact, many of these books provide positive policy suggestions of how there can be less workplace conflict and a more equitable sharing of benefits *given a balance of political power different from that which currently exists.* But a change in the balance of power will not come about merely by academic proclamation, even if unions choose to embrace the programmatic elements contained in such works. Rather, it is only by acting to alter the current imbalance that the benefits proposed by the convergence theorists will become possible. Ironically, then, the realization of the goals of the cooperation school writers are more likely to be realized by a social unionism that seeks to confront capital over a broad array of issues than by a business unionism which seek to work with management to increase productivity for mutual gain.

NOTES

1. These differences may be quite significant when discussing other issues, such as the process of formation of state macroeconomic policy, but are not significant when discussing how or why a union adopts a specific strategic orientation vis a vis capital and the state.

2. Of course, corporations often use "rules of thumb" or satisficing techniques (Simon 1957). As well, corporations may forgo a higher profit rate in one year in order to maximize market share and earn greater profits in later years. But ultimately, satisficing or maximizing market shares are techniques or tactics of profit maximization. In the case of satisficing, this involves a means of compensating for inadequate information—that is, satisficing provides an easy "rule of thumb" for gauging and monitoring overall corporate performance (Tirole 1989: 48-49).

3. As Hart points out, Russia, China, and Iran were three other countries that experienced social revolutions in the period between 1910 and 1920. As well, the twentieth century has seen social revolutions occur in a number of other countries including China again in 1949, the former Yugoslavia, Vietnam, Cuba, and Nicaragua.

4. In particular, a large group of trade unionists in Mexico City formed the "Red Battalions" which sided with the victors of the Mexican Revolution, led by Venustiano Carranza and Alvaro Obregón, among others. The support of the Red Battalions assisted Carranza and Obregón in their ultimately successful struggle against the forces of Pancho Villa and Emiliano Zapata. For its participation, labor was rewarded with the creation of Article 123, which provided constitutional guarantees for many labor benefits, such as the 8-hour day.

5. It should be pointed out that because Mexican telephone workers receive a smaller percentage of their income as their base salary and a larger percentage in the form of overtime (or, now, incentive bonus payments) and in the form of benefits (e.g., the 60-day *aguinaldo* or Christmas bonus), there is still a substantial drop-off in the income of retired STRM workers. Nonetheless, STRM pensioners do better, relative to their lower salaries, than their U.S. or even Canadian counterparts.

6. No "international" union was ever headed by a Canadian until Lynn Williams became head of the United Steel Workers (USW) in 1977 (Palmer 1992).

7. Indeed, in the 1994 Collective Agreement membership vote, the contract passed by a narrow 51% vote, a near-replay of the 1990 contract vote in which members rejected a contract by a 51% vote. Primary reasons for the low approval rate was that the wage increase was perceived to be low (2.5% in the first year, 2% in the second year) and many members objected to a new contract provision regarding same sex spousal benefits.

8. To reiterate, in Mexico, "05" operators take customer service orders, a function that is considered a "clerical," rather than an "operator," role at BC Tel.

9. See, for instance, Lovera 1990.

10. A similar process is occurring in the STRM. Although the shift was more abrupt in the STRM, the people active in the union have not changed and local activists are still important in STRM politics.

11. With apologies to Gabriel García Márquez.

12. As Maria Victoria Murrillo writes, "Several PRI-related national union centrals, which were all competing for the same constituencies in Mexico, provide an example of organizational competition that hindered resistance. Between 1982 and 1994, the PRI government compensated only those who did not voice opposition with faster union registration and special programs. This induced an 'exit' of member unions toward the favored centrals, at the expense of the less compliant ones . . . at the end, the latter reduced their opposition to recover state resources and members" (Murrillo 1996: 8).

13. Currently, all remote line testing for AT&T in the United States, for instance, is centralized in Detroit (Interview T-93-27).

14. According to Hernández Juárez, the unionization rate in Mexico has fallen to somewhere between 12 and 14 percent (Hernández Juárez and Xelhuantzi López 1993: 125). This contrasts with an estimate of 28 percent density in 1980 (De la Garza 1994b: 206). Although union density figures in Mexico are notoriously unreliable, the contrasting figures do suggest that a significant decline has occurred.

15. Not to mention the compromises that may have to be made in a "postrevolutionary" situation, which in many cases may be even greater. At least, such has been the case in many revolutions supported by unions historically.

Bibliography

Adriano Almilla, Virginia, Julio González Castillo, Lilia Herrea Ambriz, Carmen Ramírez Ruiz. 1993. *Prestaciones de los trabajadores de Telmex.* Department of Labor Sociology, paper for Prof. Enrique de la Garza. Universidad Autónoma Metropolitana, Iztapalapa.

Aguilar, Gabriela. 1994. "Suman ya 720 las Quejas Contra Telmex por Llamadas 'Fantasma'." *El Financiero.* June 13: 16.

Aguilar, Gabriela y José de Jesús Guadarrama H. 1994. "Entran de Lleno a la Globalización las Empresas Mexicanas de Telcomunicaciones." *El Financiero.* June 15: 10.

Aguilar, Gabriela and Jaime Hernández. 1994. "Presentan Empresas Objeciones al Plan de Interconexión de Larga Distancia de Telmex." *El Financiero.* May 31: 10.

Aguilar García, Francisco Javier. 1992. *La modernización, el movimiento obrero y el estado mexicano: 1983-1990.* Dept. of Political and Social Sciences, Ph. D. Universidad Nacional Autónoma de México.

Aguilar Mares, Mónica, Miguel Contreras Quirván y Miguel Rodriguez Barcena. 1993. *Democracia sindical.* Dept. of Labor Sociology, paper for Prof. Enrique de la Garza. Universidad Autónoma Metropolitana, Iztapalapa.

Aissa, Ben. 1991. *RNCC Rationalization Business Case.* Burnaby, B.C.: BC Tel.

Aldridge, Jim. 1989. *Re Reimbursement of Benefits for Operators Laid-Off in Cranbrook: Dissent 89-05-04.* Burnaby, B.C.

Almazán González, José Antonio. 1993. "Electricistas: los vientos de cambio." *La Jornada Laboral.* July 29: 3-4.

Andrews, Edmund L. 1990. "Global Markets Love Baby Bells." *New York Times.* Dec. 19: D-1, D-6.

Angeles, Luis. 1993. "Economía y telecomunicaciones." In *Las telecomunicaciones como factor de desarrollo y modernización económica*. Ed. SCT y Colegio Nacional de Economistas, 25-30. México, D.F.: SCT.

Apodaca, Patrice. 1996. "GTE May Join the Merger Bonanza: Analysts See Long-Distance Relationship With Foe AT&T." *Los Angeles Times*. April 30: D-1, D-7.

Arthur D. Little. 1985. Study commissioned by Telmex. México, D.F.

Atterbury, John III. 1994. "Southwestern Bell, Inc." *Telmex Investors' Meeting*. México, D.F.: Feb. 11-12.

Aziz Nassif, Alberto. 1989. *El estado mexicano y la CTM*. México, D.F.: Ediciones de la Casa Chata.

Babe, Robert. 1990. *Telecommunications in Canada: Technology, Industry, and Government*. Toronto: University of Toronto Press.

Bagnall, James. 1992. "Trouble on the Line." *Financial Times of Canada*. August 20: 12-13.

Barnet, Tom. 1980. "Labour troubles the background to rate rehearing." *Vancouver Sun*. November 3: A-8.

Barrera, Eduardo. 1992. *Telecommunications, International Capital, the Peripheral State: The Case of Mexico*. Dept. of Economics, Ph. D. University of Texas, Austin.

Barrera Barrera, Juan. 1992. "Las elecciones en el SME." *La Jornada Laboral*. July 30: 4-5.

Batten, Dick and Sara Schoonmaker. 1987. "Deregulation, Technological Change, and Labor Relations in Telecommunications." In *Workers, Managers and Technological Change: Emerging Patterns of Labor Relations*. Ed. Daniel B. Cornfield, 311-327. New York: Plenum Press.

Baur, Cynthia. 1995. *Incomunicado: The arrested development of telecommunication systems in Latin America*. Dept. of Communications, Ph. D. University of California, San Diego.

Bayko, John and Dan Schiller. 1984. *Labor Relations in the Information Society: The Impact of the 1983 Telephone Strike*. Unpublished manuscript.

Beaumont, P. B. 1992. "Structural Change and IR: The UK." In *Labour Relations in a Changing Environment*. Ed. Alan Gladstone et al, 203-214. New York: Walter de Gruyter.

Bell, Daniel. 1960. *The End of Ideology: On the Exhaustion of Political Ideas in the Fifties*. New York: Free Press, rev. ed. 1965.

Beniger, James R. 1986. *The Control Revolution: Technological and Economic Origins of the Information Society*. Cambridge, Mass.: Harvard University Press.

Benítez, Rodolfo. 1992. *Privatization of Telecommunications Services*. PTTI Regional Conference. Panama City, Panama. July 6-8.

Benítez Chávez, Mario Flavio. 1991. *Trabajo, organización y lucha en el caso del SME: situación actual y perspectivas (1960-1989)*. Dept. of Economics, Lic. Universidad Nacional Autónoma de México.

Bernard, Elaine. 1982. *The Long Distance Feeling: A History of the Telecommunications' Workers Union*. Vancouver: New Star Books.

———. 1996. "Outsourcing." *Boston Globe*. March 26: 60.

Bizberg, Ilán. 1986. *La clase obrera mexicana*. México, D.F.: Secretaría de Educación Pública.

———. 1990. *Estado y sindicalismo en México*. México, D.F.: El Colegio de México.

Blackwell, Richard. 1989. "Canadians happy with phone service: poll." *Business Communications Review*. August 23.

Bluestone, Barry and Irving. 1992. *Negotiating the Future: A Labor Perspective on American Business*. New York: Basic Books.

Bolton, Brian. 1993. "Negotiating structural and technological change in the telecommunications services in the United States." In *Telecommunications Services: Negotiating structural and technological change*. Ed. Brian Bolton, 123-143. Geneva: International Labour Office.

Bolton, Nathalie J. and Richard P. Choykowski. 1990. *The Impact of Technological Change on Work Organization and Wages: A Case Study in the Canadian Telecommunications Industry*. Queen's Papers in Industrial Relations. Kingston, Ontario: Queen's University.

Bothello, Antonio José J., and Caren Addis. 1994. *Privatization of Telecommunications in Mexico: Its Impact on Labor and Labor Relations*. Geneva: International Labour Office.

Boulter, Dr. Walter. 1985. *Deregulation*. Address to TWU Convention [video]. Burnaby, B.C.: TWU.

Boulter, Walter G., James W. McConaughey, and Fred J. Kelsey. 1990. *Telecommunications Policy for the 1990s and beyond*. Armonk, NY: M.E. Sharpe.

Brandenburg, Frank R. 1964. *The Making of Modern Mexico*. Englewood Cliffs, N.J.: Prentice-Hall.

Braverman, Harry. 1974. *Labor and Monopoly Capital: The Degradation of Work in the Twentieth Century*. New York: Monthly Review Press.

Breecher, Jeremy and Tim Costello. 1994. *Global Village or Global Pillage: Economic Reconstruction from the Bottom Up.* Boston: South End.

Brenner, Aaron. 1995. "Rank and File Teamster Movements in Comparative Perspective." In *Trade Union Politics: American Unions and Economic Change, 1960s-1990s.* Ed. Glenn Perusek and Kent Worcester, 111-139. Atlantic Heights, NJ: Humanities Press.

British Columbia. 1995. *The Electronic Highway Accord: Securing British Columbia's On-ramp to the Electronic Highway.* Victoria, BC: British Columbia.

British Columbia Telephone (BC Tel). 1990. *Corporate Strategic Plan Summary: 1991-1995.* BC Tel Group. Burnaby, B.C.: BC Tel.

———. 1992a. *BC Tel Annual Report: The Speed of Change.* Burnaby, B.C.: BC Tel.

———. 1992b. *Competitive Improvement Project.* Slide presentation. June. Burnaby, B.C.: BC Tel.

———. 1992c. *Why PNOC.* Burnaby, B.C.: BC Tel.

———. 1993a. *BC Tel—Customer Team Guide.* Burnaby, B.C.: BC Tel.

———. 1993b. *BC Telecom Inc., 1994-1998: Strategic Plan—Strategic Planning and Analysis.* April. Burnaby, B.C.: BC Tel.

BC Tel and FTW. 1971. *Collective Agreement.* Burnaby, B.C.: BC Tel and FTW.

BC Tel and TWU. Various Years. *Collective Agreement.* Burnaby, B.C.: BC Tel and TWU.

———. 1983. *Committee on Contracting-Out and Technological Change (COTC) Committee minutes.* May 11. Burnaby, B.C.: BC Tel and TWU.

———. 1993. *Letter of Agreement 1-25-93 [re Work Teams].* Burnaby, B.C.: BC Tel and TWU.

British Trade Unions Committee (BTUC). 1990. *Telecommunications in the 1990s: a submission to the Department of Trade and Industry on the telecommunications policy review by the British Trade Unions Committee.* Duopoly Review Submission 2. London: BTUC.

———. 1991. *Quality and Choice: A Response to the Department of Trade and Industry's Consultative Paper: 'Competition and Choice: Telecommunications Policy in the 1990s'.* Duopoly Paper Submission 3. London: BTUC.

Caballero, Alejandro, Oscar Camacho, Elena Gallegos, Roberto Garduño, Néstor Martínez and Ismael Romero. 1994. "México a debate." *Perfil de La Jornada.* May 12.

Caby, Laurence and Charles Steinfield. 1994. "Trends in the Liberalization of European Telecommunications: Community Harmonization and National

Divergence." In *Telecommunications in Transition: Policies, Services and Technologies in the European Community.* Ed. Johannes M. Bauer, Laurence Caby, and Charles Steinfield, 36-48. Thousand Oaks, CA: Sage.

Caliz Cecilia, Ana María. 1984. *Proceso de producción y avance tecnológico— estudio de caso: Teléfonos de México.* Department of Economics, Maestría. Universidad Nacional Autónoma de México.

Calva, José Luis. 1994. "Empleo y Distribución del Ingreso." *El Financiero.* May 6: 30.

Campos, Cortesana, Marisela Mejía Estrada and Rocio del Carmen. 1989. *Principales efectos laborales debido a la introducción de innovaciones tecnológicos en los centrales de Telmex.* Dept. of Social and Political Sciences (Communication), Lic. Universidad Nacional Autónoma de México.

Canadian Auto Workers (CAW). 1993. *CAW Research Overview of 1993 Negotiations with the 'Big Three'.* Willowdale, Ontario: CAW.

Canadian Federation of Communications Workers (CFCW). 1973. "Canadian Federation launched." *The Federation Paper.* December: 1.

———. 1975. "Toronto Over the Top." *The Federation Paper.* August.

———. 1979. "Traffic vote." *The Federation Paper.* September.

Canadian Radio-television and Telecommunications Commission (CRTC). 1985. *Interexchange competition and related issues (Decision 85-19).* Ottawa: Minister of Supply and Services.

———. 1990. *Unitel Communications, Inc. and B.C. Rail Telecommunications/Lightel Inc.—Applications to Provide Public Long Distance Voice Telephone Services and Related Resale and Sharing Issues: Scope and Procedure (Notice 90-73).* Ottawa: Minister of Supply and Services.

———. 1992. *Competition in the Provision of Public Long Distance Voice Telephone Services and Related Resale and Sharing Issues (Decision 92-12).* Ottawa: Minister of Supply and Services.

———. 1993. *Submission of the Director of Investigation and Research to the CRTC re: Telecom Public Notice CRTC 92-78: Review of Regulatory Framework.* Ottawa: Minister of Supply and Services.

Cano Miramontes, José del Rogelio, Ramón Evaristo Felix, Pablo A. Lugo Colín, and Jorge Salinas Jardón. 1994. *Balance de 4 años de productividad y calidad en Tel-Mex.* Paper presented at Primer Encuentro Sindical Nacional sobre Productividad. México, D.F: May 27-28.

Carr, Shirley. 1991. "Canadian Labor Strategies for a Global Economy." In *Labor in a Global Economy: Perspective from the US and Canada.* Ed.

Steven Hecker and Margaret Hallock, 25-29. Eugene, Oregon: University of Oregon.

Carrillo, Jorge. 1992. *Mujeres en la industria automotriz en México*. Tijuana: COLEF.

Carroll, Lewis. 1971. "Alice's Adventures in Wonderland." In *Alice's Adventures in Wonderland and Through the Looking Glass and What Alice Found There*. Ed. Roger Lancelyn Green, 1-111. New York: Oxford University Press.

Carter, Donald D. and Thomas McIntosh. 1990. *Collective Bargaining and the Charter: Asessing the Impact of American Judicial Practices*. Queen's Papers in Industrial Relations. Kingston, Ontario: Queen's University.

Castañeda, Jorge. 1993. *La utopia desarmada*. México, D.F.: Editorial Planeta.

Centro de Investigación Laboral y Asesoría Sindical, A.C. (CILAS). 1992. *Estudio Económico, Financiero, Productivo, Contractual y Salarial de la Empresa Teléfonos de México, S.A. de C. V.* Jan. 25. México, D.F.: CILAS.

Cepeda Salinas, Arturo. 1993. "Comunicaciones y electrónica: movimiento de la civilización." *Las telecomunicaciones como factor de desarrollo y modernización económica*. Ed. SCT and Colegio Nacional de Economistas, 252-262. México, D.F.: SCT.

Cerezo P., Adolfo. 1994. "Finance." *Telmex Investors' Meeting*. Feb. 11-12. México, D.F.

Church, George J. 1994. Reported by Bernard Buamohl, William McWhirter, and Suneel Ratan. "Unions Arise With New Tricks." *Time International*. June 13: 40-42.

Cisneros Luján, Lilia Ana. 1994. "La Iniciativa Privada no se Salva de Toda Culpa." *El Financiero*. June 14: 70.

Clark, Bill. 1984. "President's Report." In *January 1984 TWU Convention Minutes*. Burnaby, B.C.: TWU.

———. 1988. *A Background to the "Letters of Agreement," The Underlying Principle at the Beginning and Their Roots in the Collective Agreement*. Unpublished manuscript. March 24.

Clyne, J.V. Guy Fourrier, Carl Beigle, Robert Fulford, Beland Honderich, Dianne Narvik, Alphose Onimet, Lloyd Shaw (Clyne Commission). 1979. *Telecommunications and Canada: Consultative Committee on the Implications for Canadian Sovereignty*. Ottawa: Ministry of Supplies and Services.

Coates, Mary Lou. 1990. *Industrial Relations in 1990: Trends and Emerging Ideas*. Kingston, Ontario: Queen's University, Industrial Relations Centre.

Collier, David. 1995. "Trajectory of a Concept: 'Corporatism' in the Study of Latin American Politics." In *Latin America in Comparative Perspective: New approaches in methods and analysis.* Ed. Peter H. Smith, 135-162. Boulder: Westview Press, 1995.

Collier, Ruth Berins. 1992. *The Contradictory Alliance: State-Labor Relations and Regime Change in Mexico.* Berkeley, CA: International & Area Studies Research Series, no. 83.

Collier, Ruth Berins, and David Collier. 1991. *Shaping the Political Arena: Critical Junctures, the Labor Movement, and Regime Dynamics in Latin America.* Princeton, NJ: Princeton University Press.

Colombo, John Robert. 1993. *1994: The Canadian Global Almanac.* Toronto: Macmillan Canada.

Communication Workers of America (CWA). 1993. "Customer Service: Towards the Breakthrough." *Journal of the Communication Workers' Union of America.*

Communication Workers of Canada (CWC). 1991. *Our Niche in the Global Economy: CWC's position on local network convergence.* Ottawa: CWC.

———. 1992. *Prosperity and Progress: CWC's Vision for Shaping the Future.* Ottawa: CWC.

CWC and ACTWU (Atlantic Canadian Telecommunications Workers Union). 1992. *Opposing joint petition of CWC and ACTWU re Telecom Decision 92-12.* Submission to CRTC.

Conaghan, Catherine M. and James M. Malloy. 1994. *Unsettling Statescraft: Democracy and Neoliberalism in the Central Andes.* Pittsburgh: University of Pittsburgh Press.

Cook, Maria Lorena. 1990. *Organizing Dissent: The Politics of Opposition in the Mexican Teachers' Union.* Dept. of Political Science, Ph.D. University of California, Berkeley.

Cooke, P. 1992. "Some spatial aspects of regulation and technological change in telecom industries." *Environment and Planning* 24: 683-703.

Cooper, Len. 1993. *Telecom: The Lean Movement and Australia.* Lean Workplace Conference. North York, Ontario.

Cooper Tory, Jennifer. 1988. *Mujer, trabajo y nueva tecnología—estudio de caso: Teléfonos de México.* Dept. of Economics, Maestría. Universidad Nacional Autónoma de México.

———. 1989. "Cambio tecnológico: organización y resistencia. El caso de los telefonistas." In *Fuerza de Trabajo: Feminina Urbana en México.* Ed. Jennifer Cooper, Teresita de Barbieri, Teresa Rocha, Estela Suárez, and Esperanza Tuñon. México, D.F.: Grupo Editorial Miguel Angel Parrúa.

Coordinadora Democrática de Telefonistas. 1991. *Teléfonos: Modernización Privatizada.* México, D.F.: Unpublished manuscript.

Coparmex. 1989. *El Sindicato de Telefonistas de la República Mexicana: Una maestra de reestructuración tecnológica y flexibilización del contrato colectivo.* México, D.F.: Unpublished manuscript.

Corona, Rosanna et al. 1992. "Proceso de privatización en México, El: cinco estudios de México." *Procesos de privatización en América Latina.* Ed. Manuel Sánchez, 105-214. México, D.F.: ITAM/Banco Internacional de la Reconstrucción y Desarrollo.

Corona Armiento, Gabriel. 1992. *El sindicalismo oficial en el proceso de reestructuración Política del Estado Mexicano (1982-1990).* Dept. of Political Science, Maestría. Universidad Nacional Autónoma de México.

Corro, Salvador. 1987. "Las indecisiones de Hernández Juárez merman al sindicalismo oficial." *Proceso.* April 20: 16-19.

Cowhey, Peter F. and Jonathan D. Aronson. 1989. "Trade in Services and Changes in the World Telecommunications System. In *Changing Networks: Mexico's Telecommunications Options.* Ed. Peter F. Cowhey, Jonathan D. Aronson, and Gabriel Székely, 5-49. La Jolla: Center for U.S.-Mexican Studies.

Cowie, Jefferson. 1996. *Industrial Locations and the Spaces in Between: RCA Workers in North America and the Problem of Capital Migration.* Presentation to Center for Democratization and Economic Development. La Jolla: Feb. 26.

Crandall, Robert W. 1993. *Comments of Robert W. Crandall Re Telecom Public Notice 92-78.* Ottawa: CRTC.

Crandall, Robert W. and Kenneth Flamm. 1989. "Overview." *Changing the Rules: Technological Change, International Competition and Regulation in Communications.* Ed. Robert W. Crandall and Kenneth Flamm, 1-10. Washington, D. C.: The Brookings Institution.

Cregan, Alex, J. R. Aldridge, and Thomas R. Braidwood. 1986. *Re Cranbrook Office Closures/Constructive Layoff (Decision 86-10-23).* Burnaby, B.C.: BC Tel-TWU arbitration decision.

Crémieux, Pierre-Yves. 1996. "Effect of Deregulation on Employee Earnings: Pilots, Flight Attendants, and Mechanics, 1959-1992." *Industrial and Labor Relations Review* 49: 2 (January): 223-242.

Cross, Brian. 1993. "The CAW and the Big Three seal an innovative deal that emphasizes the welfare of the community." *Windsor Star.* October 16.

Cruz Cervantes, César. 1984. *Condiciones de trabajo de la industria telefónica.* Dept. of Economics, Maestría. Universidad Nacional Autónoma de México.

Cull, Greg. 1974. "10,000 workers to pull BC Tel plug." *The Province*. June 27.

Cywith, Peter and Mark Lewin. 1990. "Sounding More and More Like a Three-Man Band." *Business Week*. April 23: 30.

Darling, Juanita. 1991. "Mexico's 'Don Fidel': The Indispensable Power Broker." *Los Angeles Times*. April 23.

Davidson, Dr. William H. 1993. *National Telecommunications Policies for an Evolving Industry* [prepared for Stentor—exhibit 7]. Ottawa: CRTC.

Davis, Edmund M. 1993. "Negotiating structural and technological change in the telecommunications services in Australia." In *Telecommunications Services: Negotiating structural and technological change*. Ed. Brian Bolton. Geneva: International Labour Office.

Davis, Edmund M. and Russell D. Lansbury. 1989. "Worker Participation in Decisions on Technological Change in Australia." In *New Technology: International Perspectives on Human Resources and Industrial Relations*. Ed. Greg J. Bamber and Russell D. Lansbury, 100-116. London: Unwin Hyman.

de Buen, Néstor. 1989. "El convenio de modernización en Teléfonos de México. *El Cotidiano* 30 (July-August): 59-61.

de la Garza Toledo, Enrique. 1988. *Ascenso y crisis del Estado social autoritario: Estado y acumulación del capital en México (1940-1976)*. México, D. F.

———. 1989a "¿Quién ganó en Telmex?". *El Cotidiano* 30 (Nov.-Dec.): 49-56.

———. 1989b. "Las estructuras organizativas del SME y del SUTERM." *El Cotidiano* 26 (March-April): 33-42.

———. 1992. "Reestructuración y polarización industrial en México." *El Cotidiano* 47 (Sept.-Oct.): 142-154.

———. 1993. "Neoliberalismo y estrategia del movimiento obrero." *Productividad: Distintas Experiencias*. Ed. Enrique de la Garza Toledo y Carlos García V., 13-55. México, D. F.: Universidad Autónoma Metropolitana, Iztapalapa and Fundación Fredrich Ebert.

———. 1994a. Presentation at *Primer Encuentro Sindical sobre la Productividad*. México, D.F.: May 27-28.

———, 1994b. "The Restructuring of State-Labor Relations in Mexico." Trans. Aníbal Yañez. In *The Politics of Economic Restructuring: State-Society Relations and Regime Change in Mexico*. Ed. Kevin J. Middlebrook, María Lorena Cook, and Juan Molinar Horcasitas, 195-217. La Jolla: Center for U.S.-Mexican Studies.

de la Garza Toledo, Enrique and Javier Melgoza. 1985. "Telmex: Los foquitos te envuelvan, te cautivan, te comen." *Información obrera* 55 (March): 28-33.

del Valle Sánchez, Manuel. 1978. *El movimiento de telefonistas del 22 de abril de 1976—alcances y limitaciones en el movimiento obrero nacional.*" Dept. of Political and Social Sciences (Sociology), Lic. Universidad Nacional Autónoma de México.

Department of Communications (DOC). 1985. *Confidential brief presented to the federal Cabinet.* May. Ottawa: Unpublished manuscript.

Department of Labour, Mediation and Conciliation Branch (DOL). 1980. *Bargaining History of British Columbia Telephone Company and Federation of Telephone Workers of British Columbia—1960 to 1977.* Ottawa: Labour Canada.

Díaz B., Fabio and Carlos Salazar P. 1991. *El Libro Negro de las Telecomunicaciones.* Bogotá, Colombia: Instituto Nacional Sindical.

Díaz, Eduardo. 1994. Presentation at PTTI Conference. México, DF: Feb. 28-March 2.

Dobie, George. 1978. "Intangibles of winning or losing a labor dispute." *Vancouver Sun.* Feb. 16.

———. 1980. "BC Tel supervisors ponder crossing the line." *Vancouver Sun.* Sept. 29: B-9.

Domínguez Cruz, Rosa Ana. 1982. *La situación de las operadoras de Teléfonos de México.* Dept. of Social and Political Sciences, Lic. Universidad Nacional Autónoma de México.

Downs, Anthony. 1957. *An Economic Theory of Democracy.* New York: Harper.

Drache, Daniel and Harry Glasbeek. 1992. *The Changing Workplace: Reshaping Canada's Industrial Relations System.* Toronto: James Larimer.

Dreery, Stephen. 1989. "Unions and technological change." In *Australian Unions: An Industrial Relations Perspective.* Ed. Bill Ford and David Plowman, 269-285. South Melbourne, Australia: MacMillan.

Dubb, Steve. 1992. *Trozos de cristal: Privatization and Union Politics at Teléfonos de México.* Paper presented at Latin American Studies Association Congress. Los Angeles: Sept. 24-27.

Dumanceau, Bernie. 1992. *Sales Support and Effectiveness Integrated Work Team.* Burnaby, B.C.: BC Tel.

Ebbinghaus, Bernhard and Jelle Visser. 1996. *Social Change and Unionization: The Development of Union Membership in Western Europe, 1950-90.* Paper presented at the American Political Science Association conference. San Francisco: Aug. 29-Sept. 2.

The Economist. 1993. "The greatest assets ever sold." *The Economist.* August 21: 9-10.

Ehring, George and Wayne Roberts. 1993. *Giving Away a Miracle: Lost Dreams, Broken Promises and the Ontario NDP.* Oakville, Ontario: Mosaic Press.

Enchin, Harvey. 1993. "CRTC heads down new road: Hearing weighs competing interests for the information highway." *The Globe and Mail.* Nov. 1: B-1, B-8.

Engels, Frederick. 1958. "Preface to the English Edition of 1892." In Frederick Engels, *The Condition of the Working Class in England.*, 360-371. Translated by W. O. Henderson and W.H. Chaloner. Stanford, CA: Basil Blackwell.

Esping-Andersen, Gøsta. 1985. *Politics Against Markets: The Social Democratic Road to Power.* Princeton, NJ: Princeton University Press.

Estrada Medina, Maricela, Martín E. Navarrete Gutierrez, and Claudia M. Segura Alcantera. 1993. *Comparación de los estatutos de electricistas, estatutos de Telmex.* Dept. of Labor Sociology, paper for Prof. Enrique de la Garza Toledo. Universidad Autónoma Metropolitana, Iztapalapa.

Evans, Don. 1992a. *Engineering Effectiveness and Integrated Work Teams.* Burnaby, B.C.: BC Tel.

———. 1992b. *Engineering Interdependencies: Integrated Work Plan.* Burnaby, B.C.: BC Tel.

Evans, Mark. 1999. "BCT Telus May Have To Speed Up Its Move East." *The Globe and Mail.* Jan. 28.

Fan, Heather. 1974. "No show and Tel Trouble." *The Province.* Feb. 23.

Farmer, Anthony, Michael Terry, Jon Berry, Nick Gilman, Benson Maina, Athina Nicolaides, and Yee Mei Tong. 1994. *Developments in IR/HR Management in Telecom: Britain. International Developments in Workplace Innovation: Implications for Canadian Competitiveness.* Toronto.

Federación de Sindicatos de Empresas de Bienes y Servicios (Fesebes). 1992. *Documento de Táctica y Estrategia.* México, D.F.: Fesebes.

Federation of Telephone Workers (FTW). 1972. *Annual Plant Council minutes.* Burnaby, B.C.: FTW.

Filippelli, Ronald L. 1990. "The Historical Context of Postwar Industrial Relations." In *U.S. Labor Relations 1945-1989: Accommodation and Conflict.* Ed. Bruce Nissen, 137-171. New York: Garland, 1990.

Flanders, Tony and Anne Cohen. 1991. *Telecommunications Workers' Union Report for Executive Council.* Unpublished report.

Foucault, Michel. 1980. *Power/Knowledge.* New York: Pantheon Books.

Francés, Antonio, with Felipe Aguerrevere, Raquel Benbunan, and María Eugenia Boza. 1993. *!Aló Venezuela!: Apertura y privatización de las telecomunicaciones.* Caracas, Venezuela: Ediciones IESA.

Freeman, Jo. 1983. *Social Movements of the Sixties and Seventies.* New York: Longman.

Freeman, Richard B. and James L. Medoff. 1984. *What Do Unions Do?.* New York: Basic Books.

Fuchs, Gerald. 1993. *Do Nations Matter? Governance Structures and Regime Transformation in Telecom.* ISA Congress. Acapulco, Jalisco, México.

Fuentes, Manuel. 1994. *La imposición laboral que nos viene del norte.* México, D.F.: Comisión Mexicana de Defensa y Promoción de los Derechos Humanos, A. C.

Fucini, Joseph J. and Suzy Fucini. 1990. *Working for the Japanese: Inside Mazda's American Auto Plant.* New York: MacMillan.

Gamboa González, Victor Manuel. 1985. *El estado y el movimiento obrero en México: 1970-1976.* Dept. of Political and Social Sciences, Maestría. Universidad Nacional Autónoma de México.

Gemini. 1992a. *Objectives of Integrated Work Teams.* Burnaby, B.C.: BC Tel. Unpublished report.

————. 1992b. *Order Flow Process Coordinating Integrated Work Team.* Burnaby, B.C.: BC Tel. Unpublished report.

General Telephone and Electronics Corporation (GTE). 1992. *GTE Strategic Plan.* Unpublished report.

Geoghegan, Thomas. 1992. *Which Side Are You On?.* New York: Plume.

Gladstone, Alan. 1992. "Introductory." In *Labour Relations in a Changing Environment.* Ed. Alan Gladstone et al, 1-13. New York: Walter de Gruyter.

Globeman, Steven. 1992. "Convergence between Communications Technologies: The North American Core." In *Convergence between Communications Technologies: Case Studies from North America and Western Europe.* Ed. OECD, 25-59. Paris, France: OECD.

Glyn, Andrew and Bob Sutcliffe. 1992. "Global but Leaderless: The New Capitalist Order." In *The Socialist Register.* Ed by Ralph Milbrand and Leo Panitch, 76-95.

Golden, Miriam A. 1988. *Labor Divided: Austerity and Working-Class Politics in Contemporary Italy.* Ithaca, NY: Cornell University Press.

————. 1990. *A Rational Choice Analysis of Union Militancy with Application to the Case of British Coal and Fiat.* Ithaca, NY: Cornell University Press.

González Apaciaza, Raúl. 1993. "La formación de recursos humanos en el campo de las telecomunicaciones." In *Las telecomunicaciones como factor de desarrollo y modernización económica*. Ed. SCT and Colegio Nacional de Economistas. 149-167. México, D. F: SCT.

Gordon, David M., Richard Edwards, and Michael Reich. 1982. *Segmented Work, Divided Workers*. New York: Cambridge University Press.

Gorz. André. 1982. *Farewell to the Working Class*. London: Pluto Press.

Gourevitch, Peter. 1986. *Politics in Hard Times: Comparative Responses to International Economic Crises*. Ithaca, NY: Cornell University Press.

Gramsci, Antonio. 1990. "Our Trade Union Strategy." In *Selections from Political Writings (1921-1926)*. Ed and Trans. Quintin Hoare, 164-168. Minneapolis: University of Minnesota Press.

Grinspun, Ricardo. 1993. "The Economics of Free Trade in Canada." In *The Political Economy of North American Trade*. Ed. Ricardo Grinspun and Maxwell A. Cameron, 105-124. Kingston, Ontario: McGill and Queen's University Press.

Guadarrama H., José de Jesús. 1994. "La Pobre Infraestructura en Telecomunicaciones Obliga a Empresas a Instalar sus Propias Redes." *El Financiero*. May 3: 18.

Guzmán G., Juan. 1987a. "Reconoce Juárez que no ha descartado la reelección para un tercer periodo en el STRM." *Unomásuno*. May 4: 9.

———. 1987b. "Hernández Juárez: le inyectan dinero a la disidencia del STRM." *Unomásuno*. May 3: 1.

Haggard, Stephan. 1990. *Pathways from the Periphery: The Politics of Growth in the Newly Industrialized Countries*. Ithaca, NY: Cornell University Press.

Halarm, Dr. Albert. 1993. *The US Experience: Implications for Canada* [to CRTC on behalf of Stentor, exhibit 8]. Submission to CRTC.

Hall, Noel A. 1977. *Conciliation Report*. Ottawa: Ministry of Labour.

Hamilton, Nora. 1982. *The Limits of State Autonomy: Post-Revolutionary Mexico*. Princeton, NJ: Princeton University Press.

Hammond, Thomas Taylor. 1987. "Lenin on Trade Unions." In *Theories of the Labor Movement*. Ed. Simeon Larson and Bruce Nissen, 59-62. Detroit: Wayne State University Press.

Hanafin, Joe. 1992. *Unitel Decision and Bill C-62*. CWC: Unpublished manuscript.

Hart, John Mason. 1989. *Revolutionary Mexico: The Coming and Process of the Mexican Revolution*. Berkeley, CA: University of California Press.

Haydu, Jeffrey. 1988. *Between Craft and Class: Skilled Workers and Factory Politics in the United States and Britain, 1890-1922*. Berkeley, CA: University of California Press.

Hecker, Steven and Margaret Hallock. 1991. "Introduction." In *Labor in a Global Economy: Perspective from the US and Canada*. Ed. Steven Hecker and Margaret Hallock, 2-8. Eugene, Oregon: University of Oregon Press.

Heckscher, Charles C. 1988. *The New Unionism: Employee Involvement in the Changing Corporation*. New York: Basic Books.

Hellman, Judith Adler. 1988. *Mexico in Crisis*. 2nd edition. New York: Holmes & Meier.

Hernández Juárez, Francisco. 1990. "Privatización de empresas: perspectiva de la reforma del estado." Presentation at *Seminario: La privatización: un diálogo necesario*. Caracas, Venezuela: October.

————. 1991. *Reestructuración de capital y privatización de empresas: tendencia histórica de las fuerzas productivas*. Unpublished manuscript.

————. 1992. "Informe que rinde a la XVIIa Convención Nacional Ordinaria Democrática del STRM." *XVIIa Convención Nacional Ordinaria*. México, D.F.: STRM.

Hernández Juárez, Francisco and María Xelhuantzi López. 1993. *El sindicalismo en la reforma del Estado: una visión de la modernización de México*. México, D.F.: Fondo de Cultura Económica.

Heron, Craig. 1989. *The Canadian Labour Movement: A Short History*. Toronto: Larimer & Co.

Hiebert, Rod. 1986a. *Keep Jobs in the Kootenays*. Burnaby, B.C.: TWU. Unpublished manuscript.

————. 1986b. *Letter to Fiona McDonald*. Feb. 7. Burnaby, B.C.: Unpublished letter.

————. 1987. "Quality Circles: Why the Union Says No." *The Transmitter*. August: 6.

————. 1988. "British warning on Quality Circles." *The Transmitter*. January: 14.

————. 1992. *Brief to the Parliamentary Committee Considering Bill C-62: The Telephone Deregulation Bill*. TWU. Submission to Parliament.

Hiebert, Rod, Linda Rolufs (Hebert), Bob D'Etcheverrey, John Johnston, Ross McNicol, Bill Brewer, Jim Gordon, and Doug Harrop. 1980. *Appendix to TWU Intervention to the CRTC Hearings on BC Tel Company's request for a rate increase*. Submission to CRTC.

Hiebert, Rod, Peter Massy and Sid Shniad. 1991. *Letter to Fred Pomeroy and Joe Hanafin* (CWC). Burnaby, B.C.: Unpublished letter.

Hoerr, John. 1991 "What should unions do?" *Harvard Business Review*. May-June: 1-11.

Hoey, Kelly. 1990. *Industrial Relations Responses to Technological Change: A Case Study of BC Tel*. University of British Columbia, paper for Professor Joe Weiler.

Hogg, Peter. 1990. "Jurisdiction over telecommunications: Alberta Government Telephones v. CRTC." *McGill Law Journal* 35: 480-485.

Holson, Laura M. 1998. "2 Bells, SBC and Ameritech, Set to Rejoin in $60 Billion Deal." *The New York Times*. May 11.

Hope, H. Alan. 1981. *Return to Work Arbitration*. Ottawa: Canadian Ministry of Labour.

Horwitz, Robert Britt. 1988. *The Irony of Regulatory Reform: The Deregulation of American Telecommunications*. New York: Oxford University Press.

House, Dr. Ronald K. 1993. *The Evolution of the Canadian Perspective: Prepared for CRTC Telecommunications Public Notice 92-78—Review of Regulatory Framework—submission of Stentor Resource Centre, Inc [Exhibit 10]*. Submission to CRTC.

Hutcheon, Justice Henry E. 1978. *Interim Report of the Industrial Inquiry Commision*. Ottawa: Ministry of Labour.

Hyman, Richard. 1975. *Industrial Relations: A Marxist Introduction*. Plymouth, UK: MacMillan Press Ltd.

———— 1987. "Marxism and the Sociology of Trade Unionism." In *Theories of the Labor Movement*. Ed. Simeon Larson and Bruce Nissen, 38-43. Detroit: Wayne State University Press.

Implusora Telefónica, S. A. and Sindicato de Trabajadores de Impulsora Telefónica (Impulsora and SINATIMEL). Various years. *Contrato Colectivo de Trabajo*. México, D.F.: Impulsora and SINATIMEL

Janisch, Hudson N. and Bohdan S. Romanuk. 1994. "Canada." In *Telecommunications in the Pacific Basin: An Evolutionary Approach*. Ed. Seisuke Komatsuzaki, Eli Noam, and Douglas A. Conn, 349-392. New York: Oxford University Press.

Jenson, Jane and Rianne Mahon. 1993. "The Legacies for Canadian Labour of Two Decades of Crisis." In *The Challenge of Restructuring: North American Labor Movements Respond*. Ed. Jane Jenson and Rianne Mahon, 72-92. Philadelphia: Temple University Press.

Jeremy, Mike (assisted by Timothy Heyman and José Cuellar). 1991. *Teléfonos de México S.A. de C.V. : Mexico's Telecommunications Giant*. México, D.F.: Baring Securities.

Jones Tamayo, Claudio Gerardo. 1993. *Acción colectiva y autonomía sindical: los telefonistas y la reestructuración de Telmex (1976-1989)*. Dept. of Political Science, Lic. Instituto Tecnológico Autónomo de México.

Keefe, Jeffrey and Karen Baroff. 1994. *Telecom: Labor-Management Relations one Decade after the AT&T Divestiture*. Presentation at International Developments in Workplace Innovation: Implications for Canadian Competitiveness conference. Toronto.

Kelleher, Stephen, Roy Heenan, and Jim Aldridge. 1989. *Re Reimbursement of Benefits for Operators Laid-Off in Cranbrook (Decision 89-05-04)*. Burnaby, B.C.: BC Tel-TWU arbitration decision.

Kelley, Robin D. G. 1990. *Hammer and Hoe: Alabama Communists during the Great Depression*. Chapel Hill: University of North Carolina Press.

Kelly, William P. 1969. *Letter dated 7/15/69 to Mr. Bernard Wilson*. Elaine Bernard special collection. Vancouver, BC: University of British Columbia.

Kerr, Clark. 1983. *The Future of Industrial Societies: Convergence or Continuing Diversity?*. Cambridge, Mass: Harvard University Press.

Kerr, Clark, John T. Dunlop, Frederick H. Harbison, and Charles A. Myers. 1960. *Industrialism and Industrial Man: The Problems of Labor and Management in Economic Growth*. Cambridge, Mass.: Harvard University Press.

Kettler, David, James Struthers, and Chistopher Huxley. 1990. "Unionization and Labour Regimes in Canada and the United States: Considerations for Comparative Research." *Labour/Le Travail* 25 (Spring): 161-187.

Kingston, Maxine Hong. 1977. *The Woman Warrior: Memoirs of a girlhood among ghosts*. Alfred A Knopf: New York.

Knight, Alan, 1990. *The Mexican Revolution, Volume 2: Counter-revolution and Reconstruction*. Lincoln, Neb.: University of Nebraska Press.

Kochan, Thomas A., Harry C. Katz, and Robert B. McKersie. 1986. *The Transformation of American Industrial Relations*. Basic Books: New York.

Kochan, Thomas A. and Paul Osterman. 1994. *The Mutual Gains Enterprise: forging a winning partnership among labor, management, and government*. Boston: Harvard Business School Press.

Kochan, Thomas A. and Awil Verma. 1992. "A Comparative View of US and Canadian Industrial Relations: A Strategic Choice Perspective." In *Labour Relations in a Changing Environment*. Ed. Alan Gladstone et al., 187-201. New York: Walter de Gruyter.

Kofas, Jon V. 1992. "The Mexican Labor Movement." In *The Struggle for Legitimacy: Latin Ameircan Labor and the United States, 1930-1960*, 23-69. Tempe: Arizona State University, Center for Latin American Studies.

Kopinak, Katherine. 1995. "Technology and the Organization of Work in Mexican Transport Equipment Maquilas." *Studies in Political Economy* 48 (Autumn): 31-70.

Kumar, Pradeep, David Arrowsmith, and Mary Lou Coates. 1991. *Current Industrial Relations*. Kingston, Ontario: Henson & White.

La Botz, Dan. 1991. *A Troublemaker's Handbook: How to Fight Back Where You Work—And Win!* Detroit: Labor Notes.

———. 1992. *Mask of Democracy: Labor Suppression in Mexico Today*. Boston: South End Press.

———. 1996. "Biggest Teachers' Demonstration in Years Overwhelms Mexico City." *Mexican Labor News and Analysis* 1 (10): June 2.

Labour Canada. 1994. *Major Wage Settlements, Listing SIC 544, Telephone Systems*. Prepared by Jane Henson. Ottawa: Unpublished report.

Ladner, Hugh C. 1973. *Conciliation Report*. Ottawa: Ministry of Labour.

———. 1975. *Conciliation Report*. Ottawa: Ministry of Labour.

Laidlaw, Blair and Bruce Curtis. 1986. "Inside Postal Workers: The Labour Process, State Policy, and the Workers' Response." *Labour/Le Travail* 18 (Fall): 139-162.

Lara Sánchez, Miguel Angel. 1992a. *Proceso de trabajo y automatismo: el caso de Teléfonos de México*. Dept. of Economics, Lic. Universidad Nacional Autónoma de México.

———. 1992b. *Productividad y trabajo: el caso de Telmex*. México, D.F.: CIESAS.

———. 1994. *La productividad en Telmex: crítica a la visión oligárquica de la productividad*. México, D.F.: Unpublished manuscript.

Larson, Simeon and Bruce Nissen. "Introduction: The Labor Movement as "Pure and Simple" Business-Unionism." In *Theories of the Labor Movement*. Ed. Simeon Larson and Bruce Nissen, 131-133. Detroit: Wayne State University Press, 1987.

Laxer, Robert. 1982. *Canada's Unions*. Toronto: James Larimer & Company.

Lazarus, Morden. 1977. *The Long Winding Road: Canadian Labour in Politics*. Vancouver: The Broag Foundation.

Lenin, Vladamir. 1978. *On Trade Unions*. Moscow: Progress Publishers.

Levine, David I. and George Strauss. 1993. *Participación y Compromiso de los Trabajadores*. University of California, Berkeley: Unpublished manuscript.

Lindblom, Charles E. 1949. *Unions and Capitalism*. New Haven, CT: Yale University Press.

Línea Democrática. 1987. *La nueva tecnología y la democracia sindical*. México, D.F.: Unpublished manuscript.

Lipset, Seymour, Martin Cole, and John Coleman. 1956. *Union Democracy*. New York: Doubleday.

Lipsig-Mummé, Carla. 1990. *Wars of Position: Fragmentation and Realignment in the Quebec Labour Movement*. Queen's Papers in Industrial Relations. Kingston, Ontario: Queen's University.

Llamas Salvador, Flores. 1988. "El sindicato se opone a la privatización de Telmex." *Opciones*. April 23: 1.

Lovera, Sara. 1990. "Telmex no ha probado la inutilidad de operadoras, dice el sindicato." *La Jornada*. July 19: 14.

———. 1993 "Nuevo modelo de productividad de Telmex." *La Jornada Laboral*. June 24: 3.

———. 1994. "Telmex-sindicato, laboratorio de la modernización de trabajo: entrevista con Francisco Hernández Juárez." *La Jornada Laboral*. April 28: 3-4.

Luxembourg, Rosa. 1970. "The Mass Strike, The Political Party, and the Trade Unions." In *Rosa Luxembourg Speaks*. Ed. Mary-Alice Waters, 153-218. Pathfinder: New York.

MacEwan, Arthur. 1994. "Globalisation and Stagnation." In *The Socialist Register*. Ed. Ralph Milbrand and Leo Panitch, 130-143. Toronto: Merlin Press.

Magdoff, Harry. 1992. "Globalisation—To What End?". In *The Socialist Register*. Ed. Ralph Milbrand and Leo Panitch, 44-75. Toronto: Merlin Press.

Malone, Thomas W. and John F. Rockart. 1993. "How Will Information Technology Reshape Organizations? Computers as Coordination Technology." In *Globalization, Technology and Competition: The Fusion of Computers and Telecommunications in the 1990s*. Ed. Jerry A. Housman, Richard L. Nolan, and Stephen P. Bradley, 37-56. Boston: Harvard University Press.

Marotte, Bertrand. 1994. "Cut-throat competition costs 650 jobs at Unitel." *The Vancouver Sun* Jan. 12: D-2.

Martínez, María Teresa. 1988. *Historia del sindicato de telefonistas: 1915-1975*. Dept. of Sociology, Lic. Universidad Autónoma Metropolitana, Iztapalapa.

Martínez de Ita, María Eugenia, Roger Miranda Bengoecehea, and Gemán Sánchez Daza. 1982. *Dominación, explotación y lucha: el caso de los telefonistas*. Dept. of Economics, Lic. Universidad Autónoma de Puebla.

Martínez González, Lourdes. 1989. "Frena la falta de recursos el proceso de modernización en Teléfonos de México." *La Jornada*. May 18.

Martínez Lira, María Eugenia. 1986. *Dos proyectos sindicales, en el Sindicato de Telefonistas de la República Mexicana, 1976-1984*. Dept. of Philosophy and Letters, Maestría. Universidad Nacional Autónoma de México.

Marx, Karl and Frederick Engels. 1978. "Manifesto of the Communist Party." In *The Marx-Engels Reader*. Ed. Robert Tucker, 473-500, 2nd edition. New York: W.W. Norton.

Mather, Boris. 1980. "Worker Beware." *Canadian Forum*. November: 28-29.

Matthews, John. 1987. "Technological Change and Union Strategy." In *Union Strategy & Industrial Change*. Ed. Stephen J. Frenkel, 134-154. Kensington, Australia: New South Wales University Press.

McCubbins, Matt D. and Barry R. Weingast. 1989. "A Theory of Political Control and Agency Discretion." *American Journal of Political Science*. August 33 (3): 588-611.

McIntyre, Wayne M. and Don Evans. 1992. *Business Operations—Customer Services Integrated Work Team*. BC Tel. Burnaby, B.C.: BC Tel.

McPhail, Joy. 1991. "The Contingent Workforce in Canada, Problems and Solutions." In *Labor in a Global Economy: Perspectives from the U.S. and Canada*. Ed. Steven Hecker and Margaret Hallock, 170-173. Eugene: University of Oregon.

Medina Nuñez, Ignacio. 1993. *Telmex: Modernización y Nuevas Relaciones Laborales*. Universidad de Guadalajara: Unpublished manuscript.

Mercado Maldonado, Angel. 1993. *Telmex-STRM: Una historia política*. Toluca, México: Centro de Investigación en Ciencias Sociales y Humanidades, Universidad Autónoma del Estado de México.

Mészáros, István. 1995. *Beyond Capital: Towards a Theory of Transition*. New York: Monthly Review.

Middlebrook, Kevin. 1989. "The Sounds of Silence: Organized Labour's Response to Economic Crisis in Mexico." *Journal of Latin American Studies* 21 (2): 195-220.

———. 1995. *Organized Labor and the State in Mexico: Mass Politics in a Postrevolutionary Authoritarian Regime*. Baltimore: Johns Hopkins.

Midwest Academy. 1984. *Midwest Academy Organizing Manual*. Chicago: Midwest Academy.

Mondragón Pérez, Yolanda. 1994. *Cambio en la relación corporativa entre estado y los sindicatos: el caso del Sindicato de Telefonistas de la República Mexicana, 1987-1993*. Dept. of Political Sociology, Maestría. Instituto de Investigaciones Sociales Dr. José Ma. Luis Mora.

Moody, Kim. 1988. *An Injury to All*. New York: Verso.

Morton, Desmond. 1980. *Working People*. Ottawa: Deneau Publishers.

Mosco, Vincent. 1990. *Transforming Telecommunications in Canada*. Carleton University: Unpublished manuscript.

Moss Kanter, Rosabeth. 1991. "Championing Change: An Interview with Bell Atlantic CEO Raymond Smith." *Harvard Business Review*. Jan.-Feb.

Munroe, Donald R., David K. Didyeon, and Michael W. Hunter. 1983. *Re Staff Relocation of Departments from Kamloops/Vernon to Kelowna (Decision 83-08-01)*. Burnaby, B.C.: BC Tel-TWU arbitration decision.

Müller, Hans-Erich. 1993. *Lean Production in Germany: Learn, Don't Copy*. Presentation at Lean Workplace Conference. North York, Ontario: Sept. 30-Oct. 3.

Müller-Jentsch, Walther, Katharina Rehermann and Hans Joaquim Sperling. 1992. "Socio-Technical Rationalisation and Negotiated Work Organisation: Recent Trends in Germany." In *New Directions in Work Organization: The Industrial Relations Response*. Ed. OECD, 93-111. Paris, France: OECD.

Murrillo, Maria Victoria. 1996. *Latin American Unions and Social Sector Reforms: Institutional Constraints and Policy Choices*. Presentation at the 1996 Annual Meeting of the American Political Science Association. San Francisco: August 29-Sept. 1.

Nacional Financiera. 1992. *Fideicomiso de los Trabajadores Miembros del Sindicato de Telefonistas de la República de México: Nota informativa*. México, D.F.: Unpublished report.

Nash, June. 1989. *From Tank Town to High Tech: The Clash of Community and Industrial Cycles*. Albany: State University of New York Press.

Nelson News. 1980. "$3.6 million payroll loss—cost of BC Tel move?". *Nelson News*. May 27: 1.

New Democratic Party (NDP). 1993. *Strategy for a Full-Employment Economy: A Jobs Plan for Canada from Canada's New Democrats*. Ottawa: NDP.

Nissen, Bruce. 1990. "A Post-World War II "Social Accord?". In *U.S. Labor Relations 1945-1989: Accommodation and Conflict*. Ed. Bruce Nissen, 173-207. New York: Garland.

Noam, Eli. 1992. *Telecommunications in Europe*. New York: Oxford University Press.

Noam, Eli N. and Richard A. Kramer. 1994. "Telecommunications Strategies in the Developed World: A Hundred Flowers Blooming or Old Win in New Bottles?". In *Telecommunications in Transition: Policies, Services and Technologies in the European Community*. Ed. Johannes M. Bauer, Charles Stamfield, and Laurence Caby, 272-286. Thousand Oaks, CA: SAGE.

Noble, David F. 1984. *Forces of Production: A Social History of Industrial Automation.* New York: Oxford University Press.

Novelo, Victoria. 1991. *La difícil democracia de los petroleros; historia de un proyecto sindical.* México, D.F.: Ediciones El Caballito.

Noll, A. Michael. 1996. "Aren't We Glad They Broke Up Bell?". *Los Angeles Times.* April 24: B-9.

Nomura, Masani. 1993. *The End of Toyotism 2: Recent Trend of a Japanese Automobile Company.* Presentation at Lean Workplace Conference. North York, Ontario: Sept. 30-Oct. 3.

O'Brien, Jon. 1978. "Telephone union vows to go back next week." *The Province.* Feb. 9. Elaine Bernard special collection. Vancouver: University of British Columbia.

O'Donnell, Guillermo, Philippe Schmitter, and Laurence Whitehead. 1986. *Transitions from Authoritarian Rule: Tentative Conclusions about Uncertain Democracies.* Baltimore, Md.: John Hopkins University Press.

Offe, Claus and Helmut Wiesenthal. 1985. "Two Logics of Collective Action." In *Disorganized Capitalism: Contemporary Transformations of Work and Politics.* Ed. John Keane, 170-220. Cambridge, MA: MIT Press.

Olding, John. 1965. "'Company Union' Cry Stirs Storm." *Vancouver Sun* May 26. Elaine Bernard special collection. Vancouver: University of British Columbia.

O'Neill, Thomas P., Jr. 1987. With William Novak. *Man of the House: The Life and Political Memoirs of Speaker Tip O'Neill.* New York: Random House.

Ortega, Max. 1992. "Fesebes, paradigma del sindicalismo neocorporativo." *La Jornada Laboral.* Oct. 29: 4-5.

Ortiz Magallón, Rosario. 1993. "¿Productividad y concertación?: El caso de los trabajadores telefonistas." In *Productividad: Distintas Experiencias.* Ed. Enrique de la Garza Toledo y Carlos García V, 57-71. México, D.F.: Universidad Autónoma Metropolitana, Iztapalapa and Fundación Fredrich Ebert.

Ortiz Pérez, Guillermo y Oscar Morales Pineda. 1991. *El sindicalismo independiente en México: 1970-1976.* Dept. of Political and Social Sciences, Lic. Universidad Nacional Autónoma de México.

Osing, Roy A. and William E. Silvester. 1992. *BC Tel Credit Process Team: Business Case for combining the functions of credit verification, overdue accounts and close accounts.* Burnaby, B.C.: BC Tel-TWU Letter of Agreement.

Palmer, Earl E. 1969. *Responsible Decision-Making in Democratic Trade Unions.* Ottawa: Privy Council Office.

Palmer, Bryan D. 1992. *Working Class Experience: Rethinking the History of Canadian Labour, 1800-1991*. 2nd ed. Toronto: McClelland & Stewart.

Panitch, Leo and Donald Swartz. 1993. *The Assault on Trade Union Freedoms: From Controls to Social Contract*. 2nd ed. Toronto: Garamond Press.

Parizeau, G. and T. de Pencier. 1994. "Direct election of union officers proposed." *The Transmitter*. Dec.: 2.

Parker, Mike. 1985. *Inside the Circle: A Union Guide to QWL*. Boston: South End.

Parker, Mike and Jane Slaughter. 1988. *Choosing Sides: Unions and the Team Concept*. Boston: South End.

Payne, Douglas W. 1998. "Mexican Labor: Cracks in the Monolith." *Dissent*. Winter: 23-28.

Pazos, Luis. 1991. "El costo del sindicalismo." *El Financiero*. Jan. 28: 34.

Peck, Ed. 1980. *Conciliation Commissioner's Report in a Dispute between BC Tel and CT&S, Ltd. and TWU*. Ottawa: Ministry of Labour.

Peitchinis, Stephen G. 1983. "The Attitude of Trade Unions Toward Technological Change." *Relations Industrielles* 38 (1): 104-119.

Perlman, Selig. 1928. *A Theory of the Labor Movement*. New York: MacMillan.

Persky, Stan. 1978. "BC Tel's lock-out: workers get the 'long distance feeling'." *The Northwest Worker*. February.

———. 1980. "Reach out, reach out and . . . nationalize the BC Tel." *The Columbian*. Sept. 20: A-3.

Perusek, Glenn and Kent Worcester. 1985. "Introduction: Patterns of Class Conflict in the United States since the 1960s." In *Trade Union Politics: American Unions and Economic Change, 1960s-1990s*. Ed. Glenn Perusek and Kent Worcester, 3-21. Atlantic Highlands, NJ: Humanities Press.

Peterson, David et al. 1990. *People and Skills in the New Global Economy*. Toronto: Liberal Party of Canada.

Petrazzini, Ben Alpha. 1995. *Political Economy of Telecommunications Reform in Developing Countries*. Westport, CT: Praeger.

Phillips, Jack. 1978. "TWU needs full support in battle with BC Tel." *Pacific Tribune*. Jan. 6.

Pilgrim, Ross. 1992. *Process Improvement Integration and Key Indicators Integrated Work Team*. Burnaby, B.C.: BC Tel.

Piore, Michael J. and Charles E. Sabel. 1984. *The Second Industrial Divide*. New York: Basic Books.

Pitta, Julie. 1996. "PacTel, SBC Help Fund State's Study of Merger." *Los Angeles Times*. June 26: D-1.

Pomeroy, Fred. 1988. "Fred Pomeroy." In *Canadian Union Movement in the 1980s: Perspectives from Union Leaders.* Ed. Pradeep Kumar and Dennis Ryan, 206-224. Kingston, Ontario: Queen's University.

Ponale, Allen and Loren Falkenberg. 1989. "Resolution of Interest Dispute." In *Collective Bargaining in Canada.* Ed. Amarjit S. Sethi, 260-295. Scarborough, Ontario: Nelson Canada.

Postal, Telegraph, Telephone International (PTTI). 1992. *Multinationals in Telecommunications: Up-date.* Spring. Washington, D.C: PTTI.

———. 1994. Conference proceedings [personal notes]. México, D.F: Feb. 28-March 2.

The Province. 1980. "Long, ruthless battle seen at BC Tel." Sept. 24.

———. 1981. "'Interconnect' brings in new companies and pushes BC Tel & TWU together." June 11: C-3.

Rangel Pérez, Mario. 1989. *Los telefonistas frente a la crisis y la reconversión.* México, D.F.: Pueblo/Información Obrera.

Rebollo Pinal, Herminio. 1994. "Mesa de Negocios: Presentan Objeciones a Telmex por la LD." *El Financiero.* May 9: 18.

Reich, Robert. 1992. *The Work of Nations: Preparing Ourselves for 21st-Century Capitalism.* New York: Random House.

Reinecke, Ian. 1985. *Connecting You: Bridging the Communications Gap.* Melbourne, Australia: Penguin.

Reinecke, Ian and Julianne Schultz. 1983. *The Phone Book: The Future of Australia's Communication on the Line.* Melbourne, Australia: Penguin.

Renaud, Jean-Luc. 1992. "Convegence Between Communications Technologies: The Western European Case." In *Convergence between Communications Technologies: Case Studies from North America and Western Europe.* Ed. OECD, 60-86. Paris, France: OECD.

Richardson, Monty. 1991. *CCC Executive Director Speaks Out.* Toronto: Canadian Competition Coalition.

Robinson, Ian. 1993. "Economistic Unionism in Crisis: The Origins, Consequences, and Prospects of Divergence in Labour-Movement Characteristics." In *The Challenge of Restructuring: North American Labor Movements Respond.* Ed. Jane Jenson and Rianne Mahon, 19-47. Philadelphia: Temple University Press.

Rodriguez Reyna, José Ignacio. 1989. "El Convenio en Telmex: Modelo a seguir en la revisión de la ley del trabajo (primera parte)." *El Financiero.* June 5.

Rogaw, Robert. 1989. "Collective Bargaining Law." In *Collective Bargaining in Canada.* Ed. Amarjit S. Sethi, 44-91. Scarborough, Ontario: Nelson Canada.

Rojot, Jacques and Peter Torgeist. 1992. "Overview: Industrial Relations Trends, Internal Labour Market Flexibility and Work Organization." In *New Directions in Work Organization: The Industrial Relations Response.* Ed. OECD, 9-34. Paris, France: OECD.

Rojot, Jacques. 1992. "Structural Change and IR Strategies: Introduction." In *Labour Relations in a Changing Environment.* Ed. Alan Gladstone et al, 173-186. New York: Walter de Gruyter.

Roman, Andrew. 1980. Presentation by NAPO (National Association of Poverty Organizations) to the CRTC [video]. Burnaby, B.C.: TWU.

Romo, Horacio. 1994. Presentation at *Primer Encuentro Sindical sobre la Productividad.* México, D.F.: May 27-28.

Rosablanda Rojas, Octavio. 1994. *El desarrollo tecnológico de las telecomunicaciones y su gestión transnacional.* México, D.F.: Unpublished manuscript.

Ross, John. 1995. *Rebellion from the Roots: Indian Uprising in Chiapas.* Munroe, Maine: Common Courage Press.

Roxborough, Ian. 1984. *Union and Politics in Mexico: The Case of the Automobile Industry.* Cambridge, UK: Cambridge University Press.

Rueda Pérez, Raúl. 1986. *Los cambios tecnológicos en Teléfonos de México.* Dept. of Economics, Lic. Universidad Autónoma Metropolitana, Azcapotzalco.

———. 1989. *Antecedentes y resultados de una modernización concertada en Teléfonos de México.* Paper for Prof. Francisco Zapata. Colegio de México.

Ruíz, Ramón Eduardo. 1980. *The Great Rebellion: Mexico 1905-1924.* New York: W.W. Norton.

———. 1992. *Triumphs and Tragedy: A History of the Mexican People.* New York: W.W. Norton.

Salinas, Jorge and Rigoberto Barba. 1987. *Telefonistas democráticas: a la clase obrera y a la opinión pública.* Línea Democrática: Advertisement published in various newspapers.

Sandoval Cavazos, Jorge. 1988. "Filosofía de calidad." *Modelo de Calidad, Telmex/STRM.* Ed. Telmex and STRM, 22-26. México, D.F.: Telmex and STRM.

Sánchez Daza, Germán. 1985. "La lucha sindical en Telmex: ¿Salarios o condiciones de trabajo?" *El Cotidiano* 2 (7): 37-41.

———. 1992. *Las telecomunicaciones en las ochentas: tendencias y perspectivas.* Dept. of Economics, Maestría. Universidad Autónoma de Puebla.

————. 1993. "Teléfonos de México: ¿Una productividad concertada?" In *Productividad: Distintas Experiencias*. Ed. Enrique de la Garza Toledo and Carlos García V. México, D.F.: Universidad Autónoma Metropolitana, Iztapalapa.

Sánchez Gutierrez, Pablo. 1987. *Los sindicatos nacionales de industria al interior del Congreso del Trabajo*. Dept. of Political and Social Sciences, Lic. Universidad Nacional Autónoma de México.

Sánchez y García, Francisco. 1994. "Human Resources and Labor Relations". *Telmex Investors' Meeting*. México, D.F.: Feb. 11-12.

Schecter, Darrow. 1991. *Gramsci and the Theory of Industrial Democracy*. Brookfield, VT: Gowver Pub. Co.

Schiesel, Seth and Laura M. Holson. 1998. "Reshaping the Phone Business: Bell Atlantic Reported Set to Acquire GTE for $52.8 Billion." *The New York Times*. July 28.

Schmitter, Philippe C. 1974. "Still the Century of Corporatism?". *Review of Politics* 36: 85-131.

Schreiner, John. 1977. "New technology at heart of BC Tel dispute." *Financial Post*. Dec. 24.

Seager, Moe. 1996. "France at the Barricades, Part II; Revolt pays off, for now." *Z Magazine*. February: 29-32.

Seager, Moe and Kevin Phelan. 1996. "Let Them Eat Reform: France at the barricades." *Z Magazine*. January: 30-37.

Secretaría de Comunicaciones y Transportes (SCT). 1990. "Modificación al Título de Concesión de Teléfonos de México." *Diario Oficial de México*, Dec. 10.

————. 1993. *Evaluación del servicio de Telmex durante 1992*. México, D.F.: SCT.

Secretaría de Trabajo y Previsión Social (STyPS). 1991. "Programa Nacional de Capacitación y Productividad, 1991-94." *Diario Oficial*. June 20: 6-60.

Segovia, Raymundo. 1993. "La infraestructura de las telecomunicaciones en México." *Las telecomunicaciones como factor de desarrollo y modernización económica*. Ed. SCT and Colegio Nacional de Economistas, 234-245. México, D.F.: SCT.

Serrill, Michael S. (reported by Laura Lopez). 1996. "Mexican Prodigy: The country's richest man ventures into online services as he moves to globalize his empire." *Time International*. June 3.

Sethi, Amarjit S. 1989. "The Future of Collective Bargaining in an Information Society: Strategic Choices for Management and Unions." In *Collective Bargaining in Canada*. Ed. Amarjit S. Sethi, 482-538. Scarborough, Ontario: Nelson Canada.

Shaiken, Harley. 1986. *Work Transformed: Automation and Labor in the Computer Age.* Lexington, Mass.: Lexington Books.

———. 1990. *Mexico in the Global Economy.* La Jolla: Center for U.S.-Mexican Studies.

Shimada, Haruo. 1992. "Structural Change and Industrial Relations: Japan." In *Labour Relations in a Changing Environment.* Ed. Alan Gladstone et al., 233-241. New York: Walter de Gruyter.

Shiver, Jube. 1995. "Back to the Future." *Los Angeles Times.* June 18: D-1.

Shniad, Sid. 1986. "Quality Circles: Cat's out of the bag." *The Transmitter.* May: 10.

———. 1989. "Ma Bell tolls for us all: Deregulating phone system would leave U.S.-style mess." *The Globe and Mail.* Sept. 19: A-7.

———. 1995. "CRTC ruling could herald big changes." *The Transmitter.* Feb.: 12.

Simon, Herbert. 1957. *Models of Man.* New York: Wiley.

Sindicato de Telefonistas de la República Mexicana (STRM). 1977. Editorial. *Restaurador 22 de abril* 2 (10) Oct.-Dec.: 2.

———. 1979. *Democratización sindical.* México, D.F.: STRM.

———. 1980. "Debate para definir la Táctica y Estrategia de nuestra organización." *Restaurador.* March (no. 12): 6-57.

———. 1981. "La lucha de las operadoras." *Restaurador, 22 de abril. Nueva Época.* 1 (1) Feb.: 10-19.

———. 1987. "Propuestas tráfico." *Asamblea General Nacional.* April 22. México, D.F.: STRM.

———. 1988. *Comisión de Modernización: Proyecto (Propuesta). Informe presentado por la Comisión de Modernización a la XIII. Convención Nacional Ordinaria Democrática de Telfonistas.* September. México, D.F.: STRM.

———. 1989, 1993. *Tabuladores de Salario.* México, D.F.: STRM.

———. 1990. *Reforma estatutaria.* México, D.F.: STRM.

———. 1991a. *Relaciones laborales.* Comisión Obrero-Patronal. México, D.F.: STRM.

———. 1991b. "Acuerdos tomados por la XVI Convención Nacional Ordinaria de Telefonistas." *XVI Convención Nacional Ordinaria.* México, D.F.: STRM.

———. 1991c. Informe: Comisión de Modernización. *XVIa. Convención Ordinaria Democrática.* México, D.F.: STRM.

———. 1992a. *Análisis de nuevos servicios propuestos por el STRM.* México, D.F.: STRM.

———. 1992b. *De la materia de trabajo y el contratismo.* La Comisión de la Cláusula Novena. México, D.F.: STRM.

———. 1992c. Democracia, libertad y proyecto: la fuerza del STRM— propuesta de táctica y estrategia. *XVIIa Convención Ordinaria Democrática.* México, D.F.: STRM.

———. 1993a. "Tráfico se rebuica: se busca que la mayoría se quede en la misma localidad." *Boletín: Restaurador 25 de abril* (1) 7: 1-2.

———. 1993b. Actividades de Política Exterior: Informe. *XVIIIa Convención Ordinaria Democrática.* México, D.F.: STRM.

———. 1993c. Informe—Comisión de Modernización. *XVIII Convención Ordinaria Democrática.* México, D.F.: STRM.

———. 1993d. "Revisión salarial." *Boletín: Restaurador 25 de abril* 1 (1): 1-2.

———. 1994a. *Programa General de Incentivos a la Calidad y la Productividad: Distribución de Bolsas de Incentivos por Centro o Unidad de Trabajo: Mayo de 1994-Abril de 1995.* Comisión de Modernización. México, D.F.: STRM.

———. 1994b. *Boletín Informativo de Productividad.* April 15. México, D.F.: STRM.

———. 1994c. *Tabulador de Salarios Actualizado al mes de febrero de 1994.* México, D.F.: STRM.

———. 1994d. *PG de Incentivos a la C y P: Propuesta de modificación.* México, D.F.: STRM.

———. 1994e. "Tranquilidad laboral para el SME." *Boletín: Restaurador 25 de abril* (1) 10: 10.

Sklair, Leslie. *Assembling for Development: The Maquila Industry in Mexico and the United States.* Boston. Unwin Hyman. 1989.

Slater, David. 1985. *New Social Movements and the State in Latin America.* Amsterdam: CEDLA.

Smith, Bob. 1978. "Hot edict aids BC Tel workers." *Socialist Voice.* January: 23.

Solís Granados, Victor Javier. 1992a. *El cambio estructural y la privatización en Telmex.* Dept. of Economics, Lic. Universidad Nacional Autónoma de México.

———. 1992b. "La modernización de Teléfonos de México." *El Cotidiano.* March-April: 60-67.

Sosa, Iván. 1992. "Los telefonistas manejarán sus acciones mediante dos fideicomisos." *El Financiero.* July 13: 47.

Stacey, Clay. 1981. "Phone outfit deserves boot." *Revelstoke Herald.* March 4.

Statistics Canada. 1980-1990. *Statistiques du téléphone: Réseau téléphonique transcanadien.* Ottawa: Statistics Canada.

Steinfield, Charles. 1994. "An Introduction to European Telecommunications." *Telecommunications in Transition: Politics, Services and Technologies in the European Community.* Ed. Charles Steinfield, Johannes M. Bauer, and Laurence Caby, 3-17. Thousand Oaks, CA: SAGE.

Stentor. 1993. *Review of Regulatory Framework: Public Notice CRTC 92-78—submission by Stentor Resource Centre, Inc.* Ottawa: CTRC.

Streeck, Wolfgang. 1992. *Social Institutions and Economic Performance: Studies of Industrial Relations in Advanced Capitalist Economies.* Newbury Park, Calif.: Sage.

Suárez Azueta, César. 1989. *Movimiento obrero y el estado en México, El proceso de democratización del sindicato de telefonistas (1976-1978).* Dept. of Political and Social Sciences, Lic. Universidad Nacional Autónoma de México.

Swenson, Peter. 1989. *Fair Shares: Unions, Pay and Politics in Sweden and West Germany.* Cornell Series in Political Economy. Ithaca, NY: Cornell University Press.

Sutrees, Lawrence. 1994. "Unitel to cut almost 20% of staff by 1996." *The Globe and Mail.* Jan. 12: B-1, B-20.

Symonds, William C., with Peter Coy, Mark Maremont, and Stephen Baker. 1990. "The Baby Bells Take Their Show on the Road: Big markets beckon abroad. Can the Bells rise to the challenge?" *Business Week.* June 25: 104-106.

Syracuse Cultural Workers. 1995. *Carry It On 1996 Peace Calendar.* Syracuse, NY: Syracuse Cultural Workers.

Székely, Gabriel and Jaime del Palacio. 1995. *Teléfonos de México: una empresa privada.* México, D.F.: Grupo Editorial Planeta.

Tandon, Pankaj. 1994. "Mexico." In *Does Privatization Deliver? Highlights from a World Bank Conference.* Ed. Ahmed Galal and Mary Shirley, 59-74. Washington, D. C.: World Bank.

Telecommunications Workers Union (TWU). 1978. *Convention Minutes.* June. Burnaby, B.C.: TWU.

———. 1979. *Convention Minutes.* June. Burnaby, B.C.: TWU.

———. 1980a. *Convention Minutes.* January. Burnaby, B.C.: TWU.

———. 1980b. *Convention Minutes.* June. Burnaby, B.C.: TWU.

———. 1980c. *Press release 80-09-01.* Elaine Bernard special collection. Vancouver: University of British Columbia.

———. 1981a. *Convention Minutes.* January. Burnaby, B.C.: TWU.

———. 1981b. *Press Release 81-01-30.* Elaine Bernard special collection. Vancouver: University of British Columbia.

———. 1981c. *Press Release 81-02-05*. Elaine Bernard special collection. Vancouver: University of British Columbia.

———. 1981d. *Don Champion: Address to TWU Special Convention* [video]. September. Burnaby, B.C.: TWU.

———. 1983a. *Technological Change Conference* [video]. Burnaby, B.C.: TWU.

———. 1983b. "Company push on 'quality circles' not to workers' benefit." *The Transmitter*. July/August: 1.

———. 1984a. "How representative are TWU's structures," *The Transmitter*: Feb: 8.

———. 1984b. *Convention Minutes*. January. Burnaby, B.C.: TWU.

———. 1984c. *Executive Council Minutes*. Burnaby, B.C.: TWU.

———. 1985a. "Clark says circles are 'hypocritical'." *The Transmitter*. May/June: 12.

———. 1985b. *Alexander Graham advertisement*. [video]. Burnaby, B.C.: TWU.

———. 1986a. *Convention Minutes*. June. Burnaby, B.C.: TWU.

———. 1986b. *Keep Jobs in the Kootenays: Nelson Town Meeting* [video]. Burnaby, B.C.: TWU.

———. 1987. OEP: Don't trust honeyed words." *The Transmitter*. Dec.: 14.

———. 1988a. "British warning on Quality Circles." *The Transmitter*. Jan.: 14.

———. 1988b. "Union steps up fight against Quality Circles." *The Transmitter*. Oct: 1.

———. 1988c. *Telecommunications: The Conservative Record*. Burnaby, B.C.: TWU. Unpublished manuscript.

———. 1988d. *Executive Council Minutes*. Burnaby, B.C.: TWU.

———. 1989. Worker, union fight to keep offices open. *The Transmitter*. Dec.: 1.

———. 1990a. "Settlement rejected," *The Transmitter*. March: 1.

———. 1990b. *Convention Minutes*. June. Burnaby, B.C.: TWU.

———. 1991a. *TWU Job Classification Summary Company Wide*. January 15.

———. 1991b. The choice for British Columbians. *The Transmitter*. Sept: entire.

———. 1991c. *Final Argument Submitted by TWU; Re: CRTC Telecom Public Notice 1990-73*. Burnaby, B.C.: TWU.

———. 1991d. *Executive Council Minutes*. Burnaby, B.C.: TWU.

———. 1991e. "Rod Hiebert chosen to succeed Armstrong." *The Transmitter*. July: 1.

———. 1992a. "2-year deal hikes wages 4.5% and 4%." *The Transmitter*. Oct.: 1, 5.

————. 1992b. *"A comparison of real wages between TWU and CWC, using the same weighted average of wage rates that were used in chart CWC: TWU, but deflating TWU wages by the Vancouver CPI and deflating CWC wages by the Toronto CPI, 1981=100."* Burnaby, B.C.: TWU. Unpublished manuscript. April 22.

————. 1993a. *Convention Minutes.* June. Burnaby, B.C.: TWU.

————. 1993b. *To All Inside Sales Reps and Business Account Reps Re May 27, 1993 meeting re planned reorganization of business division.* Burnaby, B.C.: TWU.

————. 1993c. "NDP stands alone against Bill C-62." *The Transmitter.* July: 4.

————. 1993d. "Strategic Renewal Workshop". *1993 TWU Convention.* Burnaby, B.C.: TWU. Unpublished report.

————. 1993e. "Serv Reps, Phone Reps upgraded to Wage Group 7" *The Transmitter.* Dec.: 4.

————. 1994a. "Seniority List," *The Transmitter.* Feb.: 12.

————. 1994b. "SQUEAKER!: 51% say Yes to new 2-year deal: Wage hike totals 4.5%. *The Transmitter.* July: 1.

————. 1994c. "Roll Call," *TWU January 1994 Convention.* Burnaby, B.C.: TWU.

————. 1994d. "Dramatic impact likely from CRTC Changes." *The Transmitter.* Oct.: 1.

————. 1995a. "Company, union exchange bargaining proposals, talks underway soon." *The Transmitter.* Dec.: 3.

————. 1995b. "Hiebert elected to second term." *The Transmitter.* Feb.: 1, 3.

Teléfonos de México (Telmex). 1987a. *Octava Reunión de Planeación Corporativa.* México, D.F.: Telmex.

————. 1987b. *Balance Telmex 1987-2000.* México, D.F.: Telmex.

————. 1989. *Programa permanente de establización de calidad de servicio.* México, D.F.: Telmex.

————. 1991. *Historia de la telefonía en México, 1878-1991.* México, D.F.: Telmex.

————. 1993a. "Annual Report for the Fiscal Year Ended December 31, 1992." *Securities and Exchange Commission—Form 20-F.* Washington, D.C.: Telmex.

————. 1993b: *Información sobre Teléfonos de México.* México, D.F.: Telmex.

————. 1993c. *Avances del Plan Trienal 1991-1993.* México, D.F.: Telmex.

————. 1993d. *Desarrollo del Plan Trienal.* México, D.F.: Telmex.

————. 1994. *Presentación de Inttelmex* [computer presentation]. México, D.F: Telmex.

Telmex and STRM. Various years. *Contrato Colectivo de Trabajo.* México, D.F.: Telmex and STRM.

————. Various years. Convenios Departamentales. México, D.F.: Telmex and STRM.

————. 1989a. *Convenio de concertación.* México, D.F.: Telmex and STRM.

————. 1989b. Trafico Nacional e Internacional: *Perfil de Puesto—Anexos.* México, D.F.: Telmex and STRM.

————. 1993a. *Programa General de Incentivos a la Calidad y Productividad.* México, D.F.: Telmex and STRM.

————. 1993b. *Acuerdos en principio en relación de la medición de la productividad en el área de cables.* México, D.F.: Telmex and STRM.

————. 1994a. *(2o) Programa General de Incentivos a la Calidad y Productividad.* México, D.F.: Telmex and STRM.

————. 1994b. PG de Incentivos a la C y P: Bases de Aplicación: Mayo 1994-Abril 1995. México, D.F.: Telmex and STRM.

Thelen, Kathleen. 1991. *Union of Parts: Labor Politics in Postwar Germany. Cornell Studies in Political Economy.* Ithaca, NY: Cornell University Press.

Thompson, Edward P. 1966. *The Making of the English Working Class.* New York: Vintage.

Thompson, Mark Elliott. 1966. *The Development of Unionism among Mexican Electrical Workers.* School of Industrial and Labor Relations, Ph.D. Cornell University.

————. 1981. "Canada." In *International Handbook of Industrial Relations: Contemporary Research,* 71-91. Westport, CT: Greenwood Press.

Thurlow, Ann. 1978. "Telecom workers are right." *Smithers News.* Jan. 25.

Thwaites, James. 1989. "Union Growth: Dimensions, Policies and Politics." In *Collective Bargaining in Canada.* Ed. Amarjit S. Sethi, 92-131. Scarborough, Ontario: Nelson Canada.

Tirole, Jean. 1989. *The Theory of Industrial Organization.* Cambridge, Mass.: MIT Press.

Touraine, Alain. 1988. *Return of the Actor. The Return of the Actor: Social Theory in Postindustrial Society.* Minneapolis: University of Minnesota Press.

Trejo Delarbre, Raúl. 1990. *Crónica del sindicalismo en México (1976-1988).* México, D.F.: Siglo Veintiuno Editores.

Transnational Information Exchange (TIE). 1994. Convention proceedings [personal notes]. Oaxtepec, Morelos, México. Feb. 11-13.

Trueba, Alberto and Jorge Trueba. 1993. Ley Federal de Trabajo: Comentarios, Prontuario, Jurisprudencia y Bibliographia. 72a edición actualizada. México, D.F.: Editorial Porrúa.

Turner, Lowell. 1991. *Democracy at Work: Changing World Markets and the Future of Labor Unions.* Ithaca, NY: Cornell University Press.

Twigg, John. 1987. "People Turn Around." *Equity.* June: 25, 27, 53-54, 69.

Unitel. 1992. Unitel's Response to the Stentor Petition to the Governor-In-Council of August 5, 1992. Submission to CRTC.

Unomásuno. 1980. *Tres huelgas de telefonistas—hacia un sindicalismo democrático.* México, D.F.: Editorial Uno.

Urlocker, Mike. 1992. "Communications bill by Friday?" *The Financial Post.* Feb. 25.

Valdes Vega, María Eugenia. 1990. *Obreros y sindicatos: los electricistas mexicanos.* Dept. of Political and Social Sciences, Ph. D. Universidad Nacional Autónoma de México.

Valenzuela, J. Samuel. 1992. "Labour Movements and Political Systems: Some Variations." *The Future of Labour Movements.* Ed. Mariano Regini, 53-101. Newbury Park, CA: Sage, 1992. 53-101.

Vallas, Stephen Peter. 1993. *Power in the Workplace.: The Politics of Production at AT&T.* Albany: SUNY Press.

Vancouver Sun. 1969. Editorial. "After the phone strike." *Vancouver Sun.* Aug. 6. Elaine Bernard special collection. Vancouver, BC: University of British Columbia.

Vásquez, Alberto. 1994. Teléfonos de México y sus empresas filiales. México, D.F.: Unpublished manuscript.

Vásquez Rubio, Pilar. 1986. "El terremoto de digital" *Cuadernos de Insurgencia Sindical.* Puebla: Información Obrera.

———. 1987. "La requisa: Historias del sindicalismo mexicano." *Información Obrera* 7 (August): 15-31.

———. 1990. "Por los caminos de la productividad." *El Cotidiano* 38 (Nov.-Dec.): 10-13.

Velásquez, Hena Carolina. 1993. *¿A dónde desea hablar?.* México, D.F.: Aguirre y Beltrán Editores.

Verma, Awil. 1991. "Restructuring in Industrial Relations and the Role for Labor." In *Labor in a Global Economy: Perspective from the US and Canada.* Ed. Steven Hecker and Margaret Hallock, 47-61. Eugene, Oregon: University of Oregon Press.

Vivares Torres, Amabilia. 1988. *Programa de Táctica y Estrategia.* México, D.F.: Planilla Naranja.

Wada, Norio. 1993. "Negotiating structural and technological change in the telecommunications services in Japan." *Telecommunications Services: Negotiating structural and technological change*. Ed. Brian Bolton, 83-99. Geneva: International Labour Office, 1993.

Walkom, Thomas. 1993. "Union takes creative action on job creation." *Toronto Star*. October 20.

Waisman, Carlos H. *Reversal of Development in Argentina: Postwar Counterrevolutionary Policies and Their Structural Consequences.* Princeton, N.J.: Princeton University Press.

Watanabe, Ben. 1993. *The Japanese Auto Industry: Is Lean Production on the Way Out?.* Presentation at Lean Workplace Conference. North York, Ontario: Sept. 30-Oct. 3.

Watanabe, Ben and John Price. 1994. "The Japanese Model Falters." In *Working Smart: A Union Guide to Participation Programs and Reengineering*. Ed. Mike Parker and Jane Slaughter, 224-244. Detroit: Labor Notes.

Watkins, Mel. 1991. "Recent Developments in the opposition to Meech." *Labor in a Global Economy: Perspective from the US and Canada*. Ed. Steven Hecker and Margaret Hallock, 30-32. Eugene, Oregon: University of Oregon Press.

Webb, Sidney and Beatrice. 1965 [1897]. *Industrial Democracy*. New York: Augustus M. Kelley.

Weber, Jonathan. 1989. "Is the US losing the telecom edge?" *Communications Week*. May 22: 40-46.

Webster, Jack. 1985. *CNCP on Deregulation—interview of Jim McDaniel* [video broadcast]. Vancouver, BC: CTV.

Weiler, Joe. 1988. *Criteria for the Arbitration of Work Disputes*. Burnaby, B.C.: BC Tel-TWU arbitration decision.

Wever, Kirstin. 1995. *Negotiating Competitiveness: employment relations and organizational innovation in Germany and the United States*. Boston: Harvard Business School Press.

Williams, Paul. 1993. "Negotiating structural and technological change in the telecommunications services in the United Kingdom." In *Telecommunications Services: Negotiating structural and technological change*. Ed. Brian Bolton, 101-121. Geneva: ILO.

Wilson, John. 1994. *Teams—The Competitive Improvement Project and the Union*. Paper presented at January 1994 TWU Convention. Burnaby, B.C.: TWU.

Winseck, Dwayne. 1993. *A Study of the (De)Regulatory Process in Canadian Telecommunication: Labour Unions and the Struggle for the Public Interest.* Dept. of Communications, Ph.D. University of Oregon at Eugene.

Xelhuantzi López, María. 1988. *Sindicato de Telefonistas de la República Mexicana: Doce años. 1976-1988.* México, D.F.: STRM.

————. *Reforma del estado y sindicalismo.* 1992. Dept. of Political and Social Sciences, Maestría. Universidad Nacional Autónoma de México.

Zapata, Francisco. 1981. "Mexico." *International Handbook of Industrial Relations: Contemporary Research.* Ed. Albert A. Blum, 351-391. Westport, CT: Greenwood Press.

————. 1989. "Labor and Politics: The Mexican Paradox," in *Labor Autonomy and the State in Latin America.* Ed. Edward J. Epstein, 173-193. Boston: Unwin Hyman.

Zonfei, Antonello. 1993. "Patterns of collaborative innovation in the US telecom industry after divestiture." *Research Policy* 22: 309-325.

Zornilla Cosio, Raúl. 1993. "Telecomunicaciones y desarrollo económico." In *Las telecomunicaciones como factor de desarrollo y modernización económica.* Ed. SCT y Colegio Nacional de Economistas, 31-37. México, D.F.: SCT.

Zetka, James R. 1995. *Militancy, Market Dynamics, and Workplace Authority: the struggle over labor process outcomes in the U.S. automobile industry, 1946 to 1973.* Albany, NY: SUNY Press.

Zureik, Ella and Vincent Mosco. 1989. "Telephone Workers' Reaction to the New Technology." *Relations Industrielles* 44 (3): 507-527.

Zuboff, Shoshanna. 1987. *In the Age of the Smart Machine.* New York: Basic Books.

Index

competition, 45-46
Mexico City earthquake, effect on
  telephone workers 178-179,
  191, 198
microwave technology 37
Middlebrook, Kevin, 7, 13, 82
militancy
  STRM, 7, 161
  TWU, 5, 7, 8, 161
modernization program, STRM, 179-
  181, 224, 227, 350
monitoring. *See* supervision.
monopoly providers. *See* telephone
  monopoly companies.
Moody, Kim, 94, 99
Morones, Luis, 121-122
Morton, Desmond, 13
Mosco, Vincent, 54, 315
Movimiento de Acción Sindical
  (Union Action Movement), 191
multi-skilling, 35-36.
multi-tasking. *See* multi-skilling.
multidivisional corporate structure,
  29
multinational corporate influence,
  47-48
multinational corporate structure, 29
Murrieta, Francisco Raúl, 123
Murrillo, Maria Victoria
mutual gains enterprise, 89, 93
mutual insurance, 69

Nader, Ralph, 292
National Labor Relations Board
  (United States), 110
National Revolutionary Party. *See*
  Partido Nacional
  Revolucionario.
national industrial unions, Mexico,
  78, 365

national labor regime hypothesis, 19,
  80-86, 92, 318-320, 363-366
neocharrismo, 258, 304
neocorporatism, 258
New Democratic Party of Canada
  (NDP)
  and British Columbia Electronic
  Highway Accord, 299, 377
  and Canadian social unionism, 137
  election results, 304, 307, 310-311
  nature of, 14, 303
  Ontario social contract legislation,
  307-308
  strength of, 71
  TWU, relationship with, 119, 126,
  145, 256-258, 274, 277-280,
  290, 301, 370
New Voice (1995 AFL-CIO election
  slate), 106
new unionism
  Great Britain, late 19th century, 68
  Mexico, 1990s, 75, 93
no-hire, no-fire agreements. *See also*
  convenio de concertación.
  CEP, 325-326
  SME, 322
Noam, Eli, 38, 41, 53
Noble, David, 31, 33
non-party revolutionary unionism.
  See syndicalism.
Nora and Minc Report, France, 56
North Atlantic Free Trade
  Agreement (NAFTA), 5, 50,
  308, 376
Northern Telecom, 50, 121, 362
Northwest Tel, 188
Novelo, Victoria, 13, 24-25
NYNEX, 49

O'Donnell, Guillermo et al., 111

www.ingramcontent.com/pod-product-compliance
Ingram Content Group UK Ltd.
Pitfield, Milton Keynes, MK11 3LW, UK
UKHW021416040325
455677UK00033B/60